Peter Shaffer
Revised Edition

Twayne's English Authors Series

Kinley E. Roby, Editor

Northeastern University

TEAS 261

PETER SHAFFER
Roddy McDowall. Courtesy of The Lantz Office

Peter Shaffer
Revised Edition

Dennis A. Klein

Twayne Publishers • New York
Maxwell Macmillan Canada • Toronto
Maxwell Macmillan International • New York   Oxford   Singapore   Sydney

Twayne's English Authors Series No. 261

Peter Shaffer, Revised Edition
Dennis A. Klein

Copyright © 1993 by Twayne Publishers.

Twayne Publishers   Maxwell Macmillan Canada, Inc.
Macmillan Publishing Company   1200 Eglinton Avenue East
866 Third Avenue   Suite 200
New York, New York 10022   Don Mills, Ontario M3C 3N1

Library of Congress Cataloging-in-Publication Data

Klein, Dennis A.
    Peter Shaffer: Dennis A. Klein.—Rev. ed.
        p.   cm. —(Twayne's English authors series; TEAS 261)
    Includes bibliographical references and index.
    ISBN 0-8057-7024-0 (alk. paper)
    1. Shaffer, Peter, 1926–   —Criticism and interpretation.
I. Title. II. Series.
PR6037.H23Z7   1993
822'.914—dc20   92-38258
                                                                 CIP

The paper used in this publication meets the minimum requirements
of American National Standard for Information Sciences—Permanence
of Paper for Printed Library Materials. ANSI Z3948-1984. ∞™

10 9 8 7 6 5 4 3 2 1   (hc)

Printed in the United States of America

For my friends,
who have always stood by me:
Les and Linda Cohn,
Sam and Susanne Greengard,
And Mr. Howard Hoffman

In loving memory
of my sister, Irene Miller,
and my aunt, Mary Berman

Contents

Preface

Since the writing of the original preface, Peter Shaffer's reputation has been enhanced by the increased scope of his theater. It now includes the musical biography *Amadeus*, for which the dramatist won awards in London, New York, and Hollywood; and the biblical epic *Yonadab*. The playwright also made a return to comedy with *Lettice and Lovage*, a showcase for the unique talents of the actor Maggie Smith.

There are significant changes from the original edition in this text. This revised version includes six new plays—the three mentioned above, the final form of *White Liars*, the radio play *Whom Do I Have the Honour of Addressing?*, and 1992's *The Gift of the Gorgon*. The chapters on *Amadeus, Yonadab*, and *Lettice and Lovage* consider both the British and American versions. There is also a section on his latest work, *The Gift of the Gorgon*. All chapters now contain information on the dramatic productions, including significant directors, actors, designers, and composers. In addition, there are sub-chapters on the films for which Shaffer wrote the scripts—specifically, *Equus* and *Amadeus*. The new chapters are no mere appendage to the original book. Throughout the text there are references to the characters and themes of the plays that came after *Equus*, the work with which the original study ended. I am very fortunate to have the opportunity to make corrections and additions—a word here, a paragraph there—that I immediately wished I had made after I saw the work in print.

There is no attempt in this book to force the plays to fit a preconceived mold for the purposes of literary and theatrical analysis. For example, the character on *Amadeus* requires a substantial section on the sources of the play, while *Lettice and Lovage* requires no such background; the chapter on *Five Finger Exercise* does not contain a section on stagecraft, while the chapter on *Equus* does. Also, the lengthy section on the 1955 radio play "The Salt Land" has been retained so that the present volume is complete in and of itself.

As respondent to a panel on his theater at the annual convention of the Modern Language Association on 29 December 1983, Shaffer commented, "I write to illuminate my own experience through the medium of the stage." This book attempts to bear witness to that illumination.

Preface to First Edition

The scope of Peter Shaffer's theater is vast. It ranges from the hilarious antics of *Black Comedy* to the psychological tension of *Equus*, from the domestic tragedy of *Five Finger Exercise* to the historical spectacle of *The Royal Hunt of the Sun*; and in a corpus of only ten works it encompasses everything from the stark drama of *Shrivings* to the broad farce of *The Public Eye*, and misses little in between. Shaffer's plays include the sprawling epic of the Spanish conquest of the New World and the comedy of the traditional European farce; the plots are as time-honored as the conflict between an old, lackluster husband married to a spirited young wife, and as modern as the Peace Movement. Shaffer probes questions as intimate as identity crises and sexual self-doubt and as far-reaching as loneliness and humanity's need for worship.

As a dramatist, Shaffer has no social ax to grind. He does not write didactic plays of social criticism or protest, but rather he writes about individuals in conflict with themselves: a young man preoccupied with preserving his individuality; a conquering hero obsessed with eternalizing his name; a young wife living with a husband who does not understand her; a guilt-ridden alcoholic agonizing with his conscience. And his plays are about persons in conflict with each other, by twos, by threes, by fours, and by whole cultures: husbands pitted against wives, fathers against sons, believers against skeptics, Christians against Incas. The characters are domineering and oppressed, religious and atheistic, self-confident and insecure, painfully honest and benignly false. They compete with each other for love, for power, for glory, or just for the satisfaction of proving that their view of the world is correct. Shaffer's plays are as traditional as the weekend-cottage Naturalism of *Five Finger Exercise* and as contemporary as the overlapping dialogues of *Shrivings*. Shaffer uses techniques of game-playing and mistaken identity, light and darkness, music and mime, crystal balls and placebos. There are moments as tender as the playing of the love duet from *Madame Butterfly*, and others as horrifying as the blinding of horses.

Analysis of Peter Shaffer's work is a problem for critics because they cannot pigeonhole him as belonging to a "school" or "movement." His drama defies the convenient labels of Theater of Anger, of Revolt, or of

Absurdity. When Shaffer started writing for the London stage, his drama was theatrically anachronistic: while his contemporaries were producing "Angry" plays of social protest, he was concerning himself with the domestic problems of the middle class; while much of Europe was involved with the "Absurd," Shaffer was writing "well-made" plays in the tradition of Sir Terence Rattigan, in clear, precise prose. After Shaffer wrote *Five Finger Exercise*, he was afraid of being categorized as a writer of "week-end cottage naturalism." That need never have been a worry for him, because subsequently he went on to produce one of the most varied programs of any playwright's repertoire.

This study will focus on the characters, themes, and techniques as they develop throughout Shaffer's career as a writer. The organization of the book is basically chronological with the exception of *The Royal Hunt of the Sun*, which, for its characters and themes, is more logically grouped with *Shrivings, Equus, Amadeus,* and *Yonadab*, than treated between *The Public Eye* and *Black Comedy*. Each chapter begins with the stage record of the play under consideration. Then, for the benefit of the reader who is unfamiliar with Shaffer's plays, there is a substantial plot summary. Each chapter gives an analysis of the themes, techniques, and especially the characters as individuals—both in their contact with one another, and in their relationships to other characters in Shaffer's plays. The chapters conclude with a critical appraisal of the plays, from the point of view of the reviewers as well as from that of the present writer.[1] The chapters on *Five Finger Exercise* and *Equus* are especially detailed because the former play provides the key to understanding Peter Shaffer's dramaturgy, and the latter is his most widely acclaimed success.

A minimum of space is devoted to the state of the British theater when Shaffer began his career as a playwright. What discussion there is occurs at the end of the chapter on *Five Finger Exercise*, Shaffer's first play to be presented on the British stage. Considerations of the twentieth-century theater in general are available in fuller form elsewhere.[2] There is also a deliberate effort not to duplicate material already included in other works of the Twayne series.[3] There will be no attempt to "read" the playwright into any of his characters or to conclude that attitudes or situations in his plays are in any way autobiographical. To do so would be to fail to treat each work as its own artistic end. There can be no attempt yet to determine what Shaffer's influence will be on modern drama: he is in mid career and enjoying the peak of his success.

Acknowledgments

My first note of thanks must go to Peter Shaffer, for writing the plays that inspired this study; for his time and interest in meeting with me and verifying the biographical information in my first chapter; for affording me the opportunity to study the text of "The Salt Land"; and for granting me permission to quote freely from his plays. I know of no other artist of a more generous and humanitarian spirit than Mr. Shaffer.

I owe a debt of thanks to several individuals and organizations in London for helping to make my research so pleasant: to Mr. Mark Berlin of London Management; to Ms. Miranda Gregg of MCR Management; to Mr. Ben Jancovich and to Ms. Susanne Davies of the Royal Shakespeare Company; to Mrs. Molly O'Daly Woods, the playwright's housekeeper; and to the British Museum; the Theatre Museum, and the British Broadcasting Corporation. All were helpful in providing me with valuable assistance and information.

Likewise, I thank the New York Public Library, which makes scholarly research possible in the United States; the Public Library of Vermillion, South Dakota; the State Library of South Dakota; and the research library at the University of California—Los Angeles.

I must also thank my former colleagues at the University of Missouri—Rolla: Dr. W. Nicholas Knight, who encouraged me to write this book; and Dr. Larry Vonalt, for his help in locating bibliographical items and interpreting the plays. I extend deep thanks to Dr. Gerald Cohen for his intellectual suggestions, constant encouragement, interest, and friendship. And I cannot fail to mention the assistance of the interlibrary loan office at that university.

In the same vein, I thank the staff of the library of the University of South Dakota, and especially the reference department, headed by Professor David Olson and served by Professors Carolyn Hopkins-Carroll, Amy Kreitzer, Max Leget, John Van Balen, and Karen Zimmerman, as well as many other devoted professionals, including Professor Nancy Myers, the acquisitions librarian. I am very grateful for all of the work that Ms. Florence Muller of the interlibrary loan department has done on my behalf. Thanks are also in order to the Department of Modern Languages and the Student Financial Aid Office for providing secretarial xiv

ACKNOWLEDGMENTS

help. Likewise, I thank the Office of Research for providing funds for travel, as well as my former student, Mr. David Duane Davis, for his computer expertise. I deeply appreciate all of the efforts of Ms. Lindia Brady, the secretary of the Department of Modern Languages. She handled not only my correspondence, but also a thousand other details that allowed me to use my time to prepare this book. She is all that a secretary could be. I also appreciate the time that the College of Arts and Sciences granted me through a reduced teaching assignment.

I thank The Lantz Office for permission to quote from the plays, as well as permission to reproduce Mr. Shaffer's photograph. I thank Samuel French, Inc., for permission to quote from *Five Finger Exercise*, and Mr. Peter Shaffer and Atheneum Publishers for permission to quote from *Equus* and *Shrivings*. My deepest thanks go to Dr. Brent Froberg of the Department of Classics at the University of South Dakota for his close friendship, sincere encouragement, scholarly advice, and meticulous proofreading of the original version of this book. I also thank Mr. David Moore, who provided me with notes for the revised edition.

Chronology

1926	Shaffer born in Liverpool, England, on 15 May.
1951	British publication of *The Woman in the Wardrobe*.
1952	British publication of *How Doth the Little Crocodile?*
1955	On 8 November "The Salt Land" is produced on Independent Television. British publication of *Withered Murder*.
1956	American publication of *Withered Murder*.
1956–1957	Serves as literary critic for *Truth* magazine.
1957	On 14 December "The Prodigal Father" airs on BBC radio's *Saturday Matinee*. "Balance of Terror" produced by BBC television on 21 November. American publication of *How Doth the Little Crocodile?*
1958	"Balance of Terror" airs on American television on 27 January.
1961–1962	Becomes music critic for *Time and Tide* magazine.
1962	London premiere, on 10 May, of *The Private Ear* and *The Public Eye*.
1963	New York opening of *The Private Ear* and *The Public Eye* on 9 October. London premiere, on 17 December, of *The Merry Roosters' Panto*. Completes film script, with Peter Brook, of William Golding's *Lord of the Flies*. The New York production of *The Establishment* includes a sketch written for the television series "That Was the Week That Was."
1964	On 6 July *The Royal Hunt of the Sun* premieres at the Chichester Festival; it opens in London on 8 December.
1965	Chichester premiere of *Black Comedy* on 27 July. Opening of *the Royal Hunt of the Sun* in New York on 26 October.
1967	Chichester premiere of *Black Comedy* and *White Lies* on 12 February.
1968	Opening in London of *Black Comedy* and *The White Liars* on 21 February.

1970   Premiere in London of *The Battle of Shrivings* on 5 Febru-
       ary. *Five Finger Exercise* airs on BBC's "Play of the Month"
       on 24 December.

1972   Completes film script of *The Public Eye*, also called *Follow
       Me!*

1973   London premiere of *Equus* on 26 July.

1974   New York opening of *Equus* on 24 October. *Shrivings* is
       published.

1976   On 28 June *White Liars*, paired with *Black Comedy*, opens
       at the Shaw Theatre in London.

1977   Film version of *Equus* released.

1979   London premiere of *Amadeus* on 2 November.

1980   New York premiere of *Amadeus* on 17 December.

1984   Film version of *Amadeus* released.

1985   Premiere in London of *Yonadab* on 4 December.

1987   Awarded title Commander of the Order of the British
       Empire. London premiere of *Lettice and Lovage* on 27
       October.

1989   *Whom Do I Have the Honour of Addressing?* airs on BBC
       radio on 20 November.

1990   New York opening of *Lettice and Lovage* on 25 March.

1992   Premiere performance of *The Gift of the Gorgon* on 16
       December at the Pit Theatre in London's Barbican Cen-
       tre.

Chapter One
Biography: Early and Minor Works

Biography

Peter Levin Shaffer was born in Liverpool, England, on 15 May 1926, the son of Jewish parents, Jack and Reka Shaffer. His twin brother, Anthony, is the author of the prize-winning play *Sleuth*, and Brian, a younger brother, formerly a biophysicist, is now manager of the family's real estate firm, since the death of their father. Jack Shaffer worked in real estate and was always able to maintain a comfortable home for his family. In 1936, the Shaffer family moved to London, and from 1936 through 1942 they moved all over England. When they settled in London in 1942, Peter was enrolled at St. Paul's School. From 1944 to 1947, Peter and Anthony were conscripted as "Bevin Boys," and as such worked in the coal mines of Kent and Yorkshire. After completing his national service, Peter enrolled in Trinity College of Cambridge University on a scholarship and received his baccalaureate degree in history in 1950. During his years as a student, Shaffer edited a magazine at Cambridge and felt his first stirrings as a writer. Since employment in publishing was scarce in London, he decided to move to New York, but there, too, his possibilities for employment were limited, and he took a job as a salesman in Doubleday bookshops in mid-Manhattan. He was not happy forcing himself on potential customers for a sale, and so he left the bookstores to work in the acquisitions department of the New York Public Library. He remained at the library until 1954, and then, bored with a career that he did not think was benefiting him, he returned to London and accepted a position with the music publishing firm of Boosey and Hawks, where he remained until 1955. He left to become a literary critic for *Truth* magazine and subsequently became a music critic for *Time and Tide*.

Shaffer wrote three detective novels—the first alone and the other two in conjunction with his brother Anthony. In 1951 *The Woman in the*

Wardrobe, the first of the three, was published in London under the
pseudonym of Peter Antony. It is the only novel that was not subsequently published in the United States. Peter and Anthony collaborated
on *How Doth the Little Crocodile?*, which appeared under Peter Antony for
its 1952 British publication and with the authors' real names for the
1957 American publication. Their second novel together was *Withered
Murder*, which appeared in London in 1955 and in New York in 1956,
this time with no pseudonyms.

Early in his career, he also wrote three scripts for radio and television,
the first of which he completed in New York and took back to London
with him. It was called "The Salt Land"; Shaffer hoped it would be
produced on stage, but instead it was aired on Independent Television.
"The Prodigal Father" was a radio play produced on the BBC program
"Saturday Matinee," and "Balance of Terror" was produced both in
England by the BBC and subsequently on "Studio One" in the United
States.

Satisfied by the success of "The Salt Land" and "The Prodigal Father,"
Shaffer decided to dedicate himself to writing a play intended for the
West End. On 16 July 1958, *Five Finger Exercise* had its debut at the
Comedy Theatre in London, and Peter Shaffer had come into his own as
a dramatist. The play was an immediate success and won for Shaffer the
Evening Standard Award for the best new playwright of the season. It
moved to New York in 1959, and on 2 December opened at the Music
Box, this time winning the New York Drama Critics' Circle Award for
the best foreign play of the 1959–60 season.

Throughout the 1960s, there was hardly a time when Shaffer's work
was not being presented in London or New York, or in both cities
simultaneously. After having enjoyed international success with *Five
Finger Exercise*, Shaffer brought to the London stage *The Private Ear* and
The Public Eye, a pair of one-act plays of high comedy, which opened at
the Globe Theatre in 1962. The following year was one which gave
exposure to Shaffer's works in London and New York, on stage as well as
on the screen: in 1963, *The Private Ear* and *The Public Eye* opened at
the Morosco Theatre in New York; a sketch that Shaffer wrote for the
television series "That Was the Week That Was" was included in the
New York production of *The Establishment*;[1] *The Merry Roosters' Panto*
opened at Wyndham's Theatre in London; and, along with Peter Brook,
Shaffer worked on the film script of William Golding's *Lord of the Flies*.
In December 1964, less than a year later, *The Royal Hunt of the Sun* opened
at the Chichester Festival. The play began a successful run at the ANTA

Theatre in New York in October 1965. In the same year, Sir Laurence Olivier, the director of the National Theatre, commissioned Shaffer to write a comedy for the 1965 repertoire, and the result was *Black Comedy*. For its opening in New York at the Ethel Barrymore Theatre in 1967, Shaffer wrote another one-acter as a "curtain-raiser." Originally entitled "A Warning Game" the name was later changed to *White Lies*. *White Lies* was rewritten and presented in London as *The White Liars* at the Lyric Theatre in 1968, again paired with *Black Comedy*.

The success that Shaffer enjoyed in the 1960s was only a prelude to that of the 1970s and beyond, despite a less than successful production of *The Battle of Shrivings* in London in 1970. In 1972, the film version of *The Public Eye* appeared, for which Shaffer wrote the film script. In 1973, *Equus* opened at the National Theatre in London and has since been presented with overwhelming success in virtually every corner of the globe, and has won for Shaffer the universal enthusiasm of the public and the praise of the critics. The Atheneum Press edition of *Equus* includes a revised version of his 1970 play, entitled *Shrivings*. He also wrote the screenplay for the 1977 film version of *Equus*.

The production of *Equus* in New York won Shaffer both the Antoinette Perry ("Tony") Award and the Drama Critics' Award for the best play of the year. He won a similar award from the Los Angeles Drama Critics. Shaffer also earned an Academy Award nomination for the screenplay, despite the failure of the motion picture. Between the stage and the film versions of *Equus*, the final version of *White Liars,* again paired with *Black Comedy*, opened at the Shaw Theatre in London on 2 June 1976.

Six years after the premiere of *Equus*, Shaffer completed and presented *Amadeus* at the National Theatre on 2 November 1979. The following year it opened in revised form on 17 December at the Broadhurst Theatre in New York. The international success of the play and then film in 1984 eclipsed even the reception of *Equus* on stage. The playwright won the Evening Standard and London Drama Critics' awards for the best play of the year in London, and the Tony Award for the best play in New York. He also won the Academy Award ("Oscar") for the best screenplay adapted from another medium.

Again six years passed before Shaffer had another play ready for the stage, and again it was at London's National Theatre that the biblical epic *Yonadab* premiered in 1985. In a departure from the philosophical, psychological, and metaphysical *Shrivings, Equus, Amadeus,* and *Yonadab,* Shaffer returned to the genre of comedy in his 1987 play *Lettice and*

Lovage, which opened at the Globe Theatre in London on 27 October. In slightly revised form, it moved to the Ethel Barrymore Theatre in New York on 25 March 1990. Between the two openings of that work, Shaffer's radio play *Whom do I Have the Honour of Addressing?* aired on BBC radio on 20 November 1989.

Shaffer maintains residences in New York and London and divides his time between those cities. As a British playwright, he prefers to have his plays presented in London before they open in New York.

The Detective Novels

Eight pieces of Shaffer's writings fall into the categories of early or minor works: three novels, four scripts for television or radio, and one pantomime. The texts of some of these works have not been published. Yet, a study of these works, however cursory, is a necessary preliminary to focusing on the works written for the National Theatre, the West End, and Broadway. The three novels, which represent the writer's earliest creative efforts, are clearly a cut above standard detective fare. The novels, however, when read after a study of the plays of Peter and Anthony Shaffer, only hint at the talents of the authors of *Equus* and *Sleuth*. All three novels are similar in their structure and need not be treated in detail.

The Woman in the Wardrobe, subtitled "a light-hearted detective story," the earliest of the three novels, was published in London in 1951. Upon leaving his house, Mr. Verity sees a man climbing out of a window and suspects that a crime has been committed at a guest house at an English seaside resort in Sussex. Mr. Maxwell, a blackmailer and all-around scoundrel, has been murdered, and the murderer could have been anyone who knew him. Supersleuth Verity, whose vocation it is to solve mysteries between tea and supper, sets out to solve this case in his usual ingenious manner. The detective conducts his interviews of the suspects and reveals that the murder was committed by a drug addict whom Maxwell was blackmailing. More important than the details of the plot, however, are the elements in the novel that appear throughout Shaffer's writing career. There are frequent references to history and to the Greco-Roman civilizations, both of which are dominant features that span Shaffer's writing career: Mr. Verity lives in a home he calls "Perse-polis," and his hobby is archaeology. In the solution of the crime, Verity cannot resist what he refers to as a "coup de théâtre," and he uses tricks to force the murderer to reveal his guilt. (Shaffer employs a similar device in his plays, written as much as twenty-five years later.) The reader learns little about Mr. Verity the man, except that he considers his father to be nothing, a man he never knew. (He claims that when he was a boy of ten, his mother fell in love with a carpenter, and that the neighbors put it down to "religious mania.")

How Doth the Little Crocodile?, the second novel, appeared in England in 1952 and in the United States in 1957. Like *The Woman in the Wardrobe*, it was published in England under the pseudonym Peter Antony, while the American edition bears the names Peter and Anthony Shaffer. This time the supposedly murdered man is Sir Livingstone, who was involved in an adulterous affair with Miss Lovelace. She is murdered, and the killer could be either of the two jealous women in the novel or any number of men who possessed motives. The trick this time is for the detective to reveal that Livingstone staged his own "murder" and then planted clues pointing to all possible suspects. The details of the plot are incidental to the significant motifs—the game-playing among the characters, the many references to the classical world, and to the theater and actors—which are common to the larger study of Shaffer's writing. Sir and Lady Livingstone prefigure the kinds of husbands and wives who appear in almost all of Shaffer's plays.

Withered Murder is the third and last of the novels. It was published both in England (1955) and in the United States (1956) under the names A. and P. Shaffer. Once again the setting is a boardinghouse, at a seaside resort on the south coast of England. A murder takes place, and the detective-hero pledges to resolve it in one evening's time, and so he does. The list of suspects includes a spinster, two giddy maids, a professor from Germany, a minister and his wife, and an artist, all of whom possessed opportunity, means, and/or motive to commit the crime. Like the other two novels, there are the now-familiar allusions to the classical world, amorous triangles, and the theater; in addition, this time there is a defense of sadism from the mouth of the hero, as well as details which suggest lesbianism.

The three novels share more than bonds of just plot or classical references: there is a strong resemblance in their structure and style. In all of the novels, the body of the book (between the incidence of the crime and its solution) consists primarily of dialogue, much like a play, with the detective questioning his suspects one by one. The books are the work of playwrights more than of novelists.

Radio and Television Scripts

Shaffer wrote four scripts for radio and television, one of which is no longer extant. "The Salt Land" was aired by ITV on 8 November 1955. Shaffer wrote the work for the theater and describes it as a "tragedy [constructed] along loosely classical lines, not for the sake of experiment, though experiment has its own fascination, but because the subject of Israel and immigration is truly heroic, and deserves classical treatment."[2]

"The Salt Land" represents Shaffer's first attempt at writing drama and is a beautiful work, rich in the elements that appear in his later plays. Since the only copy of the script is in private hands, a detailed plot summary is in order. "The Salt Land" is a drama in two acts and five scenes.

The first scene takes place on the stern of a small boat that is bringing illegal immigrants into Palestine, in the fall of 1947. As the curtain rises, there is the sound of chanting from the Friday evening Jewish service for the Sabbath. Saul, the twenty-two-year-old captain of the vessel, is furious because the singing will attract the attention of a patrol ship, attention which he is trying to avoid. Saul belongs to a group called the Palmach, whose mission it is to help Jews escape from Europe. A conflict arises between two brothers, Arieh and Jo Mayer. Arieh, aged twenty-seven, is dressed in traditional, Orthodox garb and believes that the Jews should sit and wait, and that they will be delivered to the Promised Land when the Lord sees fit. Jo, five years his junior, wears contemporary clothes, smokes on the Sabbath, and has little tolerance for the Talmud, his brother, or the pacifist philosophy. Mr. Mayer, the father, stands in awe of his elder son but agrees with Jo that Jews have a right to their own land, as do all other people. Kulli, a young woman, sides with Arieh, and Jo says that a man of Arieh's temperament could easily kill her. Jo has lived in Paris and feels superior to his father and brother, who have spent their whole lives in the ghetto. He considers Arieh to be a man still living in the Middle Ages, whose knowledge is limited to the sacred names of God and the recipe for incense burned in the Temple; he has no practical knowledge to bring to Palestine. Mr. Mayer thinks Jo's life is all dishonesty, tricks, lies and the most abject kind of materialism—Jo has been active on the black market, for which he has spent time in prison. Jo does not think that his activities are any of his father's business and that his father should be happy that Jo, through his connections, was able to get him on the boat. Max Galinsky, another passenger, becomes filled with the thought of arriving in the Land and of living on a kibbutz, a venture the success of which Mr. Mayer doubts; he fears that people will tire of the communal life and will want their own homes. As Max cries at the thought of something preventing their entering Palestine, the first scene ends.

Scene 2 takes place the next night. Jo is with his friend and fellow passenger Mr. Mordecai, whose whole manner indicates a frenchified, German businessman, dressed in a most corrupt, worldly style. They both believe that this trip was paid for with money and that prayers had nothing to do with it. Mordecai has placed himself on a superior level to the rest of the Jews, whom he thinks of as masochists who *like* suffering and being exiles. He made his money from the Nazis and by selling passports on the black market; now he is going to Palestine to milk it for all it is worth, and Kulli is appalled. Jo is to be his partner and translator. Arieh fears that the Jewish people have abandoned the Lord, and as a result will have to inhabit a wilderness, a salt land. The captain announces that the boat is now off the coast of Palestine and that the passengers should prepare to disembark.

The third scene takes place at the command post of a settlement in the Negev, in early October 1948: a sunlit scene of destruction. Arieh is the commander of a post, seriously deficient in arms and men. He accepted the position after he heard the Voice, and he knew that the sword could be used for good purposes. Jo, who is sarcastic regarding his brother's position in Palestine, has come to offer Arieh tanks, trucks, and jeeps in return for a favor he will want later when his brother has a high position in the State. Kulli begs Arieh to have nothing to do with Jo or his deals. Arieh cannot lose the chance of turning Palestine into Paradise and he decides to accept Jo's offer. If need be, Arieh will break his word to Jo later, but he must have the weapons now. He believes (or tells himself) that Jo was sent to him by the Lord: in the fight for Israel, even the most vile must serve.

Act 2, scene 1, is a Saturday morning in late summer 1949. The scene is the communal room of a desolate settlement in the Negev. Kulli is married to Arieh, whose father is offended that work goes on, even on the Sabbath. Between acts, Jo was tried for profiteering—making money off of the homeless—but was acquitted for lack of witnesses willing to testify against him and thereby incriminate themselves as accessories. Arieh's attitude has changed: he will not order people to go to services and observe the Sabbath while there are fields to be tilled, and his father is appalled at Arieh's new, wicked ways. Jo comes to see Arieh again and tells his brother that the people no longer support a man who cannot keep his promises to them, and that he has received all of the help that the organizations are willing to give him; he has lost his position as Prophet. As Jo sees the situation, only prestige concerns Arieh. Jo has come to collect the debt that his brother owes him—and he must collect it while Arieh still has some influence: as a failure, he will be worth nothing to Jo. He wants Arieh's support in helping him and Mr. Mordecai begin a conservative political party of their own. For Mordecai, it is a business enterprise to turn Israel into a capitalistic society with restrictive immigration laws. Arieh is irrevocably opposed to the plan, and to Jo, who is always the stumbling block between him and his visions. In addition to the arms that he supplied in the past, Jo now offers Arieh the machinery that his brother cannot find but desperately needs to keep his settlement afloat. Jo will even supply engineers and most important of all, water. As Arieh is praying to God for direction, Jo slaps him, throws him across a table, and claims credit for Arieh's being in Israel. Arieh agrees to let the people of the settlement decide whether or not to accept Jo's deal, and the scene ends with Arieh praying for a curse on Jo that will follow him to his grave.

The final scene takes place in the same room that night. Mr. Mayer bemoans to the rabbi how both of his sons are a disappointment to him: Jo because he hates his father; Arieh because he killed savagely on the battlefield, and so Mayer fears him. When Arieh asks for his father's opinion, Mayer speaks in favor of Jo's plan, which will improve life in Israel: the people will live with dignity and not like animals. Arieh sees no hope and thinks that he has been abandoned by God as well as by his wife, from whom he feels emotionally distanced. Jo presents the alternatives to the members of the kibbutz: they can accept his help and become an up-to-date settlement, or reject it and go on living in misery. In speeches of overwhelming emotional impact, Saul and Kulli speak out against any plan that will keep their Jewish brothers and sisters out of the Promised Land. All pledge to support Arieh. In another emotional speech, Arieh recalls the history of ancient Israel and in doing so is overcome with passion and hate against his brother, who contradicts the mission of the Promised Land. Arieh strangles Jo in front of the other settlers. Kulli, like Mr. Mayer, remains incredulous, stunned with grief. Arieh believes that God brought his hands to Jo's throat, but now Arieh must suffer punishment for the act. Saul takes command and orders Arieh to wait in his room until the police come for him. As the curtain falls, Mr. Mayer muffles the grief on his face in his prayer shawl.

Reduced to its simplest terms, "The Salt Land" is about two brothers, each with a dream for the State of Israel, each with an ulterior motive: Arieh, who wants to recreate the Garden of Eden in the middle of the Negev desert, but whose motivations are pride and stubbornness; and Jo, who wants to see the people of Israel living with dignity, but who is motivated by ambition and greed. It is also the story of a father who suffers disillusionment over his sons: one because he has turned to crime in order to realize his dream, and the other because he comes to put material goals before Jewish law. And it is about a young wife watching her husband—and her marriage—fall apart.

The script of "Balance of Terror," which is no longer available, was aired by BBC television on 2 November 1957, and then on "Studio One" in the United States 27 January 1958. The BBC explains that their contractual agreement obligated them to erase the tapes and destroy the scripts. The following description of the play appeared in the *New York Times* on 28 January 1958:

> International intrigue also was involved somewhat in "Balance of Terror" on "Studio One" over Channel 2 [CBS] last night.
> This was a drama purporting to tell of British intelligence operations against Soviet agents in Berlin. The presentation on a network television program of such an inept production, presuming to deal with as important a subject as control of intercontinental ballistic missiles, was inexcusable. (55)

Shaffer agreed with the *Times*'s evaluation of the rewritten American version, and is quoted as having described the production as follows: "The good guys were clean-limbed, overgrown Boy Scouts. The bad guys were wicked, dreadful Communist agents. It was boiled down to the lowest common denominator of American television rubbish."[3]

The last play, "The Prodigal Father," was presented on BBC radio's "Saturday Matinee" on 14 September 1957. The play takes place in Glenister Hall, which has been in Lady Sylvia Glenister's family since 1670. It was built as a retreat from the cares of the town. There are eight identifiable scenes in the play, although they are not so designated in the script. The first is a conversation between father and son. Leander Johnson is considering buying Glenister Hall principally to give his son, Jed, some "class," which Leander feels is definitely lacking in his son's character. At once it becomes evident that the two are not comfortable around each other; there is no understanding between them, much less respect. The father's personal motive for buying the house is to try to make up to his son for the many years of paternal neglect. Leander and his wife were separated when Jed was only four, and since then Jed was reared by just his mother in America, while Leander was off in Europe. This is the first time that father and son have been together in sixteen years, and Jed does not let his father forget it.

The second scene introduces Lady Glenister, who is upset about having to sell the family manse, which she can no longer afford to maintain. Rather than giving us any information about Lady Glenister's past, the scene fills in more information about Leander's character. Jed's bitterness toward his father arises from having been deprived by him of a real home. While Jed accuses his father of pretentiousness, Leander rebuts Jed, accusing him of trying to be *too* manly, and of wanting everything that is the coolest, the latest, the snazziest. Jed fled five years ago at the time of his mother's death, and Leander spent those years trying to locate him. Leander is ready to unburden himself to Sylvia, and to reveal the sordid details of his childhood. It was his father who made the money, and he merely inherited it. His childhood was far from happy: Leander's mother died when he was eleven years old, and his father moved to the American Midwest with him, a move that left the youngster's aspirations totally unfulfilled. At eighteen, he ran away from his father to realize his frustrated dreams. When he married, Leander's wife wanted a rustic life, but his dreams were grander than that. Nevertheless, Sylvia has more respect for Jed's honesty toward life than for Leander's airs. All that Sylvia reveals about her life is that she never had children and that she brought up Lucy, whose parents were killed in an accident.

The third scene is between Jed and Lucy. Jed has gone through life feeling that he was a mistake as far as Leander was concerned. He admits that his self-image is very low; he considers himself a moron because he does not have interests such as the study of history. Jed's attention now turns to Lucy's problem: he suspects that Sylvia never lets her out of the house. Lucy will not explain herself and draws away when Jed tells her that she is pretty.

The fourth scene returns to Lady Glenister and Leander, and this time it is she who talks of her past. After her husband died, she spent a good deal of her time traveling, just like Leander. She was lonely, and when the opportunity to rear Lucy presented itself, she seized it. Sylvia's insight is more penetrating than Leander's and, at the risk of not selling her house, she tells him that it is not a house that Jed needs, but a sense of security.

In the final three scenes the denouement proceeds rapidly. Leander is going to forget about buying Glenister Hall in order to go back to

America with his son and start over; for the moment at least, father and son have reconciled their differences. Jed wants Lucy to see him again, but she does not comply; Jed knows it is because of Lucy's sense of obligation to Sylvia. Lucy does consent to write to Jed, and this is supposed to leave their relationship on a hopeful note. Likewise, Leander wants to see Sylvia again. In the final moments, Sylvia tells Lucy that she thinks that it is time they have weekend company, her way of letting Lucy know that the outside world is now welcome in her home. Lucy, of course, is delighted.

"The Prodigal Father" is a bridge from a historical drama and an espionage thriller to Shaffer's bona fide, serious dramatic writing, which begins in the following year with *Five Finger Exercise*. If "The Prodigal Father" seems to have too happy an ending and to be too pat, critical appraisal of the script must take into consideration its function of filling a spot on a Saturday afternoon radio program and not of being a believable piece of theater. The father–son relationship as described in "The Prodigal Father" is one of the axes on which most of Shaffer's drama revolves, beginning with *Five Finger Exercise* and continuing through *Yonadab*. To some extent, the figure of the father in this play is to become the figure of the mother in *Five Finger Exercise*: both characters are pretentious souls, impressed by wealth and stature. Young women often play marginal roles in Shaffer's plays, and Lucy is typical: she is young, attractive, and appealing to Jed. She is not an individual, but rather one of many women to whom Jed could be attracted, and she refuses the attention of a young man abandoned emotionally by his father. Finally there is Lady Sylvia Glenister, mature, perceptive, and in many ways Leander's double. She is the outsider who unites the family, if only temporarily.

A Pantomime

The Merry Roosters' Panto is the only work written after *Five Finger Exercise* included in this chapter. It is a Christmas pantomime for children, produced at Wyndham's Theatre by the Theatre Workshop Company.[4] As with "Balance of Terror," for which the script is no longer extant, information on this play is available from secondary sources. The play (which calls for the participation of the children in the audience) is Shaffer's interpretation of the Cinderella story, in which Prince Charming is a spaceman, the Fairy Godmother is the Duchess of Margate, Cinderella is a blonde suburbanite, and her stepsisters are played by men.

Lional Bart wrote the lyrics and Stanley Myers set them to music for slapstick entertainment. Not all reviewers were in agreement about the pantomime. Philip Hope-Wallace in the *Guardian*[5] thought it was a spirited little show, while T. C. Worsley in the *Financial Times*[6] found it to be a dismal failure and did not even mention Shaffer's name in the review. Hubert Kretzmer, critic for the *Daily Express*[7] saw an underlying moral in the work: why *should* Cinderella get to go to the ball? Has she *earned* the rights of leisure? Kretzmer's interpretation is in keeping with Shaffer's purpose in writing the pantomime. Also there is disagreement on the issue of whether or not the musical is for children. W. A. Darlington, writing in the *Daily Telegraph*,[8] found it very much for children, but Milton Shulman in the *Evening Standard*[9] wrote that the work was more for adult tastes than for children's. A blurb in the theater section of the *Observer* alerts that "private and progressive jokes may deter some parents, but [there is] plenty of audience participation for non-political children."[10] Thirty-two years passed before Shaffer's next radio play, *Whom Do I Have the Honor of Addressing?* was aired on BBC radio on 20 November 1989. A treatment of that work appears in chapter 9.

Summation

Some of the works treated in this chapter may not seem of much importance in and of themselves. They are generally early attempts at writing—for radio, for television, for children's entertainment. Their shortcomings aside, the works do have value taken in the text of Shaffer's *opera*: from the detective novels, Shaffer said that he learned a great deal about plot development, and from the radio and television scripts, he was able to make the leap to the serious stage. Most importantly, these early works contain the themes, the types, and the motifs which are prominent in the major works on which Shaffer's reputation has been built.

Chapter Two
Five Finger Exercise

Encouraged by the success of "The Prodigal Father" and "The Salt Land," Shaffer decided to devote himself to writing a play for the London stage. He wanted his material to be of more substance than that of the drawing-room dramas and comedies on which the London theatergoers had been nurtured, but he knew that in order to keep the attention of his audience his medium had to be one with which that audience could feel comfortable. What he had to do was construct a play that *seemed* traditional and that brought his respected predecessors to mind, and yet maintain the integrity of his subject matter. Shaffer brought the play to H. M. Tennant, an important London theater producer, and six months later received a call to come to Tennant's office. *Five Finger Exercise* opened at the Comedy Theatre in London on 16 July 1958 under the direction of Sir John Gielgud, with Adrianne Allen in the role of Louise, Brian Bedford as Clive, Ronald Culver as Stanley, Juliet Mills as Pamela, and Michael Bryant as Walter. Frederick Brisson, the theater producer, saw the play and wanted to produce it in New York. His plans were realized, and once again Gielgud directed the play, which opened at the Music Box Theatre on 2 December 1959. Jessica Tandy played Louise, and the rest of the cast remained the same as in London. By winning the Evening Standard Award in London and the Drama Critics' Circle Award in New York for *Five Finger Exercise*, Peter Shaffer established himself as a playwright of the first order.

Structure and Plot

Five Finger Exercise is a meticulously crafted play in two acts and four scenes, the basis of which are conversations among the members of the Harrington household. Little "action" takes place in the course of the drama, yet the work is continuously engrossing for the fine individual characterizations and the portrayals of the intricate relationships. In each of the conversations Shaffer plants seeds that finally reveal the personal desires and interpersonal dependencies of the characters. It is necessary to set down the essentials of the plot before delving into the needs and intrigues of the personalities.

The play takes place in the Harringtons' weekend cottage in Suffolk, England, in the 1950s. Act 1 begins at breakfast on a Saturday morning in early September and continues on a Saturday night after dinner, two months later. Act 2 occurs on the following Sunday morning at breakfast and concludes that evening, after dinner. Shaffer describes in intricate detail the scene that serves as the setting for the entire play. It is a multi-level set in which the living room occupies the lower floor, and the hall and study room compose the upper level. The living room is well furnished and "almost aggressively expresses Mrs. Harrington's personality. We are let know by it that she is a 'Person of Taste,' but also that she does not often let well alone."[1] As the curtain rises, Louise is serving breakfast to her nineteen-year-old son, Clive, and she wastes no time in ridiculing her husband to Clive. When Stanley (Mr. Harrington) enters the room, Clive, who was previously described as nervous, feels even more so. The family disagreement this morning is over the necessity of a private tutor for their adolescent daughter, Pamela. For Louise it is essential, but as Stanley sees it, the only reason Louise insists is that "the best people have tutors, and since we're going to be the best people whether we like it or not, we must have a tutor, too" (*FFE*, 3). It is immediately apparent that the issue of a tutor is only the latest detail in a continual battle between husband and wife—Louise's pretentiousness versus Stanley's commonness—which Clive describes as a battle between "the salon and the saloon" (*FFE*, 32).

Clive tells his parents that he was out last night reviewing a production of *Electra* for a magazine, and the quarrels start again: Louise feigns shock over Stanley's ignorance of the play; Clive has to justify his literary interests to his father; Stanley criticizes Clive's impractical nature and his "arty-tarty" friends. Stanley knows that his offer will be refused, but, in an attempt to improve his relationship with Clive, he invites his son to go shooting with him. Clive prefers to stay behind and help Louise clear the breakfast table and, on her suggestion, do the breakfast dishes together.

Pamela enters with Walter (her tutor) and tries to talk him out of her French lesson. She is interested in learning about his past life and tries to get him to talk about Germany, his homeland, and his family, but to no avail; he claims that he has no family besides the Harringtons and that England will be his home. Clive lets him know that he is doing himself no favor by allowing the Harringtons to "adopt" him in this way. Louise goes for a music lesson with Walter, and Clive plays games with the material in Pamela's history lesson. In the last moment of the scene, Walter enters the room, and Clive is upset by his presence.

Two months pass between scenes, and Clive is now a student at Cambridge University. In the interim, he has started to drink whiskey rather steadily; he has lost his interest in helping Louise around the house; and he has had a talk with the manager of Stanley's furniture company, during which he criticized his father's "grotesque," "shoddy and vulgar" products. Stanley is no more impressed by his son's lifestyle than Clive is by his father's furniture. Stanley wants Clive to be practical about the future, to make the right friends, to choose a profession in which he can make money: "it's the one thing that counts in the end" (*FFE*, 24). Clive has no such concerns and is happy to be at Cambridge where, he says, people "speak his language." In Clive's conversation with Walter, the subject, as usual, is filial obligation: Walter does not approve of Clive's disparaging attitude toward his parents and feels that children owe their parents respect. In contrast, Clive feels only scorn for his own parents. Louise talks to Walter of her French ancestry and of how she married beneath herself. She, too, wants to know everything about Walter—about his family, about his past. He insists that there is nothing to tell and reveals only that he hates everything German. When Clive enters, drunk, he sees Louise holding Walter's head in her hands. He ridicules Louise's family tree to Walter and again warns him about his family. Clive needs a friend badly and asks Walter to take a trip with him during the forthcoming vacation. Walter refuses; Clive insults him and resumes drinking. Stanley tries to have a heart-to-heart talk with Clive, an attempt that serves to reveal once again how much father and son do not understand each other. He sees his son crying and forces him to tell the cause. Clive lies and says he saw Louise and Walter together intimately.

Act 2 takes place the following morning. In the first scene, Pamela gets the chance to speak and to show how perceptive a young woman she is. She tells Walter that her brother has never had a girlfriend (and only once a female acquaintance), and that her parents are always having a row that is not really *about* anything. Then she confides that Clive has a recurrent dream about Stanley coming into his room while he is asleep and peeling the blankets from him one by one. Stanley is distracted today, and Clive is more uneasy than usual, to the point of being sharp even with Louise. She has no trouble in recognizing that Clive is jealous of Walter's relationship with her.

Pamela trips on the stairs, and Walter rushes over to help her. He picks her up and carries her in a way that makes her feel like a baby rather than like the young lady that she would prefer him to consider her, and she tells her mother that he makes her feel ashamed. Walter is clever and penetrating but never heeds Clive's warnings about the personality of the Harringtons. He allows himself to feel too comfortable with them, even to the extent of giving them advice and revealing the skeleton in his own closet to Clive: he does have a family back in Germany; his father is a Nazi who worked at Auschwitz and who brutally beat him as his mother watched uncritically. Clive still insists that Walter must leave the Harrington home for his own sake. Now Louise has her chance with Walter and speaks to him tenderly, wanting to hear more than anything else that he loves her; what she hears instead is that he thinks of her as a mother. She is distraught, and try as she might to hide it, her bitterness is evident.

The final scene of the play takes place after supper, for which Clive never appeared. Husband and wife battle over who is responsible for Clive's state: Louise blames Stanley for unfatherly treatment of his son, and Stanley counters by accusing Louise of ruining him by making him into a mama's boy and turning his son away from him. Stanley offers Louise the chance to ask him for a divorce, but the whole subject is "too vulgar" for her to consider. On the pretext that Walter is having a bad effect on Pamela, Louise asks Stanley to dismiss him from his duties. Stanley goes to Walter, but is sidetracked into talking about Clive and what a bitter disappointment he has been to Stanley, and never accomplishes his mission of firing Walter. Once again Clive and Walter talk, and this time Walter reaches the heart of the problem: Clive has to be forgiving toward his parents and not hold them responsible for the fact that he "has no girl friend." Walter's advice to Clive is the same as Clive's to Walter: leave the house and never come back.

Stanley verbally assaults Walter; he blames him for turning Clive into a "sissy" and fires him, not because he believes that he is having a bad effect on Pamela, but ostensibly because he thinks that Walter is trying to make love to his wife. (He later reveals that he never believed Clive's lie.) Furthermore, Stanley is going to see to it that Walter will never get his British naturalization papers, and Walter's pleading to the contrary is in vain. There is a rapid denouement of accusations and counteraccusations: Clive accuses Louise of being jealous of her own daughter, and Louise rebuffs him, insinuating that it is Clive who is really attracted to Walter. As the family squabbles, Walter tries to commit suicide in his room, and Clive prays for the courage for all of them to go on living.

Characters

Five Finger Exercise is a play of individual and family crises—husband and wife, mother and son, father and son—and the relationship of each of the Harringtons to Walter. As such, the body of any study on *Five Finger Exercise* must focus on the characterizations. Clive's recurrent dream, which Pamela relates to Walter, is a metaphor for Shaffer's mode of writing the play: just as Mr. Harrington methodically strips the covers from his son, so the playwright strips the characters of their facades.

Act 1:

1. ***Louise and Stanley.*** With the possible exception of the Mozarts in *Amadeus*, there is not one happy marriage in all of Shaffer's plays, and the trend goes back even further than *Five Finger Exercise* to "The Prodigal Father." Shaffer portrays husbands and wives whose basic values conflict to the point that harmony is impossible, and the prototype is the marriage of Louise and Stanley Harrington. Louise is described as "a smart woman in her forties, dressed stylishly, even ostentatiously for a country week-end. Her whole manner bespeaks a constant preoccupation with style, though without apparent insincerity or affection. She is very good-looking, with attractive features . . ." (*FFE*, 2). The manner in which Louise dresses is indicative of her pretention: her home is expensively furnished; her son is going to Cambridge; her daughter has a private tutor. Her special pride is her French ancestry and her family background. She tells Walter,

You see, when I married I was a young girl . . . I had hardly met anybody outside of Bournemouth [her home town]. My parents didn't consider it proper for me to run about on my own. And when I met Stanley they did everything in their power to arrange a marriage. You see, they weren't exactly very dependable people. My mother was an aristocratic little lady from France who'd never learnt to do a thing for herself. . . . Naturally, father had reservations about the marriage. I mean, socially the thing was far from ideal. . . . His people had always been professional men. Marrying me into the furniture business—(*with a faint smile*) well, was rather like going into trade in the old days. (*FFE*, 27–28)

She entered into a marriage in which she felt she was compromising herself and has spent her life proving just what a sacrifice she made in marrying a vulgar and common man, for whom she has felt nothing but contempt.

Stanley is described as "a forceful man in middle age, well-built and self-possessed, though there is something deeply insecure about his assertiveness" (FFE, 3). Unlike his wife, he is a down-to-earth, hard working person, with no pretentions and no education. He denies his family nothing and receives nothing in return. It is Louise who is in charge of the household—with little argument from Stanley about their relative positions—and she is absolute in her control: authoritarian, scheming, and ultimately vicious. Just as she furnished her house in such a way that Stanley always feels out of place, so her whole raison d'être seems aimed at the same goal: she speaks of the theater, which Stanley has never learned to appreciate; she punctuates her speech with French words, which Stanley cannot understand; and she loves having her house filled with music, which gives Stanley a headache. If Louise has no understanding of Stanley, his understanding of her is perfect: she has to do whatever will make her one of the "Best People."

The basic theme of their continual row is always the same; only the details change. In the first act the topic of argument is the need for a private tutor for Pamela. Stanley complains, "What's money after all? We had a town place so we simply had to have a country place, with a fancy modern decorator to do it up for us. And now we've got a country place we've simply got to have a tutor" (FFE, 4). Stanley does not understand why the things over which Louise becomes so excited are considered cultural at all: plays about "people having their eyes put out" (FFE, 5), or the music that Pamela is learning to play on the piano. Of course, Louise can never seem to remember the name of that Greek play that Sir Laurence Olivier was in, or tell the difference between pieces of music by Bach or Mozart, and she depends on her son for her knowledge of drama, music, or anything that is intellectual and edifying.[2]

2. *Louise and Clive*.   The emotion that Louise withholds from her husband she lavishes on her son, a "quick, nervous, taut and likeable" young man (FFE, 2). What Clive has to do to remain in the number-one place in his mother's affections is to correct her errors uncritically, side with her against his father, and play verbal games with her:

Clive: (rising) Votre Majesté. My Empress!

Louise: (permitting her hand to be kissed) Levez!

Clive: (Moving down L of the table) The Empress Louise, ill-fated, tragic, dark-eyed queen from beyond the seas. What is your wish, ma-dame? (He makes a low bow to Louise) I am yours to command. (. . .)

Louise: *(rising)* I've told you already, my little Cossack. *Sois content.* (. . .) Be happy.

. . . .
             (They embrace very fondly) (FFE, 8)

Another game that Louise likes to play is that of giving nicknames, and the one that she uses for Clive is Jou-Jou, aptly enough her little plaything. (The techniques of games and nicknames will remain throughout Shaffer's works.) Not only is it fun for her to have a human toy, but games help her forget that she is old enough to have a college-aged son. For playing games like this with her, Clive is rewarded with her loyalty: she defends and encourages his interests, kisses the top of his head as she passes, and lays his napkin across his lap. But Clive's compliance with the ground rules that Louise has established is only superficial, and he wishes that he did not have to sacrifice his father in order to secure the love of his mother, but so it is. Clive is to be pitied for his relationship with his mother: Louise holds tight, psychological reins on him, and he plays along with her both for the security of her love and the safety from her wrath. Louise deserves some sympathy, too: her marriage is passionless, and she must express emotion where she can.

3. *Clive and Stanley*. Worse than the marriages in Shaffer's plays, are the relationships between fathers and sons. In "The Prodigal Father," the distance was a physical one—Leander and Jed were on different continents; in *Five Finger Exercise* the distance is emotional: Clive and Stanley do not share each other's values. Shaffer's description of Clive specifies that he looks like his mother. He also acts and thinks like her, as far as Stanley can see. If the contention between husband and wife is a continuous conflict between practicality and pretention, with father and son it is one of realism versus idealism. Stanley is a good father, but despite his concern with his son's well-being, conflicts arise between them, both because there are real differences between Clive and Stanley, and because Clive fears betraying Louise.

From the first scene, it is clear that Clive would like to get along with his father, but he just does not know how. He wants to support his father on the issue of the need for a tutor, but he has to be certain that he in no way contradicts his mother's point of view:

Stanley: [to Clive] . . . We don't send our girl to anything so common as a school. You like the idea, I suppose?

Clive: *(eager to agree)* As a matter of fact, I think it's ridiculous—I mean, well—unnecessary, really. (*FFE*, 3)

When Stanley informs Louise that Clive agrees with him and not with her, she presses Clive, and he avoids the subject:

> *Stanley:*   . . . Clive agrees with me.
>
> *Louise:*   *(pouring coffee for Stanley)* Oh? Do you, Clive?
>
> *Clive:*   *(quietly)* Isn't it a little early for this sort of conversation? (*FFE*, 4)

Stanley is interested in Clive's plan for the future. He would like for his son to forget the nonsense of college and certainly of the arts. He urges him instead to become interested in business and in making money. Stanley questions Clive about his whereabouts the night before, and with some reluctance Clive reveals that he was reviewing a play for a magazine that a friend edits, and that he plans to study literature at Cambridge. Stanley wants to know why he would study anything like that, and Clive's answer is incomprehensible to him: "Well, because—well, poetry's its own reward, actually—like virtue. All Art is, I should think" (*FFE*, 6).

Stanley finally gets around to the real issue at hand, that of making money: "You don't seem to realize the world you're living in, my boy. When you finish at this university which your mother insists you're to go to, you'll have to earn your living" (*FFE*, 6). After a round about Clive's impracticality, the subject is his choice of friends, on which Stanley has definite views: Clive should be making contacts in the world of business with people who can be useful to him and help him get ahead: "I mayn't be much in the way of education, but I know this: if you can't stand on your own two feet you don't amount to anything. And not one of that pansy set of spongers you're going round with will ever help you do that" (*FFE*, 6). Stanley may object to the "pansy set of spongers" as not being able to help Clive professionally, but his real concern is that a son of his should associate with people like the "arty-tarty boys," "giggling and drinking and talking dirty, wearing Bohemian clothes, tight trousers," as they hang around Chelsea looking down on people who have interests more important than "*operah*—and *ballay* and *dramah*" (*FFE*, 6). Stanley goes on until Louise intervenes on her son's behalf.

     4. *Pamela and Clive.*   Pamela, the fourteen-year-old daughter, "as volatile as her brother, and wholly without his melancholy" (*FFE*, 9), is the least-developed character in the play. The only two people with whom she converses at length are her brother and her tutor. Stanley seems too preoccupied with the problems of his son to give her much

thought, and Louise does not go beyond fulfilling her motherly obligations toward the girl and using her as a pawn for her own ends. Pamela
feels affection and genuine respect for Clive, although her relationship
with her brother is more frivolous than serious: they play verbal games
with each other (not unlike the games Clive plays with his mother, but
much more innocent); they speak to each other in make-believe voices;
and Clive quizzes Pamela on history by making a game of it:

> *Clive:* . . . Which was the most uncertain dynasty in Europe?
>
> *Pamela:* . . . I haven't the faintest.
>
> *Clive:* (*as if reading*) The Perhapsburgs. . . . Thomas the Tenta-
> tive—a successor of Doubting Thomas, of course—and— . . .
> Vladimir—the Vague. (*FFE*, 17)

Pamela and Clive's is the only family relationship in which there is love
and respect for as well as an enjoyment of each other, and in which there
are no ulterior motives.

   5. *Pamela and Walter.*   Walter is the common denominator and
the catalyst, the outsider who is all things to all people: a tutor for
Pamela, a friend for Clive, a confidant for Louise, and a sounding board
for Stanley. But for her light-hearted games with Clive, Pamela hardly
speaks to anyone in the play except for Walter. She talks about
everything—American English, her friends, her family—to avoid her
studies, but mostly she is interested in talking about Walter. Where is he
from? What is Germany like? What about his family? She is a budding
adolescent with interests more personal than French verbs. She speaks to
Clive of Walter in superlatives:

> *Pamela:* (*listening*) He's the best, isn't he?
>
> *Clive:* Just about.
>
> *Pamela:* Oh, you can tell. I knew just as soon as he came in the door.
>
> *Clive:* How d'you get on together?
>
> *Pamela:* (. . .) Oh, we simply adore each other.
>
> *Clive:* Is he going to teach you anything?
>
> *Pamela:* (. . .) Everything, my dear. (*FFE*, 16–17)

   6. *Louise and Walter.*   Misunderstanding characterizes the relationship between Louise and Walter. Louise is thrilled to have in her
home an intellectual-in-residence to give her daughter private tutoring,

to play music on the piano, but most of all to fill her own emotional gap, left by the rift between herself and her husband. Walter is "a German youth, secret, warm, precise but not priggish" (*FFE*, 9); he is a mystery and a challenge to Louise. Treating him like another son in her house, Louise gives him the nickname Hibou (Owl), because of his appearance when he wears his glasses. But it is not as a mother that she wants Walter to regard her. She unburdens herself to him and speaks of her family background and of her marital problems, explaining that only for the children's sake does she stay with Stanley. She wants to know about his past, but all that he is willing to tell her is that his parents died when he was too young to remember them and that he was brought up by an aunt and uncle—a situation similar to that of Lucy in "The Prodigal Father."

Walter also lets Louise know that he hates everything German: "I am German. This is not so poetic—even the name—I hate. . . . You are too good to understand what I mean. I know how they seem to you, the Germans: so kind and quaint. Like you yourself said: millers' daughters and woodcutters. But they can be monsters" (*FFE*, 30). To Walter, England is Paradise, and he wants nothing more than to become a British subject and spend the rest of his life there. Slowly, Louise leads Walter into talking about his feelings for her. She begins by recalling the day they met: "at that terrible cocktail party in London, [you were] standing all by yourself in the corner pretending to study the pictures. Do you remember? Before even I spoke to you I knew you were something quite exceptional. (. . .) I remember thinking—'Such delicate hands—and that fair hair—it's the hair of a poet. And when he speaks, he'll have a soft voice that stammers a little from nervousness, and a lovely Viennese accent . . .'" (*FFE*, 29–30). Walter bends and kisses Louise's hands just as Clive does when he is game-playing with his mother. This is Louise's opportunity to establish the relationship that she wants with Walter, and she acts upon her desires: she takes his head in her hands and holds it close to her and speaks to him tenderly just as Clive enters the room.

7. *Clive and Walter.*   Walter's presence in the Harrington home has its influence on the whole family, but more so on Clive than on any of the others: his effect on Stanley is minor; Louise is strong enough to recover from any disappointments she suffers because of him; Pamela is too young and emotionally immature to take him seriously. Such is not the situation with Clive: he has not yet defined himself in adult terms, independent of his mother's subtle pressures that he never grow up, and of his father's that he start accepting adult responsibility and thinking about the future. Walter's presence in the house is a source of relief at the

same time that it is a threat and a torment for Clive. In their first conversation, Clive warns Walter about the family with which he is living: "This isn't a family. It's a tribe of wild cannibals. (. . .) Between us we eat everyone we can. . . . Actually, we're very choosy in our victims. We only eat other members of the family" (*FFE*, 13–14). Clive, who has always had a family to take care of him, has been spoiled by it and can see only its shortcomings. Walter, on the other hand, considers himself fortunate to be living with a family and to feel the security of a home for the first time.

Jealousy, at first subdued and later pronounced, mars their friendship, as Walter, the intruder, threatens Clive's relationship with his mother. Rather than coming to Clive now when she has questions about music, Louise goes to Walter, who should know; after all, he is German, which is almost Viennese. When Louise decides to give Walter a nickname, just as she has given one to Clive, and she selects Hibou, Clive instead suggests "Pou" as being even better: it means "louse."

8. *Clive, Act 1, Scene 2.* Two months pass between the two scenes of act 1, and they are crucial months in Clive's life: he has started college, and being away from home has produced profound changes in him. The most dramatic change at home is in his relationship with his mother, who is now critical of him for taking so late a train that he missed dinner (she had prepared all of his favorites); for leaving his suitcases in the dining room rather than putting them in his room; for drinking more whiskey than she approves of; and for not trying to learn to play the piano. The first real blow to Louise comes when Clive is no longer interested in helping her with the dinner dishes; it is the first sign in Clive's behavior that he is asserting himself as an individual, unconcerned with his mother's disapproval. Her second disappointment is induced by Clive's reluctance to play their old games together:

> Louise: Oh, Jou-Jou! *Mon petit Cossack. Embrasse-moi. (She pauses) Non? (She pauses)* It's your empress.
>
> Clive: *(rising)* Your Majesty. *(He crosses to the sideboard and pours a whiskey for himself)* (FFE, 25).

And Louise exits into the kitchen. Later, on her suggestion that Walter recite some poetry for them, Clive becomes furious and goes out to a pub. When he returns, drunk, he finds Louise holding Walter's head in her hands, and Clive is distressed.

What little there was of his relationship with his father has deterio-
rated also. In the interim, Clive visited his father's factory and was openly
critical with the manager about the grotesque, shoddy, and vulgar
furniture that his father produces. Louise rushes to Clive's defense: "Just
because *you've* got no taste," she tells Stanley, "it doesn't mean we all have
to follow suit" (*FFE*, 21), which she says as much to offend her husband
as to support her son. Stanley defends the practicality of his approach to
producing furniture: he sells the people what they want and has been
quite successful; and he reminds Clive that his own business expertise has
kept the family well maintained. Clive is sorry for what he said about his
father's business and tries to apologize to him. Characteristic of the good
father that he is, Stanley is more concerned with Clive's life at Cambridge
than with the incident at his factory. Has Clive made friends? Joined any
clubs? Participated in any sports, perhaps? To Stanley's disappointment,
Clive is active only in the Dramatic Society. Stanley turns the conversation around to what Clive is making of his education, and Clive's poetic
explanation is not what Stanley had hoped to hear:

Look, education—being educated—you just can't talk about it in that way. It's
something quite different—like setting off on an expedition into the jungle.
Gradually, most of the things you know disappear. The old birds fly out of the
sky and new ones fly in you've never seen before—maybe with only one wing
each. Yes, it's as new as that. Everything surprises you. Trees you expected to be
just a few feet high grow right up over you, like the nave of Wells
Cathedral. . . . Anyway, if you had seen all this before, you wouldn't have to
go looking. I think education is simply the process of being taken by surprise,
don't you see? (*FFE*, 23)

No, Stanley does not see it. This is the time for Clive to be making the
right friends, not just because he will be judged by the company he
keeps, but also because the contacts that he makes now can help him
professionally later in life. The question of who are Clive's friends is
touchy for him ("Do you want a list?" *FFE*, 23), and this scene with his
father is an unpleasant reliving for Clive of his life before he started
college. Clive goes through another round of trying to explain to his
father who are the people that he, Clive, considers important, like a fellow
student from Bombay: "He's completely still. . . . I mean that deep
down inside him there's a sort of happy stillness that makes all our family
rows and raised voices seem like a kind of—blasphemy almost. That's
why he matters—because he loves living so much. Because he understands birds and makes shadow puppets out of cardboard, and loves Ella

Fitzgerald and Vivaldi, and Lewis Carroll . . ." (*FFE*, 36). Stanley is both bewildered and impatient. He tries to tell Clive that he is happy that his son has some nice friends, and Clive accuses him of being patronizing. He is tired of being the one who has to try to understand his father; why does his father not try to understand him sometimes? Why must he be considered no more than an extension of his father rather than an individual in his own right, complete just as he is right now?

I am myself. Myself. Myself. You think of me only as what I might become. What I might make of myself. But I am myself now—with every breath I take, every blink of the eyelash. The taste of a chestnut or a strawberry on my tongue is me. The smell of my skin is me, the trees and sofas that I see with my own eyes are me. You should want to become me and see them as I see them—as I should with you. But we can never exchange. Feelings don't unite us, don't you see? They keep us apart. (*FFE*, 38)

Clive is naive not to realize that it is precisely this kind of language that keeps him and Stanley apart because Stanley cannot begin to understand what his son means. Stanley sincerely tries to get close to him; he asks if Clive would like to go over to visit a friend of his father and maybe stop off for a drink on the way. But Clive excuses himself on the pretext that he has some reading to do, and Stanley leaves discouraged. When he returns, Clive tells him dramatically, tearfully, and deceitfully that he caught Walter and Louise together; she was half undressed and Walter was kissing her on the mouth and on the breasts.

Jealousy gets the best of Clive when he finds Walter with his head in Louise's hands, and he cannot find it in him to be cordial any longer. He alludes to Walter's unkempt state: "Hair is being worn dishevelled this year. The Medusa style. What would have happened if Medusa had looked in a mirror? Are monsters immune against their own fatal charms?" (*FFE*, 31). And then he attacks his mother's ancestors to Walter, to set the record straight on the half-truths that Louise must have been telling him.

In actuality, I regret to say, they weren't as aristocratic as all that. My great-grandpa despite any impression to the contrary, did not actually grant humble petitions from his bedside—merely industrial patents from a run-down little office near the Louvre. The salary was so small that the family would have died of starvation if Helene, my grandmother, hadn't met an English solicitor on a cycling tour of the Loire, married him, and exchanged Brunoy for Bournemouth.

Let us therefore not gasp too excitedly at the loftiness of mother's family tree. Unbeknownst to father it has, as you will see, roots of clay. (*FFE*, 31)

So much for his mother's family; now for his mother. Louise suffers from what Clive calls a "plaster-gilt complex": she imagines herself "*ormolu*" in a sitting room of plaster gilt; the only place she feels really at home is in a salon, because there is no other place where she can be so continuously dishonest. And why does she have Walter in her household? Because he is a precious ornament, a dear little Dresden owl, who sooner or later will be used and then cast out when he can no longer help one member of the family score a point against the others.

When Pamela comes home, Clive can only think: "*(to himself)* She's the only one who's free, with her private star of Grace. *(louder)* It's a marvelous dispensation: to escape one's inheritance" (*FFE*, 33). For all of his lofty ideas, he envies his sister for the freedom to be herself, just as he envies his friend from Bombay for his inner peace.

Clive's attitude toward Walter changes, and he asks Walter to go away on a vacation with him, maybe to the West Country at Christmastime. Walter refuses because he does not want to be away from the family then, and he has his tutoring obligations for which he has been paid until the end of January; besides, he has an obligation to Mrs. Harrington. Clive pleads in quiet desperation: "If you come away with me, it would be for my sake not yours. I need a friend so badly" (*FFE*, 34). Walter pities Clive but does not change his decision, and Clive lashes out against him:

Is that all you can say—"I'm sorry?" Such an awkward position I put you in, don't I? The poor little immigrant, careful not to offend. So very sensitive. *(with sudden fury)* When the hell are you going to stop trading on your helplessness— offering yourself all day to be petted and stroked? Yes! Just like I do . . . O.K., you're a pet. You've got an irresistible accent. You make me sick!" (*FFE*, 34)

Walter excuses himself from the room as Clive tries to apologize.

B. *Act 2*. Act Two is built upon the conversations that each member of the Harrington family has with Walter. He has become important in their lives, a part of the family, and at the same time he almost remains enough of an outsider to be considered an objective observer by his confidants.

1. *Pamela and Walter*. The conversation that Pamela has with Walter begins appropriately enough as one between pupil and tutor and then proceeds to become more encompassing and more penetrating. In it, Pamela shows that she is an intelligent observer and a force to be reckoned with, not a silly child whose thoughts are dismissed by her mother (though not by her brother) as insignificant and unworthy of consideration. It is a Sunday morning, and Pamela, who is dressed in her jodhpurs for riding, demonstrates her interest in sports—an interest not shared by her brother. She reads the word *salacious* in the *Sunday Times*, and Walter tells her what it means. She thinks that he is brilliant and ought to be teaching English. Gradually, though not at all cautiously, she brings the conversation around to her family:

> Pamela: *(impulsively)* Are you happy here? Are you really, really happy?
>
> Walter: Of course.
>
> Pamela: Who do you like best?
>
> Walter: You.
>
> Pamela: No, seriously.
>
> Walter: I like you all. You and your mother . . .
>
> Pamela: And Clive?
>
> Walter: Of course, and Clive. (*FFE*, 42)

Walter feels sorry for Clive because he is so unhappy, but Pamela attributes his unhappiness to his having been spoiled when he was young. She thinks marriage would be the best thing for her brother, and that Walter must help him find a girlfriend.

> Walter: Has he not had friendships with girls before?
>
> Pamela: *(in her affected voice)* Not even acquaintances, my dear. *(in her normal voice)* Except one . . . Clive said they used to go down on the beach and neck, but I bet he was just bragging. (*FFE*, 42)

Pamela suggests that Clive needs a girl who will pay attention to him because, as his sister sees it, "Clive spends his whole time not being listened to" (*FFE*, 43).[3] Furthermore, she thinks (and Clive later reveals) that he is no more than a weapon that mother and father use in their ongoing battle, and: "With mother and daddy the row is never really *about*—well, what they're quarrelling about. I mean—behind what they say you can feel—well, that mother did this in the past, and daddy did that. I don't mean anything *particular*" (*FFE*, 43). Pamela tries to see her parents objectively, and believes that each has a legitimate complaint against the other:

I know mother's frightful to him about culture, and uses music and things to keep him out—which is terrible. But isn't that just because *he* made *her* keep out of things when they were first married? You know he wouldn't even let her go to concerts and theatres although she was dying to, and once he threw a picture she'd bought into the dustbin. . . . But then, mightn't *that* just have been because being brought up by himself he was afraid of making a fool of himself. Oh, poor daddy. Poor mother, too. *(FFE, 43)*

Pamela gives details and a point of view on her family's struggles not heard from the other members of her family; and her concern is her family, not herself.

Later in the act, Pamela trips on her way down the stairs, and Walter rushes over to help her. Unfortunately, his manner of helping does not conform to her romantic fantasies about him, and she complains to her mother.

> Pamela: (exasperated) . . . And that idiot Walter has to come in and pick me up as if I was a chandelier or something. Holding me that way.
>
> Louise: (carefully) What way, darling?
>
> Pamela: Well, trying to carry me, as if I was a baby. (FFE, 51)

Pamela regrets what she said about Walter and hopes that he did not hear any of it. It has, however, been well recorded in Louise's memory.

2. *Louise and Walter.* Just as in Act 1, Louise finds a private moment with Walter. All of the preliminaries finished, all pretenses stripped away, Louise quickly brings up the subject of love and introduces one of the tenderest moments in the play:

> Louise: (warmly) I don't believe you can ration love, do you?
>
> Walter: (admiringly) With someone like you it is not possible.
>
> Louise: Nor with you, my dear. You know, last night held the most beautiful moments I've known for many years. I felt—well, that you and I could have a really warm friendship. Even with the difference—I mean in—in our ages.
>
> Walter: Between friends there are no ages, I think.
>
> Louise: (tenderly) I like to think that, too.

> *Walter:* Oh, it's true. Like in a family—you never think how old people are, because you keep growing together.
>
> *Louise:* Yes.
>
> . . . .
> What's the matter, Little Owl, are you embarrassed?
> (WALTER *shakes his head*)
> That's the last thing you must ever be with me.
> (WALTER *smiles*)
> What are you thinking? Tell me.
>
> *Walter:* Some things grow more when they re not talked about.
>
> *Louise:* Try, anyway. I want you to.
>
> *Walter:* (. . .) It is only that you have made me wonder . . .
>
> *Louise:* (*prompting eagerly*) Tell me.
>
> *Walter:* (*lowering his voice*) Mrs. Harrington, forgive me for asking this, but do you think it's possible for someone to find a new mother? (LOUISE *sits very still and stares at Walter*) (*He kneels beside Louise and puts his hand on hers*) Have I offended you?
>
> *Louise:* (*smiling without joy*) Of course not. (*She slips her hand from under his*) I am—very touched. (*FFE*, 58)

What she really is is very crushed, and much to Louise's dismay she is herself partially to blame. While she tries to interest Walter in her as a woman and thus fill the emotional void left by her husband's indifference, she is also playing the same game with him that she plays with Clive, calling him "Hibou" and "my dear boy." She has, in effect, created an Oedipal triangle among the three of them. (Lyons, 45). She is equating Walter with her son and making him regard her as a mother. She fulfills his need for a family but lets herself in for a serious disappointment. Louise is well versed in the art of revenge; if she cannot have Walter, neither can her daughter or her son. Walter tries to express his concern over Clive's unhappiness, and Louise dismisses him brusquely: "As you said yourself, you *are* only a newcomer to the family" (*FFE*, 59). Pamela has given Louise the excuse that she needs to get Walter out of the house. Her daughter regards Walter as she would a character in a Romantic opera who "should wear a frock-coat and have consumption," and as someone who always makes her feel "ashamed" (*FFE*, 52): he is having an undesirable effect on a girl who is at an impressionable age.

 3. *Clive and Walter.* The seeds that Shaffer plants in the first act come to fruition in the second. Thus Clive's sexual preoccupation, which

is only hinted at earlier, becomes a focal point in act 2. He is forced
to come to grips with his ambiguous feelings toward Walter: on the
one hand, jealousy toward the intruder on his private territory—his
mother—and on the other, an emerging closeness that he feels toward
the strange man now living in their house. Walter mischievously asks if
Clive thinks that he will make a good father someday, but Clive is feeling
too cheerful for so deep a conversation. Soon his briskness and gaiety
wane, and he talks about his future, which seems dim to him because he
can identify only those things that he does *not* want to be in life and has
no idea of what he *does* want to be. Clive is still waiting for his calling,
aware that if he does not decide for himself how he wants to spend his life,
other people will decide for him. His self-doubts begin to surface: "I
always seem to be talking about things that don't matter" (*FFE*, 55). He
does not say this as an appeal for sympathy but out of conviction, hoping
for Walter to supply an answer. There is a pause, and Walter changes the
subject by apologizing for walking out on Clive last night. He thinks
that it was kind of Clive to suggest that they take a vacation together and
he encourages him to talk about the things that he has on his mind. Clive
would rather forget those issues, and, making an about-face from the
stand he took last night, he asks Walter to leave the house, to go back to
Germany, to leave the Harringtons for his own good. If Walter will not
go for his own sake, then he should do so for Clive's, who can't bear to
watch. Clive never finishes his thought, but there are any number of
things he cannot bear to watch: Louise's emasculation of Walter, or her
affection for him, or Clive's own attraction to the man.

Clive's cheer has now changed to depression, and Walter thinks that
he has identified sexual self-doubt as the reason for which Clive hates his
parents and himself. Walter reveals to Clive the details of his first sexual
encounter. He thought that it would change him, make him a man,
make him so strong that nothing could hurt him again, but it did none
of those things. He wants Clive to forgive his parents for "being
average," for any mistakes that they made in bringing him up that have
resulted in problems for him, and to forgive himself for his real problem
which, as Walter sees it, is having fears and doubts. Walter insists that
"sex by itself is nothing, believe me. Just like breathing—only important when it goes wrong. And Clive, this only happens if you're afraid of
it. What are you thinking? *(He pauses)* Please talk to me" (*FFE*, 69). Clive
mistakes Walter's concern for pity, as he violently seeks answers:
"What's wrong with me? . . . What have they done to me?" (*FFE*,
69). Walter, in his turn, now advises Clive that he must leave his parents'

house and never come back: "At the end of term in Cambridge, don't come back here. Go anywhere else you like. Join your American friend singing. Go into a factory" (*FFE*, 69). Walter reveals what he wants out of life: a wife, children, and many English friends. Clive's desires are less concrete: he wants to fall in love with just one person and to know what it is to bless and to be blessed. Clive consents to take Walter's advice and quips about how they spend their time ordering each other out of the house.

Similarly, Walter is ready to confide his secret to Clive, a secret which apparently nobody else in England knows. Walter is not an orphan; his parents are alive in Muhlbach, Germany. And it is not surprising that Walter has suppressed the facts about his past: his father was a Nazi and one of the most efficient officers at the Auschwitz concentration camp. Walter confesses:

He was a great man in town. People were afraid of him, and so was I. When war broke out, he went off to fight and we [Walter and his mother] did not see him for almost six years. When he came back, he was still a Nazi. Now, everyone else was saying, "We never liked them. We never supported them." But not him. "I've always supported them," he said. "Hitler was the best man our country has seen since Bismarck." . . . Every night he used to make me recite the old slogans against Jews and Catholics and the Liberals. When I forgot, he would hit me—so many mistakes, so many hits. (*FFE*, 56)

His mother worshipped his father. As he was beating Walter, she would look away; her husband was only doing his duty. Thus, Walter's denial of having a family and his hatred of everything German becomes understandable, as does his game of false identity, which will be a theme in the one-act plays.

4. *Stanley and Walter.* Everybody's feelings have been exposed except Stanley's, and he, like his son, turns to Walter. Walter is as nervous around Stanley as Clive is. Stanley is concerned that his son may be developing a drinking problem, and that Clive uses alcohol to escape from his father. He presses for Walter's opinion on what he has seen of the family's relations, and Walter is frank in his reply: Clive does not believe that his father loves him; he feels that his father is judging him when they are together; that his father considers him useless. Stanley sees the situation from a parent's point of view: children are the selfish ones; they think only of their own problems; Clive hates him and thinks that he is too busy making money to care about his family. He imagines that when

Clive is looking at him, he is thinking, "How common he is" (*FFE*, 66). Walter urgently defends Clive: a boy should not have to apologize for enjoying Greek or opera. Walter oversteps his bounds when he suggests that Clive needs help, and the angered Stanley tries to blame Walter for his son's attitudes. Once calm, Stanley reflects out loud on his life, in a manner reminiscent of another father, Mr. Mayer in "The Salt Land":

What's it matter? You start a family, work and plan. Suddenly you turn around and there's nothing there. Probably never was. What's a family, anyway? Just—just like kids with your blood in 'em. There's no reason why they should like you. You go on expecting it, of course, but it's silly, really. . . . You can't expect anybody to know what they mean to somebody else—it's not the way of things. . . . Perhaps he'll make the rugger fifteen or the cricket team or something—anything—and then his first girl friend and taking her home—or perhaps just keeping her to himself till he's sure. (*frankly*) But nothing— nothing. And now he hates me. (*FFE*, 67)

He has spoken his mind, and now the subject is closed.

Moments later, in a rage, he returns to dismiss Walter as Pamela's tutor, and Walter suddenly is blamed for all of the Harringtons' problems. Stanley resents Walter for speaking so freely about his adopted family; for being patronizing with his employer; for turning Clive into a "sissy"; for advising Clive to leave home and never come back; and finally for having a bad effect on their daughter (which Stanley admits that he does not believe to be true). Stanley brings the scene to a climax by revealing the real reason that Stanley wishes to get him out of the house. Walter is trying to make love to Louise. Stanley tells it to him as brutally as he knows how: "You filthy German bastard. . . . Once a German, always a German. Take what you want and the hell with everyone else" (*FFE*, 71). One cruel blow follows another: Walter finds it incomprehensible that his friend Clive would betray him to Stanley by saying that he was making love to Louise. Worst of all Stanley will see to it that Walter is made to leave England for alleged indiscretions with Pamela:

I'm going to fix it so you never get your naturalization papers. I'm going to write to the immigration people. I'll write tonight, and tell them all about you. I'll say—let's see: "Much though I hate to complain about people behind their backs, I feel it my duty in this case to warn you about this young German's standard of morality. Whilst under my roof, he attempted to force his attentions on my young daughter, who is only fourteen." Try to get your papers after that. They'll send you back to the place where you belong. (*FFE*, 72)

Walter's every hope and illusion has now been destroyed: he has lost his "new mother," been betrayed by his only friend, been asked to leave the house in which he considered himself a member of the family, and been denied the chance of becoming a British subject. He even now faces the most dreaded of all possibilities, that of having to return to Germany. There is no reason left for him to go on living.

5. *Stanley and Louise.* In the last scene of the play, Stanley and Louise really discuss the family's problems. Since his conversation with Walter, Stanley is preoccupied with Clive and takes the offensive with Louise: "You know what the trouble is? Your son's turning into a drunkard," he says (*FFE*, 61). Louise counters by blaming Stanley for their son's drinking: "The way you've been behaving lately's enough to make anyone drink. . . . No-one would think he's your son. You treat him abominably" (*FFE*, 61). Tempers flare, but both believe that they are speaking frankly. Louise believes that Stanley has made no attempt to understand Clive, and Stanley accuses Louise of turning their son into a sniveling little neurotic mother's boy, whose speech is starting to sound like that of a lunatic; it is all Louise's fault because every time Stanley tried to interest Clive in sports and thereby establish a decent relationship with his son, Louise interfered with excuses that Clive was too delicate and that his time was better spent reading. Stanley's closeness with Clive threatened Louise's selfish interests: if he had snipped Clive from her apron strings, she would have been left with nothing—no husband and no son.

Louise admits that she was afraid that Stanley would have tried to force him straight into his "third-rate" furniture business for the rest of his life: "Well, that's not good enough for *me*, Stanley" (*FFE*, 62). Whether it would have been good for Clive never occurs to her. After Stanley accuses Louise of destroying a son for him, Louise can stand no more. There is a moment in which, despite all of her flaws, Louise expresses seriously what has always been a thorn in Stanley's side, and she appears as a character who deserves some sympathy: "My life was never meant to be like this—limited this way. I know I'm unpredictable sometimes. I say things I don't mean. But don't you see I'm just so frustrated, I don't know what I'm doing half the time? . . . There are times I feel I'm being choked to death—suffocated under piles of English blankets. . . . I've never been able to take your world of shops and business seriously. Can't you understand?" (*FFE*, 63). Stanley is willing to offer Louise a divorce, but the idea is too vulgar for her to consider. He wants to improve their relationship (maybe a weekend away together would help), but Louise is not interested.

Stanley worries about the effect that a divorce would have on Pamela; Louise thinks only of herself and of Clive. She manages to change the topic to get Stanley to do her dirty work for her: she wants him to fire Walter on the pretext that he is having an adverse effect on Pamela. Stanley's unpleasant task of dismissing Walter is made easier since he has heard Walter express himself on how Clive is a troubled man. And so Stanley does his wife's bidding.

6. *Louise and Clive.*   The final confrontation is between mother and son, the two most explosive characters in the play. The scene brings to a culmination their disillusions compounded by jealousies and frustrations, and they show a complete lack of sympathy for each other. Clive has just returned home from a day's drinking, and Louise tells him that "your father and I have been worried to death" (*FFE*, 65). Louise's choice of words sparks Clive's jealousy, which knows no boundaries, and even extends to his own father: "Do I detect a new note in the air? Your father and I. How splendid! The birth of a new moral being. Your-father-and-I When did you last see your-father-and-I? Or is it just a new alliance? All the same, I congratulate you. I always thought you two ought to get married" (*FFE*, 65).

Clive wants to know why Walter is upset, and, although Louise does not want to discuss the matter, Stanley tells him that he has just dismissed him for paying too much attention to his wife, and Louise hears for the first time the lie that Clive fabricated for his father's benefit. Clive still believes that "what I felt under the lie—about you and Walter—was that so untrue?" (*FFE*, 75). Now Louise's jealousy is activated as Clive expresses concern only for his father: "Can't you *see* what you've done? There isn't a Stanley Harrington any more. We've broken him in bits between us" (*FFE*, 75). What Clive wants to see is an end to the war that Louise and Stanley declared at the time of their marriage, the cultural war in which they use Clive as emotional ammunition. Louise tells Clive that Walter has been dismissed in order to protect Pamela, and he cries out: "*(in sudden despair)* He can't go away from here" (*FFE*, 75). Clive, uses his strongest weapon against his mother when he accuses her of being jealous of her fourteen-year-old daughter: "What was it? Jealousy? Shame, when you saw them so innocent together? Or just the sheer vulgarity of competing with one's own daughter?" (*FFE*, 76). When Clive finishes his tirade, Louise bursts into tears, and Clive, desperate for tenderness, tries to resort to the reliable "French game," but he has gone too far, and even games do not help. Louise is provoked as never before; she circles her son, preparing to humiliate him by insinuating that he feels an attraction for Walter: "D'you think you're the only one can ask terrible questions? Supposing I ask a few. Supposing I ask them. You ought to be glad Walter's going, but you're not. Why not? Why aren't you glad? You want him to stay, don't you? You want him to stay very much. Why?" (*FFE*, 77). Clive panics, screams, falls across the table, and accuses Louise of killing him. While this scene is taking place in the living room, Walter is upstairs attempting suicide. Stanley saves him just in time, and Clive ends the play with a prayer: "The courage. For all of us. Oh, God—*give* it" (*FFE*, 78).

C. *Summation*. Except for Pamela, an innocent girl going through adolescent growing pains, no character is presented as all good or all bad. Louise is vicious, but she is suffering from cultural suffocation and lacks an outlet in her marriage for her emotional needs. She lavishes attention on Clive to protect herself from nothingness—to assure herself of a partner in her battle against the mundane. Stanley is the picture of the upright family man, but he is ready, based on a lie, to inform the immigration board of an alleged indiscretion and thereby ruin Walter's chances of establishing a life for himself in England. Clive receives a sympathetic treatment, but is guilty of jealousy and of deceit. Although he apparently feels nothing but love for his mother and contempt for his father, the situation is really more complex than that. Clive is a poseur, who, in his attempt to be liked, is whatever people want him to be: he plays games with his mother to keep her love, while at the same he harbors hate, jealousy, and resentment for what she had made of him. The contempt that he has been conditioned to feel for his father is really concern, and he senses an identification between himself and Stanley: both men are fighting to keep from being devoured by Louise. Walter's mask is the most blatantly misleading: he has been living a lie concerning his past, but only in order to protect himself from a world that would be harsh in its judgment of him and from a psyche that would otherwise be relentless.

Structure

Characterizations aside, much of the beauty of *Five Finger Exercise* derives from the simplicity, subtlety, and hence, elegance of its structure, which is faithful to the spirit of the classical unities. The play is divided into two acts, with each act divided into two scenes. The first scene of each act takes place in the morning and the second scenes take place after dinner. Two months pass between the scenes of act 1 but the effect of the play is that it takes place in a single weekend. Each scene involves a series of conversations among the members of the Harrington family and the tutor, with only a bit of new information given at one time, all of which comes together in the climactic scenes of the second act.

Shaffer explains his intention in writing his first play as he did: ". . . I worked deliberately in the dead-ended convention of week-end-cottage naturalism in *Five Finger Exercise*, but without any desire to be tricksy: the convention is utterly appropriate to the subject, and far from dead if handled with seriousness and desire. . . ." ("Labels," 20–21). In another interview, he expressed his contempt for the British drama that fails to go below the surface of family life: "I was using the stock properties of the artificial, untrue and boring family plays the English never seem to tire of in order that the audience should feel solid ground under its feet and so follow me easily into my play" (Ross, 3).

The title of the play suggests a piano exercise for one hand, five fingers, hence five characters,[4] and shows Shaffer's intention in its structure. Each conversation, usually between two characters at a time, is only moderately revealing as to the depth of intrigue within the Harrington household, but like a good fugue, all of the elements (here, characters) depend on each other, and thus the relationships are shown to be mutually dependent: Louise's relationship with Clive takes place within the context of a passionless marriage; Clive's apparent scorn for his father is a consequence of his relationship with his mother; Pamela is neglected because she cannot serve as ammunition between Louse and Stanley as easily as her brother can. Walter serves as a catalyst; all of the Harringtons can speak freely to him, unburden themselves to him, and win his sympathy. Thus, one and all use him.

Critical Interpretation

The play seems to be as straightforward as possible: it is a slice of life on two significant weekends in the lives of the Harringtons. Yet the reviewers and critics found all kinds of implications in the work. For Gore Vidal[5] the Harringtons are a family of stereotypes: four strangers with nothing in common, forced by blood to share the same house. Taking the Harringtons as a microcosm, Vidal sees the theme of the play as the downfall of the Western family. He takes a dangerous critical position by projecting the Harringtons beyond the limits of Shaffer's two acts, and predicts that Louise will live in a fantasy world, that Pamela will marry, and that Clive will be a homosexual. John Russell Taylor[6] thinks that Louise is unjustified in seeing homosexual overtones in Clive's relationship with Walter, while the unidentified writer for McGraw Hill[7] maintains that it is Walter who encourages a homosexual relationship to develop between himself and Clive. Ignoring Clive's psychological problems brought on by his relationship with his mother, Kenneth Tynan[8] sees Clive as a rebellious youth fighting against a rich, philistine father. In a review in the *New Yorker*,[9] Tynan expanded his interpretation to include that of five individuals in need of love, each one seeking it where it is least likely to be forthcoming. As such, it is a play of mutual unfulfillment. John McClain[10] sees the theme as the inability of people to unburden themselves honestly to one another, an interpretation which probably comes closest to what Shaffer had in mind when he wrote the play. Loftus quotes Shaffer on the play's meaning as that of a treatment of various levels of dishonesty (Loftus, 1). Robert Coleman[11] sees the problem delineated in the play as one of a lack of communication between the generations and jealousy between Louise and Pamela over Walter. George Wellwarth[12] probes an understanding of the playwright via his drama: *Five Finger Exercise* is Shaffer's attempt to exorcise his personal, drab, middle-class background by producing a work which denigrates his past. This interpretation is both speculative and nonliterary: the critic is not trying to understand a work of art, but rather to use it as a tool for analyzing its author. Shaffer views his play as "morally based": "It is about the fabric of life itself. Life itself is continuous"[13] Shaffer contrasted the reception by the British audience, who found the play a bit daring, with that of the American audience—accustomed to castration and cannibalism in Tennessee Williams's plays—who found the hint at a homosexual attraction rather restrained.

Critical Acclaim

Five Finger Exercise opened in London to enthusiastic critical acclaim and was an immediate success: Shaffer won the Dramatist Award of the *London Evening Standard* and the award for the Best Play by a New Playwright for the 1958–59 theater season from the drama critics of the London newspapers. Most reviewers were eager to praise the work and welcome the new playwright to the London stage. The *Daily Express*[14] praised Shaffer's flair for characterization and dialogue and called him an overnight great of the British theater. The *Times*[15] drew attention to the subtlety of the dialogue. The *Illustrated London News*[16] found in Shaffer's

writing a feeling for phrase demonstrated by few other recent playwrights. And on and on. But there were also some critics who restrained
themselves in their praise. *Punch*,[17] while it admitted that Shaffer had
something to say and said it skillfully, believed that other reviewers were
overly enthusiastic about the play. The *Spectator*[18] found the pace and bite
of the dialogue to be praiseworthy, but criticized its lack of wit. In 1959,
Five Finger Exercise moved to New York and received such an enthusiastic
reception that, on 4 December 1959, the *London Times* included an article
which echoed the New York reviewers.[19] The *New York Times*[20] was
impressed by the subtle characterizations and the precise prose. The
Journal American[21] found *Five Finger Exercise* to be nothing less than great
theater. There was little dissension among the reviewers, and they
presented to Shaffer the New York Drama Critics' Circle Award for the
Best Foreign Play of the 1959–60 season. In 1962, Columbia Pictures
released the film version of *Five Finger Exercise*, directed by Daniel Mann.
Shaffer did not write the script, which was the work of Frances Goodrich
and Albert Hackett. Rosalind Russell (the wife of Frederick Brisson, who
produced the movie and co–produced the stage version in New York)
played Louise; Jack Hawkins, Stanley; Maximilian Schell, Walter; An-
nette Gorman, Pamela; and Richard Beymer, Clive.

The success of *Five Finger Exercise* is even more impressive and surprising when it is considered in the context of the historical moment of
British and continental European drama. It was produced only two years
after John Osborne's *Look Back in Anger*, which many authorities on
British drama consider a turning point in the English theater.[22] It was
produced in the same year as such "Angry" and revolutionary plays as
John Arden's *Live Like Pigs*, Arnold Wesker's *Chicken Soup with Barley*,
and Shelagh Delaney's *A Taste of Honey*. Shaffer's play was not only out of
line with the British protest plays of the late 1950s, but was also in sharp
contrast with the technically innovative drama being written by his
British contemporary Harold Pinter, and such towering figures of European drama as Samuel Beckett and Eugène Ionesco.[23] The immediate
appeal of *Five Finger Exercise* did not wane; as mentioned above, it was
produced as a film in 1962 and presented on the BBC "Play of the
Month" in 1970. The play deserves its success and lives up to every line
of praise bestowed on it by the critics. For its elegant structure, penetrating characterizations, and poetic and witty dialogue, *Five Finger
Exercise* remains Peter Shaffer's finest play to date. There is not a play that
Shaffer wrote after it that does not contain some element already found
here.

Chapter Three
The One-Act Plays

Almost four years had passed since the respective openings of *Five Finger Exercise* in London and New York, before *The Private Ear* and *The Public Eye* debuted at the Globe Theatre in London, on 10 May 1962, and later opened at the Morosco Theatre in New York, on 9 October 1963. For the *Private Ear*'s London premiere Terry Scully played the role of Bob, Douglas Livingstone portrayed Ted and Maggie Smith acted as Doreen. Brian Bedford, Barry Foster, and Geraldine McEwan played the corresponding parts in New York. Kenneth William was Julian, Maggie Smith played Belinda, and Richard Pearson portrayed Charles in the roles of *The Public Eye* in London. The parts were played in New York by Barry Foster, Geraldine McEwan, and Moray Watson, respectively. Peter Wood directed both plays in New York and in London.

Shaffer wanted to experiment with new techniques and enjoyed great success with the variety of devices that he employed in his one-act plays. He also dispelled any ideas that he was a writer of only weekend-cottage naturalism. In addition to *The Private Ear* and *The Public Eye*, *Black Comedy*, paired in New York with *White Lies* and then in London with *The White Liars* (and later *White Liars*), proved that Shaffer is a master of a genre in which relatively few modern dramatists have managed to be successful with the critics as well as with the public. The plays are generally skeletal in their plots (except for *Black Comedy*) and are vehicles for Shaffer's character studies, themes, and techniques.

The Private Ear

The action of *The Private Ear* takes place in slightly over two hours in Bob's attic sitting room in the Belsize Park section of London. The room is shabbily furnished and dominated by the twin speakers of a stereo system. The argument of the plot is linear and simple: for the first time in his life, awkward and insecure Bob has invited a young lady for dinner. Lacking any confidence in his ability to prepare a proper dinner for her, much less sustain a conversation, he invited Ted, a more knowledgeable friend of his, to help him through the evening. Ted arrives a few minutes before Doreen is supposed to come and is disappointed to find that Bob is not dressed yet, that he has forgotten to buy an aperitif, and that he has no interest in any sexual activity with the young lady; he berates Bob on each account. Ted shows Bob a photograph of the girl with whom he could have been spending the evening had he not agreed to help his friend. Bob upsets a vase, thus wetting the photo, which Ted puts on Bob's mirror to dry. Bob tells that he met Doreen at a concert; she dropped her program; he picked it up for her and asked her to have coffee with him after the concert. She accepted, and to his dismay, he could find nothing to say to her. Believing that she must share his love for classical music, he invited her for dinner.

When Doreen arrives, she is as nervous as Bob and not at all looking forward to the evening. Ted carefully combs his hair and comes in from the kitchen to serve wine. As is his custom, Bob does not drink. The conversation between Ted and Doreen is animated and slick, but when Ted returns to the kitchen to prepare dinner, Bob and Doreen are left alone groping to find something to say to each other. Bob begins talking about music, the only topic that he really knows. He speaks of his stereo set (which he has personified and named Behemoth) and of how pleased he is that Doreen was at the Bach concert. She confesses that Bach is not really her favorite composter; she prefers someone more modern, which Bob takes to mean Stravinsky and Shostakovich. No, she meant someone more tuneful; and Bob interprets this to mean a composer such as Britten.

Again Ted intervenes just in time to announce that the soup is ready, thereby saving Bob and Doreen from having to invent any more conversation. The dinner is painful for Bob. Ted begins by ridiculing opera and opera lovers, and Bob calls him "dead ignorant." Ted becomes obvious in his attempt to win Doreen's affection, and Bob begins to drink wine. By the end of dinner, nothing remains of the wine or of Bob and Ted's former friendship. While Bob is in the kitchen preparing the coffee, Doreen confesses to Ted that she was at the concert by accident; a friend gave her the ticket, and she did not want to see it go to waste. Ted slips her a pencil for her telephone number, and she excuses herself so that she may write it down. In her absence, Bob confronts a suddenly defensive Ted and orders him out of the house. When Doreen returns, she is unhappy that Ted left without so much as saying good night, and without her knowing where she can reach him.

As Doreen prepares to leave, Bob becomes urgent about losing her and makes attempts at telling her how pretty she is. He continues by telling her that he hates his job and confides that at times he spends his evenings "conducting" the records on the phonograph. (Pamela "conducted" a record in *Five Finger Exercise*.) Doreen is anxious to leave, but reluctantly agrees to listen to the love duet from *Madame Butterfly*, which Bob assures her will take only three minutes. In the six-minute pantomime that follows, Bob awkwardly tries to seduce Doreen and receives nothing for his efforts but a slap. Acknowledging his failure, Bob gives Doreen Ted's business address, which she had requested earlier, and lies by telling her that the photograph on the mirror is of his (Bob's) girlfriend, to whom he is soon to be married. Left alone and desperate, he plays *Madame Butterfly* again and deliberately scratches the record beyond repair.

The Private Ear is a sensitive character study, and, as is the case with *Five Finger Exercise*, any examination of the play must focus primarily on the characters. Doreen is hardly developed and may be dismissed with little more than a casual comment. She is an antagonist, introduced in the play only so that Bob may go through his moment of self-realization, and so that he and Ted have a chance to confront each other. Ted may not be dismissed quite so quickly as Doreen, but he is not so complex as Bob.

Like Clive in *Five Finger Exercise*, Bob is a discontented and confused young man, emotionally isolated and unable to communicate his deep feelings to prosaic individuals. His life consists of a job that he does not like during the day and of going to concerts or "conducting" his records alone in his room at night. On the evening that the play takes place, he is trying to change his pattern, to get acquainted with a young woman for the first time. In his imagination, he has idealized Doreen, a work-a-day stenographer, into the living image of Botticelli's Venus. All physical evidence to the contrary, Bob sees her as having "exactly the same neck—long and gentle," which is a sign of "spiritual beauty. Like Venus. That's what the picture really represents. The birth of beauty in the human soul."[1] Before Doreen arrives, Ted tries to make Bob see her more realistically, but to no avail, and the difference between his picture and her reality can cause Bob only disappointment. Ted also makes broad references to the sexual activity in which he expects Bob to engage Doreen, and this only angers Bob and makes him tell Ted things like: "Look, Ted, it's not that way at all" (*PE*, 16) and, "Oh, Ted, I wish you'd stop talking like that" (*PE*, 19). Ted accuses Bob of *wanting* to fail with women and he may be correct: Bob is not the first or the last young man in a Shaffer play whose sexual desires for women are, at best, minimal.

The feelings that Bob has bottled up inside of him are deeper and more spiritual than either Ted or Doreen can understand. Bob is unhappy and feels that his life is being wasted: "Some mornings I can hardly get out of that bed thinking how I'm going to spend the day. When I wake up I've got so much energy. I could write a whole book—paint great swirling pictures on the ceiling. But what am I *actually* going to do? Just fill in about five hundred invoices" (*PE*, 53). He marvels at the miracle of creation and despairs at how people waste the precious gifts of life. In a poetic manner worthy of Clive Harrington, he expresses himself to Doreen:

Eyes. Complicated things like eyes, weren't made by God just to see columns of pounds, shillings, and pence written up in a ledger. Tongues! Good grief, the woman next to me in the office even sounds like a typewriter. A thin, chipped old typewriter. Do you know how many thousands of years it took to make anything so beautiful, so feeling, as your hand? People say I know something like the back of my hand, but they don't know their hands. They wouldn't recognize a photograph of them. Why? Because their hands are anonymous. They're just tools for filing invoices, turning lathes around. They cramp up from picking slag out of moving belts of coal. If that's not blasphemy, what is? (*PE*, 53)

The object of Bob's worship is his music, a theme that will recur in *Amadeus*. He has not only personified his stereophonic equipment by giving it a proper name, but in the last scene, after he loses Doreen, he turns to his phonograph as if it were a lover or a god: *"He stands by it as it plays. He looks down at the record turning. He kneels to it, stretching out his arms to enfold it"* (*PE*, 59). When he fails with Doreen, he turns against the thing he loves most, his music, and tries to destroy it. His act is a pale foreshadowing of Alan's in *Equus*.

Ted is the antithesis of Bob; he is *"cocky and extroverted, fitted out gaily by Shaftesbury Avenue to match his own confidence and self-approval"* (*PE*, 13) and a self-proclaimed success with the ladies. He is also insulting and insincere. From the moment he enters Bob's room, he begins criticizing his friend's forgetfulness and carelessness, his music and his clothes. Of Bob's ties, he says, "What is it? The Sheffield Young Men's Prayer Club?" and of another: "Look: that sort of striped tie, that's meant to suggest a club or an old school, well, it marks you, see? 'I'm really a twelve pound a week office worker,' it says. 'Every day I say, Come on five thirty, and every week I say, Come on Friday night. That's me and I'm contented with my lot.' That's what that tie says to me" (*PE*, 15). He is just as unkind when he attacks Bob's taste in music, a very important and private part of his friend's life:

. . . Opera! How so-called intelligent people can listen to it I just can't imagine. I mean, who ever heard of people singing what they've got to say? *(singing to the Toreador Song in* Carmen.*)* "Will you kindly pass the bread?" "Have a bowl of soup?" "Champignon"—"I must go and turn off the gas." Well for heaven's sake! If that's not a bloody silly way to go on, excuse language, I don't know what is. I wish someone would explain it to me, honest. I mean, I'm probably just dead ignorant. *(PE,* 37)

His worst characteristic is his insincerity, his pretense at being Bob's friend. (False friendship reaches fatal proportions in *Yonadab*.) He claims at the beginning of the play that he refused a date with a particularly luscious woman just so that he could come and help out his friend on his first date. There may never have been such an offer, and he might have thought that he would take the opportunity to build himself up by knocking his friend down, as well as to steal Doreen from him. He wastes no time on either score; the moment Bob makes the mistake of offering Doreen the Dubonnet that he has forgotten to buy, Ted appears with a bottle of wine and asks: "Cocktails, madame?" *(PE,* 29) and continues with his charms to make himself attractive to her.

Ted makes his second appearance after Bob and Doreen suffer a complete lack of communication regarding her taste in music. This time he enters wearing a grocery bag, which is intended to make him look like a chef. All through dinner he charms Doreen, as Bob proceeds to get drunk. As soon as Bob is out of the room, Ted tries to put Bob in a poor light in Doreen's eyes by revealing that she is the first woman that Bob has ever had in his apartment. Ted's cruelest cut of all is making Bob face himself during their final confrontation: "You *want* it all to be a bloody total disaster. Christ knows why. Well, you've got your wish" *(PE,* 50). Bob recognizes how Ted has been using him and finally he reacts: "I'm just someone to look down on, aren't I? Teach tricks to. Like a bloody monkey. You're the organ grinder, and I'm the monkey! And that's the way you want people. Well—go home, Ted. Find yourself another monkey!" *(PE,* 50). Ted shares some common traits with Louise: affected speech and the use of nicknames. As does Louise, Ted spices up his speech with French with the intention of impressing Doreen, and to that end he is successful. He also uses a nickname for Bob: "Tchaik," since Tchaikovsky was once Bob's favorite composer. The nickname is fitting, but also demeaning, both to Bob and to classical music, which Bob takes seriously. The kind of relationship that exists between Bob and Ted—with its elements of admiration and ridicule—is a dominant theme in many of Shaffer's plays.

There is no information about Bob's family, except that he has a mother who lives in Sheffield (no mention of a father), but there is some significant information about Ted's and Doreen's families. Ted describes his father as "Mr. Alcohol, 1934" and as a man so completely dominated by his wife that he has not made a decision since he married. His mother is not much better: when she is not out at a bingo hall, she is at home with a bottle of gin. Doreen's father is much like Mr. Harrington, serious and practical, a man who spouts lines like: "Unpunctuality's the thief of time" and "Drink is the curse of the working classes" (*PE*, 24). He is also a forerunner of the hard-working, Socialistic father in *Equus*.

Three dramatic techniques prevail in *The Private Ear*: music, tapes, and pantomime. The musical motif, well developed in *Five Finger Exercise*, plays a prominent role in this play also: the love duet of *Madame Butterfly* inspires amorous longings in Bob that he never knew existed and gives him the courage to attempt making love to Doreen. The music serves as a backdrop for a second technique, a pantomime, a six-minute sequence for Bob's fumbling attempt to seduce Doreen. (In this play's companion piece, silence is taken to its extreme and is one of the play's themes.) Of at least equal importance is Bob's enthusiasm for Benjamin Britten and particularly for his opera *Peter Grimes*. What few details Bob tells Doreen of the opera mirror his whole life: a lonely man who has visions of an ideal woman. In the opera, Peter, a well-intentioned misfit, refuses the help of his friends, an action which gives added significance to Ted's final speech to Bob: "Don't lecture me, boy. It's not me who doesn't help. It's you, who doesn't want it" (*PE*, 50). Opera as a reflection of a character's life will be prominent in *Amadeus*. The use of tapes appears twice in Shaffer's dramas, in this play, and in *The White Liars*. Its functions here are to speed up the time that passes on stage, to give a stylized appearance to the scene that is taking place; and to convey to the audience the drunken perspective with which Bob views the dinnertime conversation.

The Public Eye

The Public Eye is Shaffer's contribution to European farce and deals with a problem as old as the genre itself: the young wife and the older husband. It is a straightforward piece, rich in the elements of traditional farce, from Plautus to Lorca. As in *The Private Ear*, there are only three characters, and the play is constructed on their mutual misunderstandings and the games that they play with each other. The comedy takes place in the outer office of Charles Sidley's Bloomsbury accounting firm. The office, well furnished and lined with books, reflects the presence of a prosperous professional. Julian Cristoforou, an eccentrically dressed man in his mid thirties, is staring at his large turnip watch and mixing packets of raisins and nuts, which he produces from the large pockets of his raincoat. Charles Sidley, a meticulous man of forty, appears and is surprised to find someone in his office on Saturday. Sidley does not know Cristoforou, nor does he know why he has come to see him. Julian's remarks serve to enhance rather than diminish the confusion in the ensuing conversation:

> *Charles:* . . . Now, if you don't mind—perhaps I can make an appointment for next week.
>
> *Julian:* (*ignoring him, staring at the shelves*) Websters! Chambers! Whittakers Almanac! Even the names have a certain leathery beauty. And how imposing they look on shelves. Seried ranks of learning!
>
> *Charles:* (*brutally*) Are you a salesman?
>
> *Julian:* Forgive me. I was lapsing. Yes, I was once. But then I was everything once. I had twenty-three positions before I was thirty.
>
> *Charles:* Did you really?
>
> *Julian:* I know what you're thinking. A striking record of failure. But you're wrong. I never fail in jobs, they fail me.
>
> *Charles:* Well, I really must be getting home now. I'm sorry to have kept you waiting, even inadvertently. May I make an appointment for you early next week?
>
> *Julian:* Certainly. If that's what you want.
>
> *Charles:* Well, as I say, I don't receive clients at the weekend. Now let me look at my secretary's book . . . What about next Tuesday?
>
> *Julian:* (*considering*) I don't really like Tuesdays. They're an indeterminate sort of day.
>
> *Charles:* Would you please tell me when you would like to see me?
>
> *Julian:* It's rather more when *you* would like, isn't it?

Charles: I suppose I could squeeze you in late on Monday if it's urgent.

Julian: I had imagined it was. In fact, I must admit to feeling disappointed.

Charles: I'm sorry—

Julian: No, if the truth be known, extremely surprised.

Charles: Surprised?

Julian: At your being so off-hand. I had imagined you differently.

Charles: Are you in some kind of trouble?

Julian: Your trouble is mine, sir. It's one of my mottoes. Not inappropriate, I think. Still, of course, I mustn't be unreasonable. It's your decision. After all, you're paying.

Charles: I'm what?

Julian: Paying. *(He pretends to go out).*

Charles: Mr. Cristoforou, come here. I had assumed you were here to see me professionally.

Julian: Certainly. (*PE*, 65–67)

And so the conversation goes in vaudevillian manner until Julian lets Charles know that he is the private detective (public eye) from the firm that Charles has employed to follow his wife and determine whether she is being unfaithful to him. In the month since the detectives last reported to Charles, they have still found no reason to believe that Belinda, Charles's wife, is having an affair with another man. Julian has determined, however, that Belinda is seeing another man on a daily basis, a man whom Julian describes as handsome and debonair; a diplomat, perhaps. Julian does not know his name or where he lives. Charles becomes violent and threatens Julian with physical harm if he does not have more information on the man by nighttime. At this point, Charles hears Belinda approaching and orders Julian down the fire escape.

Belinda is a pretty young woman of twenty-two, who is wearing unconventional clothes—a characteristic which links her with Julian— and carrying an armload of flowers for her husband's office. Just as there was no understanding on either part when Charles and Julian were speaking to each other, neither is there when Charles tries to get Belinda to understand what he considers to be the role of a wife: his definition is tight and conventional; his wife is neither. Charles claims that he loves Belinda very much, but she finds it hard to believe and denies that there is any life left in their marriage. Charles is hurt and announces that he knows she is seeing another man. She tries to deny it, but Charles insists that she be as honest as she presumes to be and forces her to reveal the details of the relationship. (Such was the situation in *Five Finger Exercise* and will be again in *Shrivings* and *Equus*.) Yes, she is *seeing* another man, no more and no less. He follows her all over London—to parks cinemas, coffee bars—and in three weeks they have not exchanged a single word. The man, as Belinda describes him, is not handsome and debonair, but: "a goofy-looking man with spectacles, eating macaroons out of a polythene bag" (*PE*, 96); Charles knows that she can only be describing Cristoforou. Belinda opens the door to water the flowers and discovers Julian, who has been eavesdropping on the entire conversation.

Belinda suffers two hurts in rapid succession: first, that her husband has employed a private detective to spy on her; and second, that Julian is being paid to follow her around London. She wants nothing more to do with either of them. Julian asserts himself: he orders Belinda not to speak to her husband for thirty days. As he sees it, without speaking, he and Belinda have managed to form a close relationship, and he believes that it can be the same way with Belinda and Charles. He tolerates no questioning, commenting, or interfering with his plan: Charles is to follow his wife around London for a full month looking at anything she chooses to point out: "Sit, stand, skip, slide, or shuffle entirely at her will" (*PE*, 115). If Charles refuses, Julian will tell Belinda that her husband has been paying calls to a Notting Hill Gate prostitute—an idle threat, since Julian found out this bit of information from Belinda. Charles reluctantly agrees. And while Charles is performing Julian's job, Julian will perform Charles's: for the next thirty days he will play at being an accountant. That switch begins in the final speech of the play, with Julian on the telephone: "Well, permit me to introduce myself. My name is Cristoforou. Julian Cristoforou. Diplomas in Accountancy from the Universities of Cairo, Beirut, Istanbul, and Damascus. Author of the well-known handbook 'Teach Yourself Tax Evasion.' What seems to be your particular problem?" (*PE*, 119).

Like Louise Harrington, Belinda is a fully developed female character and not a mere antagonist with whom the male characters may interact. Belinda spent the first eighteen years of her life in Northampton with parents whose ambitions for her were a job at the library and marriage to a local man. Belinda rebelled by running off to London and moving in with two bohemian artists. When Charles met her, she was a waitress at a club in Soho. She was swept off her feet by Charles's encyclopedic knowledge, and they were married. She traded her circle of friends (which included an artist who spat paint directly from his mouth to express his contempt for society) for Charles's in the financial world, and the exchange has been impossible for her to accept. She refuses to submerge her individuality by renouncing her routine of seeing horror films and eating ice cream concoctions, for cutting cigar ends and pouring port for old men. Within her value system, her time is better spent in concern over the plight of the Yaghan Indians of Southern Chile than in the routine details of keeping house. Like Louise Harrington, she was being suffocated in her husband's world of business affairs and had to break out. Her needs are diverse and cannot be satisfied by one man: "You've got to be faithful to all sorts of people. You can't give everything to just one. Just one can't use everything. And you certainly can't *get* everything from just one. Just because you get sex from a man, it doesn't mean you're going to get jokes as well, or a someone who digs jazz. Oh I know a husband claims the right to be all these things to a woman, but he never is. The strain would be appalling" (*PE*, 91–92).

Charles is a most unlikely husband for Belinda. He is a staid accountant, a man of the most traditional and conservative nature. He met Belinda when a friend of his invited him to the club where she was working. He married her with the idea of playing Pygmalion and of making her over in his own image, something that she pretended to want, and that he proceeded to do. Now, he claims the credit for everything she knows, from selecting hats to viewing statues. Charles says he was "infatuated" with her when they were married, and his reasons for wedding her were completely selfish:

> *Charles:* . . . She was young and that was enough. Youth needs only to show itself. It's like the sun in that respect. In company with many men of my age, I found I was slipping away into middle life, journeying, as it were, into a colder latitude. I didn't like it. I didn't like it at all.
>
> *Julian:* So you went after the sun. Tried to bottle a ray or two.
>
> *Charles:* Foolish, imbecile attempt. Within a year I had to recognize that I had married a child. Someone with no sense of her place at all. (*PE*, 81)

(Charles's attempts "to bottle a ray or two" of sun is similar to that of Pizarro in *The Royal Hunt of the Sun*, the subject of the next chapter.) As Charles defines Belinda's place, it is at home, catering to his friends from investment companies in the City; behaving as the wife of a professional man and not as that of a "jazz trumpeter in New Orleans" (*PE*, 82).

Charles began to suspect that his wife was seeing another man when, for the last three months, she completely avoided him: "Well, she is averting her face, her look, her mind. Everything. Whole meals go by in silence. . . . Now she's up and out of the house sometimes before eight. As if she can't bear to lie in my bed another minute . . . (*PE*, 83). There is a double standard in Charles's sexual attitudes: he complains that when Belinda was single she went to bed with three different men in the same week, but he, as a married man, has no trouble accepting his regular visits to a prostitute.

The presence of Julian Cristoforou turns domestic drama into true farce: *"his whole air breathes a gentle eccentricity"* (*PE*, 63), his conversation borders on the absurd and no less so his manners and dress. He speaks in paradoxes, describing his name, Cristoforou, as a "little downbeat" and his appearance as "nondescript." He is well intentioned and yet confesses that his motives are somewhat selfish: after spending three years as a detective who broke up marriages, he would like to cement just one. But it is more than that: like Bob, he is a social misfit, and just as Bob hides from himself and from the rest of the world by conducting records in his room at night, so Cristoforou adopts a way of living that is compatible with his personality:

Most of my life has been spent making three where two are company. I was hardly out of puberty before I started becoming attracted to other men's wives. Women who were unattainable obsessed me. . . . I was always in the middle, getting nothing and being generally in the way. Finally I made myself so unhappy that I had to sit down and think. One day I asked myself this fateful question: "Would you like to know a beautiful, tender, unattached girl to whom you were everything in the world?" And the answer came back: "No!" . . . Revelation! At that moment I realized something shattering about myself. I wasn't made to bear the responsibility of a private life! Obviously Nature never intended me to have one! I had been created to spend all my time in public! . . . Alone, I didn't exist; I came alive only against a background of other people's affairs. . . . I immediately resigned from Private Life, and became a Public Eye. (*PE*, 104)

The problem with the Sidleys' marriage is that it has lost the spark that made it successful at the start—Charles is no longer attracted by Belinda's youth, and Belinda no longer worships Charles's learning. Cristoforou is the personification of that which can cure the ills of their marriage: a little imagination. As eccentric as he may be, he is the one person who can reunite Charles and Belinda; he has the creativity which appeals to her and the assertiveness which appeals to him. He has been successful at establishing a relationship with Belinda and now encourages Charles to speak to him freely of his marital problems and personal shortcomings. In his attempt to save their marriage, the games he plays with the Sidleys range from describing himself as handsome and debonair (to make Charles jealous) to making idle threats of telling Belinda about her husband's visits to a prostitute (to make him vulnerable).

The situation on which the play is constructed fits within the tradition of European farce; it is a mélange of the time-honored tales of the old man in pursuit of the young girl, and that of the imaginative and spirited young wife married to a dull, lifeless, older man. As such, Belinda and Charles Sidley are the two characters in Shaffer's dramatic creation most profoundly steeped in literary tradition. The greatest writers of comedy all tried their hands at the problem. Plautus established the prototype of the *senex amator* in *Mercator* (The Merchant); Molière adapted the situation for his seventeenth-century *L'École des femmes* (The School for Wives). In the eighteenth century, Regnard altered Molière's plot enough to produce another masterwork of comedy, *Le Légataire universel* (The Residuary Legatee). In *El sí de las niñas* (The Girls' Consent), Leandro Fernández de Moratín, the most successful Spanish playwright of manners of the eighteenth and early nineteenth centuries, has a fifty-nine-year-old man in pursuit of a sixteen-year-old girl, to whom he would be more of a father than husband if the marriage were to take place. More recently, in the twentieth-century theater, Federico García Lorca uses the same plot in four of his plays, two of which were written for puppets— *Los títeres de cachiporra* (The *Malicious* Puppets) and *Retablillo de don Cristóbal* (The Little Puppet Stage for don Christopher)—and two of which were written for human actors—*La zapatera prodigiosa* (The Shoemaker's Prodigious Wife) and *Amor de don Perlimplín con Belisa en su jardín* (The Love of don Perlimplin with Belisa in the Garden). Throughout the centuries the moral of the play has been the same; Charles confesses to Cristoforou: "The moral, of course, is that men of forty shouldn't marry girls of eighteen. It should be a law of the church like consanguinity: only marry in your generation" (*PE*, 81).

There is another message in the play, too: imagination and fantasy are essentials in life (especially in marriage) and they keep the everyday realities of life from becoming overbearing. Lorca has that same message for his readers in his poetic farce *La zapatera prodigiosa*, but the play that is the closest to Shaffer's is Jacinto Grau's *Las gafas de don Telesforo o un loco de buen capricho* (Telesforo's Spectacles or a Well-Intentioned Misfit). The name of the title character recalls that of the detective in *The Public Eye*, and Grau's comedy is subtitled "Farsa en tres ratos de la vida de un hombre singular" (A Farce in Three Episodes in the Life of an Unusual Man). The two men are similar in name, appearance, and function. Telesforo's prescription for solving problems is much the same as Cristoforou's, too: suspend reality for a while, let go, and allow the imagination to take over. (Imagination will be a major force in *Lettice and Lovage*.)

The Private Ear and *The Public Eye* share themes of misunderstanding, absence of love, loneliness, and fantasy. Bob invited Doreen to his flat for dinner because he mistook her presence at a concert and misidentified her as a music-lover. Similarly, Charles thought that marrying an eighteen-year-old girl would give him back the joie de vivre that the years had taken away from him. Neither woman understands what the men are trying to say to them. In both plays, the women are the innocent victims: Doreen subjects herself to a near-seduction, and Belinda to a joyless marriage. There is an identification between Bob and the Sidleys, all of whom lead lonely and loveless lives, and even more strongly between Bob and Cristoforou, whose lives are little more than their fantasies: alone at night Bob privately imagines himself a conductor; and publicly during the day, Cristoforou plays at his various professions, from private eye to public accountant. Both Bob and Julian escape from the real world and hide from relationships with women: Bob retreats to his music, and Julian to his professional games. Bob and Belinda are related, since both have turned themselves over to another person (Ted and Charles, respectively) to be made over in the other's image. The two plays contrast different kinds of silence. Julian's with Belinda is a positive silence, which helps them establish a relationship. But there is also the negative kind—the dinners that Charles and Belinda spend in complete silence, or Bob and Doreen's awkward moments in the coffee bar after their meeting at the concert. The subject will reappear in the emotionally sterile marriage between the psychiatrist and his wife in *Equus* as well as in Alan's refusal to speak to the doctor in that play.

Criticism

Criticism on the relative merits of *The Private Ear* and *The Public Eye* is mixed. For W.A. Darlington,[2] *The Public Eye* is clever and very funny but artificial comedy, and *The Private Ear* is a gem of writing. Emory Lewis[3] considers *The Public Eye* to be a vivacious work while *The Private Ear* is the more pensive piece. John Gassner[4] finds both to be expertly fashioned, but criticizes *The Public Eye* as being rather slight. For both J. C. Trewin[5] and Milton Shulman,[6] *The Private Ear* is the more successful of the two works. John Chapman[7] finds both plays silky smooth, literate, artful, witty, and irresistibly human. Some reviewers were so impressed with *The Public Eye* that *The Private Ear* seemed to them the less important of the two plays. Harold Hobson and Hubert Kretzmer belong to this group of critics; Hobson[8] calls *The Public Eye* the "sure-fire hit," and Kretzmer[9] believes that Shaffer intended the more important piece to be *The Public Eye*.

The film version of *The Private Ear*, written by Thomas C. Ryan and Ben Starr, was called *The Pad (And How to Use It)*. Brian G. Hutton directed Brian Bedford, James Farentino, and Julie Sommars, in the roles of Bob, Ted, and Doreen, respectively. Shaffer wrote his own screenplay for the 1972 film version of *The Public Eye*, called *Follow Me!* While Meg Matthews[10] does not fault Shaffer's script, she does lament that what should have been a soufflé turned out to be a flat pancake. For Jay Cocks,[11] the film, under Sir Carol Reed's direction, is a sad travesty. Mia Farrow played Belinda; Chaim Topol (of *Fiddler on the Roof* fame), Julian; and Michael Jayston, Charles.

Black Comedy

Shaffer wrote *Black Comedy* under circumstances that normally do not appeal to him: a deadline, imposed by the National Theatre, directed by Sir Laurence Olivier.* The comedy had its debut on 27 July 1965, on a program with Strindberg's *Miss Julie*. Derek Jacobi played Brindsley, Maggie Smith was Clea, Albert Finney was Harold, and Louise Purnell played Carol. John Dexter directed the plays in 1965, 1967, and 1968. For the New York opening at the Ethel Barrymore Theatre on 12 February 1967, Shaffer wrote *White Lies* (originally titled "A Warning Game") as a curtain raiser. Michael Crawford (the musical stage's original Phantom of the Opera) played Brindsley in *Black Comedy* and Tom in *White Lies*; Geraldine Page, Clea and Sophie; Donald Madden, Harold

---

*Olivier was knighted Lord Olivier in 1970.

and Frank; and Lynn Redgrave was Carol. After a successful run in New York, with reviews that were as enthusiastic as those in London, there was a second London production, which opened at the Lyric Theatre on 12 February 1968, accompanied by *The White Liars*, a rewritten version of *White Lies*. This time Ian McKellen took the role of Tom, James Boham had the roles of Frank and Brindsley, Dorothy Reynolds played Sophie, and Angela Scoular portrayed Carol.

Black Comedy is based on a conceit of traditional Chinese drama so that when the lights are on onstage, the actors behave as if they were in complete darkness, and when the lights are off, they act as if nothing were amiss. Using a reversal of darkness and light, Shaffer created one of the best farces in the modern English theater. As in the other one-act plays, Shaffer is faithful to the classical unities of time, place, and action.

The storyline is simple, but the confusion resulting from mistaken identities and misunderstood motives keeps the farce moving at a lively pace. The scene is the South Kensington, London, flat of Brindsley Miller, a sculptor in his mid twenties, intelligent and handsome, but like Clive and Bob, nervous and unsure of himself. On the Sunday evening in question, Georg Bamberger, a millionaire art collector, is coming to inspect, and perhaps purchase, some of Brindsley's work. On the same evening, his fiancée, Carol, a silly and spoiled debutante, is bringing her father, the Colonel, to meet Brin and give his consent to their marriage. In order to impress Colonel Melkett, Brin had borrowed some of his neighbor's most treasured antiques. The neighbor, Harold Gorringe, is the owner of an antique shop and treats his possessions as if they were his children. Brin helped himself to Harold's treasures for the evening, while his neighbor was away for the weekend. At the height of Brin's anxiety over meeting Carol's father, nervousness over Bamberger's appraisal of his art, and fear of Harold's early return, a fuse blows. Until this point, Brin and Carol have been acting on a completely dark stage as if they could see perfectly: Brin compliments Carol on her yellow dress, which brings out the color of her hair; Carol tells Brin to straighten his tie because he looks sloppy. Now that the fuse has blown, the lights come up onstage, and the characters pretend to be in darkness.

While they are groping for matches, Brin has a telephone call from Clea, his ex-mistress, who wants to come to see him. Brin has just lied to Carol that he has not seen Clea in two years, that their affair lasted for three months, and that she was "about as cozy as a steel razor blade."[12] He follows up those lies with another: Clea is "just a chum," he tells Carol. As Brin is about to go out to a pub for matches, in comes Brin's upstairs neighbor, Miss Furnival, the spinster daughter of a Baptist minister. As befitting her station, she is prissy, refined, and unaccustomed to alcoholic beverages. While Brin is calling the electric company for help and going to Harold's apartment in search of a candle, Carol informs Miss Furnival of the background of the evening. She also asks her to be a good sport and not divulge that Brin has borrowed Harold's china and furniture, which Miss Furnival recognizes immediately as belonging to her friend; this is Brin's only hope of convincing the Colonel that Brin can support his daughter.

During Brin's absence, the Colonel has also arrived and has begun criticizing Brin's lack of organization. Brin returns, not knowing that the Colonel has arrived, and refers to Carol's "monster father." From then on, it goes from bad to worse between Brin and Carol's father; in his nervousness, everything the young man says is wrong. Brin was unable to find candles in Harold's apartment and is now on his way to the pub, when he encounters Harold, who has returned unexpectedly. To keep him from discovering that the furniture is missing from his apartment, Brin leads him into his own flat. Thinking that they are alone and that he is finally going to get the attention from Brin that he has long wanted, Harold takes Brin's arm and mentions how cozy it is in the dark. To Harold's dismay, they are not alone, but he consents to stay for a drink. Brin uses Harold's raincoat to cover the Wedgwood bowl which he has taken from Harold's apartment.[13] Harold has matches, and each time he lights one, Brin blows it out so that Harold will not see the furniture. (When a match is lighted on stage, the lights dim a little in keeping with the complete reversal of light and darkness.)

Without the benefit of light, Brin attempts to return Harold's furniture to his apartment without being discovered. In a desperate attempt to keep her father's attention away from her fiancé, who is being taken for a madman, Carol decides that it is time to serve drinks. Naturally, in the darkness they are all confused, and Miss Furnival receives a glass of scotch. She takes a long drink before returning it, and after having her first taste of alcohol, makes several trips to the bar for large doses of gin. The Colonel discovers that Brin is still in the apartment, and Brin feels compelled to say that he has been to the pub and back and that it was closed. The Colonel is enraged at Brin's lying and threatens not to let Brin marry his daughter. This is the first time that Harold has heard that there is marriage in Brin's immediate future, and he is incensed at not having been told before and about having to hear the news in a room full of strangers. There is no making up to the moody Harold for keeping a secret from him.

In the midst of an already frantic situation, Clea arrives and in the darkness goes unnoticed. To Brin's dismay, the subject turns to his former girlfriends, and he tries, none too successfully, to keep Harold from volunteering any information about Clea. But Harold is still hurt at having been slighted by his friend and speaks spitefully of how ugly Clea was: "teeth like a picket fence—yellow and spiky" and skin that was "like new pink wallpaper, with an old grey crumbly paper underneath" (*BC*, 89). Miss Furnival joins in and comments not only on Clea's "lumpy" appearance but also on how "tiresomely Bohemian" she was. When Clea can stand no more, she takes careful aim and slaps Brin's face. Brin assumes that Harold slapped him, and further confusion ensues. Groping about in the dark, Brin catches Clea by the bottom, recognizes her immediately, and begins talking of how beautiful, witty, and loyal she was. He also takes the opportunity to start kissing her and to ask her to go up to the bedroom and wait for him to come up and explain. Harold, standing nearby, thinks that Brin is inviting *him* to the bedroom, but asks whether this is "quite the moment." In the bedroom, Brin lies to Clea about his relationship with Carol and about the purpose of her father's visit. He begs her to leave quietly and kisses her passionately, but she does not go.

As Carol is beginning to suspect that there is something going on in Brin's bedroom, Schuppanzigh, the electrician, enters, and since he has a German accent and a knowledge of art, he is mistaken for Bamberger and is treated accordingly. Bamberger is supposed to be "stone deaf," and so Brin, Carol, and Miss Furnival shout in Schuppanzigh's ear, and he cannot imagine what is happening. All gather to listen to him as if he were giving the last word on sculpture, until he reveals his identity. He is assaulted with insults and goes through the trapdoor to replace the fuse in the cellar. Carol mentions her forthcoming marriage to Brin. Clea's mouth falls open, and she is determined to have her revenge. First she takes a bottle of vodka from the bar and goes to the bedroom level from which she soaks Carol, Brin, Harold, and the Colonel. Improvising wildly, Brin tries to make his guests believe that the cleaning woman is upstairs and gets Clea to play along for the moment. Cautioning her to watch her language, the Colonel tells Clea that she is in the presence of Brin's fiancée, and in an inspired moment she asks: "You must be Miss Clea's father" (*BC*, 109). Brindsley falls face down on the floor. She continues that it is a good thing that Brin finally asked her to marry him since her "little bun in the oven" was getting "a bit prominent" (*BC*, 110). Clea reveals her identity, and by using Carol's affectations of speech proceeds to insult Miss-Laughingly-Known-As and her Daddipegs. The Colonel, in an attempt to comfort his daughter, mistakenly takes Clea's hand, and this gives her another idea. They will all play Guess the Hand. Clea puts Carol's hand in Harold's, which she mistakes for her fiancé's. Then she puts Brin's hand in Harold's, and Harold has no trouble identifying it. This puts Brin in the position of having to explain to Carol how Harold could identify his hand so easily.

Miss Furnival is drunk by now, and Harold takes her home. In a moment he returns, wild-eyed with rage: he has seen his apartment. He accuses Brin of being everything from a "skunky, conniving little villain" (*BC*, 117) to a "light-fingered Lenny." Still angry from before, he attacks Brin with: "Don't tell Harold about the engagement. He's not to be trusted. He's not a friend. He's just someone to steal things from!" (*BC*, 118). And he goes on hysterically about how he has always been a good friend to Brin, listening to all his "boring talk about women, hour after hour" (*BC*, 118). Dramatically, he lists all of the items which have been "stolen" from his apartment, and taking his raincoat from Brin's table, breaks his most valuable antique, which the coat was hiding. While Harold and the Colonel, armed with the metal prongs from Brin's sculpture, are chasing Brin around the room, Bamberger appears, and since he sounds so much like Schuppanzigh, he is taken for the electrician. Schuppanzigh reappears through the trapdoor and thinks that the rude Englishmen are making fun of him by imitating his accent. The electrician fixes the fuse, and the stage goes black.

Unlike the other plays, *Black Comedy* is populated by stock characters—a dizzy debutante, a middle-aged spinster, a military bully, an effeminate antique dealer—and is less easily identifiable as a character study or as a play with a message. Yet it does convey a message on the theme of identity; the media for the message are the personage of Brindsley and the technique of the reversal of light and darkness. This reversal is no mere theatrical gimmick; it is necessary to the meaning of the play. The events of the entire play lead up to the moment of truth between Brin and Clea. Brin tells Clea that she had no right to ruin his chances with Carol, since it was *she* who walked out on him:

Brindsley: *You* walked out on me. (*He joins her on the low stool.*)
   Clea: Is that what I did?

> *Brindsley:* You said you never wanted to see me again.
>
> *Clea:* I never saw you at all—how could you be walked out on? You should live in the dark, Brindsley. It's your natural element.
>
> *Brindsley:* Whatever that means.
>
> *Clea:* It means you don't really want to be seen. Why is that, Brindsley? Do you think if someone really saw you, they would never love you? (*BC*, 114)

Brindsley avoids the subject, because it is too painful for him to confront. For all of his success with women, Brindsley remains basically insecure and unsure of himself. He almost marries Carol Melkett because she does not present him with confrontations or force him to face himself as Clea does; rather she flatters his ego:

> *Clea:* Stop pitying yourself. It's always your vice. I told you when I met you: you could either be a good artist, or a chic fake. You didn't like it, because I refused just to give you applause.
>
> . . . .
>
> Is that what *she* gives you? Twenty hours of ego-massage every day?
>
> *Brindsley:* At least our life together isn't the replica of the Holy Inquisition you made of ours. . . . (*BC*, 115)

Brindsley is not the only character who is playing identity games; the farce in the play is based on mistaken identities. Miss Furnival would have the world believe that she would never let a drop of liquor pass her lips, but drink she does, when she, as Brindsley, is protected from life's revealing light; and Clea plays the part of a charwoman. Even in a play that uses stock characters, there is a relationship between the individuals in this work and others of Shaffer's dramas. Brindsley, for all his sexual bravura, is just as nervous and unsure of himself as are Bob and Clive, perhaps even more so than Clive, who makes a sincere attempt to assert his individuality and present himself honestly to the world. Carol Melkett is a paler version of Louise Harrington; both play at nicknames (Carol calls whiskey, Winnie; vodka, Vera; and gin, Ginette) and both value material things: "Then we can buy a super Georgian house and live what's laughingly known as happily ever after. I want to leave this place just as soon as we're married. . . . I don't want to live in a slum for our first couple of years—like other newlyweds" (*BC*, 105).

Colonel Melkett, the father and figure of authority in the play, has the
same doubts about Brin's future that Stanley Harrington has about
Clive's: how will he make a living when his interests are the arts? The
arts, then, link Brindsley with his predecessors: Clive's interest is drama,
Bob's is music, Brin's is sculpture. Brindsley's identity problem—his
fear of facing himself—is the "black" element in the comedy; it gives a
frantic farce a serious message and helps make the play truly a Black
Comedy. The themes of lying and identity link *Black Comedy* with the
three following one-act plays.

White Lies

As in *The Private Ear* and *The Public Eye*, there are only three characters
in *White Lies*: Sophie (Baroness Lemberg), Frank, and Tom. The play
takes place at Sophie's fortune-teller's parlor, a seedy living room facing
the sea, on the promenade of a rundown seaside resort on the south coast
of England. On the window are printed the words *"'BARONESS LEM-
BERG, PALMISTE. CLAIRVOYANTE.'* and in smaller letters 'CONSULT-
ANT TO ROYALTY'" (BC, 9). It is six o'clock on a mid-September afternoon.
The two most important items in the room—which shows obvious signs
of poverty—are a portrait of Vassili, Sophie's former boyfriend, and a
parakeet named Pericles; Sophie speaks to both of them as if they were
human beings. Sophie, who is forty-eight years old, speaks with a
German accent. On the evening of the play, she is talking to Vassili and
Pericles of her financial problems: she has not had a client in days and has
not been able to pay the rent since June. When Sophie sees that not one
but two clients are waiting to see her, she is overwhelmed.

The first is Frank. He is about twenty-five years old, "cold, watchful,
ambiguous" (BC, 13). Frank is given to practical jokes and will do
anything for a laugh. He has come to Sophie to arrange for her to tell his
friend's fortune based on the information that Frank supplies; he wants
to "stage the best joke ever played," to get Tom "so brilliantly he'd never
forget it" (BC, 16). Sophie is offended. She thinks of herself as a
professional and maintains that she lives by the slogan "Lemberg never
lies." As Frank tells the story, Tom (who is lead singer in the group called
the "White Lies," which Frank manages) has taken an interest in Frank's
girl friend, and Frank wants Sophie to see a tragic end for Tom if he does
not leave the woman alone. Sophie will not consent to such a prostitution
of her profession, but at the offer of twenty-five pounds she changes her
mind, rationalizing that "it is the duty of the aristocracy to maintain

itself, no matter what!" (*BC*, 23). Frank tells Sophie Tom's history: he came from a poor working family in a mining town; his mother is dead, and his father is a drunkard who used to beat him.

After Sophie has had a few minutes to study the notes that Frank left for her, Frank returns with Tom. Unlike Frank, Tom is a "shy-looking boy of twenty-two, with a thick Cheshire accent" (*BC*, 23). Sophie insists that Frank leave them alone if she is to achieve an accurate reading. Tom is impressed that she knows that he is a musician, but in order to establish credibility, she admits that she learned that much from Frank. She likes Tom immediately and does not want to go through with Frank's scheme, for which she has already been paid, and she claims to feel a headache on the way. As he starts to leave, she changes her mind again, either because she does not want to lose the money or because she does not want Tom to go.

Sophie tells Tom's life story just as Frank related it to her. Tom is startled and cannot believe that she could possibly be getting that information from her crystal ball. When Tom has heard as much as he cares to hear, he tells Sophie that it is all a lie: he comes from a middle-class family, with a mother who is indeed alive and a father who is an accountant. His whole present life is one enormous lie, which he invented in order to be successful in the rock-music business because "middle class is right out. No one believes you can sing with the authentic voice of the people if you're the son of an accountant" (*BC*, 31). Sophie is stunned. She has been found out, and by a person she likes and with whom she identifies closely. Tom describes his deplorable living situation to her: he, Frank, and Helen all live in the same house, he upstairs and they downstairs. Every morning Tom has to come down and see Helen in Frank's bed, with Frank smiling at him, as Tom prepares their breakfast. Tom has never been able to tell Helen about his true identity for fear that he would lose her: "Look! Truth's the last thing she wants. She's 'in love'—that's what she calls it! She's in love with a working-class boy—even though he doesn't exist. And I'm in love with feelings I see in her eyes—and I know they don't exist. They're only what I read into them" (*BC*, 33).

Tom's talk about love and about eyes triggers associations in Sophie's mind. She, too, was in love, with Vassili, the man in the photograph; she loved his immense black eyes. She continues to tell Tom the truth about her past. When her husband died, he left her penniless, and in order to make a living she worked as a landlady, and it was then that she met Vassili. He was a student looking for an inexpensive room; she rented one to him and was immediately attracted to him. But he had a fiancée (chosen for him by his father), whom he could not marry for another two years until he completed his studies. Sophie allowed Vassili to invite Irina to his room, and Sophie, all the while filled with hate, served them tea. One day, he revealed that he knew Sophie's secret: she was not an aristocrat, just a girl named Sophie Harburg from a poor Jewish family, and she had never been the manager of a grand hotel, just a barmaid in a pub. She could no longer see him and advised that he marry Irina, for Sophie's sake. Before leaving her, Vassili presented Sophie with Pericles, the parakeet, as a gift. Vassili told her that Pericles was a bird of truth, in whose presence no one must ever tell a lie. Until today, she has spent her life protecting her white lies, but now she is through with them. Sophie advises Tom to go to Helen, to tell her the truth and to run off with her.

When Frank returns and Sophie tells him what happened, he demands that Sophie return his money, and when he becomes violent and throws Pericles out of the window, she does, but not until she tells his fortune. "Five of pounds: card of cruelty. Five of pounds: card of vanity. Five of pounds: card of stupidity. Five of pounds: card of fantasy. Five of pounds:—card of a loveless life. It's all in the cards, mister" (*BC*, 42). Left alone, she stares at the photograph and tells it, "Harburg never lies" (*BC*, 42), and discards it on the floor along with the images she has spent her life protecting.

In many of Shaffer's plays, beginning with *White Lies*, there are conflicts between two characters who care for and identify with each other. Sophie and Tom have just such a relationship: they have both created false identities for themselves (Sophie as nobility and Tom as working-class poor) and they go about life living a lie.[14] Just as Walter serves as a catalyst for the members of the Harrington family, Sophie's encounter with Tom is the turning point in her life: he reminds her of her past, upsets her present, and determines her future. Her attraction to Tom is immediate: she comments first on his eyes and next on his paleness, the two aspects of Vassili to which she refers during her scene of self-revelation. She looks at Tom and comments on their first common trait: they are both winter people; neither one likes the sun: sunlight equals truth. Sophie thereby unites, Tom—and herself—with Brindsley. Tom tells her how he likes the isolation and desolation of winter: "I went to Herne Bay last March. . . . All the sea gulls . . . looked like rows of old convalescents, huddled down in their coat collars" (*BC*, 25–26). She feels Tom's sensitivity and hears his poetic language (which approaches Clive's and Bob's) and she knows that he is one of her people; she cannot betray him for the likes of Frank. When she finally does tell his fortune, she turns it, more for his benefit than for hers. She intimates that she can no longer lie to him, and having reestablished her credibility proceeds to protect him with her white lies. She tells him that Frank's warning game was that Tom's punishment would be loneliness, not violence, and she makes him see that he is afraid of himself and not of Frank. She gives him the courage to leave Frank and his illusionary past behind and to take Helen and start an honest future; he gives her the strength to discard her pretentions and to begin facing the world as Sophie Harburg, who never has to lie again.

Tom is linked with Clive by more than their sensitive natures and their poetic language: they share the same kind of parents—his father has almost nothing to do with his son, and his mother belongs to the bridge set and puts on airs. Tom says, "They've virtually disowned me, after all. Dad calls me 'Minstrel Boy' now every time I go home, and mother has a whole bit with her bridge club that I'm in London 'studying' music. Studying is a better *image* than singing in clubs. She can *see* herself as the mother of a student. Both of them are talking about themselves, of course, not me" (*BC*, 31–32). Tom's parents are configurations of Stanley, who wants Clive to go into business, and Louise, who will not hear of it because Clive's being in the business world is not good enough for *her*.

Sophie's past life is also another glimpse of Louise; in her attempt to be an aristocrat, she has to belie her heritage and denigrate middle-class life, be it her taste in music or her weekend sightseeing outings with Vassili:

Now *there* was a fan! He taught me everything: what groups were good, what lousy, Top Ten, Pick of the Pops! Secretly I liked it, but it was vulgar to admit to. After all, I was the Baroness Lemberg. His own family was just middle class. . . . He was absolutely intoxicated by history! And because I was an aristocrat, you see, I was supposed to know all about it. Every Sunday we went on a bus—up to Windsor castle, down to St. Paul's Cathedral. And what he never knew was that every Saturday night I would sit up, secretly memorizing the facts—then speaking them next day, almost yawning, because tourism, after all, is a little common, my dear . . . (*BC*, 35)

History and tourism will be paired motifs in *Lettice and Lovage*.

Both Tom and Sophie are denying their pasts—she by creating a finer image than is true of her, and he by creating a lower one than his true status in life. Tom no longer believes in truth, in presenting himself to the world sincerely, because nobody does it; honesty is impossible: "Believe me, Baroness: I've worked it out. Look—everyone makes images—*everyone*. It's like no one can look at anyone direct. The way I see it, the whole world's made up of images—images talking at images— that's what makes it all so impossible" (*BC*, 31).

Sophie feels no identification at all with Frank: he is too brutal, too candid. He begins by asking not if she is the Baroness Lemberg, but if she is "the witch." He insults her, bribes her, and forces her to compromise her ideals. He also instills as much fear in her as he has instilled in Tom and Helen. Around Frank, Sophie dwells on all that makes her unhappy in her life—its truth. He forces her to realize that her parlor is not filled with duchesses waiting for a reading and that thrones are not tottered at the flip of her predictions. She is no longer holding the hands of governors, princes, and ministers of justice. She has fallen desperately since then—if ever there indeed was any glory in her past:

Look, mister, I'm not mad, you know, there are no Duchesses out there, I know that. Just crazy spinsters, stinking of moth balls, old red men with gin in their eyes, begging me to predict just one horse race, one football pool, to make them rich for life. Rubbish people, all of them, boring me to death with their second-rate dreams. Nevertheless, I make adjustment. Other years—other tears! I spend my life now casting prophetic pearls before middle class swine." (*BC*, 21)

While Tom and Sophie are engaged in image games with themselves and the rest of the world, Tom and Frank have a relationship based on practical jokes, with shades of the relationship between Bob and Ted in *The Private Ear*. Ted and Frank are older than Bob and Tom, have had more success with women, and take their friends under their wings— Ted seemingly instructs Bob in the facts of life, and Frank gives Tom a job as lead singer with the White Lies. The relationship between Tom and Frank is presented second-hand; that is, but for one moment when Frank brings Tom into Sophie's parlor, they are never on stage together. Their relationship parallels those of the other plays in which two men are pitted against each other in a power struggle, this time for the love of a woman who thinks she loves Frank (according to Tom) and whom Frank (again according to Tom) does not even pretend to love—Frank does not believe that such a thing as love exists at all. Sophie, Tom, and Frank all live by her adage, that "nothing is *just* anything" (*BC*, 25); there is always another level beneath the apparent one. Sophie's adage is Shaffer's message, echoed by the characters as well as by the props.

Shaffer's two major props in *White Lies* are the parakeet Pericles and the photograph of Vassili; Pericles reminds Sophie that she is supposed to tell the truth, and the photograph accuses her (or so she imagines) of being a fraud. The photograph is really a physical representation of her conscience. In her opening monologue, she "hears" the photograph calling her a fraud and she responds: "It takes a fraud to call a fraud . . ." (*BC*, 12–13). When she is considering Frank's proposition to tell Tom's fortune, again she imagines that the photograph is accusing her, and she replies in kind: "Look, everyone cheats a little, my darling, even your Greek witches. What do you think your famous oracle at Delphi was doing?—one silly cow sitting in a lot of smoke, saying exactly what she was paid to say!" (*BC*, 22). When she discards the photograph, she is discarding her lies, her games, her guilts, and her insecurities. She has told her last lie. Likewise, when Frank throws Pericles out of the window, she tells her first truth: as she predicted in her opening monologue of the play, Pericles is going on a long, long journey. She is once against Sophie Harburg, and Harburg never lies.

The White Liars

Before writing *White Liars*, Shaffer called *The White Liars*, loosely based on *White Lies*, a new play and the final version. He specified that it should be played before *Black Comedy* and that "the two plays represent a complete evening's entertainment, on the theme of tricks."[15] As in *White Lies*, the play takes place in Sophie's fortune-teller's parlor, on a run-down amusement pier. The names of the characters are the same, and the plot line remains very close to that of *White Lies*. There are, however, some significant changes in the characters' personalities, in the details of Sophie's relationship with "Vassi," and in the techniques: Shaffer has eliminated the parakeet and the photograph—at the end of *White Lies*, Pericles was sent on a long journey, and Sophie discarded Vassi's picture—and they have been replaced by tapes, which play Sophie's thoughts, both present and remembered.

Frank and Tom have effectively exchanged the identities they had in *White Lies*. Now Frank is shy, soft-spoken, and gentle; and Tom is casual to the point of what Shaffer terms "brutality." He has a heavy midlands accent and wears long hair and bright clothes. Frank, the manager of a rock music group called "The White Liars," wants Sophie, via her crystal ball, to warn Tom to keep away from his girlfriend, Sue. Frank tells Sophie how much he has done for Tom: he took him out of a filthy cellar in the slums, gave him a room in his flat, and formed a musical group for him. After she gets over the insult of being bribed to tell a fortune, she feels a strong identity with Frank and wants to join him in his plan against Tom; both she and Frank are "Givers"; Tom, like Vassi, is a "Taker," and "Takers" should be taught a lesson. Sophie divides the whole world into the "Givers" and the "Takers": "The Givers are the world's aristocrats. . . . The Takers are the Peasants, emotional peasants" (WL, 19).

Tom is superstitious, a great believer in fortune-tellers, and is anxious for his reading, despite Frank's act at being disappointed by Sophie. Sophie takes an immediate dislike to Tom, in no small measure because he brings to Sophie's mind Vassi and the advantage he took of her:

Pay the rent. "More, please!" Hellas Restaurant. "More, please!" Shop at Jaeger's, twenty pounds one jacket. Riding lessons in Richmond Park, two pounds one hour! Seats for the theatre, that boring *Elektra*—of course we must sit close to watch the faces—seventy shillings for two places, just to see bad make-up! . . . And always more. Always the same cry of More! Take and take, and take, until the cows are at home. And then what? Surprise! "Sophie, I've met this girl Irina. She's the daughter of my father's oldest friend. We are suited to each other, absolutely. We are both young. We both tell the truth. We don't pretend to be Baronesses. And so, bye-bye!" (WL, 30–31)

Nothing that Tom says convinces Sophie that she may be wrong about him, but he wants her to consider just three facts: he was not living in a slum, he had money, and he had formed "The White Liars" a year before he ever met Frank. He tells of how Frank and Sue would come week after week and watch him perform. Frank pretended to be a journalist who wanted to write a story about Tom, which would mean being around him for a whole month. Frank invited Tom to move into his flat, on which he owed three months' rent, and which Tom paid. Frank, it turned out, was not a journalist at all, but an employee in a boutique on Kings Road in Chelsea, until he lost his job. Tom cannot take the responsibility of making up the lies about his past, because, as he sees it, Frank and Sue *made* him lie:

Once I'd spoken—actually spoken a lie out loud—I was theirs. They got excited, like lions after meat, sniffing about me, slavering! . . . Who was I? I didn't exist for them. I don't now! *(He rises violently.)* They want *their* Tom: not me. Tom the idol. Tom the Turn-on. Tom the Yob God, born in a slum, standing in his long-suffering maltreated skin—all tangled hair and natural instinct—to be hung by his priests in white satin! . . . Our uniform for The Liars. He designed it—she made it—I wear it" (*WL*, 35–36).

That is all that Tom can see that the "Givers" give: they give out identities and roles until the "Takers" are their emotional prisoners. Yet Sophie will not be convinced that Tom is telling the truth. Finally, he has to tell her that Frank and Sue were never lovers, and that the person that Frank really wants is Tom. When Frank returns and Tom is gone, Sophie is forced to tell Frank that Tom has left him, and Frank tells Sophie that she should not believe everything that Tom might have said about him.

Just as lies exist between Frank and Tom, so they existed between Sophie and Vassi. Five years have passed since Sophie has seen Vassi, and yet their final conversation still echoes in her ears; she still hears him telling her how it is impossible to live with liars and her replying that he should get out—words she has lived to regret and tried to retract, but to no avail.

While the relationship between *White Lies* and *The White Liars* is striking, the relationship between *The White Liars* and *Black Comedy* is more subtle. Both plays examine lies and identity crises: Frank, Tom, and Sophie cannot be honest about their identities; they live in their own private worlds of fabricated images of themselves. Only Sophie verbalizes a rationale for so deceitful a lifestyle: "All right, lies, so what? *So what?* So he tells a couple of—of tales just to make himself a little more important—just to shield himself a little from the sordidness of life!" (*WL*, 33). Life is easier for her to face as the Baroness Lemberg than as Sophie Weinberg, Fraulein No-one. Tom is Sophie's reminder of Vassi; he acts on her emotions as well as on her conscience: in his presence, Sophie relives her unhappy moments as well as the guilt and suffering that her lies brought her; she thinks that Tom, as did Vassi, is calling her a fraud. Shaffer describes Tom as looking like a parakeet, the symbol that represented both Vassi and truth in *White Lies*. Tom and Brindsley share the need for adulation, for worship; Brindsley preferred the company of Carol to that of Clea because he received "ego-massage" from Carol every day. Similarly, Frank tells Sophie that, like a Greek monster, Tom lives on worship: "He can hardly get through a day without two tablespoons of sticky golden worship poured down his throat, preferably by a girl" (*WL*, 16). Both Tom and Vassi are represented by animals: in *White Lies*, the parakeet has the function of acting as Sophie's conscience and as a constant reminder of Vassili; in *The White Liars*, the toy dog that Tom wins at the shooting gallery serves as a symbol of Tom. When Frank sees at the end of the play that Tom has left his toy in the waiting room, he realizes that it is all he has left of a former friendship. The theme of male jealousy in *Black Comedy* is echoed in *The White Liars*. Harold Gorringe would like Brindsley to spend his time and affection on him instead of "wasting" it on Clea and Carol; Frank wants Tom, and the only way to keep Tom in his home is by pretending to be interested in Sue.

The White Liars also shares common bonds with *The Private Ear*, *The Public Eye*, and *Five Finger Exercise*. Its link with *The Private Ear* is the situation of two men vying for the attentions of the same woman—one man is shy and gentle, while the other is aggressive and dominant. *The White Liars* is related to *The Public Eye* through Frank, who takes on a role of bogus journalist and claims that he has to shadow Tom for a month and take notes on his activities for an article that he is writing. Julian assumes professional roles that do not belong to him and recommends following people around as a means of solving marital problems. There is also a common thread between *The White Liars* and *Five Finger Exercise*. Tom's mother is a reincarnation of Louise—both putting on airs and trying to re-create their children in their own images; and Tom's father is as unimpressed with him as Stanley Harrington is with Clive. Frank exhibits the same kind of possessiveness as Louise: if he cannot have Tom, neither can Sue.

White Liars

Shaffer wrote a third version of this play, which he titled *White Liars*. The revival of *Black Comedy*, along with this curtain raiser, opened at the Shaw Theatre in London on 28 June 1976. The director was Paul Giovanni, who also directed the record-breaking production of *Equus* in Buffalo, New York, and wrote and directed the 1978 play *The Crucifer of Blood*. The cast included Maggie Fitzgibbon (Sophie), Peter Machin (Frank and Brindsley), Timothy Dalton (Tom and Harold), Gemma Craven (Carol), and Celia Bannerman (Clea). *White Liars* is the version of the play that appears in *The Collected Plays of Peter Shaffer*. The progression from *White Lies* to *The White Liars* and finally to *White Liars* demonstrates Shaffer's ability to pare from his plays all extraneous elements and superfluous techniques. That process will also be evident in the chapters on *Amadeus* and *Yonadab*. Gone from the last version are the offstage tapes representing Sophie's memories, as well as all references to Sophie's having had a lover, Vassi, in her past. The prop that does remain is a photograph—this time of her father. Sophie speaks to her Papa in her opening monologue, in which she complains of her present situation and fondly remembers life with her family in Austria before the Nazis.

The play's theme continues to be false appearances. The "Baroness Lemberg" is Sophie Plotkin. Frank isn't in love with Sue, but with Tom. He wants Tom to leave Sue alone so that Frank and Tom can resume their six-month, intimate relationship. Even the faded photo of Sophie's father is deceptive. In it he is dressed for a production of *The Count of Luxembourg*, and his medals came from a shop on Portobello Road. In real life, he ran a kosher delicatessen in Innsbruck before Hitler's reign and then continued in that business in London. Sophie's mother no more approved of her daughter telling fortunes, which is beneath her, than her father approved of a lady drinking. In this version, Sophie can no longer handle reality and has turned to the bottle—a rose-colored decanter—to give her and the world around her a pleasant glow. This new detail not only picks up on Miss Furnival's enjoyment of what she calls her first drink, but also looks ahead to *Lettice and Lovage*, in which drink serves as the tie that binds the two women in the play.

Other elements also link *White Liars* to plays that came before it and to those that will follow. Frank describes Sue in terms that suggest a younger version of *Five Finger Exercise*'s Louise Harrington and a variation on *Black Comedy*'s Carol Melkett. Sue is the picture of respectability and is devoted to golf and gardening. Tom represents to her everything that her parents hate. However, she like Clive Harrington, is tired of being surrounded by phonies. Frank insists that Tom is the kind of monster out of Greek fable: "Tom the yob god standing in his long-suffering maltreated skin—all tangled hair and natural instinct" (*CP*, 175). This is a description that could easily fit Alan, the young man in *Equus* who worships horses. Alan does not have Tom's invented "flagellant father," but does flagellate himself; and Sophie's criticism of Tom for trying to "borrow suffering" parallels an idea that Dr. Dysart, the psychiatrist in *Equus*, will also condemn.

Whereas in *The White Liars* Sophie tells Frank that Tom has left him, in *White Liars* an actual confrontation between the two men takes place on stage. Tom overhears part of Frank's complaint to Sophie and decides to honor Frank's pleas for him to get out of Frank's life. As Sophie sees it, Frank got what he wanted out of his visit to her: no more monster. Exorcising another kind of monster from Alan is going to be Dr. Dysart's job. There is also a connection with *Amadeus* through music, which of course dominates that play about Mozart. Sophie's father was a musician in Austria; he played the clarinet in a chamber group "like a lover" (*CP*, 159).

At the end of the play Sophie turns against her father, whom she loved and admired—the man she thought knew everything and now believes knew nothing—by smashing his photograph, much as Bob scratches his beloved recording of *Madame Butterfly*. Alan makes sure that his horse-god can see "NOTHING"; and David, the young man in *Shrivings* who lived by his mentor's philosophy, comes to realize that it was words that meant "NOTHING." Tom's aunt, like the emperor in *Amadeus*, likes the kind of music that "you can chew tea cakes to" (*CP*, 137), the kind that goes down easily, that doesn't challenge the listener. The connection between *White Liars* and Shaffer's other works continues to *Lettice and Lovage*. Both Sophie and Lettice end their respective plays with toasts, Sophie to the sea gulls and Lettice (in the revised version) to the audience. And, like the mention of Frank and Tom's sexual relationship, there is also an overtly homoerotic point of reference in the radio play *Whom Do I Have the Honour of Addressing?*

Summation

Of the six plays in this chapter, the critics were most enthusiastic about *Black Comedy*. It has been praised for its humor, originality, surprises, and grace. The only reservation that some reviews had was that the play went on too long to sustain the initial appeal of Shaffer's technique. *White Lies* and *The White Liars* received less laudatory reviews, ranging from "thin" and "stretched"[16] to "wise" and "earnest."[17] Irwing Wardel[18] was pleased to see the removal of the tapes from the final version of the play, *White Liars*, but found the speeches still too long and literary; he claimed they failed to establish believable characters. He was apparently not aware of the second version of the play because he comments that "the homosexual punchline removes the situation further from reality." For Benedict Nightingale,[19] *White Liars* "remains a miss," but he expresses the wish that Shaffer become a major writer in the minor genre of comedy instead of remaining a minor writer in the major genre of drama.

Five of the plays are dominated by intense relationships between men in competition with each other: Bob and Ted, Tom and Frank; and even Charles Sidley and Julian Cristoforou, to some extent. This battle of the wills between two men is the focal point of the plays in the following chapters: *The Royal Hunt of the Sun*, *Shrivings*, and *Equus*, *Amadeus*, and *Yonadab*.

Chapter Four
The Royal Hunt of the Sun

Following a delay of six years, during which time financially cautious impresarios were reluctant to make the large outlay necessary to stage the spectacle, *The Royal Hunt of the Sun* was finally produced at the Chichester Festival on 6 July 1964. The opening in London took place at the Old Vic Theatre by the National Theatre Company on 8 December 1964. *Royal Hunt* has the distinction of being the first nonclassical play to be presented by the National Theatre. John Dexter directed the cast headed by Colin Blakely as Pizarro, Robert Stephens as Atahuallpa, and Robert Lang as Old Martin. Michael Annals designed the sets and costumes, Marc Wilkinson composed the music, and Claude Chagrin choreographed the movement on stage. Its New York debut was at the ANTA Theatre on 26 October 1965. In New York Christopher Plummer, David Carradine, and George Rose played the parts of Pizarro, Atahuallpa, and Martin, respectively. Shaffer has provided more background information and commentary concerning the writing of this play than of any earlier work. He stated that, during a period of mandatory bedrest, he filled his time by reading William Prescott's classic *History of the Conquest of Peru*, which inspired him to write *The Royal Hunt of the Sun*, his interpretation of Pizarro's conquest of the Incan Empire. In an introduction to the published version of the play, which he wrote at least a year after the play had already been produced, Shaffer set forth his intentions in writing the play:

Why did I write *The Royal Hunt?* To make colour? Yes. To make spectacle? Yes. To make magic? Yes—if the word isn't too debased to convey the kind of excitement I believed could still be created out of "total" theatre.

The "totality" of it was in my head for ages: not just the words, but jungle cries and ululations; metals and masks; the fantastic apparition of the pre-Columbian world. . . . I did deeply want to create, by means both austere and rich . . . an experience that was *entirely and only theatrical*.[1]

The themes, he wrote, were to be "an encounter between European hope and Indian hopelessness; between Indian faith and European faithlessness. I saw the active iron of Spain against the passive feathers of Peru: the conflict of two immense and joyless powers. The Spaniards suspected joy as being unworthy of Christ. . . . The Conquistadors defied personal will: the Incas shunned it" (*RH*, v). Unlike anything else Shaffer has written, *The Royal Hunt of the Sun* is epic in its conception and mammoth in its production. It takes place on two continents over a period of four years, and has an emperor and a conqueror as its protagonists. The play is divided into two acts, "The Hunt" and "The Kill," with each act subdivided into twelve sections intended solely for reference and not for indicating any pauses or breaks in the continuity of the action. The set described is that used at the Chichester Festival.

Plot

When the play opens, Old Martin, the narrator, grizzled, in his mid fifties, and dressed in the black costume of a Spanish *hidalgo* of the sixteenth century, says that he is a Spanish soldier who has spent most of his life fighting for land, treasure, and the Cross. He has been closer to Pizarro than any other man alive, and as a youth, he would have died for Pizarro, the object of his worship. The scene fades to that of a town in Spain in 1529; Pizarro enters accompanied by Hernando De Soto, his Second-in-Command, and Fray Vincente de Valverde,[2] a Dominican priest. Old Martin interrupts the action to give more background information: Pizarro had already made two trips to the New World, and now over sixty years old, he is back in Trujillo, the town of his birth, to recruit men for a third expedition. One of his recruits is the literate Young Martin, who idolizes Pizarro. Pizarro warns his men to have no illusions about the impending journey: ". . . I'm promising you swamps. A forest like the beard of the world. Sitting half-buried in earth to escape the mouths of insects. You may live for weeks on palm tree buds and soup made out of leather straps. And at night you will sleep in thick wet darkness with snakes hung over your heads like bell ropes—and black men in that blackness: men that eat each other" (*RH*, 4). But Pizarro promises his men gold as a reward for enduring—and surviving—those hardships, more gold than they could ever imagine, and slaves who are theirs for the taking. Next, Valverde appeals to the men's religiosity: this is their chance to save the souls of heathens otherwise condemned to eternal damnation. Valverde promises that "he who helps me lift this dark man into light I absolve of all crimes he ever committed" (*RH*, 5). Pizarro's motive is different from that of the other men: as was Arieh in "The Salt Land," he is trying to attain immortality, and a name that will be remembered in legends for centuries to come. He is also trying to overcome his image of an illegitimate peasant who worked as a swineherd.

The scene quickly changes to Panama, where the soldiers of fortune are having their weapons blessed so that those weapons might be able to turn savages into Christians. Fray Marcos De Nizza, the Franciscan friar on the expedition, tells the men of the noble purposes for making their trip: "You are the bringers of food to starving peoples. You go to break mercy with them like bread, and outpour gentleness into their cups. You will lay before them the inexhaustible table of free spirit, and invite to it all who have dieted on terror. You will bring to all tribes the nourishment of pity. You will sow their fields with love, and teach them to harvest the crop of it, each yield in its season. Remember this always: we are their New World" (*RH*, 8). Estete, the Royal Veedor and Overseer, is the representative of the Crown of King Carlos the Fifth of Spain. Disagreement arises over his position relative to that of Pizarro's: Estete professes that he speaks with royal authority, and Pizarro recognizes no higher power than his own on the expedition.

Pizarro doubles over with pain and explains to a concerned Young Martin that he is still suffering from a wound inflicted on him by a savage long ago. Pizarro tries to dispel Martin's illusions of chivalry: a soldier's mission is to kill, no more and no less; in the army's tradition there is no glory. He advises his disciple to forget Peru and to go back to Spain, but Martin will not leave the man who has become his idol.

To the strains of exotic music, Atahuallpa, sovereign Inca of Peru, appears in the medallion of the sun, a second acting stage used as a part of the play's set. His priests warn him that Pizarro is trouble, but Atahuallpa is determined to meet the White God. While the Spaniards are making their way toward the Inca, they seize one of his chiefs, who explains that Atahuallpa is the illegitimate Son of the Sun; his father had two sons and divided his empire between them, but Atahuallpa, wanting it all, declared war against his brother and killed him. Valverde is appalled to hear Atahuallpa referred to as God and instructs the men to convert the heathen Incas by any means necessary. Again Pizarro tries to destroy Martin's faith, this time in him. Pizarro insists that he is a man who is not to be trusted and that Young Martin is a target for disillusionment because he is a worshiper: "You belong to hope. To faith. To priests and pretences. To dipping flags and ducking heads; to laying hands and licking rings; to powers and parchments; and the whole vast stupid congregation of crowners and cross-kissers. You're a worshipper, Martin. A groveller. You were born with feet but you prefer your knees. It's you who make Bishops—Kings—Generals. You trust me, I'll hurt you past believing" (*RH*, 17–18).

Later the soldiers meet the head of a thousand families who explains the Incan modus vivendi: in the seventh month they pick corn; in the eighth, plow; in the ninth, sow maize; in the tenth, mend roofs. From Atahuallpa, the Spaniards learn how Incas have their whole lives planned for them: from the ages of nine until twelve, they protect harvests; from twelve to eighteen, they care for the herds; from eighteen to twenty-five, they serve as his warriors; at twenty-five, they marry and receive a plot of land. At fifty, all retire and live honorably in the community. Later in the play, De Nizza attacks the Incas' system as depriving its people of the right to hunger—which, as he sees it, gives life meaning—as well as the right to be unhappy: . . . "happiness has no feel for men here since they are forbidden unhappiness. They have everything in common so they have nothing to give each other. They are part of the seasons, no more; as indistinguishable as mules, as predictable as trees. All men are born unequal: this is a divine gift. And want is their birthright. Where you deny this and there is no hope of any new love; where tomorrow is abolished, and no man ever thinks 'I can change myself,' there you have the rule of Anti-Christ" (*RH*, 51).

Pizarro thinks that his whole life may have been a path to this day, which offers perhaps his death, perhaps new life. The hours pass as the soldiers agonizingly wait for a messenger to summon them to Atahuallpa. Martin spots thousands of heavily armed Incas approaching. Before they reach Pizarro, they put down their arms because "you don't approach gods with weapons" (*RH*, 35). Atahuallpa enters to an explosion of color and music and asks to see the Spaniards' God. Valverde and De Nizza try unsuccessfully to explain Christianity to him and are enraged by what they consider his blasphemy: Atahuallpa cannot accept the idea that a God can be killed by men, and he calls the Pope a madman who gives away countries that are not his; finally he casts the Bible to the ground. In "The Mime of the Great Massacre" that follows, three thousand Incas are slaughtered, and Atahuallpa is led off stage at sword-point. The act ends with screams from the Indians, and a blood-red cloth is drawn across the stage.

There is no break in the action between act 1, which ends with the arrest of Atahuallpa, and act 2, much of which is composed of scenes between the two leaders. In their first conversation, Pizarro is employing the talents of Felipillo (a slim, delicate Indian, whom he captured on a previous expedition) as translator, until it becomes apparent to Martin, who understands a little of the Incan language, that Felipillo is distorting what Pizarro and Atahuallpa are saying in order to benefit his own selfish ends. In the future, Martin will learn Incan and serve as Pizarro's translator.

The priests try to explain Communion to Atahuallpa, and it sounds to him like something ridiculous, bordering on cannibalism and vampirism: "First he becomes a biscuit, and then they eat him. . . . At praying they say 'This is the body of our God.' Then they drink his blood. It is very bad. Here in my empire we do not eat men. My family forbade it many years past" (*RH*, 49).

Atahuallpa suspects why the Spaniards have come to his land and offers to fill the room with gold in the next two months in return for Pizarro's promise to free him. De Soto cautions Pizarro about giving his word when it may not be possible to keep it, but Pizarro feels certain that Atahuallpa could never keep his part of the bargain, and so he consents. Atahuallpa orders that gold be brought in from every corner of his empire, and so "The First Gold Procession" takes place, during which the most elaborately worked objects are delivered, but not enough to fill a room; Pizarro finds Atahuallpa wanting in honesty. He reminds Atahuallpa of his promise to listen to the Christian priests; Atahuallpa has listened and thinks that they are fools. He also sees in Pizarro's eyes that the Spaniard agrees with him. Pizarro faults Atahuallpa for killing his brother and seizing the land, but Atahuallpa forces Pizarro to admit that he would have done the same thing. Pizarro mentions incidentally that sooner or later he is going to kill Atahuallpa. Nevertheless, Atahuallpa removes one of his golden earrings and hangs it on Pizarro's ear; it is the sign of Incan nobility. Next, he tries to teach Pizarro one of the indigenous dances, but Pizarro's attempt at it is so funny that Martin starts laughing. Pizarro starts laughing, too, extends his hand to Atahuallpa, and they leave the stage together.

A month has passed, and De Soto returns from a reconnaissance. He reports that, for hundreds of miles, men are standing in their fields waiting for Atahuallpa, their God, to return to them. Also, in the course of the month, the men notice that Pizarro is a changed man; never before so content as now, he spends several hours every day with the Inca. They know that Pizarro is going to find it hard to kill Atahuallpa when the time comes. As the Spaniards talk, the Incas mime "The Second Gold Procession," and the Spaniards are anxious for the division of the treasure. Only under threat of death do the soldiers disperse and postpone "The Rape of the Sun."

Just as Atahuallpa tries to teach Pizarro to dance, so Pizarro tries to teach the Inca the Spanish language and the art of fencing. Pizarro acknowledges that Atahuallpa has fulfilled his promise concerning the gold and declares Atahuallpa a free man. But his release is not so simple an issue as it appears: he must first promise that none of the Spanish soldiers will be harmed. Atahuallpa can make no such promise because he still has to avenge the death of the many men he lost at the hands of the Spaniards. Martin further complicates Pizarro's decision of whether or not to release Atahuallpa by telling Pizarro that Atahuallpa trusts him, and that he cannot betray that trust.

After the division of the gold, there is tension and violence among the soldiers: greed has overcome them. As the men are in open conflict with each other, Pizarro continues to struggle internally. What is he to do with Atahuallpa? For advice, he turns to his Second-in-Command and the representatives of the Crown and of the Church. De Soto insists that Pizarro must live up to his promise and give Atahuallpa his freedom, but Pizarro is afraid that if his army is wiped out, nobody will remember his name. Pizarro feels no obligation to the king, and Estete finds Pizarro's attempt to keep a promise of life to Atahuallpa nothing more than quaint. It is Valverde's decision that "no promise to a pagan need bind a Christian. Simply think what's at stake: the lives of a hundred and seventy of the faithful. Are you going to sacrifice them for one savage?" (*RH*, 71). From De Nizza, Pizarro gets advice that he interprets to mean: "To save my own soul I must kill another man!" (*RH*, 72). In order to protect Atahuallpa from being killed, Pizarro binds the two of them together with a rope: if the men want to kill Atahuallpa, they will have to kill Pizarro first. Atahuallpa is less concerned about his life than is Pizarro: Atahuallpa is a god and cannot be killed by a man; only his father can take his life from him. Just as Pizarro is trying to save Atahuallpa's physical life, the Inca is trying to save the Spaniard's spiritual life: "Pizarro. You will die soon and you do not believe in your God. That is why you tremble and keep no word. Believe in me. I will give you a word and fill you with joy. For you I will do a great thing. I will swallow death and spit it out of me" (*RH*, 76).

In a hopelessly unfair trial, Atahuallpa is found guilty of killing his brother, of worshiping idols, and of having more than one wife, and he is sentenced to death by burning. Pizarro pleads with him to accept baptism and thereby have his sentence reduced to death by strangling.

He accepts, and is baptized and killed. When Atahuallpa does not regenerate his own life, Pizarro cries out at the lifeless body: "Cheat! You've cheated me!" (*RH*, 79) and he lies down next to Atahuallpa's body. That day, Pizarro dies spiritually, and, shortly after, he dies physically in a quarrel with the soldier who brought up the reinforcements. Spain brought the New World "greed, hunger and the Cross: three gifts for the civilized life. The family groups that sang on the terraces are gone. In their place slaves shuffle underground and they don't sing there. Peru is a silent country, frozen in avarice" (*RH*, 80).

Characters

Chronologically *The Royal Hunt of the Sun* should be considered after *The Private Ear* and *The Public Eye* and before *Black Comedy, White Lies* and *The White Liars*, but for its character studies and themes it is grouped more logically with Shaffer' later plays, *Shrivings*, and later *Equus*, *Amadeus*, and *Yonadab*, since these plays examine the theme of worship, relationships between an adolescent and a mature man, and intense relationships between two men.

A. *Martin.* Young Martin worships Pizarro. He relates in his opening monologue to the audience: "He was my altar, my bright image of salvation. Francisco Pizarro! Time was when I'd have died for him, or for any worship" (*RH*, 1). The rest of the play traces the decline of this intense love and respect that Martin once felt for his hero. Martin is a fifteen-year-old orphan whom the illiterate Pizarro employs as his page because the boy can read and write. Pizarro promises Martin nothing in return for his services except disillusionment about chivalry and the boy's noble ideals. Honor and glory for Pizarro are "dungballs. Soldiers are for killing: that's their reason" (*RH*, 10). Despite all of Pizarro's negativism, Martin is not discouraged and is determined to serve Pizarro, whom he calls his lord. The discomforts of traveling through the forest in the New World do not diminish Martin's reverence for Pizarro, to whom he claims to belong, to whom he can declare, "You are all I ever want to be" (*RH*, 17). But Martin's "ever" is shortlived: he loses his respect for the conquistador, when Pizarro fails to keep his word to Atahuallpa, a man who trusts him. This is the turning point in Martin's life: "I went out into the night—the cold high night of the Andes, hung with stars like crystal apples—and dropped my first tears as a man. My first and last. That was my first and last worship too. Devotion never came again" (*RH*, 63). The narration, as given by Old Martin, does not deify Pizarro, or anything else. He says that the play is about ruin; the ruin is both personal as well as national.

   B. *Pizarro*.   Pizarro's whole life has been a road from ruin and an attempt to find glory and thus transcend his humble origins—that of an illegitimate swineherd in a drab Spanish village—which denied him the respect of men and the love of any woman he could consider for marriage. He is the empty shell of a man who, like Clive and Bob, is given to pondering the big questions in life, the kind that philosophers never resolve: Religion, Time, Immortality. His manner of speech, however, is more rhetorical than that of his earlier dramatic colleagues. His motivation in making another expedition to the New World is not the greed for gold (which he uses in order to entice the other men to come along), but something much deeper than any material gains: as was Charles Sidley, Pizarro is searching for the sun, for the source of life and of eternity. Gene A. Plunka[3] suggests that he wants to become the god of an "inferior people." Pizarro sees no value in institutions such as the Court, the Military, or the Church. The sun, he believes, is worthy of worship, and for pagans he thinks that it must make a fine god, something that they can see and whose power they can experience.

   Pizarro's disillusionment in life extends to women, in whom he no longer has any real interest: as everything else, women have served to be only one more disappointment in his life of shattered dreams. He blames his loss of love for women on Time, the culprit guilty of all failure in life:

I loved them with all the juice in me—but oh, the cheat in that tenderness. What is it but a lust to own their beauty, not them, which you never can: like trying to own the beauty of a goblet by paying for it. And even if you could it would become you and get soiled. . . . I'm an old man, Cavalier, I can explain nothing. What I mean is: Time whipped up the lust in me and Time purged it. I was dandled on Time's knee and made to gurgle, then put to my sleep. I've been cheated from the moment I was born because there's death in everything. (*RH*, 32)

   Pizarro almost finds the object of worship that he has been looking for when he discovers the Incan religion and meets Atahuallpa.

   C. *Pizarro and Atahuallpa*.   Pizarro is a different man in act 2 after Atahuallpa becomes his fountain of new life, at least temporarily; his nihilistic attitudes and chronic pessimism diminish when he is with the Son of the Sun. There is a strong identification between the two men: both are illegitimate and both are the leaders of men. Of even greater importance is that each one considers the other a god. Atahuallpa wants to meet Pizarro in order to receive the blessing of the White God, and Pizarro finds more meaning in the Incan religion than he ever found in Christianity, and comes to believe that perhaps the Incas have the answers to questions that the white man has never been able to receive: "I myself can't fix anything nearer to a thought of worship than standing at dawn and watching it [the sun] fill the world. Like the coming of something eternal, against going flesh. What a fantastic wonder that anyone on earth should dare to say: 'That's my father. My father: the sun!' . . . Since first I heard of him I've dreamed of him every night. A black king with glowing eyes, sporting the sun for a crown" (*RH*, 32–33).

During Atahuallpa's captivity, Pizarro grows closer to him than he ever has to anyone else in life. They teach each other their respective skills (dancing and fencing) and learn to read together, like brothers. So much does Pizarro come to love and respect Atahuallpa, that he cannot let the man to whom he has promised life be killed. When finally Atahuallpa is killed, Pizarro suffers his last disillusionment: the Inca does not regenerate himself as Pizarro believed he would. His final attempt at worship becomes his ultimate disappointment.

   D. *Atahuallpa*.   Unlike Pizarro's, Atahuallpa's convictions are simple and firm: his father is the Sun; he is the Son of the Sun; any human being who can be killed is not a real god. Shaffer includes details about Atahuallpa which are intended to make him a Jesus figure, such as placing his age at thirty-three. Atahuallpa and Pizarro are mutually dependent: Atahuallpa depends on Pizarro to preserve his physical life, and Atahuallpa is Pizarro's last hope for acquiring the ability to worship, a wish he tries to suppress but secretly envies in the Inca. All three characters—Martin, Pizarro, and Atahuallpa—are united by common bonds. Martin needs Pizarro for his worship, and Pizarro in turn needs Atahuallpa for his. In Pizarro's hands rests Atahuallpa's only hope for existence.

   Atahuallpa is not nearly so complex a figure as his Spanish counterpart and functions as an antagonist rather than a protagonist. However, he shows himself to be a master of understatement when he tells his priests that the Spaniards may come to meet him because he wants them "to see [his] mountains." Thus, the soldiers suffer the perils of the Andes in "The Mime of the Great Ascent." Shaffer uses the technique of a song to show that Atahuallpa is no fool and that he understands perfectly why Pizarro and the other Spaniards have come to the Incan empire:

You must not rob, O little finch.
The harvest maize, O little finch.
The trap is set, O little finch.
To seize you quick, O little finch.

Ask that black bird, O little finch.
Nailed on a branch, O little finch.
Where is her heart, O little finch.
Where are her plumes, O little finch.

She is cut up, O little finch.
For stealing grain, O little finch.
See, see the fate, O little finch.
Of robber birds, O little finch. (*RH*, 53)

Atahuallpa explains that this is a harvest song, and that Pizarro is the robber bird.

E. *Other Characters.* The other characters in the play have secondary roles: Valverde and De Nizza act on behalf of the Church. Hernando De Soto is at once the most practical, noble-minded, and sensitive character in the play. He regrets that Pizarro ever made a bargain with Atahuallpa, but now that he has, he expects Pizarro to honor it. De Soto cannot advise that Atahuallpa be killed after Pizarro set the conditions for his release and certainly not after he learns that the Inca trusts Pizarro. For all the priests' talk about saving the souls of the Indians, only De Soto understands that the goal of Christianity is love and that the means should not contradict the missionary ends in Peru.

Sources

Shaffer used Prescott's *History of the Conquest of Peru* as his historical source for *The Royal Hunt of the Sun* and made such changes as were necessary for his dramatic purposes. For the most part, he was faithful to history in the development of the fictionalized-historical characters and in the storyline. Francisco Pizarro was born ca. 1471 in the Spanish town of Trujillo, in the region of Extremadura. He was left as an illegitimate foundling and might have been nursed by a sow. As a boy, he worked as a swineherd and never learned to read or write. In January 1531 he left on his third and last expedition for the conquest of Peru. Shaffer is faithful also to the inclusion of the secondary characters. Prescott mentions that Pizarro was accompanied by a veedor appointed by the Crown; by Fray

Valverde, who attempted to explain the Creation, the Trinity, and the Pope to Atahuallpa; by Felipillo, a malicious youth who acted as interpreter between Pizarro and Atahuallpa; and by Hernando De Soto, who, along with Hernando Pizarro (Francisco's brother), went to meet Atahuallpa as representatives of the chief of the expedition. Prescott explains that the Spaniards arrived during a period of internal strife in the Incan empire, and that the moment was right for the conquest. Conflict had arisen between the two brothers who controlled the empire, and when Atahuallpa, the more ambitious of the two, emerged victorious, he had his brother killed. The Incan emperor was an absolute despot in a totally socialistic society and was a representative of the Sun, and there was a belief that a departed monarch would return after his death to reanimate his body on earth. (The process, however, was never believed to be so immediate as Pizarro expected of Atahuallpa.) Prescott is not so specific as Shaffer concerning the number of Incas who were slaughtered, but puts the number between 2,000 and 10,000. Atahuallpa was not led off by the soldiers at sword-point, but rather by Pizarro himself, and without any violence; Pizarro considered the emperor a guarantor of his own safety. Pizarro assured him that in the Spanish camp he would be received as a friend and a brother. Prescott estimates Atahuallpa's age to be about thirty, which Shaffer interprets as thirty-three in order to sustain his Atahuallpa/Jesus identification.

Atahuallpa was astute enough to realize that the Spaniards had not come to the New World just to save souls, and offered them a room full of gold and a smaller room filled twice with silver. The soldiers took Atahuallpa's promise as idle boasting in an attempt to gain his freedom. The Spaniards of authority agreed that the most expedient way of disposing the problem was just, and that setting Atahuallpa free was too dangerous an act. Atahuallpa was found guilty on twelve charges, including usurpation of the crown, assassination of his brother, idolatry, adultery, and insurrection against the Spaniards (the last was the most important charge in the trial). A mere four paragraphs of Prescott's monumental work mention the friendship that the Incan extended to Pizarro and of Pizarro's visible emotion when Atahuallpa pleaded for his life.[4] Pizarro's first concern, however, had to be for his men. On 29 August 1533 Atahuallpa was taken to the town square in chains. Just as Atahuallpa was to be burned, Fray Valverde promised him that if he accepted Christianity, his penalty would be reduced to death by strangulation. Atahuallpa agreed and he was thus executed. Historically, Pizarro did not die quite so soon after Atahuallpa as he does in the play.

It was not until 26 June 1541 that a band of rival conquistador Pedro de Almagro's men (whose leader Pizarro had executed in 1538 and whose lands he denied them) attacked and murdered him. The spectacle of the play too, has its origins in Prescott: he describes the soldiers' painful ascent of the Andes; the procession of the Incas and of Atahuallpa, royally attired; the decorations made from the plumes of tropical birds; and the gold processions bearing the largest booty in history.

Some critics find Shaffer's source of inspiration in Antonin Artaud's "La Conquête du Mexique,"[5] an outline of which appeared in published form in 1950.[6] There Artaud describes his work of "Theater of Cruelty" as the struggle of Christianity against primitive religion and the question of racial superiority. He mentions such details as music, dance and pantomime, poetic lamentations, and philosophical discussions, all of which appear in *The Royal Hunt of the Sun*.

Critical Appraisal and Interpretation

Reviewers were more sharply divided over *The Royal Hunt of the Sun* than over any of Shaffer's earlier plays. Writing in the *New York World Tribune and The Sun*, Norman Nadel praised the symmetry of poetry, the noble speech and strong wisdom, and placed Shaffer in the highest rank of twentieth-century British playwrights: "No Englishman in the century, save Shaw and Christopher Fry, has achieved such sensible beauty with words, such noble clarity of ideas. *The Royal Hunt of the Sun* might well be a masterpiece."[7] The *Saturday Review*[8] called it the season's most thrilling, imaginative and beautiful event, and *America*[9] called it the finest play of the season. The *New York Daily News*[10] praised Shaffer's use of language in this beautiful play, Peter Coe[11] praised *The Royal Hunt of the Sun* as a towering event of theater and literature, and Martin Esslin[12] shows considerable respect for the text of the play. Other critics had good words to say about Shaffer and his work, but found his play to be overwritten, overscrutinized, and too long.[13] Many critics praised Shaffer's daring and the vitality that he put back into the theater.[14] Those who criticized the play found the script to be heavy and self-conscious,[15] of "bloated form, pretentious theme, mundane prose and sentimental sermonizing,"[16] and a play that, for its lack of characters and language, has a hole in the middle that the spectacle cannot conceal.[17] Howard Taubman[18] reconciled the critical excesses when he stated that the play was first hailed as a masterpiece and later condemned as a showy fraud, and that the truth is somewhere between those extremes.[19] Stanley

Richards saw fit to include it in *Best Plays of the Sixties*. *The Royal Hunt of the Sun* was made into a film in 1969. Irving Lerner directed a script by Philip Yordan and the cast included Robert Shaw (Pizarro) and Christopher Plummer (Athuallpa). Iain Hamilton adapted Shaffer's script for the libretto of the operatic version, which was produced by the English National Opera. To criticize *The Royal Hunt of the Sun* as being empty, as lacking in characters or themes, is unjustified; Shaffer accomplished all that he had intended in the play. The themes are big, perhaps grandiose, the characters are heroic, and the mise-en-scène is formidable. The criticism of the language is only slightly more justifiable. The language is grand, but in its attempt to be poetic as well as profound it sometimes loses the quality of spontaneity that characterizes the speech of Clive Harrington, for example. But if Pizarro's language seems to lack lyricism, then De Nizza's poetic speech compensates for it. *The Royal Hunt of the Sun* may not be judged on literary criteria: it was Shaffer's purpose to create a work of "total theater" for the stage and not a piece of dramatic literature for the printed page.

As for Shaffer's comments on the play, in one statement he said: "Ultimately, the play is about a man's search for immortality."[20] And in another article, Shaffer called it "a play about two men: one of them is an atheist, and the other is a god. . . . The relationship . . . is intense, involved and obscure, between these two men, one of whom is the other's prisoner. . . . They are mirror-images of each other. And the theme which lies behind their relationship is the search for God, the search for a definition of the idea of God. In fact, the play is an attempt to define the concept of God."[21]

With *The Royal Hunt of the Sun*, Shaffer brought to the stage all of the spectacle he had imagined for a long time. In addition, he developed themes contained originally in his television script "The Salt Land." The play brought to life the Peru of the Incas, a land that in fact was "a natural gold mine," an expression used by Jo to describe the land of Israel. It gave another treatment of the epic theme of the settling of the New World.[22] It developed the idea of worship and man's need for God, as well as that of the search for immortality, which obsesses both Arieh and Pizarro. Thus, in one sense, *The Royal Hunt of the Sun* completed work that Shaffer had begun earlier; in another sense, it was a precursor of his portrayal of the intense struggles between two men, which dominates *Shrivings*, and tells of the death of a god, which is one of the themes of *Equus*.

Chapter Five
Shrivings

In a note written in 1974 for the published version of *Shrivings*, Shaffer stated that this play is a substantially rewritten version of *The Battle of Shrivings*, which opened at the Lyric Theatre in London on February 5, 1970, to mixed reviews from the critics.[1] The play is the result of dual sources of inspiration: Mahatma Gandhi's decision to renounce sex, which he considered a source of aggression, and the student protests of the 1960s, which grew out of the Vietnam War and the killings at Kent State University. For Shaffer, it is his "American play," which he associates with his sojourns in 1968 and 1969 in New York, then plagued by violent confrontations between Flower Children and construction workers. The play, in its published form, has never been professionally produced. Shaffer wrote *Shrivings* with John Gielgud and Lawrence Olivier in mind. Olivier was unavailable, and the parts went to John Gielgud and Patrick Magee. Wendy Heller played the part of Enid Petrie, which does not appear in the revised, published version. Dorothy Lyman and Martin Shaw completed the cast. H.M. Tennant, who had launched Shaffer's career with *Five Finger Exercise*, produced the play. John Bury, who would later design the sets for *Amadeus* and *Yonadab*, created a set so bone-white that the bowl of green apples in act 2 "riveted every eye."[2]

Shrivings, Shaffer's first three-act play, is divided into five scenes. Just as is *Five Finger Exercise*, it is true to the spirit of the classical unities: it transpires during a single weekend, treats a single problem, and takes place in a house called Shrivings, in the Cotswold Hills of England. Like the house in *Five Finger Exercise*, there is a multi-level set with the living room, study, and kitchen on the lower level and the bedrooms on the upper level. The atmosphere is one of tranquility and dedication, as was the original medieval Shrivings, a house of retreat, confession, and penance.

Structure and Plot

The play begins at five o'clock on a Friday afternoon in 1970. Without any preliminaries, the story starts with the first speech, as Lois Neal, Sir

Gideon Petrie's secretary, answers the telephone and tells the caller that Sir Gideon will stage a peace vigil by sitting in Parliament Square on Saturday and Sunday to protest the production of all arms in the United Kingdom. This weekend, the house is closed to travelers in anticipation of the arrival of Mark Askelon, a noted poet and former student of Gideon. On Monday, Mark and Gideon are going to receive awards, Gideon for the publication of his twenty-fifth book on philosophical explorations and Mark for the publication of his collected poems. Gideon is excited about Mark's expected arrival, and he wants everything to be perfect for him. Rather than being excited, Mark's son, David, who lives at Shrivings, is apprehensive about receiving his father, whom he has not seen in six years. Gideon reminds David that life has not been easy for his father since his wife's death, and that perhaps Mark is coming to Shrivings because he needs both Gideon and David.

Mark, a relic of the man he used to be, has a less-than-spectacular arrival. From the moment he enters Shrivings, he begins to fulfill his intention of making himself unwelcome, and he surprises Shrivings in a manner for which no one in the house is prepared. He criticizes Lois's vegetarianism; he calls Shrivings a "Commune for Transients"; he questions Lois's adulation of Gideon; and he callously ridicules the peace movement. But Mark receives a surprise, too: his son has left Cambridge University and has devoted himself to making furniture in Gideon's home. (Since Mark does not read letters, he never knew the news about David's life.) Mark is disappointed, but makes light of the situation by calling carpentry the only profession with "an indisputable patron saint!" (*ES*, 135). David's latest piece is a chair, almost a throne, for Gideon, and Mark is more than a little jealous. Gideon alarms Mark by describing the vigil that will take place. First Mark reacts by attacking the question of nonviolence. He asks Lois, Gideon, and David what they would do if an attacker with a weapon were to threaten one of them. Then he describes his insensitivity during a riot in New York in which he saw young protesters being mercilessly beaten by gangs of construction workers—Mark claims to have watched uncritically as he sipped martinis. Having upset the household sufficiently for his first afternoon, Mark retreats to his room and prays to the ashes of his dead wife to keep Gideon, David, and Lois safe from his own abuse of them, while at the same time he decides to become, metaphorically, the attacker, by using his tongue as a weapon.

It is 10:30 at night in the second scene. Mark, half-drunk in his room, alternately tries to blame David ("master carpenter to Gideon Petrie,"

ES, 143) and alternately himself for getting carried away in verbal abuse against the prevailing values at Shrivings for the sake of Lois, "one pretentious American slit" (*ES*, 143). Downstairs, as David rolls marijuana for a smoke, Lois admonishes him for not having warned her in advance of his father's character. David would like to have a plate represent his father, and then smash it. Lois rebuffs David's attempt to steal a kiss, which for her would violate the spirit of Gideon's renunciation of sexual activities. She also decides for David that he will attend the peace vigil, for which Gideon thinks a two-day hunger strike will add pathos to the situation. Lois suggests fasting for everyone who plans to attend. Mark, having rejoined the others, proposes that for all the love they claim to feel, he can make Shrivings reject him in just one weekend; Gideon insists that that could never happen. The Battle of Shrivings has begun.

Mark confesses that he *wants* to be proven wrong and agrees that if Shrivings can survive a weekend of him with its gentleness intact, he will return to Sir Gideon's humanitarian fold. If not, it is really Gideon and his philosophy that lose, and the philosopher must never preach improvability again. Mark begs Gideon to save him. He was not so unfeeling as he said at the New York demonstration; in fact, he was so upset that he vomited down the side of the building. He also admits to having murdered his wife but offers no details.

Act 2 begins on Saturday night, after the first day of the vigil. Mark listens over the radio to the report on the demonstration, and Gideon, David, and Lois return home, intoxicated with the vigil's success. In defiance of the hunger strike, Mark has prepared himself "the very smallest repast" (*ES*, 160) of lamb chops, salad, roll, and wine, and, to Lois's horror, David accepts his father's invitation to join him. After a six-year absence, Mark sits down to talk with his son. Because of the jealousy that he feels for David's relationship with Gideon and his guilt at having alienated himself from David, Mark thinks that David is trying to tell him to mind his own business when he asks about his son's plans for the future. Lois questions Mark's motives for coming to Shrivings; she used to admire him as a poet, but now she has lost all respect for him and finds him contemptible.

At this point, Mark wants to adapt an experiment in which total strangers were asked to inflict electric shock on innocent victims. He designates four apples as representing various degrees of punishment, from mild pain to death, and given license to say anything he would like, he attempts to provoke so much anger against him that he will be asked to leave the house. To bring the experiment to its conclusion, he reveals "secrets" about Gideon's sex life, even accusing him of stealing David, his own friend's son, to satisfy his sexual appetite for young boys. David picks up the death apple and smashes it over and over again. Mark returns to his room in repentance, and ends the scene by throwing brandy in the face of the statue on his late wife's shrine.

In the second scene of act 2, it is ten o'clock in the morning following what has been a bad night for all. Lois is furious with David because he pressed the death apple, and thereby did exactly what Mark wanted. For David, it was worthwhile to lose Mark's Apple Game because it "stopped the voice." Gideon tries to convince Lois that they must smother Mark with acceptance. Despite Mark's allegations that Gideon is a homosexual, Gideon maintains that he gave up sex with his wife because he considered it the main source of aggression in himself; his wife found the decision too rigorous for her and she left him. David wants to protect Gideon from the impending harm to him: he knows his father and wants Gideon's permission to ask Mark to leave Shrivings. Gideon is now alone in his resolution that Mark must stay. Meanwhile, Mark is planning to thicken the plot by seducing Lois, and with charm and cunning he does just that.

Act 3 takes place following the Sunday afternoon vigil, which Lois missed because she was in bed with Mark. Mark is eager for Lois to get downstairs so that their secret might be revealed to David and Gideon. He becomes adamant, and she realizes that the sex act was just one more move in his game to enrage Gideon. Mark hints broadly to Gideon and David at what was going on in his room while they were at the demonstration. Gideon is appalled that Mark, even within the context of the battle, could have stooped so low.

Mark, who has tried to win the battle by using first Gideon, and then Lois, finally uses his own son. In a last effort to turn David against Gideon, he advises Gideon that it is no longer necessary to withhold the secret of David's origins, and he assails his son: "Look at you! Is that my face? Dirty olive out of the standard wop jar! Is that my body? Slack-waisted camel-walk: the harbour hump! Get with it, you lump of Italy—it took a lot of pasta to make you!" (*ES*, 198). David asks that Gideon stop the voice, and Gideon in return only wrings his hands. David can stand no more of the philosopher's passivity and lashes out against him: "Theories and hopes and vigils and fasts! And *nothing! Lovely nothing!*" (*ES*, 200). He ends by howling at his former idol to "FUCK OFF!" David rushes out of the room, and Mark congratulates

Gideon on his victory; he acknowledges that Gideon has won the Battle of Shrivings, even if (as he alleges) it meant torturing an innocent boy in the process. Gideon faints, and Lois tries to revive and encourage him to eat, and then in a tirade against him she tells Gideon that he is a phony. In the climactic scene, he betrays his philosophy of nonviolence and strikes her.

In his room, Mark tries to make David believe that he was lying about his son's supposed illegitimacy so that he would not have to tell him how he killed Giulia, the boy's mother. One night, as his wife lay crippled in bed, Mark brought another woman into their room and had sex with her in front of his wife. Three weeks later, Giulia died. Mark, David, Gideon, and Lois are four lost souls: Lois does not know where she is; Mark has nowhere to go in life; Gideon has just one word for Mark, "Dust"; David stretches out his arms to Lois, but she remains motionless and expressionless, as the light fades.

Characters

The types of the estranged father, the abandoned son, and the reluctant young woman first appeared in "The Prodigal Father." Here they appear in fuller form. Mark is a troubled man. The manifestations of his problems are cruelty, jealousy, and alcoholism; the root is guilt, for the death of his wife, for his estrangement from his son, and for disappointment in himself. Mark and Giulia's marriage was one more in a series of bad unions in Shaffer's plays. At the core of the marital problems there was mutual canonizing between husband and wife which, ironically for Mark, led to an ambiguous love-hate relationship. The marital problems of Mark and Giulia were far deeper than those of the Harringtons, in part because Mark was an atheist who "wrote about Catholicism like it was a disease" (*ES*, 124), and Giulia, devoutly religious, was forced to read her devotional books in secret. Unlike Belinda's shortlived idealization of Charles Sidley, Giulia's adoration of her husband endured to the end. After her death, Mark regarded Giulia as a saint, much as she revered him during her lifetime. Mark loved Giulia intensely, and his love was so profound that it produced a change in his poetry: he gave up his biting criticism of the Catholic Church to sing of his love for his wife. Strangely enough, the resentment that Mark came to feel for his wife was an outgrowth of the love and admiration that she felt for him, and of which he never considered himself worthy.

Mark's plan at Shrivings is to divide and conquer, to turn Gideon, David, and Lois against one another and thereby destroy Gideon's ideas on the perfectability of humans; to prove that "the Gospel According to Saint Gideon is a lie. That we as men cannot alter for the better in any particular that matters. That we are totally and forever unimproveable" (*ES*, 156). In fact, Mark wants to *lose* the verbal battle that he declares against Gideon, because Mark needs him; he needs to have Gideon win him back to the humanist philosophy and not let him stumble into the arms of Mother Church. The battle that Mark initiates against Gideon, then, is really a manifestation of his own internal struggle. He, like Pizarro, and later Dr. Dysart and Yonadab is desperate for something in which he can believe.

Mark is and always has been a joyless man. Life has never held the excitement and passion for him that it offers to other people. He confesses to Lois how desperate and jealous his lack of passion has made him: "I was never quite alive. . . . Inside me, from my first day on earth, was a cancer. An incapacity for Immediate Life. When I was a boy, the crowd at football matches jumped to its feet, shouting. All I could see was a ball and legs. At student dances, I hopped in silence. . . . The only music I ever heard was words, and the clear thought of Gideon Petrie" (*ES*, 189–90). Joy never came to him even as an adult, and the lack of it turned to poison in him and made him hate the people who *could* feel it, the people whom he envied, including his wife and his son. He tells David: "When you were six, I watched you race your bike through the olive trees. Your mother was standing beside me. Your mouth opened with glee. Hers too. All I got were the mouths opening and shutting. No glee. Just physical movements. I stood there hating you both" (*ES*, 203).

Mark also suffers from an identity crisis; he neither knows who he is, nor identifies with his heritage. He goes about the world as a spiritually dead Christian; yet like Sophie's in *White Lies* and *The White Liars*, his heritage is Jewish. He also believes that David is lost because he never knew either a home or a homeland: "We are not Place People, David or I. My father was not called Askelon, but Ashkenazy. Israel Ashkenazy, of the ghetto face. He bequeathed me no home on earth: only envy of home in others. That boy will never walk a Dorset lane like an Englishman— rock a Vermont porch like a Yankee—doze under a Corfu cypress like a Greek. He's a mongrel! Russo-Jewish-English-Neopolitan! Whelped in one island, weaned in another" (*ES*, 152).

In several respects, Mark's situation is similar to Pizarro's. Just as Pizarro tried to drive the admiration of him out of Young Martin, so

Mark proved to Giulia how undeserving he was of her love. Also like Pizarro, he lashes out against worshipers in general, while secretly a need of something to worship engulfs him. Furthermore, he condemns the Church and all that it represents as he goes through life in search of an ideal worthy of him. Like Pizarro, he, too, is attempting to immortalize his name: Pizarro did it through his conquest of Peru; Mark is trying to do it through his poetry. And Mark and Pizarro are both joyless, empty men. Mark is also like Arieh in "The Salt Land"—both men thirst for a homeland.

David is the only issue of Mark's union with Giulia and the most disturbed son in any of Shaffer's plays before *Equus*. (David speaks in "Wows" and expresses his emotions in shrugs.) He grew up with ambiguous feelings toward his parents. There is no indication that he did not love his mother while she was alive, but after her passing he speaks of her with a total lack of feeling or respect. In words strikingly similar to those of Walter to Clive in *Five Finger Exercise*, Lois reminds David that he owes respect to Giulia, who, after all, was his mother, and he replies: "Once. Since then, Father immortalized her in poetry. Now she belongs wholly to Penguin Books" (*ES*, 125). He suffers from a complete lack of self-confidence, and he talks of how he has nothing to offer the world: "I can't give anybody anything. Sometimes I think all the opposite things I feel should just cancel me out, and make me invisible" (*ES*, 127). David lacks Clive's poetic approach to life and his understanding—or at least a sincere attempt at an understanding—of his problems. His thoughts are concerned with getting from day to day and gratifying his immediate physical desires, principally by smoking marijuana. His talents are manual, and he finds creative escape in carpentry.

As a son abandoned by his father, David more nearly approximates Jed, the son in "The Prodigal Father," than any of Shaffer's other characters. David grew up away from his father and for a six-year period received no communication from him except telegrams that said that it was still inconvenient for Mark to return home. When Mark finally attempts to communicate with his son, he assumes that David's curious manner of expression is a brusque way of telling his father that Mark has lost the right to ask him personal questions.

In the absence of any other father figure, David has adopted Gideon—or allowed Gideon to adopt him—as his only family. It is again the Young Martin–Pizarro relationship of a young boy overcome with admiration for the man he idolizes, until disillusionment turns him irrevocably against the object of his reverence. Gideon's is apparently the only friendship and love of which David can feel secure: his mother (a former ballerina, who used to dance him to sleep) is dead; his father estranged himself long ago; there are no lovers or other friends in his life. In Gideon, David has found a substitute for the relationships that his life lacks. Gideon is a surrogate father who encourages David's interest in carpentry—and is handsomely rewarded in return. David's finest work is the chair, which Mark labels "The Chair of Paternal Wisdom," for the "First Pope of Reason" (*ES*, 136). David saved the chair to present to Gideon on the day of Mark's arrival, perhaps to show off his masterwork, or perhaps, as Mark suspects, to demonstrate that the bestowal of such a gift has to be earned.

David does not share his father's reputation for success with women. There is no mention of girls in David's past, and his present consists of half-hearted attempts to win the attention of Lois, six years his senior, who is uninterested in the young man, and repelled by the very thought of sex. Mark is as strongly opposed to his son's behavior as Stanley is toward Clive's. He reveals his displeasure and jealousy by intimating on the one hand that David and Gideon are lovers, and on the other that David and his whole pot-smoking generation "can't get it up to save [their] stoned lives!" (*ES*, 197). He speaks, too, of how Giulia could not stand her son: "Even in her, deep down, was the natural Italian horror of the Unmale" (*ES*, 197). David passively accepts whatever Lois tells him to believe. He is too bewildered by the absence of a past in his life to be concerned with the present, much less the future. David never knew a real home before Shrivings, and the concept, even the word *home*, is sacred to him. As Mark envies the ability to feel emotion, David envies the quality of inner peace, and when his father asks what he would really like to be, he says that he wants to experience the serenity of an old woman whom he once met—the kind that Clive's friend from Bombay knows.

Lois, the pretty American secretary, had her personality shaped by a strict Catholic upbringing, and she demonstrates the disastrous constraints that a zealously religious childhood can have on an adult's sexual attitudes. She describes her childhood to Gideon and David: "D'you know the last thing *I'd* see at night when I was a kid? A beautiful plastic Jesus, like the ones they have in taxis to prevent crashes, only bigger. It had these great ruby tears on its face, and I'd have to pray to it before turning out the light: 'Dear Lord, make me a Good Catholic and a Good American. Amen!'" (*ES*, 127). David makes two attempts to kiss Lois. On the first occasion she turns away coolly, and on his second attempt she *"lets herself be kissed, but remains inert"* (*ES*, 145). Mark accuses her of living with Gideon because with him she is safe from sex and free to make the

meals and the rules without ever losing her virginity. He is appalled by
her hypocrisy: "Forever a Vestal Virgin . . . ! Sagging Jesus, protect
me from all Liberal American Virgins!" (*ES*, 177). In part, to prove to
David that he is sexually superior to both a nineteen-year-old and to
Gideon (whom Mark insists "is completely queer"), Mark feels compelled to seduce Lois, and becomes the first man ever to have sex with her.

In addition to proving that he is more of a man than either David or
Gideon, Mark takes Lois to bed in order to raise the level of hostility in
the house against him. The experience is not spectacular for either of
them; Mark found Lois to be as "cold as haddock. . . . Deep Freeze
Dora, the Tundra Gash!" (*ES*, 197), and for Lois it was "just a fat old
man, dropping his sweat on me!" (*ES*, 207). Lois is Mark's double: she
does not know what enjoyment is, either.

Gideon's excessive passivism, coupled with Mark's antagonism, cause
Lois to rebel against her former mentor. Mark is successful in convincing
Lois that Gideon is a phony, and she is quick in repeating those ideas to
Gideon in the final scene of the play. While Mark is trying to reconcile
his relationship with David, Lois is downstairs ending hers with Gideon:
"Do you know what a phoney is, Giddy? . . . Someone who says Peace
because there's no war in him. I don't mean he drove it out—I mean he
never had it. It's easy to be chaste when you've got no cock, Giddy. . . .
No wonder she left you, your wife. No wonder she just got out, poor
stupid Enid. She found out what a phoney she was hitched to"
(*ES*, 208).

Mark's former professor and once the object of Lois's and David's
worship is Sir Gideon Petrie, author, philosopher, and President of the
World League of Peace. He is a hybrid of Mahatma Gandhi and Bertrand
Russell, and the mouthpiece of the humanist philosophy, which he
embraces. Most of the information about his past life is revealed by Mark
in tirades designed to make Gideon angry enough to ask him to leave
Shrivings. It is not a personal hatred of either Gideon or his philosophy
that motivates Mark to humiliate the professor, but rather jealousy of the
love and respect that Gideon has won from Mark's son and a displaced
self-hate brought on by the death of his wife and the loss of his son.

The battle between Mark and Gideon is philosophical. Is Gideon's
self-proclaimed pacifism so highly developed as to overcome any attack
that Mark might make on him and his two disciples? Mark asks Gideon
to justify his attitude given the most extreme case, that of Hitler, and
Gideon maintains that "the evil you do fight you enlarge. . . . You

arm yourself to destroy gas chambers in Poland. Five years later, you are melting the eyeballs of fishermen on the Yellow Sea. We've had centuries of fighting back for Freedom and Justice. It doesn't work" (*ES*, 138).

When Mark can make no inroads against Gideon's goodness by using remote examples, he decides to attack the man personally in front of his two disciples. Since Gideon renounced sex with his former wife, Mark considers this to be the vulnerable area, which for Gideon will be indefensible:

Why do you imagine, Miss Neal, that your employer gave up sex? Because he found you ladies such a block on his path to virtue? Don't you know the only sex Gideon ever really enjoyed was with boys? Slim brown boys with sloping shoulders. He used to chase them all over Italy on our walking tours. And then, of course, the guilt would chase him: and I'd have to endure boring vows of repentance all the next day—to be broken again, naturally, all the next night, in the very next piazza! In the end he gave everything up. Guilt, nothing but guilt! The world saw only a Great Renunciation on the grandest philosophic grounds: but not so Enid. All she saw was a self-accusing pederast, pretending to be Ghandi! (*ES*, 177)

Gideon feels compelled to defend himself, or at least to explain himself, to his Owl (David) and his Falcon (Lois). David protests that homosexuality is a boring subject, but once Gideon begins to speak, David sits on the floor to enjoy the talk:

When I was young, I had, as they say, sex on the brain. I meant by that, that even when I worked on equations, or read Political Science, the impulse of my attention was somehow sexual. Sex was everywhere. A girl's hair bobbing down the street. The sudden fur of a boy's neck. The twitching lope of a red setter dog. In flowers, even—the smell of cow parsley in a field of poppies would almost make me faint. To say I was bisexual would have been a ludicrous understatement. I was tri-sexual. Quadri. Quinti. Sexi-sexual, you might say! (*ES*, 182)

Although there is more reason to believe Gideon than Mark, the subject of Gideon's sexual preferences remains ambiguous.

The names of the three men are of biblical origin and are rich in symbolic value. Mark was a first-century Jew who took a Roman name and who authored the earliest of the four Gospels. Likewise, Mark Askelon's heritage is Jewish, but he goes through life oblivious to his past, living an atheistic present, and toying with the idea of returning to Mother Church (either Roman or Greek) in the future. His last name derives from Ashkelon, one of the five major cities of Philistia, and his actions bear out the biblical associations of the Philistines. Gideon's name is that of a tribal leader in Israel who defeated the Midianites in the twelfth century B.C.E. and who was offered the kingship of Israel but refused it on the grounds that only the Almighty is Israel's King. Just as the biblical Gideon overcame a philistine people, so the dramatic Gideon wins the Battle of Shrivings, even if it means losing everything else in the process. David's name has the Hebrew meaning of the Beloved, and beloved he is to both Mark and Gideon, but his character is antithetical to that of the biblical soldier and king. He is not the heroic David slaying Goliath, nor the majestic, marble David that Michelangelo sculpted, but rather more the innocent, childlike David of the bronze statue by Donatello. Shaffer will present another view of King David in *Yonadab*.

Themes

The play is as much concerned with exposition of philosophical questions for which Gideon and Mark are spokesmen as it is with plot and character development. Some of the questions are constants in Shaffer's theater; others appear for the first time. The basis of the play is the conflict between aggression and passivism—the aggression represented by Mark, and the passivism by Gideon. The very core and pride of Gideon's life is his philosophy of non-violence; as President of the World League of Peace, he is its foremost proponent. He believes in peaceful demonstrations—vigils and fasts—rather than in violent revolution. He carries his philosophical ideas to the extreme in refusing to defend a person who is dear to him against an attacker, since that would reduce Gideon to the level of the ruffian. His belief is that humans are good and that human nature is improvable to the point of near-perfection. His strongest statements are those on humankind's alterability, the area in which he and Mark are most at odds: "If we know *one thing* about Man, it is that he cannot *stop* altering—that's his condition! He is unique on earth in that he has *no* fixed behavior patterns! . . . There is no proof whatever that man is born inherently aggressive" (*ES*, 170–71). His only objection to the philosophy of the flower children is their desire for oneness with Nature, which is aggressive: "The Drug Children of today cry: 'Unite with Nature!' I say: Resist her. Spit out the anger in your daddy's sperm! The bile in your mother's milk! The more you starve out aggression, the more you will begin yourselves!" (*ES*, 148). He objects to sex because he sees it as the major stumbling block to people's peace with each other; for him it is a separating rather than a unifying act: "This supreme experience of union appeared to me with more and more force each time, to be simply a twin act of masturbation, accompanied by murmurs designed to disguise the fact. . . . I grew to hate the very shape of desire. Its parody of closeness. Its separating climax. Finally, I came to know that for me, it was the main source of aggression. That before I could even start on my innocence, I would have to give it up" (*ES*, 183).

The institutions that were attacked by Pizarro in *The Royal Hunt of the Sun* are further attacked by Gideon. The smallest unit is that of the family. Shrivings, he insists, is "not a family, as so many people know it—a box of boredom for man and wife—a torture chamber for the children. That idea of family must soon be obsolete, surely?—a miserable little group, marked off by a flat door, or a garden fence!" (*ES*, 152). Gideon believes that home is not the place given by birth, but the place taken by adoption: "Country can be a mental prison, and patriotism an ape's adrenaline" (*ES*, 137). He also assails materialism, patriotism, and, of course, religion: "Mangerism, or worship of Family; Flaggism, or worship of Tribe; Thingism, or worship of Money. In our theatres and on our screens, we have taught you to find the act of killing men exciting, and the act of creating them obscene. You can go to Church, and respect the stopped mind. You can go to the war memorials, and respect the stopped body. What more do you want?" (*ES*, 147).

Mark agrees with Gideon in his criticism of social institutions. In a speech that calls to mind those of Pizarro, he denigrates the flag-worshipers and shows how something that begins as innocently as good citizenship can become uncritical allegiance. He also remarks that the clergy, who start by making laws, eventually destroy individuality. Mark can feel only contempt for "the insane Popes! the Rabbis of Repression!" (*ES*, 190). (Shaffer takes on Christian fundamentalism in *Equus*, Catholicism in *Amadeus*, and biblical Judaism in *Yonadab*.) Mark sees no glory in Europe's past, no shining heritage for the young to honor, no heroes for them to worship; just doom, death, and destruction. He advises Lois at the beginning of the last act that the best thing she can do is return to the United States and leave Europe behind: ". . . Everything bad started here. The pox. The subjugation of woolly heads. The social layer cake, which God's hand alone is allowed to crumble. Above all, the Police State. That's our main gift to the world. We've never been without it" (*ES*, 191). And again, in words much like Pizarro's, he curses "the kneelers! The followers of carriage axles. The motorcade boys. The smart saluters" (*ES*, 191). The only ideals that Mark once held were Gideon's: he, too, believed that humanity could be better than it is, but he lost his faith the day of the New York riots; he lost the faith he had and discovered no other with which to replace it.

Mark confesses that life as he is living it can never be happy for him. He needs something in which to believe because he is Man, and Man needs to live with a dream: "I wish I was an animal, and could live without a dream. I wish I was a child, and could live in a Church. But I'm a man, and I've known you [Gideon]. Where else can I go?" (*ES*, 210). Gideon sees the root of all of Mark's problems in his pessimism: "Smugness! The endless smugness of pessimism! Under all that litany of woe I heard only one note: *relish!* Comfort in the idea of your own perpetual failure" (*ES*, 169).

Just as are Mark and Gideon, Lois, too, is in favor of people and opposed to labels:

I believe in the people, yes. And I believe that most of them don't want any part of the world they've been given. They don't want war. Or politics. Or organised religion. They've been taught to want these things by the ruling class, just desperate to keep its power. If they could ever get their heads straight, ordinary people would realise what history is all about. How it's just the story of a great big lie factory, where we've all been made to work every day, printing up labels: Serf. Heretic. Catholic. Communist. Middle-class. And when we're through, we're made to paste them over each other till the original person disappears, and nobody knows who the hell he is any more! (*ES*, 165)

Summation

The characters of *Shrivings* are already evident in the radio script, "The Prodigal Father," and even earlier in "The Salt Land." The situation is that of a father and son who have been estranged throughout the formative years of the son's development, and consequently they are strangers to each other when finally they meet at the mansion of Shrivings. Mark bears resemblance to any number of characters in previous plays of Shaffer. His function is something like that of Walter in *Five Finger Exercise*: the stranger who comes into a family situation and leaves it forever changed. He also assumes the role of Ted in *The Private Ear*, in his competitiveness: Ted against his friend Bob; Mark against his son David. He shares characteristics with Stanley and Bob from the same two plays: Like Stanley, he is a father out of touch with his son; and like

Bob, he has to admit that he could never dominate a woman (despite his reputation as a sexual wonder). He is similar to Pizarro in his lack of faith in organized religion. He characterizes the Old and New Testaments as "vengeful Daddy, wrapped in clouds," and "Mobile Mary, whizzing up to Heaven" (*ES*, 169). He suffers the same disappointment in his son as the fathers in "The Prodigal Father," "The Salt Land," *Five Finger Exercise*, *White Lies*, and *The White Liars*. Finally, just as with Jed and Leander and Clive and Stanley, the indication at the end of the play is that father and son have reached some temporary reconciliation. The joylessness of Mark's life makes him both a descendant of Pizarro, and a forerunner of both Dr. Dysart in *Equus* and *Yonadab*.

David shares traits of the young men in "The Prodigal Father," *Five Finger Exercise*, and *The Royal Hunt of the Sun*, as well as of Alan in *Equus*. He is the rejected son, just as is Jed, but unlike Jed he is not bitter toward his father. Indeed, like Clive Harrington, he wants very much to get along with his father and is willing to go further than Clive in his pursuit of a relationship with him. Clive is willing to agree with his father only to the point that he does not contradict his mother or side with his father against her. David is willing to reject Gideon's fast and to defy Lois's rules of vegetarianism for Shrivings by eating during the two-day fast—and meat at that. David's needs are the same as those of Young Martin: both need someone to love and respect. For Young Martin it is a conquering hero; for David, a renowned philosopher.

Lois had two idols: Mark for his forceful poetry and (like David) Gideon for his gentle philosophy. She shares with Pizarro a loss of faith in Catholicism. (She loves Mark's anti-Catholic collection of poems *Wafers of Death*.) And, like Young Martin, before the end of the play Lois loses her respect for her two heroes. She shares an intimate bond with Lucy in "The Prodigal Father," not so much as an individual, but in her relationship to other characters: Lois had a repressive, Catholic rearing imposed by her parents; Lucy is an orphan who lives under the suppression imposed by Lady Sylvia Glenister.

Gideon is the play's philosopher and bears a strong resemblance to De Nizza, who speaks of spreading love in the midst of a crowd bent on killing and looting. Gideon resembles Pizarro in his speeches, which blast the flag-wavers and cross-kissers. Mark introduces the question of Gideon's sexuality, a topic which concerns Clive, Frank (*The White Liars*), Harold Gorringe (*Black Comedy*), and later Alan in *Equus*, Yonadab, and the two male characters in *Whom Do I Have the Honour of Addressing?* His marriage, which ended in divorce, was as problematic as those of the Harringtons, the Sidleys, Arieh and Kulli Mayers, and also of the Askelons.

The theme of lying and the technique of game-playing in *Shrivings* have their origins in earlier plays. Lies dominate the plot of *Five Finger Exercise*, *White Lies*, *The White Liars*, *Black Comedy*, and *The Royal Hunt of the Sun*. (In "The Salt Land," too, Arieh is willing to agree to help Jo in the future as repayment for a favor in the present, knowing that he may very well break his word to his brother.) The pivotal point of the play is the Apple Game, similar to but more drastic than the games that Tom and Frank (*White Lies* and *The White Liars*) are accustomed to playing with each other. (No less a precedent are the games that Clea plays with everybody else in the room in *Black Comedy*.) A final technique that deserves mention is the effective use of overlapping dialogues in the last act, with conversations taking place among characters who are on two different levels of the stage (a staging device also used in *The Royal Hunt of the Sun*). There is a sequence of Mark and David's conversations, then a sequence of Gideon and Lois's. Each builds to its own climax, while each complements the other.

The short run of the original *The Battle of Shrivings* and the lack of a professional staging of the revised *Shrivings* suggest that this play does not merit its own chapter. But it does: the characters, themes, techniques, and stagecraft serve as a transition between *The Royal Hunt of the Sun* and Shaffer's next play, *Equus*.

Chapter Six
Equus

After the cool reception that *The Battle of Shrivings* received, Shaffer rebounded with the play that was to become his most successful play prior to *Amadeus*. *Equus* was presented in London by the National Theatre at the Old Vic Theatre on 26 July 1973, and then opened in New York at the Plymouth Theatre on 24 October 1974. In London, Alec McGowen originated the role of Dr. Martin Dysart. In New York, Anthony Hopkins, Leonard Nimoy, and Richard Burton all played Dysart. Peter Firth had the role of Alan in both cities. However, to focus on just the London and New York successes of *Equus* is to do Shaffer an injustice; the play has enjoyed runs in every corner of the globe, and has made theatrical history in Spain by ending the taboo of nudity on the Spanish stage. The story is based on an event that a friend of the playwright related to him. One night in a stable in Britain, a boy from a "Thou-shalt-not family" blinded twenty-six horses. Shaffer never confirmed the event, and the man who told him of the incident died before Shaffer could learn any more about the case. The story fascinated him, and he had to write his own interpretation of the tragedy. The event is historical; the treatment that it receives in the play is fictitious and bears the Shaffer trademark.

Just as is *The Royal Hunt of the Sun*, *Equus* is a play in two acts, subdivided into scenes (twenty-one in act 1 and fourteen in act 2), and the action is continuous. The changes of scene indicate a change of time, place, or mood. A substantial portion of the play is information presented through flashbacks, which examine an adolescent's past for clues that would motivate the commission of his bizarre crime. The principal action of the play is set in the Rokeby Psychiatric Hospital in southern England; the time is the present. The production that Shaffer describes in the text is the one directed by John Dexter (who also directed *Black Comedy* and *The Royal Hunt of the Sun*) at the National Theatre.

Plot

As the play opens, in silence and darkness, Alan Strang is fondling a horse's head, and the horse is nuzzling his neck. Dr. Martin Dysart, a child psychiatrist, breaks the silence with a monologue. He is troubled not about the boy, but about the horse, and he confesses that he is lost in asking questions that are unanswerable. He begins his narration with the day that Hesther Salomon, a magistrate, came to beg him to accept Alan as a patient. Only after hours of pleading the case could she persuade a court to allow the boy to enter a psychiatric hospital rather than be put into prison for life, and she is convinced that Dysart is the only man within a hundred miles who can help him. (She feels the "vibrations.") Dysart finds a fascination in the case, and, despite the fact that he is overworked, accepts the new patient. At his first session with Dysart, Alan is silent except for the television jingles that he sings in response to the doctor's questions. Dysart concludes that at least one of Alan's parents forbids him to watch television. When the nurse comes to take Alan to his room, he is reluctant to leave Dysart's office, and as he exits he passes "dangerously close" to the psychiatrist. Dysart's fascination grows. Like Alan, the doctor has been having nightmares, and he blames them on Hesther for having brought Alan to him. Dysart achieves his first breakthrough with Alan: the patient is now speaking and tells Dysart that his father forbids him to watch television, a prohibition which Alan's mother considers extreme.

In order to assess clearly the parents' religious attitudes, Dysart decides to pay the Strangs a visit on a Sunday. Frank Strang is still at work (Sundays are nothing special to him), and Dora Strang tells the doctor that Alan was always especially fond of horses. As a child he had her read to him over and over again the story of a talking horse called Prince, which only one boy could ride. Alan also learned by heart the passage about horses in the Book of Job. Alan loved the word *equitation* and savored the word *equus*, the only word he had ever encountered with a double "u."[1] Mrs. Strang also tells the psychiatrist that hers was always a "horsey family." When he returns home, Frank gets the doctor alone to fill him in on some information that he considers significant and that he is certain his wife did not mention. Frank blames Alan's problems on his mother's reading to him biblical passages about the death of Jesus night after night. For Frank, it is all just so much "bad sex." What little instruction Alan has about sex, he received from his mother, who linked sex to love and love to God.

Dysart must find out about Alan's screams of "Ek" in the night, but Alan will only answer Dysart's questions if the doctor answers his, one each in turns. Dysart needs to know what was Alan's first memory of a horse in his life; Alan especially wants to know if Dysart is married.

When Dysart dismisses the boy for reverting to singing television jingles instead of answering the question, Alan sullenly tells of his first experience at the age of six with a horse. A horseman let Alan join him on Trojan and ride as fast as he liked. His parents saw him, became worried, and caused Alan to fall. Alan claims that that was the last time he ever rode. To make it easier for Alan to release further details to him, Dysart gives the boy a tape recorder. Alan calls the technique stupid, but takes the machine nonetheless.

In three unexpected visits, Dysart acquires a wealth of information about Alan. Mrs. Strang pays a call on the doctor and tells him that when her husband tore an exceptionally objectional religious picture from the wall over Alan's bed, her son put in the same place one of a horse, photographed head-on, that appeared to be all eyes. Dysart's next visit is from Mr. Dalton, the owner of the stables at which Alan blinded the horses. Dalton reveals that Alan was introduced to the stables by a young woman named Jill Mason. Although Alan never admitted it, Dalton suspected that he was riding secretly at night. And so he was, Alan admits, because "it was *sexy*" (ES, 47). Finally, Mr. Strang appears with information that he was embarrassed to convey in his wife's presence. One night he caught Alan reciting a parody of a biblical genealogy and then kneeling in front of the photograph of the horse and beating himself with a coat hanger. Before leaving, Frank tells Dr. Dysart to ask Alan about the girl he was with on the night he blinded the horses. Frank refuses to say any more.

In their next conversation, Dysart asks Alan how he found the job at the stables and how Jill instructed him in grooming horses. Alan remembers how he loved touching the horses, but goes into a rage when Dysart wants to know about Jill: he accuses him of being a "Bloody Nosey Parker! Just like Dad" (*ES*, 57). It is Alan's turn to ask the questions, and he wants to know if Dysart has sex with his wife; it is Alan's guess that Dysart never touches her. Dysart orders Alan out of his office and has to admit to himself that Alan has pinpointed the psychiatrist's "area of maximum vulnerability" (*ES*, 59). Dysart uses Hesther's shoulder to cry on as he relates the details of his sterile marriage. She reminds Dysart that it is his job to return Alan to normality, but Dysart is not certain that he considers it a blessing to be "normal."

Dysart's techniques of getting Alan to talk have become more and more sophisticated: first answering questions in turn, then using a tape recorder, and now playing a game called Blink, through which he hypnotizes Alan and gets him to talk in detail of his naked midnight

rides on Equus. The rides begin as religious rituals and end in masturbation. This poetic and overpowering scene ends act 1 with a blackout.

Act 2 begins with another one of Dysart's monologues; it begins with
the same sentence that he used to begin the first act: "With one
particular horse, called Nugget, he embraces" (*ES*, 74). Again he asks
rhetorical questions regarding his profession and his position within it.
While he is speaking, the nurse rushes in to report a terrible scene that
has just taken place between Alan and his mother, Mrs. Strang brought
her son his lunch; he threw it at her, and she slapped him. Dysart orders
her out of the room. She tries to explain what she has been going through
as a mother, and that anything that Alan has done is a result of what *he* is
and not anything that his parents have done to him. This is Dysart's first
indication that Alan resents not only Frank, but Dora, too. Alan denies
anything that he said under hypnosis, but at the same time suggests that
he would take a truth drug, which will "make" him say things that he is
withholding. Dysart confesses to Hesther that he is reluctant to cure
Alan if it means taking away his worship, the very core of the boy's life.
Furthermore, he envies Alan for having the passion that is missing in his
own life. Hesther believes that in Dysart Alan has found a new god, or at
least a new father.

Alan is repentant and sends the doctor a note with an apology for
having denied what he said under hypnosis, and further he acknowledges
that he knows why he is in the hospital. Dysart is elated and sends for
Alan for a session in the dead of night. He gives him an aspirin and lets
him believe that it is the truth pill, and Alan begins to speak freely. He
likes the consulting room and finds it hard to believe that Dysart would
give up his job as Nosey Parker in order to move to a place where the old
gods used to bathe before they died, the Mediterranean Sea. Alan also has
difficulty believing that gods die. He lets it "just slip out" that he knows
the extent of his doctor's unhappiness. Alan requests that Dysart ask him
a question, just to see if the pill has had its effect yet; Dysart wastes no
time in asking about Jill Mason. One night after work, Jill started
talking to Alan; she told him what beautiful eyes he had and that she had
noticed him looking into Nugget's eyes "for ages." She suspected that,
like herself, Alan found horses, especially their eyes, sexy. She knew that
Alan no more enjoyed going back to his home than she enjoyed returning
to hers, and she invited him to go to a skin flick with her. When Alan saw
in the film a nude woman for the first time, he was transfixed. Then
suddenly he noticed his father in the audience. Frank caught his son
watching a "dirty" movie, but what was worse, Alan caught his father.

Mr. Strang insisted that he was at the theater on a business matter with the manager, and Jill assured him that it was her idea and not Alan's that they go to the film. Alan refused to go home with his father, insisting that it was proper that he see the young lady home first. Alan realized then that his father is just another man like all others; he also realized that he wanted to be with Jill—he wanted to see her breasts, just as he saw the breasts of the woman in the film. When Jill suggested that they go off together, Alan eagerly accepted. She took him to the stables, and they both undressed. But every time Alan touched Jill, he felt horsehide; when he tried to kiss her, he "heard" Equus disapproving; when he tried to make love to her, he was impotent. In a rage, he ordered her out of the stable, took a metal pick and with it put out the eyes of six horses. Then, left alone and naked, he begged to be found and killed.

The play ends with Dysart's final monologue, his strongest indictment of the work he is doing: he will not only relieve Alan of his pain, he will relieve him of all feeling. The play ends where it began, with Dr. Dysart feeling that he is as much a slave as is a horse: "There is now, in my mouth, this sharp chain. And it never comes out" (*ES*, 106).

Characters

The play is the story of Dr. Martin Dysart, a talented child psychiatrist in his mid forties. Unlike Clive Harrington, Mark Askelon, and Bob (*The Private Ear*), Dysart is not known to the reader through the opinions of the other characters; he is revealed exclusively through his own words, often spoken in extended monologues similar to those of Shaffer's Pizarro. Dysart's speeches are much like those of Pizarro and of De Nizza: Pizarro's laments are personal, but the implications are religious and philosophical; De Nizza's contradict conventional thought and contain unexpected twists, which shock the audience.[2] The opening monologues of both the first and second acts are startling speeches: on seeing a boy and a horse in tender embrace, Dysart's concern is not for the boy, but rather for the horse, another way of saying that Dysart is concerned about himself.

Throughout the play, Dysart insists on an identification between himself and the horse. He sees the horse as "nudging through the metal some desire absolutely irrelevant to filling its belly or propagating its own kind. What desire could that be? Not to be a horse any longer? Not to remain reined up for ever in those particular genetic strings?" (*ES*, 17). And that is Dysart's problem exactly: "I'm wearing that horse's head myself. That's the feeling. All reined up in old language and old assumptions, straining to jump clean-hoofed on to a whole new track of being that I only suspect is there" (*ES*, 18). He acknowledges that the questions he asks should remain unspoken, unthought: they are not only useless, they are subversive. They strike at the very heart of his life's work and convince him that what he is doing clinically is wrong ethically.

Dysart is suffering from a malaise both personal and professional, one which he prefers to call "professional menopause." The problem is that Dysart has lost faith in what he is doing—he no longer thinks that eliminating individual passions and restoring his patients to normalcy is a service to them. Like Julian in *The Public Eye*, Dysart believes that his job is failing rather than fulfilling him. He even doubts that he *knows* what he is doing: "In an ultimate sense I cannot know what I do in this place—yet I do ultimate things. Essentially I cannot know what I do—yet I do essential things. Irreversible, terminal things. I stand in the dark with a pick in my hand, striking at heads!" (*ES*, 106).

The head at which he is currently striking is that of Alan Strang, the adolescent boy who blinded six horses. Dysart's reaction to this case is his strongest ever, not because he is horrified, but because he envies Alan; he wishes that he could know the kind of passion that brought his patient to that savage act. Alan and Dysart both have private passions and fantasies: Alan's consists of ritualistically riding Equus, his god, once every three weeks; Dysart's passion is for the ancient Greek civilization, about which he spends night after night reading books and looking at photographs. He cannot resist contrasting his impotent attempts at recapturing the Greek civilization with Alan's wild midnight rides:

Such wild returns I make to the womb of civilization. Three weeks a year in the Peloponnese, every bed booked in advance, every meal paid for by vouchers, cautious jaunts in hired Fiats, suitcase crammed with Kao-Pectate! Such a fantastic surrender to the primitive. And I use that word endlessly: "primitive." "Oh, the primitive world," I say. "What instinctual truths were lost with it!" And while I sit there, baiting a poor unimaginative woman [his wife] with the word, that freaky boy tries to conjure the reality! I sit looking at pages of centaurs trampling the soil of Argos—and outside my window he is trying to *become one*, in a Hampshire field! . . . Then in the morning, I put away my books on the cultural shelf, close up the kodachrome snaps of Mount Olympus, touch my reproduction statue of Dionysus for luck—and go off to hospital to treat him for insanity. (*SE*, 81)

Dysart's marriage surpasses, in its sterility, all of the other empty unions in Shaffer's plays. For all of Alan's pain and suffering, Dysart envies him because he experiences, expresses, and receives emotion. Dysart says of his own wife: ". . . If you're kinky for Northern Hygienic as I am, you can't find anything more compelling than a Scottish Lady Dentist. . . . I see us in our wedding photo: Doctor and Doctor Mac Brisk. We were brisk in our wooing, brisk in our wedding, brisk in our disappointment" (*ES*, 60). Dysart would like to believe that his wife has caused their barren marriage—that it is her fault for sitting and knitting for other people's children night after night, as he admires the classical world via photographs. But it is untrue: "I imply that we can't have children: but actually, it's only me. I had myself tested behind her back. The lowest sperm count you could find" (*ES*, 81). As much as passion, as much as knowing worship, Dysart craves someone unbrisk, whom he can take to Greece and instruct: he wants a son. In his bitterness, in his rationalization, he makes himself believe that, if they did have a son, he would turn out as passionless as his mother.

Since he accepted Alan Strang as a patient, Dr. Dysart has been having a nightmare, which serves as a microcosm of his problem. He is chief priest in Homeric Greece, and his job is that of cutting the insides out of young children and offering them up as sacrifices to the gods. He has two assistants, and he is afraid that one day they will notice that behind his mask he is green with nausea over his task. If they ever discover his secret, he will be the next victim. On every child on whom Dysart is supposed to perform the sacrifice, he sees the face of Alan Strang.[3] Alan's stare, Dysart imagines, is accusing him: Alan lives his passions; Dysart does not.

Alan, the lean seventeen-year-old boy, is Shaffer's most troubled character. He exists on the periphery of society; as Dysart puts it, "He can hardly read. He knows no physics or engineering to make the world real for him. No paintings to show him how others have enjoyed it. No music except television jingles. No history except tales from a desperate mother. No friends to give him a joke, or make him know himself more moderately. He's a modern citizen for whom society doesn't exist" (*ES*, 79). In order to fill the void in his life, Alan depends on an object of love and worship. As a child, he spent night after night with his mother reading from the Bible, and thus he developed a religious worship. He never learned anything about the essence of Christianity or about the message of Jesus; his fascination was for the violence of the march to Calvary. Instead of a peaceful Jesus illuminated from within, Alan had over his bed a picture that even his mother had to admit was ". . . a little extreme. The Christ was loaded down with chains, and the centurions were really laying on the stripes" (*ES*, 44). When his father tore the picture down, Alan replaced it with a picture of a horse, which emerged as the new object of his worship.)

The first picture had a masochistic effect on Alan. One night, when Alan was supposed to have been asleep, Frank passed his room and heard his son reciting a parody of biblical genealogies, in which the Jesus/horse identification is obvious: "Prince begat Prance. . . . And Prance began Prankus! And Prankus begat Flankus! Flankus begat Spankus. And Spankus begat Spunkus the Great, who lived three score years! . . . *(kneeling)* and Legwus begat Neckwus. And Neckwus began Fleckwus, the King of Spit. And Fleckwus spoke out of his chinkle-chankle! . . . And he said 'Behold—I give you Equus, my only begotten son!'" (*ES*, 49–50). The biblical influence is clear; the names that Alan chose are associated with the experiences that he had had with horses. Prince is the horse in the storybook that he enjoyed as a child. The *Neck*wus and the *Flank*us are the parts of the horse with which his body comes in contact. The *Spit* catches Alan's attention when he sees it coming from the horse's mouth. The *Spank*us is what he is doing to himself while he recites the genealogy: he beats himself with a wooden coat hanger.[4]

Alan's beliefs about horses are based on elements from the Old and New Testaments. Equus, like Jesus, is in chains for the sins of the world, and he lives in all horses. In turn, for taking him out of his chains, Equus promises Alan salvation by making the two of them into one: horse and rider shall be one beast—the kind of being that the South American Indians considered to be a god until a Spaniard fell from his animal. Alan went into Equus's stable—that is, his Holy of Holies's—to wash and brush him, and he "heard" the horse say that Alan should mount and ride him. The first time, it was ride or fall—that is the Straw Law. (Equus was born in the straw.) The preparations for his ride every three weeks were religious rituals that he performed for his god. First Alan put on Equus's sandals, sandals of majesty, made of sack. Next he put on the chinkle-chankle—the reins: Equus did not like it ". . . but he takes it for my sake. He bends for me. He stretches forth his neck to it" (*ES*, 68). Then Alan took Equus to his place of Ha Ha, his field, and withdrew from the Ark of the Manbit, the stick that Alan put into his own mouth. It was a sacred stick for him, and he used it during every ride: "So's it won't happen too quick" (*ES*, 70). Then Alan touched Equus all over, as one would touch a lover: "Everywhere. Belly. Ribs. His ribs are of ivory. Of great value! . . . His flank is cool. His nostrils open for me. His eyes shine. They can see in the dark . . . Eyes!—" (*ES*, 70.) Finally he gave Equus his Last Supper, a lump of sugar, which Equus accepted as a sin offering. At last, he was ready to mount his god! Equus's naked hide against Alan's naked skin hurt the boy: "Knives in his skin! Little knives—all inside my legs" (*ES*, 71).

The horse was not only the object of his worship, but also his invitation to freedom and the source of his sexual release.[5] Alone and naked at midnight on Equus, Alan freed both himself and his horse from society's restrictions. Together they rode against their foes: the Hosts of Philco—the electrical appliances that Alan sold as a job—and the Hosts of Jodhpur—the clothes with which horses are adorned for shows. The speech that Alan recited during his ritualistic-orgasmic rides is fraught with historical, religious, and sexual implications. His rides began as invocation and ended in orgasm:

And Equus the Mighty rose against All!
His enemies scatter, his enemies fall!
TURN!
Trample them, trample them.
Trample them, trample them.
TURN!
TURN!!
TURN!!!
   The Equus noise increases in volume.
(shouting) WEE! . . . WA! . . . WONDERFUL! . . .
I'm stiff! Stiff in the wind!
My mane, stiff in the wind.
My flanks! *My* hooves!
Mane on my legs, on my flanks, like whips!
Raw!
Raw!
I'm raw! Raw!
Feel me on you! *On* you! *On* you! *On* you!
I want to be *in* you!
I want to BE you forever and ever!—
Equus, I love you!
Now!—
Bear me away!
Make us One Person!
   He rides Equus frantically.
One Person! One Person! One Person! One Person!

He rises up on the horse's back, and calls like a trumpet.
Ha-HA! . . . Ha-HA! . . . Ha-HA!
The trumpet turns to great cries.
HA-HA! HA-HA! HA-HA! HA-HA! . . . HA! . . . HA! . . .
HAAAAA!
He twists like a flame.
Silence.
The turning square comes to a stop in the same position it
occupied at the opening of the Act.
Slowly the boy drops off the horse on to the ground.
He lowers his head and kisses Nugget's hoof.
Finally he flings back his head and cries up to him:
AMEN!
Nugget snorts, once. (*ES*, 72–73)

From his mother, whose word he respected, Alan learned that there is a progression from sex to love to God. It was natural, then, for him to turn the object of his worship into the object of his sexual attraction.[6] His mother also taught him that God knows and sees everything.

Alan's blinding of the horses was brought about as a result of suffering three disappointments in rapid succession. First, he saw his father at a pornographic cinema. Then he realized that his mother was the cause of his father's having to go to such a place. Finally, he experienced impotence, brought on by the religion that his mother had taught him. The impotence was Alan's final shame. He warned Jill never to tell anyone, and even tries to hide the truth from Dr. Dysart. Over and over again he insists that: "I put it in her! . . . All the way! . . . I shoved it. I put it in her all the way" (*ES*, 100). But Dysart knows better; he knows that if Alan had been sexually successful with Jill, he would have had no cause to blind the horses. Alan's reasons for the blindings were two: first, Equus "saw" him in his moments of failure and disgrace; second, he turned away from Equus, and like other gods, Equus is jealous and vengeful. Alan knew that Equus would never allow him to be successful with a woman. Hiding the pick behind his back, Alan approached Equus gently: "Equus . . . Noble Equus . . . Faithful and True . . . God-slave . . . Thou—God—Seest—NOTHING!" (*ES*, 103).

Martin Dysart and Alan Strang are individually well-drawn characters. Both are presented with deep penetration into their motivations; even more profound is their relationship with and mutual effect upon each other. Many of the play's finest scenes take place between Alan and Dysart in his office, described in the stage directions as having the appearance of a railed boxing ring. The vibrations of which Hesther spoke are apparent from their first scene together. Dysart immediately identifies that one or both of Alan's parents forbade him to watch television. From the first, Dysart is affected by Alan to the point of having nightmares, and Alan has found the man he could trust. The nightmares show how Alan and Dysart mirror each other. In their subsequent encounters, Alan proves he is every bit as astute as the doctor. When the psychiatrist asks Alan if he has a special dream, Alan returns the question to him. Unlike Alan, Dysart answers it: "Carving up children" (*ES*, 36). His truthful answer gets the first smile out of Alan. And Dysart knows perfectly well how to handle Alan: when to let Alan stew in his own anxiety; when, at the first sign of regression (more television jingles), to dismiss him from the office. The threat of having to leave Dysart's office and not unburden himself is enough to make Alan talk—even about horses.[7]

Much like those in *Shrivings*, the characters in *Equus* have the double function of serving as human beings with individual preoccupations as well as acting as mouthpieces for philosophies and ideologies. There is the classical struggle between Apollo, the Greek god of healing and medicine, of morality and ethics; and Dionysus, the god of fertility, for whom the worship was ecstatic and orgiastic, and whose enemies seemed to be turned into animals and were driven mad. Alan's interest in Dysart extends beyond the man's professional capacity of a psychiatrist and into the realm of his private life. Alan's concern is Dysart's marriage. He knows that a special bond exists between the doctor and himself, and that Dysart, therefore, cannot be enjoying a good marriage. He also wants to know if the Dysarts have children. If they do, Dysart is not the sexual failure that Alan is; also it will be that much more difficult for Alan to be emotionally adopted by Dysart.

For Alan, Dysart has become Alan's new object of reverence. Equus was a destructive god and led Alan to a criminal act; Dysart is helpful and is trying to relieve Alan of his pain. In his first monologue, Dysart establishes an identification between himself and a horse. Alan has established a relationship between the horse and a god. When Dysart takes away Alan's old god, which Alan is ready to give up, the boy has to be able to replace it with a new one, and so his new object of respect becomes Dysart. Alan and Dysart share a mutual dependency (as did Pizarro and Atahuallpa): Alan is looking, if not for a god to worship, at least for a father to love and respect. Dysart is looking for a son, someone whom he can instruct. The fact that Dysart has come to grow so close to

Alan, that he has come to doubt the value of his profession, that he envies the level of raw passion and instinct on which Alan lives, make him reluctant to cure his patient. Alan *knows* worship and *acts* upon it; Dysart can only read and think about it. He is envious, but does not want to take away the one thing that gives focus to Alan's life: "Without worship you shrink, it's as brutal as that. . . . I shrank my *own* life. No one can do it for you. I settled for being pallid and provincial, out of my own eternal timidity. . . . I watch that woman [his wife] knitting, night after night—a woman I haven't *kissed* in six years—and he stands in the dark for an hour, sucking the sweat off his God's hairy cheek!" (*ES*, 81).

Dysart is only too aware of what curing Alan will do to him: it will make him "normal." He will never again blind a horse (or do anything else with one, either); he will no longer be tormented by nightmares of Equus, but at what cost? Dysart has promised Alan that he can take away the nightmares, but in another monologue he confesses the price Alan will have to pay for that relief: "When Equus leaves—if he leaves at all—it will be with your intestines in his teeth. And I don't stock replacements" (*ES*, 105). Later, to the audience, he expands on how much of a disservice he is doing to Alan by curing him:

I'll take away his Field of Ha Ha, and give him Normal places for his ecstasy— multi-lane highways driven through the guts of cities, extinguishing Place altogether, *even the idea of Place!* He'll trot on his metal pony tamely through the concrete evening—and one thing I promise you: he will never touch hide again! With any luck his private parts will come to feel as plastic to him as the products of the factory to which he will almost certainly be sent. Who knows? He may even come to find sex funny. Smirky funny. Bit of grunt funny. Trampled and furtive and entirely in control. Hopefully, he'll feel nothing at his fork but Approved Flesh. *I doubt, however, with much passion!* . . . Passion, you see, can be destroyed by a doctor. It cannot be created. (*ES*, 105–6)

Dysart has been living a life devoid of any real passion and he wants Alan to escape the same fate. However, professional considerations prevail, and he has begun the process that might turn Alan into one more unfeeling, normal member of society, one who will never know ecstasy again. Dysart will turn Alan into a man who one day might marry and thereby be reduced to his own unfeeling level.

Frank and Dora Strang's marriage is not so stormy as that of the Harringtons, but it does have one seemingly insurmountable problem: she is devoutly religious, and he is an atheist. Thus, Frank holds his wife responsible for Alan's condition and for his crime. As he sees it, religion is at the root of the problem. Against her husband's wishes, Dora has spent much time reading to Alan from the Bible, and in Frank's opinion that reading could lead to nothing but trouble: "A boy spends night after night having this stuff read into him: an innocent man tortured to death—thorns driven into his head—nails into his hands—a spear jammed through his ribs. It can mark anyone for life, that kind of thing. I'm not joking. The boy was absolutely fascinated by all that. He was always mooning over religious pictures. I mean real kinky ones, if you receive my meaning. . . . Call it what you like. All that stuff to me is just bad sex." (*ES*, 33–34). In addition, he is opposed to Alan's watching television, formerly Alan's only pleasure in life. Frank resents, too, that his wife did not respect his wishes and allowed Alan, unbeknownst to him, to steal off to the neighbor's house to watch television. More than the programs per se, Frank resented the conspiracy that existed between his wife and his son, whom he feels (as does Mr. Harrington) has been stolen away from him. He has to admit that Alan has always been closer to his mother than to him, and in keeping with his nature, Frank was never able to talk to his son about sex, and any knowledge that Alan has of the subject, he gained from his mother's point of view.

Dora defends her marriage, the familial atmosphere, and the way in which she and Frank reared their child. She blames Alan's actions on the devil:

We've done nothing wrong. We loved Alan. We gave him the best love we could. All right, we quarrel sometimes—all parents quarrel—we always make it up. My husband is a good man. He's an upright man, religion or no religion. He cares for his home, for the world, and for his boy. Alan had love and care and treats, and as much fun as any boy in the world. . . . Whatever's happened has happened *because of Alan*. Alan is himself. Every soul is itself. If you added up everything we ever did to him, from his first day on earth to this, you wouldn't find why he did this terrible thing—because that's him: not just all of our things added up. . . . I know only he was my little Alan, and then the Devil came. (*ES*, 77)

Dora's reasoning about Alan's character is no mere rationalization: it is her sincere belief, and one that appears also in Clive's highly poetic speech on individuality to his father in *Five Finger Exercise*. What is unconvincing is her sudden about-face of blaming Alan's problem on the devil.

If Dora's ideas on her son's individuality are correct, they contradict Dysart's theory that Alan's condition is the result of all of his experiences with horses, with his parents, with religion, and with sex: "Moments snap together like magnets, forging a chain of shackles. Why? I can trace them. I can even, with time, pull them apart again. But why at the start they were ever magnetized at all—just those particular moments of experience and no others—I don't know. And nor does anyone else (ES, 75). Dysart believes in Alan's individuality and in his right to keep it, yet he proceeds to add the "moments of experience" together and then to take them apart, in order, so to speak, to defuse Alan's problem. It is apparent from his concluding monologue that he endorses Dora's ideas that Alan is Alan, but he has to deny his heart, follow his head, and cure the boy, and thereby reduce Alan to his own level of reason over instinct, a trait that he so much dislikes in himself. In the opening monologue of the play, Dysart asks rhetorically, "Is it possible, at certain moments we cannot imagine, a horse can add its sufferings together—the non-stop jerks and jabs that are its daily life—and turn them into grief?" (ES, 17). In the opening monologue of the second act, Dysart asks a similar question about Alan and thus establishes an identity between Alan and the horse; he now establishes the link between himself and his patient.

As Dora stated, Alan did know security in his parents' home—until he suffered the disillusionment of finding his father at a pornographic movie theater. Despite the prohibitions that Frank placed on Alan, and even despite his low opinion of his son's aptitudes, Alan had a basic respect for Frank. Alan even quotes him to Dr. Dysart: "Who said 'Religion is the opium of the people'?" (ES, 28), which Alan took to originate with his father. Alan's former image of his father and subsequent disillusionment are what C. G. Jung calls *enkekalymmenos*, a phenomenon in which what a child considered to be a true image of his parents is destroyed, when, for one reason or another, the veil is lifted from the child's eyes and he sees his parents as they really are.[8]

Catching his father as he did was not entirely bad for Alan: it improved his self-image and showed him that even the most upright people have secret lives. It showed him that he and his father are not really so different after all: "I suddenly thought—*They all do it! All of them!* . . . They're not just Dads—They're people with pricks! . . . And Dad—he's just not Dad either. He's a man with a prick too. You know, I'd never thought about it" (ES, 94). So Alan has a clearer picture of his father. For all of Frank's raving at the ill effects of watching mindless television programs and his insistence on the importance of reading to improve the mind, he is just a man. For the first time, too, Alan saw his mother in a new light as a wife: "She doesn't give him anything. . . . She likes Ladies and Gentlemen" (*ES*, 94), and Ladies and Gentlemen are never naked. Alan is forced to reevaluate his parents, and his sympathy now rests with his father: "Poor old sod, that's what I felt—he's just like me! He hates ladies and gents just like me! Posh things—and la-di-da. He goes off by himself at night, and does his own secret thing which no one'll know about, just like me! There's no difference—he's just the same as me— just the same!" (*ES*, 95). The realization that all men, including his father, "do it," gave Alan license to accept Jill's suggestion that they go off together for sex.

The remaining characters in the play are Jill Mason, Harry Dalton, Horseman/Nugget, Hesther Salomon, and a nurse. The last character is minor and requires no comment. Jill Mason is hardly individualized: she is a young woman who is necessary to the play because she introduces Alan to the world of heterosexuality and thus brings about his failure, his shame, and finally his crime. She is also the product of a broken home—yet another bad marriage. Harry Dalton, the owner of the stables, represents the voice of society: Alan is a criminal and should be behind bars, not in a hospital at the taxpayers' expense. Significantly enough, the same actor portrays both the Horseman on Trojan and Nugget, the "horse" that Alan rides at the end of act 1. Having the same actor play both roles establishes the identification between them and serves to reinforce the importance of Alan's first ride at the age of six and the role that horses play in his adolescent life. Finally, there is Hesther Salomon, the magistrate who leads Alan to Dr. Dysart. She is a sounding board for Dysart as well as a shoulder for him to cry on. She accepts none of his arguments about his disservice to Alan by making him normal. From her point of view, Alan is in pain, and Dysart's obligation is to relieve that pain. In her name, Shaffer has revealed her essence. Her given name is a form of Esther, the beautiful and compassionate biblical queen whose sense of justice saved her people from destruction. Her last name symbolizes the wisdom of her biblical namesake. Dysart's name is also not without its symbolic value. The Greek prefix *dys* indicates difficulty,[9] and therefore shows that although he is performing his art (the second syllable of his name) masterfully, he does it in spite of himself. Ironically, the name of one of Dysart's colleagues is Dr. Thoroughgood, in whose abilities Mrs. Salomon has no faith.

Sources, Symbols, and Themes

Shaffer did extensive research before writing *Equus*, and the play is therefore enhanced by psychological, biblical, mythological, historical, and literary references. The time-honored symbols are horses, eyes, and tunnels. The compelling story aside, *Equus* is constructed on the basis of modern psychiatry, about which Shaffer consulted a child psychiatrist. The basic psychological issue in the play is presented in the writing of Dr. R. D. Laing, who questions the value and justice of curing many of those individuals society considers insane. He believes that a person is born into a world where alienation awaits (as with Alan), and that the diseases psychiatrists purport to cure are really perpetuated when an individual is regarded as "object-to-be-changed" rather than "person-to-be-accepted." He further believes that more attention should be paid to the experience of the patient, and that that experience should not be considered ipso facto invalid or unreal. Laing also objects to the denigration the patient suffers when he or she is subjected to the process of psychiatric examination, diagnosis, and treatment.[10] Similarly, Anthony Burgess, in his popular novel and film, *A Clockwork Orange*, questions the right of the society to cure patients by removing from their personalities the antisocial traits that make them unique. Martin Dysart exemplifies Jung's theory, too, that the more complicated and sophisticated one becomes, the more one loses the ability to act upon instincts.

The central symbol of the horse figures prominently in literary sources from Homer to the Bible, from Lawrence to García Lorca, as well as in sources both mythological and historical. Biblical references to horses in *Equus* come from the Book of Job and from Revelation. The quotation in Job 39:19–15 refers to the horse's strength, speed, and fierceness:

Hast thou given the horse *his* might? Hast thou clothed his neck with the quivering mane? Hast thou made him to leap as a locust? The glory of his snorting is terrible. He paweth in the valley, and rejoiceth in his strength: He goeth out to meet the armed men. He mocketh at fear, and is not dismayed: Neither turneth he back from the sword. The quiver rattleth against him, The flashing spear and the javelin. He swallowth the ground with fierceness and rage; Neither believeth he that it is the voice of the trumpet. As oft as the trumpet *soundeth* he saith, Aha! And he smelleth the battle afar off, The thunder of the captains, and the shouting.[11]

Many of the words in this selection are prominent in Alan's orgasmic rides: the *might*, the *neck*, the *mane*, the *trumpet*, and the *"Aha!* And at the end of Alan's ride in act 1, the stage directions specify that the horse snorts, as in the selection. Similarly, the equine references in Revelation figure prominently in the play and in Alan's ideas of horses. Revelation 9:19 speaks of the "power of the horses [that] is in their mouth"; 6:2–8 attribute to horses the power of speech and the authority to kill with the sword; from Revelation 19:11–12 come the references to horses' eyes and the words that Alan uses in the blinding scene: "And I saw the heaven opened; and behold, a white horse, and he that sat thereon called Faithful and True. . . . And his eyes *are* a flame of fire . . . and he hath a name written which none knoweth but he himself." The first time Dysart asks Alan for the name of his horse-god, the boy refuses to answer because "no one knows but him and me" (*ES*, 65). In Revelation 19:16, the identification between the horse and Jesus is established: "And he hath on his garment and on his thigh a name written, KING OF KINGS, AND LORD OF LORDS." Lastly, in the first chapter, verse fourteen, of Revelation, Jesus is described: "And his head and his hair were white wool, *white* as snow; and his eyes were as a flame of fire. . . ."

It is significant that Dysart's interest is in the classical world, since horses held an honored place in the ancient Greek society, even to the point of being considered beings of godly origin from the union of Poseidon and Demeter.[12] Significantly, too, the first horse that Alan ever rode was called Trojan, recalling the wooden horse in Book Eight of the *Odyssey*. Simpson[13] says that the Greeks raised aesthetic appreciation of horses to a pitch that has never been surpassed. The classicist Julian Ward Jones, Jr., in his article "The Trojan Horse, *Timeo Danaos et dona ferentis*," underscores the religious value of horses to the Trojans: "We can in no way consider it strange if to the Trojans—horse tamers extraordinary—the horse should sooner or later be regarded as a sacred animal. I suggest that this is exactly what happened and that the wooden horse was a religious object."[14] Lewinsohn, again in *Animals, Men and Myths*, sums up the role of horses in Homeric poetry and after: "In Homer's verse and thereafter the horse was an adjunct of the great heroes of ancient Greece, the greatest warriors rode on wonder beasts given to them by the gods. Most of these horses had wings, and many were able to talk" (85). Like Xanthos in Book Nineteen of the *Iliad*, Equus is a "talking" horse. Many of the other horses in epic literature were named and prominent in legend: Alexander's Bucephalus, Roland's Veillantif, and El Cid's Babieca. In *Don Quixote*, the ingenious hidalgo spends four days deciding upon a name for his horse before settling on Rocinante. In ancient art, horses abound on Greek pottery and appear in the caves of Altamira, whose paintings are among the oldest in the world. The cave dwellers of what is now northern Spain depicted on their walls the animals that they feared and revered.

D.H. Lawrence is a major link between ancient Greek mythology and modern British literature. In his *Etruscan Places* there are numerous references to horses in classical civilization. In the essay on "The Painted Tombs of Tarquinia," Lawrence refers to the young noblemen, who, according to Lawrence, surely rode with their own naked limbs against an almost naked horse. For Alan, nakedness is a sine qua non for riding Equus, and horses for him are: ". . . the most naked thing you ever saw! More than a dog or a cat or anything" (*ES*, 48). Christopher Ford quotes Shaffer on the Homeric importance of the nakedness: "There's something Homeric about these encounters. I'm sure Ulysses was really naked when he chopped up all of those suitors."[15] Lawrence describes riding a horse as: ". . . A surge of animal power that burned with travel, with the passionate movement of the blood . . ."[16]—the same power and passion that Alan experiences when he mounts Equus. Lawrence asks rhetorically, "What is it that man sees, when he looks at a horse?—what is it that will never be put into words?" (Lawrence, 72). In "Volterra" he answers his own question: "The horse is always the symbol of the strong animal of man; sometimes he rises, a sea-horse, from the ocean: and sometimes he is a land creature, and half-man. And so he occurs on the tombs, as the passion in man returning into the sea, the soul retreating into the death-world at the depths of the waters: or sometimes he is a centaur . . ." (Lawrence, 108). In a short story, "The Rocking-Horse Winner," the horse becomes Lawrence's central image, in a way that closely parallels Shaffer's use of it in *Equus*. In the Lawrence story, Paul, the young protagonist, "hears" the voice of the rocking-horse predicting winners in horse races; and the gardener becomes terribly serious when he is discussing horses, ". . . as if he were speaking of religious matters. . . ."[17] Lawrence makes repeated references to the fire in Paul's eyes; and most important, the boy rides his rocking horse with the orgasmic furor with which Alan rides Equus.

García Lorca used horses as a major symbol in both his plays and his poems.[18] In "Quimera" (Chimera), a one-act play, Viejo (Old Man) speaks of his fear of horses: "Los caballos, ¡jajajá! Nadie sabe el miedo que a mí me dan los caballos. Caiga un rayo sobre todos sus ojos."[19] (Horses, ha-ha-ha! Nobody knows how afraid I am of horses. I wish lightning would strike out their eyes.)[20] He later makes another statement which equates sexual satisfaction and fecundity with love of horses, and hip-pophobia with sexual unfulfillment. In *La zapatera prodigiosa* (previously mentioned), *La casa de Bernarda Alba* (The House of Bernarda Alba), and *Bodas de sangre* (Blood Wedding), horses appear as symbols of manhood, force, and sexual desire. At the time of García Lorca's murder, the playwright had not yet completed all of the plays that he wanted to write—a body of works that was to examine love in all of its many facets. One of the plays that was never written was going to be about a boy who is so devoted to his horse that, when the boy's father kills the horse, the boy, in turn, kills his father.[21] The fact that the story of *Equus* is based on an actual happening in no way diminishes the importance of the equine imagery. The account that Shaffer heard of the event was merely the spark that ignited his imagination and creative powers on the archetypal symbol.

Eyes, too, are rich in symbolic value and have held a place in literature at least since St. Matthew wrote "And if thy right eye causeth you to stumble, pluck it out, and cast it from thee . . ." (5:29) Latin uses the same word *testis* for both *witness* and *testicle*, thereby showing the relation-ship between eyes, which are literal witnesses, and testicles, which are figurative witnesses.[22] In the first scene of the play in which Alan is willing to talk to Dysart without resorting to television jingles, he displays his knowledge of English history, knowledge that he acquired from his mother and of which he is very proud. His favorite king, he tells the doctor, is John: "Because he put out the eyes of that smarty little—" (*ES*, 28). This reference helps to unravel the connection of imagery as it exists in Alan's mind. It is known, for example, that of the men whom John took prisoner, some were blinded; and that when Arthur became a rival of John, John was advised to have Arthur blinded and castrated.[23] The instance that most closely approximates the situation in *Equus* occurs in a one-act play entitled "Los ojos" (The Eyes), by José Ruibal. In this play, a child who can no longer stand his mother's nagging and her insistence that her eyes see everything—including through walls and into dreams—takes a knife, stabs out her eyes, and ends the play by telling her, "Tus ojos ya no lo verán todo . . . , todo . . . , todo . . ."[24] (Now your eyes won't see everything . . . , every-thing . . . , everything. . . .)

Animals' eyes appear in the writing of many authors. In any number of works by García Lorca, for example, he refers to eyes, and in one poem, "Oda al rey de Harlem" (Ode to the King of Harlem), in his collection *Poeta en Nueva York* (Poet in New York), he uses crocodiles to symbolize unadulterated, primitive society, and a spoon to represent destructive civilization; the spoon is used to gouge out the eyes of the crocodiles:

> Con una cuchara,
> arrancaba los ojos a los cocodrilos
> y golpeaba el trasero de los monos.
> Con una cuchara. (García Lorca, 478)

(With a spoon, he pulled out the crocodiles' eyes and beat the monkeys' behinds. With a spoon.) Another example is the short story "Axolotl" (Salamander), by the Argentine writer Julio Cortázar—a story in which the protagonist is metamorphosed into a lizard by staring into its eyes. Through his deep attraction for the animals he becomes one of them, just as Alan attempts to become One Person with Equus. An old superstition holds that boys who masturbate excessively will go blind. Ironically, in the play it is the masturbator who blinds the object of his lust. Christopher Ford mentioned that Shaffer would like to write a play on the Faust theme.[25] For Shaffer, the blinded Faust got something positive and even ecstatic from his transformation to blindness.

One final symbol is that of the tunnel. The set calls for two onstage sections of seats, which are separated by a central tunnel. It is through this tunnel that horse/horseman Nugget enters into and exits from Alan's life. Tunnels are womblike, and this one may be interpreted as the place where Alan receives *his* sexual gratification. It may also be thought of as the dark recess of the psyche, which Lawrence considered the place where the spirit of the horse prances. For Alan, horses are like graceful girls in a ballet.

Structure and Stagecraft

The two acts of which *Equus* is composed are parallel in their structure. Each act begins with a monologue in which Dysart wonders about the horse, the boy, and himself. Many of the scenes take place between two characters having a go at each other, as in a boxing ring. The last scene of each act has a highly dramatic moment with sexual and religious overtones, acted out by Alan. The first act ends with the young man riding Equus to orgasm and with words from the Old Testament; the second act contains an equally dramatic nude scene of attempted intercourse, the blinding of the horses, and words from the New Testament.

The temporal and the spatial organization of the play merit special attention. Dysart's opening monologue in each act takes place in the present, as do some of the therapy sessions with Alan. The scenes in which Dysart is narrating events that happened in sessions that took place between scenes, and the incidents that involve Alan's childhood and the night of his crime, are flashbacks. Most of the play takes place in the doctor's consultation room, with departures for scenes in the Strangs' home, the movie theater, the electrical shop, and, of course, the stables. In scenes in which Alan is not present but rather in his hospital room, he is able to hear the conversation taking place and to comment on it as if he were together with the other characters. For example, when Dora Strang is telling Dysart of the passage about horses in the Book of Job, she recites one line, and Alan responds with the next. When Frank is telling the psychiatrist about the scene in the bedroom, where Alan was beating himself and reciting a parody of biblical genealogies, Alan speaks the words that he was reciting that night.

The text of the play is preceded by notes on the set, the chorus, and the horses. The set is described as a square of wood set in a circle of wood, with rails on three sides containing benches. The stage has the aspect of an operating theater from which the part of the audience seated onstage witnesses at close range Dysart's metaphorical operation on Alan's mind.[26] Also, the theater has the appearance of one appropriate for the performance of Greek tragedy. Shaffer has the seated members of the cast—that is, the chorus—making "Equus Noise" of humming, thumping, and stamping. "This Noise heralds or illustrates the presence of Equus the God" (*ES*, 13). The horses are actors wearing chestnut-colored tracksuits, high metal shoes, and masks made of alternating bands of wire and leather. The playwright specifies that "any literalism which could suggest the cosy familiarity of a domestic animal—or worse, a pantomime horse—should be avoided. . . . Great care must also be taken that the masks are put on before the audience with very precise timing—the actors watching each other, so that the masking has an exact and ceremonial effect" (*ES*, 13). Shaffer's intent is that the horses have an archetypal character about them, appearing as ceremonial gods, as is most evident in the stage directions of the blinding scene:

He stabs out Nugget's eyes. The horse stamps in agony. A great screaming begins to fill the theatre, growing ever louder. Alan dashes at the other two horses and blinds them too, stabbing over the rails. Their metal hooves join in the stamping.

Relentlessly, as this happens, three more horses appear in cones of light: not naturalistic

*animals like the first three, but dreadful creatures out of nightmare. Their eyes flare—
their nostrils flare—their mouths flare. They are archetypal images—judging, punish-
ing, pitiless. They do not halt at the rail, but invade the square. As they trample at him,
the boy leaps desperately at them, jumping high and naked in the dark, slashing at their
heads with arms upraised.* (ES, 103)

Five Finger Exercise and *Shrivings* are true to the spirit of the classical
unities, but *Equus*, both in its dramatic theory and in its execution, much
more nearly approximates true Aristotelian tragedy. According to Aristotle, "A tragedy, then, is the imitation of an action that is serious and
also, as having magnitude, complete in itself; in language with pleasurable accessories, each kind brought in separately in the parts of the work;
in a dramatic, not in a narrative form; with incidents arousing pity and
fear, wherewith to accomplish its catharsis of such emotions."[27] He
further says that "tragedy is essentially an imitation not of persons but of
action and life, of happiness, and misery" (Aristotle, 231), preferably
based on historical events, and with personages of distinctive qualities of
character and thought, and consistent in their behavior throughout the
play. *Equus* fulfills all of the master's requirements for tragedy. Aristotle
recommends that the tragedian describe what *might* have happened, not
what did happen. *Equus* imitates an actual event, modified to proportions
suitable for the stage and interpreted in the inimitable manner of Peter
Shaffer. The characters contrast the emotions of ecstasy and joylessness.
The incidents in the play inspire pity for Dysart and both fear and pity for
Alan. Shaffer also satisfies the six qualitative parts of Aristotelian tragedy: plot, character, diction, thought, spectacle, and melody. Aristotle's
intention in the category of "thought" is that the play enunciate a
general truth. The truth that Shaffer presents is one that shocks the
audience, but also one that wins its approval.[28]

Shaffer, like Aristotle, believes that the most important element of a
play is its story.[29] An essential element of the plot according to Aristotle
is that of discovery. *Equus* is based on the discoveries or insights that Dr.
Dysart makes into Alan's problem, often via information brought to him
from characters who function as the messengers in Greek tragedy: Frank
Strang, Dora Strang, and Harry Dalton. He also makes perceptive
discoveries about himself. For the Greek theoretician, melody was the
greatest of the pleasurable accessories of tragedy, and in *Equus* it is found
in Alan's wild song to Equus the lover and Equus the god during his
frantic ride. Spectacle is found in every aspect of the play, from the
onstage seating to the stylized horse masks. Perhaps Shaffer's greatest
success in *Equus* is fulfilling the requirements that the story of the play

represent "one action, a complete whole, with its several incidents so closely connected that the transposal or withdrawal of any of them will disjoin and dislocate the whole" (*Aristotle*, 234). Shaffer's crafting is meticulous; ingeniously he presents the details of Alan's case bit by bit and has Dysart reach his conclusions by connecting each piece of new information to that which he already knows. If any of the information were omitted, there would be no play, or at least not in the state of perfection that Shaffer has designed. Aristotle prefers that the plot be episodic, with neither probability nor necessity in the sequence of its episodes. To that end, Shaffer moves back and forth in time in Dysart's search for the root of Alan's motivations. Shaffer, as Aristotle, specifies that the action of the play is continuous.

Both writers knew that the events that arouse fear and pity are most effective when they occur unexpectedly yet at the same time in consequence of one another. In the case of *Equus*, those events are Alan's midnight ride and his blinding of the horses, an act that also displays the Aristotelian property of suffering or torture. The final monologue, which follows Alan's reenactment of his crime, is equivalent to the catharsis in Greek tragedy. For the quantitative parts of the play, Aristotle specifies prologue, episode, exode, and chorus. Dysart's opening monologue is the prologue; his closing speech is the exode; the therapy sessions are the episodes; and the actors onstage making the "Equus Noise" are the chorus. An equally important aspect of classical tragedy that Shaffer observes is the change from ignorance to knowledge. By examining the events that led up to Alan's crime, Dysart comes to understand not only his patient but also himself, and it is he who is the truly tragic hero, whose flaw, over which he has no control, is his joylessness, his emotional sterility. Russell Vandenbroucke[30] likens Dysart to a modern-day tragic hero in the manner of Arthur Miller's Willy Loman.

Critical Appraisal

No other of Shaffer's previous plays has received so much attention from the critics as did *Equus*. From one extreme, it has been interpreted as a play about humanity's overwhelming need for transcendence, a play that urges the spectator to examine the mysteries of the Christian faith.[31] At the other extreme, critics have seen in it a homosexual attraction between doctor and patient.[32] One reviewer went so far as to say that the play is an attempt on the part of the author to present a defense of homosexuality, and a dishonest one at that.[33] Most criticism falls between those extreme positions and views the play as a confrontation between reason and instinct in a well-constructed, psychologically intriguing setting. Reviewers generally showed a keen understanding and appreciation of the play and did not spare superlatives in their reviews. *Equus* has been called an electrifying theatrical experience[34] and a theatrical event of the greatest importance,[35] it has been hailed as one of the most powerful and provocative theatrical events of our time.[36] And so it is. The *New York Times*[37] raved about the play's stagecraft and sensibility, and praised the work for reanimating the spirit of mystery that makes the theater a place of breathless discovery. The *New York Daily News*[38] thought that the psychoanalysis left something to be desired, but that the play made for gripping theater and powerful entertainment—results which, after all, fulfill Shaffer's intentions in writing it. Some reviewers voiced the same criticism of *Equus* that had previously appeared about *The Royal Hunt of the Sun*: the staging compensates for the faults of the script.[39] The *New Yorker* viewed the play as a "continuously exciting dance of exploration through the mind of a boy who loves horses, worships the quality of 'horseness,' and commits a dreadful crime in the name of that worship."[40] The last statement is at once the most precise and concise evaluation of the play's meaning and spirit. *Equus* is a masterfully crafted play, and if it is to be criticized at all, it is for being *too* perfect, too pat. The playwright has so carefully constructed it that there are no loose ends left for the audience to tie together; and yet the play has inspired such diverse interpretations. Barry B. Witham sees *Equus* as continuing in the tradition of the British "angry young man" plays of the 1950s and compares it to *Look Back in Anger*.[41] Plunka[42] calls Alan the perfect antihero of the 1970s—a nonconformist surrounded by role-players and phonies.

Equus has received considerable attention from the psychiatric community. Dr. Jules Glenn,[43] a psychiatrist in Great Neck, New York, has written considerably on Shaffer's plays; at a meeting of the Association for Applied Psychoanalysis, there was a discussion of this play. But psychiatrists have not unanimously acclaimed it. In an article in the *New York Times*, Dr. Sanford Gifford, a professor at the medical school of Harvard University, objected that the analysis that Dr. Dysart uses on Alan is medically unsound and that the play fosters the fantasies that patients have of their therapists.[44] Whatever the medical community may decide, taking the play so seriously is a credit to Shaffer's talents: Alan Strang has been elevated to the level of a prototype.

The success of *Equus* has been overwhelming in part because of its visual spectacle and its thought-provoking theme. But the reason for its widespread appeal is deeper than that; *Equus* touches the spectators at their most basic level of emotions. However sophisticated, the audience applauds the speech in which Dysart finds it ironic—ridiculous—that he, a passionless man, should be curing Alan, who knows ecstasy; however conventional their beliefs, the spectators deeply desire to be Alan—that is, to allow themselves to live on an instinctual and primitive level, free from societal restrictions, if only for an hour every three weeks. The appeal is so deep that one does not respond with polite applause, but with glee. Shaffer completely wins the audience over to Dysart's point of view of doing Alan a disservice by curing him. *Equus* compels spectators to reevaluate "the old language and old assumptions" (*ES*, 18) that they may have accepted uncritically and never before questioned. *Equus* is a guilt-relieving play; average theatergoers come to realize that whatever their little fantasies may be, they are trivial compared to Alan's. Perhaps the imagery is, by intention, transparent; but *Equus* has given the theatergoers something for which they had been starved: compelling drama that keeps them on the edge of their seats with their eyes riveted to the stage.

For writing the best play of the 1974–75 New York theater season, Shaffer won the New York Drama Critics' Circle Award, the Antoinette Perry ("Tony") Award, as well as the Outer Critics Circle Award and the Los Angeles Drama Critics Award. The Los Angeles Critics also honored Brian Bedford as best actor. Some twenty years earlier, he had created the role of Clive in *Five Finger Exercise*, as well as the role of Bob in *The Private Ear*. But Shaffer's greatest critical success to date was yet to come in *Amadeus*.

In 1977 Sidney Lumet directed the film version of *Equus*. The motion picture was so bad that it was rejected by the critics and the public alike. Not even the sensationalism of the nudity and the blinding sequence were successful in attracting an audience. The problem with the movie was its literalism, while the beauty of the play was in its stylization, which evoked the mythical proportions that the play's title intended to convey. While Dysart's soliloquies were perfectly suited to the stage, speaking directly into the camera made for a deadly dull film. The sequence of the blinding of the horses was nothing short of disgusting. Shaffer himself was terribly disappointed with the film that resulted from his script. In his remarks to the Modern Language Association on 29 December 1983, he was willing to say publicly that "it was lugubrious and overly literal. I did not care for it." The uninspired directing notwithstanding, Peter Shaffer, Richard Burton (as Dysart), and Peter Firth (as Alan) all received nominations for Oscars, but none of them won an award.

In 1980, the Maryland Ballet Company produced a balletic interpretation of *Equus*, an art form well suited to the story. Shaffer supervised the entire production in collaboration with choreographer Domy Reiter-Soffer and composer Dr. Wilfred Josephs. Two years later, the Harlem Dance Theatre presented the work in New York.

Chapter Seven
Amadeus

Even the enormous, international success of *Equus* was no preparation for the overwhelming reception that *Amadeus* was to receive on both stage and screen, nor for what it was to do for Peter Shaffer's career and his stature in modern drama. When Sir Peter Hall of London's National Theatre, who had promised to turn Shaffer's script into a "black opera," read the play, he declared it undirectable; the first act alone would have required two hours of stage time. Shaffer reports that he spent about a year writing a new opening scene virtually ever week until he was satisfied. The play went through thirty to fifty versions before the final product, which found its way to the stages of London, New York, and the rest of the world. Finally on 2 November 1979, *Amadeus* had its premiere performance in Olivier Hall at the National Theatre. The play broke all prior records for the National Theatre and played to full houses for over a year. After its American debut at the National Theatre in Washington, D.C., *Amadeus* opened at the Broadhurst Theatre in New York on 17 December, 1980.

One problem in writing on *Amadeus* is that of selecting a text. Different versions are familiar to different audiences: the audience in Washington did not see the play as it was performed in London, and the audience in New York saw yet another version. The version that has become most familiar around the world is the one on film. This study will use the script of the original production in London for the sections on the play's structure and characters. There will be separate subchapters on the changes that Shaffer made for the New York audiences, and then for the film. The sections on themes and sources are applicable to all versions of the play, as well as to the film.

Set, Structure and Plot

While Shaffer maintains that *Amadeus* can and should be produced in a variety of ways, in the published text he describes the sumptuous production under Hall's direction, for which John Bury designed the set to evoke the court life of eighteenth-century Vienna, and Harrison Birtwistle, a composer in his own right, made subtle changes in Mozart's musical compositions so that they "suggested the sublime work of a genius being experienced by another musician's increasingly agonised mind."[1] It is important for readers of the text and viewers of the play and film to keep in mind that the picture that Shaffer is presenting of Mozart is Salieri's subjective view of him, and that the music is Salieri's interpretation of it. The playwright was exceedingly pleased with the collaboration of Paul Scofield as Salieri, Simon Callow as Mozart, and Felicity Kendal as Constanze in the original production.

    A. Set.   Just as the set of *Equus* was essentially a wooden square that became office, home, or stable, as required, the basic element of the set for *Amadeus* is a wooden rectangle on a blue plastic stage. The rectangle becomes Salieri's salon, Mozart's apartment, reception rooms, and opera houses. The various locations are given detail through the use of backdrops and projections. The first projection the audience sees looks like a street at night—a picture, in fact, that came from the lid of one of Mozart's snuffboxes.

    B. Structure and Plot.   There are strong parallels between the structure of *Amadeus* and that of the plays already discussed in this study. As in *The Royal Hunt of the Sun* and *Equus*, the play is introduced by its narrator and the story line is presented in flashbacks. Here Salieri narrates in 1823 the episodes that took place from 1781 to 1791. As in *Equus*, the narrator is also the play's protagonist, and the action is presented from his point of view. Once again the play is divided into two acts; while the scenes are numbered, as in *Equus*, the numbers are intended to indicate changes of location, and the action is wholly continuous. While *The Royal Hunt of the Sun* begins immediately with the narrator's (Old Martin's) monologue, *Amadeus*, like *Equus*, has a dramatic introduction that places its opening monologue in context. In *Equus*, it consists of a brief moment that allows the audience to see Alan in an affectionate pose with the horse Nugget. That tableau makes Dr. Dysart's first remarks about Alan understandable to the audience. The opening segment of *Amadeus* is longer and more complex than *Equus*'s; it consists of an entire scene, and involves several characters. After that segment—which has the intended effect of an overture to an opera—is over, the structure of *Amadeus* bears strong resemblance to that of *Equus* through its use of a narrator in the present relating scenes from the past in flashback. While far more happens in *Amadeus* than in *Five Finger Exercise*, for example, its plot is easy to summarize. It is the very complexity of the play that makes its plot of less consequence than the other dramatic elements that compose *Amadeus* characters, themes, and techniques.

The two acts of the play depict Court Composer Salieri's dual battle over Mozart, first with himself and then with God; in both stages Mozart is the loser. The first act treats Salieri's growing awareness of Mozart's genius vis-à-vis his own mediocrity, and his plans for revenge against divine injustice. Salieri's lengthy opening monologue and his subsequent conversation with his valet are both subjects for the section on characters in this book. Suffice for the moment to say that he announces that this is the last night of his life. The story really does not start until the fifth scene, in which Salieri is required to commission an opera in German. Salieri confesses in the final line of the fourth scene that "that night changed my life" (*A*, 32). In that single sentence, Salieri identifies himself with Pizarro and Dysart, both of whom make similar admissions—Pizarro's concerning his meeting with Athuallpa, and Dysart's regarding his with Alan. Salieri's meeting with Amadeus changed the common view of Mozart and caused quite a bit of controversy among modern-day admirers of the musician. While attending a concert at the home of Baroness Waldstädten, Salieri is seated in a chair in the library that hides him from view. However, he is able to see and hear the man that he comes to realize is Mozart. What he sees is the musical genius playing a cat-and-mouse game with Constanze Weber, the woman he soon marries; what he hears is the basest, scatological wordplay emanating from the mouth of the man capable of creating "Absolute Beauty" at the keyboard. In contrast to the filth that comes out of Mozart's mouth, Salieri hears the concert in the next room; it is Mozart's Adagio of the Serenade for 13 Wind Instruments (K.361), and its perfection leaves Salieri trembling. At their next meeting, Salieri plays a march that he composed to welcome Mozart to the Viennese court. With a few deft changes, Mozart turns Salieri's pedestrian work into a masterpiece. At that point, the idea of murdering Mozart passes through Salieri's mind for the first time.

Mozart's marriage to Constanze is not the bliss that their courtship was. He can't find students, and she blames the problem on her husband's propensity for taking to bed every woman who comes to him for music lessons. Their marriage goes from bad to worse as their financial situation becomes desperate. In an attempt to help her husband, Constanze—unbeknownst to Mozart—brings some of his music to Salieri so that he may secure for Mozart the position of musical tutor to the Princess Elizabeth. The wonderment of Mozart's having written the music without correction and with every note perfectly in place makes Salieri declare war on his enemy—not Mozart, but rather the unjust God who endowed the "creature" with the musical abilities denied to him.

In act 2, Salieri uses his power in Vienna's musical and courtly circles to ruin Mozart and thereby take revenge on his divine enemy. First, Salieri tries to block the production of Mozart's new opera, *The Marriage of Figaro*, at the court. He fails at that attempt, but succeeds in limiting its exposure in 1786. In the course of act 2, Mozart loses his father, and his need to make money is more desperate than ever before. His health is also deteriorating. After *Così Fan Tutte* fails, Mozart must beg for money from his Masonic Lodge brothers because Salieri has seen to it that Mozart's financial compensation for his musical duties at court is absolutely minuscule. Salieri comes to realize that it will take little effort on his part to finish off his musical rival.

In the final stage of his diabolical scheme, Salieri enlists the assistance of his valet Ignaz Greybig. He has Greybig dress in a manner reminiscent of the Commendatore in *Don Giovanni*, and sends him to commission a Requiem Mass of Mozart. In Mozart's failing condition, he responds exactly as Salieri anticipated he would—by believing that he is being commissioned by a representative of Death to write a Requiem Mass for himself. Mozart also believes, again as Salieri predicted he would, that the two months that he is given to write the Mass is the amount of time he has left to live. In addition to enduring this psychological torment, Mozart develops severe cramps in his stomach and attributes them to an attempt to poison him; someone has been anonymously leaving bottles of wine at Mozart's door. When Greybig is no longer willing to be a part of his employer's vicious scheme, Salieri himself torments Mozart, who by now is in a demented state. Finally, at a particular moment, Salieri unmasks himself and affirms that he has been poisoning Mozart, that he is his assassin, and that because of Mozart he will go to hell.

Shortly thereafter Mozart dies, and the play calls the cause of death typhus, a deposit on the brain, kidney failure, and mercury poisoning from a cure for "sexual rot." He is given a pauper's funeral and his body is dumped into a common lime pit with twenty other corpses. Constanze remarries and becomes the self-proclaimed authority on all matters pertaining to her late husband's music, for which she charges "by the ink, so many notes so many schillings" (*A*, 117). With perfect circular structure, the plays ends where it began, in November 1823, in Salieri's salon, where he attempts suicide by cutting his throat. Such is the story line of *Amadeus*. An understanding of the play requires a detailed examination of the characters, themes, and techniques that Shaffer employs.

Characters

While Shaffer sustains the readers' and viewers' interest with the story of his drama, the play is essentially a character study. In the same vein as *The Royal Hunt of the Sun* and *Equus*, *Amadeus* is a study in the contrast between the protagonist, Salieri, and his antagonist, Mozart. It is important to examine both of these characters as individuals as well as in their relationship to each other. Despite the title of the play (to be discussed later), any study of this work must begin with Salieri.

A. Salieri. *Amadeus* is written from the point of view of Antonio Salieri, the main character of the play. Salieri is the work's narrator and the one who is allowed to make long speeches on his own background, objectives, and struggles, as well as on the playwright's themes of divinity and the conflict between genius and mediocrity. It is the latter theme that is characterized by Salieri's battle with Mozart. Salieri is really a two-dimensional character. There is on one side his self-proclaimed virtue, and on the other his malicious attempt to destroy Mozart. Since the play begins at its conclusion—on what Salieri believes to be the last night of his life—there really is little room for him to grow in the course of the drama.[2] Much of the same argument can be made about Dr. Dysart, who knows how the story ends before he gives his first speech, and of Pizarro (and even Martin, his parallel character), who view the events of the play through the eyes of bitterness. The following analysis will begin with the second scene of the play, since the first falls within the realm of techniques rather than characters.

Just as Old Martin and Martin Dysart begin *The Royal Hunt of the Sun* and *Equus*, respectively, by addressing the audience and setting down the background information of the plays, so does Salieri. But he goes a step further than Old Martin and Dr. Dysart by asking the audience to participate in the drama; the theatergoers are to be his confessors. There is thus an Artaudian quality to the play, in which the members of the audience are participants rather than merely observers. The playwright had a practical reason for Salieri's monologue in the second scene of the play; since Antonio Salieri's name was not immediately recognizable at the time the play opened, he has to tell everyone who he is. (Shaffer will do something similar in *Yonadab*.)

In his old age, Salieri addresses the members of the audience, his confessors, as *Ombri del Futuro* (Ghosts of the Future). He is simultaneously trying to win the audience's sympathy and to receive absolution for his actions, as he explains how he turned from an innocent and idealistic youth from a working-class family in the Lombardy region of Northern Italy, into a bitterly jealous (and perhaps murderous) adult in the Viennese Court. He explains what he wanted as a child and the deal he made with God to achieve his goal:

> I wanted . . . Fame. . . . I wanted to blaze like a comet across the firmament of Europe! And yet only in one special way. Music. It alone has ever told me that there is any value in life. . . . By twelve, I was stumbling about in the countryside, humming my arias and anthems to the Lord. My only desire was to join all the composers who had celebrated His glory through the long Italian past. . . . The night before I left Legnago [his home town] forever, I went to see Him, and made a bargain with Him myself. . . . "*Signore*, let me be a composer! Grant me sufficient fame to enjoy it. In return I will live with virtue. I will strive to better the lot of my fellows. And I will honor you with much music all the days of my life!" (*A*, 23–24)

And Salieri was true to his word—until he met Mozart. As he says, that night changed his life. Now he is about to play for the audience his last composition, *The Death of Mozart; or, Did I do It?*

In his earnest supplication to God and in his belief that God granted his request, Salieri shows himself to be a man of Young Martin's faith and idealism. But, just as Pizarro found only fault with Spanish Catholicism, so Salieri grew up to ridicule the faith of his childhood, his parents, and his region. He speaks in a manner that recalls Mark Askelon in *Shrivings*: "The Christs of Lombardy are simpering sillies with lambskins on their sleeves. . . . and old candle-smoked God in a mulberry robe, staring at the world with dealer's eyes. . . . Those eyes made bargains—real and irreversible" (*A*, 23). And in the second act, he tells the Emperor that "Italians are fond of waxworks. Our religion is largely based upon them" (*A*, 86). Until Salieri met Mozart, he got everything he wanted out of life. He reports in the opening monologue of background information that in the fifty-seven years since he left home to pursue his musical career, he has composed forty-one operas for Italian, German, and French librettos, a Requiem Mass, and a vast amount of sacred music. He reveals directly the decided lack of passion in his own music and of that of the court composers in general: "Much of it was dull as stale bread" (*A*, 27). In that same speech, Salieri contrasts himself with one of his former pupils, Ludwig van Beethoven, and thereby reveals in a subtle way that his music lacks passion. The metaphor for the revelation is a carpet. Salieri criticizes the German master for having worn out eight carpets from pacing as he composed his music, while Salieri has used just one all his life. Salieri is thus telling the audience—without actually saying so— that his music is as lifeless as Beethoven's is stirring.

He also got what he wanted in his personal life: "I own a respectable house and a respectable wife—Teresa. . . . I require only one quality in a domestic companion—lack of fire. And in that omission Teresa was conspicuous" (*A*, 26). His is another emotionally sterile marriage, much like Martin Dysart's. The one real passion he reveals is for sweets, and for them he demonstrates a zeal that as much approaches religious adoration as it does sexual desire. The playwright describes his indulgences in sweets and the effect that they have on him: "*He turns to the cake-stand with a reverence akin to lust—hesitates for a delicious second about which pastry to take—and finally selects a custard. In deep silence, punctuated only by a little moan of ecstasy, the old man devours it. His body shudders with pleasure*" (*A*, 25). The juxtaposition of the words *reverence* and *lust* bind Salieri with Alan in a confusion between religion and sex; here the adored object is a piece of cake instead of a horse. It is this same quality of emotion that Bob experiences for music in *The Private Ear*.

If Salieri's sexual passion is not evident around women, it is in the presence of music. There are distinct sexual overtones in two instances of his reactions to music: "Already when I was ten a spray of notes could make me dizzy—quite literally—almost to falling down" (*A*, 23). His words here are reminiscent of *Shrivings*'s Gideon, who found sexual stimulation as a youth in everything from a red setter dog to the smell of cow parsley. That type of response reaches the extreme in his reaction to hearing the Adagio from Mozart's seranade No.10 for 13 Wind Instruments in B-flat Major (K.361):

It started simply enough: just a pulse in the lowest registers—bassoons and basset horns—like a rusty squeezebox. . . . And then suddenly, high above it sounded a single note on the oboe. . . . It hung there unwavering—piercing me through—till breath could hold it no longer, and a clarinet withdrew it out of me, and softened it, and sweetened it into a phrase of such delight it had me trembling. . . . the squeezebox groaned louder, and over it the higher instruments wailed and warbled, throwing lines of sound around me—long lines of pain around and through me. Ah, the pain! Pain as I had never known it. (*A*, 36)

Salieri is convinced that what he heard was more than music—it was the voice of God. Why that realization disturbed him so much will be made clear in the section on Mozart. How Salieri reacts to this piece of music is fully consistent with the vow he made before he left home to study music: he took on more pupils, joined more committees, and wrote more music to God's glory than ever before in his life. And he makes a new request of God: "Let your voice enter me! . . . Let *me* conduct you!" (*A*, 37).

Salieri avoids meeting Mozart as long as he can, but finally it has to happen, and does at the Royal Court. In an effort to please and impress the Emperor more than to honor the new arrival on the musical scene, Salieri composed a march of welcome for Mozart. From the moment Mozart improves on the piece for Salieri, there is nothing but conflict between the two musicians. It begins when Salieri becomes convinced that Mozart "had" his prize pupil, Katherina Cavalieri, with whom Salieri claims to be very much in love, "or at least in lust" (*A*, 43); his vow of virtue, however, has forced him to keep his hands off her. It is then that Salieri decides on his first act of revenge against Mozart: he will have Mozart's wife Constanze in the same way he is certain Mozart had Katherina. Constanze warns Salieri that her husband must not know that she has come to his apartment to deliver her husband's music because he is a very jealous man. Salieri has to admit that jealousy is not a passion that he understands. Ironically enough, his envy and jealousy of Mozart become the driving passions that control his every action throughout the rest of the play. In a manner as clumsy as Bob's in *The Private Ear*, Salieri attempts to charm Constanze; he confesses that "When I met you, last night, I envied Mozart from the depths of my soul" (*A*, 43). It is an envy that parallels Dysart's for Alan in *Equus*.

Salieri's reaction to the music that Constanze leaves with him brings the first act to its dramatic climax. It makes him see his own emptiness and makes him realize that God has given him just enough talent to recognize Mozart's genius—and his own mediocrity. And he blames God:

Grazie Signore! You gave me the desire to serve you—which most men do not have—then saw to it the service was shameful in the ears of the server. *Grazie!* You gave me the desire to praise you—which most men do not have—then you made me mute. *Grazie tanti!* You put into me perception of the incomparable—which most men never know!—then ensured that I would know myself forever mediocre. . . . Until this day I have pursued virtue with rigour. I have laboured long hours to relieve my fellow men. I have worked and worked the talent you allowed me. . . . And *my* only reward—my sublime privilege—is to be the sole man alive in this time who shall clearly recognize your Incarnation [in Mozart's music]. (*A*, 67)

And so Salieri declares war not on Mozart but on God, and will have his revenge against God by blocking Mozart. Salieri is going to defeat God's plan to be celebrated through Mozart's musical talents: "From this time we are enemies, You and I! . . . *Dio Ingiusto!*—You are the Enemy! I name Thee now—*Nemico Eterno!* And this I swear. To my last breath I shall *block* you on earth, as far as I am able!" (*A*, 67–68). At that moment Salieri decides that the "creature" (Mozart) has to be destroyed. Act 1 depicts the virtuous Salieri's mounting frustration with Mozart and God. Act 2 shows the depths to which Salieri is willing to stoop in pursuit of his quest.

Salieri is fully aware of his great power in the musical circles at court and he decides to use those powers to destroy Mozart. He doesn't do it by taking sexual advantage of Constanze; that act, he rationalizes, would be petty in exchange for the advantage that Mozart took of Katherina Cavalieri. And, he admits, that his invention in love (as in art) has always been limited. In that trait he joins the parade of Shaffer's other male characters, from Bob to Dysart, and certainly including Mark Gideon and Pizarro. But mostly, Salieri's quarrel was merely *through* but not *with* Mozart.[3] Instead, he takes Katherina as his mistress behind his wife's back and thereby renounces his vow of sexual virtue. He also resigns from his committees and thereby betrays his vow of social commitment. And, Salieri recommends a man with no talent, instead of Mozart, as a musical instructor for Princess Elizabeth. Salieri shows himself to be hypocritical as well as devious by telling the emperor how he commiserates with the man he could not recommend for the position—but there are just too many rumors about Mozart's low morals.

While Salieri expects God to take revenge against him for his evil deeds, he finds himself rewarded rather than punished. In the years 1784–1785, Salieri was regarded by the public as the infinitely superior composer, and his opera *La Grotta di Trofonio* became the talk of the city and a great success: his rewards were all external. His punishment, on the other hand, was internal. He was forced to recognize Mozart's concerts for what they were: "the finest things made by Man in the whole of the eighteenth century" (*A*, 74). Salieri can appreciate Mozart's music, but he is determined not to let the rest of Europe know of it and to deny Mozart the success he deserves. As such, Salieri must prevent *The*

Marriage of Figaro from being performed, and the wedding dance in the opera's third act provides the opportunity; the emperor has forbidden ballet in opera. Salieri finds it quite easy to limit *Figaro*'s run in Vienna to nine performances between May and December of 1786. As Salieri works to destroy his rival, he also works to make Mozart believe that he is his friend, and that he is doing what he can on the young man's behalf.

Salieri attempts to reverse his guilt and accuses Mozart of speaking badly of the court composer all over Vienna—saying things like Salieri is trying to ruin him. Mozart denies those charges and swears that he speaks only kindly of his mentor. Mozart must now live up to that claim, so Salieri is more or less free to do whatever he wishes against the young composer. But Salieri can't fool himself; he recognizes the qualitative difference between Mozart's operas and his own. While Mozart was composing *Don Giovanni* after the death of his father, Salieri completed *Axur, King of Ormus*, and could not deny to himself that "from the ordinary [events of life] he created legends—and I from legends created only the ordinary!" (*A*, 93).

Salieri confesses to the audience four specific ways in which he worked at ruining Mozart. First, he poisoned the emperor's opinion of the young musician through constant slander. Second, he worsened Mozart's economic situation by recommending that the emperor pay Mozart as little as possible for the post that the emperor wants him to occupy. Salieri's evil deeds are once again rewarded rather than punished—again externally, not internally. Upon the death of the First Chapelmaster, the position goes to Salieri. Salieri understands that while the emperor can bestow honors upon him, God continues to make Salieri recognize the true value of his own work: "What *He* could do was crown me *King* of that world: indisputable darling of the meretricious! . . . I was imprisoned in Fame for life!" (*A*, 97). While it sounds like Salieri has received the Fame he prayed for as a child, such is not the case; it was "*the fame of work I knew to be worthless!*" (*A*, 97). While honors are being hurled at Salieri for his mediocre work, Mozart composes *Così Fan Tutte*, and Salieri starts to hear Mozart's giggle as God's laughter in his ear: "*Dio inquisto*, I could stand no more! I had to end it!" (*A*, 97). So Salieri decides on a third plan against Mozart, this one designed "to hasten him toward madness, or toward death" (*A*, 104). That is the episode, already mentioned in the section above, in which Salieri sends his valet to commission Mozart to write what he believes will be his own Requiem Mass. The fourth act to which Salieri confesses is that of taunting Mozart as the Ghostly Messenger while the musician is trying to compose *The Magic Flute*: "I confess that for one entire week, whilst he was writing *The Magic Flute* at night—his wife convalescing at Baden with the new baby—I would walk to the Rauhensteingasse in the moonlight. And precisely as the clocks of the city struck one, I would halt outside his window and be his more terrible clock. Every night I showed him one day less—[he retracts his fingers] then stalked away" (*A*, 109). What Salieri does not confess to is Mozart's physical poisoning. That is a lie Salieri created in the hope of winning fame; if he could not be remembered for his music, he would be remembered as the man who murdered Mozart: "As his fame grew, so would mine. 'Salieri: the poisoner of Mozart.' Just that. A horror for all eternity. *Bene e bene ancora!*" (*A*, 114). But Salieri is not even permitted that consolation prize. He admits, "I survived to see myself become extinct" (*A*, 118). Salieri could not stand being extinct, so he deliberately revived the scandal.

Salieri begins his final monologue in the last moments of the play, in the manner of Dysart and later, Yonadab. The speech indicates the feelings of alienation that have already appeared prominently in *The Private Ear*, *The Public Eye*, *The Royal Hunt of the Sun*, *Shrivings*, and *Equus*. They will appear again, forcefully, in *Yonadab*. Salieri addresses the members of the audience in a manner that will win him their sympathy—despite everything that he has done: "*Amici cari*. The gulf that separates me from other men is exact. I was created a pair of ears and nothing else. . . . If I cannot be Mozart, then I do not wish to be anything. . . . Now I go to become a ghost myself" (*A*, 119–120). He also admits that he has written a false confession stating that he poisoned Mozart, and goes on to proclaim himself Patron Saint of Mediocrities, to whom all other mediocrities may pray. It is on this note that Salieri speaks the last line of the play: "Mediocrities everywhere—now and to come—I absolve you all! Amen!" (*A*, 122). He closes the play with a gesture of benediction meant to embrace the entire audience. Why Salieri's reaction to Mozart is so extreme will become clear in the following section.

   B. Mozart.   Just as Shaffer demythologized the historical Pizarro in *The Royal Hunt of the Sun*, so he does Mozart in *Amadeus*. This section will serve the dual function of treating Mozart as a character in his own right—the antagonist whose words and actions set the play in motion—and in his relationship with Salieri. It was in the year that Salieri entered the Viennese Court that he first heard of Mozart, a ten-year-old prodigy who was touring Europe. Years later he learns that he is required to commission a comic opera in German from Herr Mozart. Although

Salieri has not yet met Mozart, he confesses that "from the start I was alarmed by Mozart's coming. . . . What worried me were reports about the man himself" (A, 31). Before the audience—or Salieri—meets Mozart, they hear that he is spirited and charming, qualities that Salieri knows he himself lacks.

The first word, or rather sound, that Salieri and the audience hear from Mozart is "Miaouw." In attendance at a private concert, Mozart and his future wife Constanze Weber are unaware of the presence of Salieri, who is seated in such a way in the Baroness Waldstädten's library that he is invisible to anyone entering from upstage. And so the young lovers, believing that they are alone, play a cat-and-mouse game with each other. Salieri hears Constanze "squeak" offstage and then sees her enter pursued by a "small, palid, large-eyed man in a showy wig and showy set of clothes" (A, 33) who runs after her: it is Wolfgang Amadeus Mozart. Mozart drops on all fours and pursues Constanze as if he were a cat: "I'm going to pounce-bounce! I'm going to scrunch-munch! I'm going to chew-oo my little mouse-wouse! I'm going to tear her with my paws-claws!" (A, 34). His piercing giggle, reminiscent of Brindsley's in *Black Comedy*, is infantile and irritating to Salieri. Nor does Salieri approve of all of Mozart's scatological references. When Mozart has caught his prey and sees that she is trembling, he tells her intimately, "I think you're going to shit yourself!" (A, 34), and then he makes the sound of a fart. Like Dysart, Mark Askelon, and later, Yonadab, Salieri can observe but not participate in passionate or spirited behavior. Mozart is as impulsive as he is playful, and on the spot asks Constanze to marry him.

If Salieri does not grow in the course of the play, Mozart has not grown in the course of his life. At the age of six he impulsively proposed to Marie Antionette, and during his first appearance in the play he does the same to Constanze Weber. Here Constanze introduces a subject that is a constant in Shaffer's plays, that of father-son relationships. She reminds him that his father would never consent to the marriage and that the younger Mozart would not go against his father's wishes because he is afraid of incurring his father's disapproval. Later in the play, the composer reveals his true feelings about his boring father—and his irreverence: "He stays up in Salzburg year after year, kissing the ring of the Fartsbishop, and lecturing me! . . ." (A, 92). Constanze hates his father for having kept her husband a baby all his life.

It is while Salieri is still in shock over Mozart's behavior that he hears from the next room the Seranade for 13 Wind Instruments. What upsets him so much is not just the fact that he could never hope to write music of that caliber, but that it came from the most obscene person—and yet represented the Divine Spirit: "It seemed to me I had heard the voice of God—and that it issued from a creature whose own voice I had also heard—and it was the voice of an obscene child" (*A*, 37). That is why Salieri has to declare war on God—for giving his most precious gift to a person who does not deserve it and for denying it to someone who does. It is a great big cruel and ugly divine joke, and Salieri must state his anger to the *Dio Inguisto* who has made him the butt of the joke: "*You know how hard I've worked!*—Solely that in the end, in the practice of the art which alone makes the world comprehensible to me, I might hear Your Voice! And now I do hear it—and it says only one name: MOZART! . . . Spiteful, sniggering, conceited, infantile . . . shit-talking Mozart with his botty-smacking wife!—*him* you have chosen to be your sole conduct!" (*A*, 67).

Mozart's words and actions are such that they earn him no friends and in fact make him enemies at court. The problem isn't that he is mean, but honest—and excessive in his behavior. His second appearance in the play is before the emperor, whom Mozart last saw when he himself was six years old. Mozart's greeting goes beyond enthusiastic: "Majesty! Your Majesty's humble slave! Let me kiss your royal hand a hundred thousand times!" [*He kisses it greedily over and over, until its owner withdraws it in embarrassement.*]" (*A*, 39). Also present at this exhibition are Count Johann Kilian von Strack, groom of the Imperial Chamber; Count Franz Orsini-Rosenberg, director of the Imperial Opera; and Salieri. The subsequent conversation shows Mozart's lack of tact, which stems from his ignorance of protocol. First, Mozart tells the emperor that he has already chosen a libretto for the opera that he was commissioned to write. Unfortunately, Mozart never made his choice known to Orsini-Rosenberg, who is startled by the news and offended by the slight. Second, he reveals with a giggle, that the opera will take place in a seraglio—a pasha's harem. Third, he proclaims that it is "full of proper German virtues." Salieri makes a point of asking "what are those? Being a foreigner I'm not sure" (*A*, 41). Mozart's explanation only makes matters go from bad to worse: "manly love, Signore. Not male sopranos screeching. Or stupid couples rolling their eyes. All that absurd Italian rubbish" (*A*, 42). Fourth is Mozart's choice of a leading lady: Katherina Cavalieri. And last is Mozart's reworking of the march of welcome that Salieri composed in his honor. If Mozart had handled the situation delicately, there might have been no problem, but there is nothing delicate about Shaffer's Mozart. He is oblivious to the fact that his exhibitionistic playing and reworking of the banal piece into the march "Non più andrai" in *The Marriage of Figaro* is deeply offensive to the court composer.

The aftermath of the performance of *Seraglio* also does Mozart nothing but harm. He could have selected better words than *excessive* and *insatiable* to describe Katherina to Salieri, who becomes convinced during the performance that Mozart must have made sexual demands of her in exchange for the "showiest" aria that Salieri has ever heard: "Ten minutes of scales and ornaments, amounting in sum to vast emptiness . . . what might be demanded by a foolish young soprano" (*A*, 45). Salieri tries to pass on to Mozart a lesson that he learned from his teacher Gluck, that music should not call attention to the virtuosity of the composer. But Mozart is not about to take the advice of a composer who "creates people so lofty they sound as though they shit marble" (*A*, 47). He follows up his comment about Chevalier Gluck with "only stupid farts sport titles" (*A*, 48).

Mozart's situation only worsens in the next conversation, this time in the home of Chapelmaster Bonno. Mozart is complaining to Strack of how he has been in Vienna for seven months and still does not have a single job. He blames the situation on foreigners: "Worthless wops like Chapelmaster Bonno!" He goes on to call Salieri's latest opera, *The Chimney Sweep*, "dried dogshit!" (*A*, 50). He even criticizes the emperor, who is in a position to do him some good, by reporting that behind his back he is known as Kaiser Keep It, for his stinginess. And he takes the opportunity to boast of himself as the best musician in Vienna. Time and again, he reminds his listeners of his greatness. On the day he announces that he will be composing *Figaro*, he reveals that it is already finished in his head: "The rest's just scribbling" (*A*, 79). After its performance, he tells Salieri, "It's the best opera yet written. That's what it is. And only I could have done it. No one else living!" (*A*, 89). And yet, Mozart can't understand why everyone at court is against him: "I'm a frank man. I like people. Before God I declare I like people. It's just that in this city there's such a *cabal* against me, I don't know where to turn!" (*A*, 91). He never stops to think that his insults and self-aggrandizement might be the cause of his problems.

He is also having problems in his marriage. When Mozart reproves his wife for having disgraced him by allowing men at a New Year's Eve party to measure her calves (as her penalty for having lost a game), she snaps back that *she* is the one who is shamed in the marriage because her husband drags to bed every female student who comes to him, and Salieri does not. When Mozart defends himself, he doesn't lie to his wife—he blames Salieri: "He can't get it up, that's why! Have you heard his music?

That's the sound of someone who *can't get it up!* At least I can do that!" (*A*, 55). Mozart uses his charm—and a game—to get Constanze to stop crying. In this particular game, Constance gets to whack her husband's bottom with a ruler, and he pleads: "Do it again! I cast myself at your feet, Madonna!" (*A*, 56). When Salieri appears unexpectedly, they freeze, and are as embarrassed as Alan and his father when they run into each other at the pornographic cinema in *Equus*.

By the second act, Mozart's situation is desperate. He has hardly a pupil to teach, and by the end of the play, two children to support. Mozart continues to get himself deeper and deeper into trouble by not taking his father's advice and controlling what comes out of his mouth. If Salieri expresses how much he enjoyed Paesiello's *The Barber of Seville*, Mozart calls it "musical piss" and proceeds to ask, "Why are Italians so scared of complexity in music? They really are the most simple-minded people in the world" (*A*, 77). And if the Baron Gottfried Van Swieten wants to know why Mozart is composing *The Marriage of Figaro* instead of something on a more elevated theme than that of Beaumarchais's play now that he has joined the Brotherhood of Masons, Mozart angers him by responding that "the only thing that a man should elevate is his doodle" (*A*, 77). Finally, when Van Swieten and Strack unite with Salieri in defense of grand, heroic themes in opera, rather than in the lives of servants, Mozart lets them have it: "You're all up on perches, but it doesn't hide your arseholes! You don't give a shit about gods and heroes!" (*A*, 78).

Of course, none of Mozart's detractors could ever complain that he is less than frank or that he does not know what is going through their minds. After the tirade detailed in the previous paragraph, Mozart tells his listeners exactly what they are thinking: "Herr Chamberlain thinking 'Insane Mozart: I must speak to the Emperor at once!' Herr Prefect thinking 'Ignorant Mozart: debasing opera with his vulgarity!' Herr Court Composer thinking 'German Mozart: what can he finally know about music?' And Mozart himself in the middle, thinking 'I'm just a good fellow, why do they all disapprove of me?'" (*A*, 78). He sees the group as a perfect quartet, as if in an opera, and sees the job of a composer as combining the inner minds of his characters into a new sound. Then, the audience experiences the music as God himself must hear it: "Millions of sounds ascending at once and mixing in His ear to become an unending music unimaginable to us!" (*A*, 79). The complexity of Mozart's thoughts so fascinate Salieri, that all he can do is stare at the young composer. So Mozart blows a raspberry and giggles.

The salary that Salieri convinces the emperor to pay Mozart at the court is so little that it is not only insulting, but, in Mozart's words, "It wouldn't keep a mouse in cheese for a week" (*A*, 95). And so he is reduced to begging money from his Masonic brothers. However, their support does not last long because Mozart betrays them by putting their rituals into *The Magic Flute*, and because he explodes at Van Swieten: "You're made of excrement, Baron. Like all grand men" (*A*, 108). He also turns Rosenberg against him by calling him "Rosencunt," "Rosenbugger," and "Woppy, foppy, wet-arsed, Italian-loving, shit-tube!" (*A*, 84).

Mozart is looking gray and hollow and is at the end of his wits when he goes to Salieri for help. In a manner of speaking, Salieri grants Mozart his wishes—yet brings him to the brink of insanity. He sends Greybig to commission the Requiem Mass at a time when Mozart is growing demented and drinking all day. Mozart believes the bottles of wine that someone leaves daily at his door are poisoned, and that is the cause of his terrible stomach cramps. When Salieri unmasks himself, Mozart is forced to admit to himself that the man he trusted is the one who caused all of the problems that have besieged him. Mozart has become another Martin (*The Royal Hunt of the Sun*) or Alan (*Equus*), with the scales removed from his eyes. In a frenzy, Mozart begs Constanze not to let death claim him. As she speaks consolingly to her husband about their children, she becomes aware that Mozart is dead. A subsequent section, on the source of the play, will examine how faithful the playwright is to the real-life Mozart.

C. Other characters.   The character of Salieri dominates the play, and that of Mozart sets Salieri's battle against God in motion. The other characters flesh out the play, but are of minor consequence in comparison to the two composers. The first character to appear on stage is Salieri's valet, Ignaz Greybig, a man in his sixties in 1823, the year in which the play begins and ends. The reader sees in Greybig that Mozart was not Salieri's only victim. While Salieri is implicated in Mozart's death, he is also directly responsible for Greybig's degeneration from a faithful and religious servant to a gaunt figure who lives by the bottle. Greybig has never been entirely convinced that his master killed Mozart; he used to believe that the composer died of "sexual rot," but now, thirty-two years later, is not so sure. Greybig has the function of being the narrator's narrator. Before Salieri begins to recall the events of 1781 through 1791, early in the play Greybig sets the scene for the audience to meet Salieri. He, in fact, presents the current state of Salieri's life: "What a scandal! The great musician Antonio Salieri, sitting alone in his own house, shoe-deep in dust, talking to himself night and day. Night and day I have to hear it" (*A*, 16). Perhaps having to hear over and over Salieri's retelling of the tale is his punishment for his role in Salieri's scheme to hasten Mozart's death. Before Salieri attempts suicide, Greybig smells death, not God, in Salieri's home, and sends for a priest. Greybig cannot help but suspect that even after forty years of serving Salieri, he really does not know him. "Secret Salieri," he calls him, as secret about his private life, it seems, as is the father in *Equus*. Yet, while Greybig admits to not understanding his employer, he has always given him the benefit of the doubt. He has considered Salieri a man of virtue for trying to reclaim Mozart and bring him back to God. He must finally conclude that "either Mozart went mad and accused my master—or else Mozart was really murdered and my master did it" (*A*, 18). Greybig serves as Salieri's conscience. He tries to keep Salieri from blasphemy when Salieri—about to indulge his passion for sweets—asks Greybig to pray for him to the Patron Saint of Stomach Ache. Later, as Salieri awaits Constanze's arrival at his home, he suspects that Salieri is about to do something that he is going to regret. He announces the arrival of *Frau* Mozart, and by emphasizing her married status adds a light moment to a tense situation.

Greybig's major function in the play is that of acting as the *Memento Mori*, the ghostly messenger who commissions Mozart to write the Requiem Mass. Greybig agrees to help only because he thinks that in some small way he is contributing to Mozart's return to God. He realizes later that he never should have agreed, and finally refuses to continue taking part in the devilish scheme. It is then that Salieri takes his place. Unlike Greybig, Salieri relishes haunting Mozart, as an earlier quotation reveals. Unlike the compassionate Greybig, who is hoping to have a positive spiritual effect on Mozart, Salieri enjoys seeing the look on the young composer's face grow more and more crazed with each passing day. Greybig feels implicated not only in Mozart's death, but also in Salieri's attempt at suicide. It is he who brings his master the shaving razor, and then watches in horror as Salieri slits his throat. After witnessing the act, Greybig's life is reduced to haunting taverns and telling the tale to anyone who will pay for his next drink.

The secondary characters at the court occupy higher social positions and sport more impressive titles than the valet Greybig, but none is so pure of spirit as he is. And Mozart is right on the mark when he suggests that there is cabal against him in Vienna. Salieri's principal accomplice in the conspiracy against Mozart is Count Franz Orsini-Rosenberg, the director of the Imperial Opera, a superstitious, sixty-year-old man. From the start he does not like Mozart, who did not bother to tell him that he has already selected a libretto for his first commissioned opera. He also finds Mozart a "young fellow trying to impress beyond his abilities. Too much spice. Too many notes. . . . I believe we are going to have trouble with this young man" (A, 30). He is put off by child prodigies in general and by this one in particular—the son of Leopold Mozart, "a bad-tempered Salzburg musician who dragged the boy endlessly round Europe making him play the keyboard blindfolded, with one finger, and that sort of thing" (A, 31). He then joins Salieri in a conspiracy against Mozart. When they are conspiring, they speak to each other in Italian.[4] Salieri knows that he must turn to Rosenberg to see to it that *The Marriage of Figaro* fails. Again they speak in Italian about the inclusion of a dance sequence in the third act that can be construed to violate the emperor's prohibition against ballet in an opera. When Rosenberg insists that Mozart remove the offending portion of the music, Mozart can feel Salieri's hand in that decision.

Count Johann Kilian von Strack, groom of the Imperial Chamber, and Baron Gottfried Van Swieten, prefect of the Imperial Library, start out favorably inclined toward Mozart. It is Mozart's mouth that turns the stiff and proper Strack against him at the precise moment when Mozart calls *The Chimney Sweep*, Salieri's latest opera, "dogshit." Strack is further outraged when Mozart refers to the emperor as "Kaiser Keep It." Moments later, when Strack asks Mozart to lower his voice and the musician responds "Lower your breeches" (A, 51), Strack can only contemplate Mozart with "cold dislike," and leave the scene. His next appearance is in the second act, and once again he has an unpleasant exchange of words with the young genius. He disapproves of Mozart's choice of Beaumarchais's play as the basis for an opera, and points to Salieri's recent opera *Danaius* as a subject befitting the genre. For Mozart, that opera avoids real life and succeeds only in boring the audience. The opera is less the subject under discussion than is Mozart's language and apparent lack of respect for the emperor. Strack is offended. On Salieri's instigation, he reports to the emperor on the subject matter of *Figaro*.

On the subject of Mozart's language, Van Swieten, a serious and cultivated man of fifty, is of an opinion akin to Strack's. Neither one wants to hear unkind nicknames for the emperor, Salieri's work compared to "dogshit," or about an opera (*Figaro*) with sheets still warm from a woman's body and a "pisspot brimming under the bed" (A, 77). While Van Swieten, a devoted member of the Brotherhood of Masons, finds Mozart's begging money from his Masonic brothers disgraceful, he does continue to help Mozart's financial situation by finding him small jobs arranging music; however, he does not generate enough money for Mozart to support his family. Brother Van Swieten is not able to find him any subscribers, due to Mozart's reputation as a libertine. He also suggests that Mozart start spending his time giving concerts instead of writing "dirty comedies." Wolfgang finally loses the support of his last benefactor, when Van Swieten learns that Mozart is planning to put the Masonic rituals into "a vulgar show" (*The Magic Flute*).

Shaffer depicts the Emperor Joseph II as kindly, if simple. He is a dapper and cheerful man of forty, pleased with himself and the world. He likes "fêtes and fireworks," and like Louise Harrington, sprinkling his speech with French. Shaffer presents Joseph as he did the Incan emperor, in bright light and surrounded by gold—here, gilded mirrors. He adores music, provided it makes no demands on the royal ear. The emperor listens to bad advice and has a way of reducing subjects to their simplest elements. For example, he dismisses *Seraglio* as having "too many notes," words obviously put into his mouth by Rosenberg. His response to *Figaro* is that Mozart is "coming along nicely." He also falls victim to the plot to ruin Mozart by taking Salieri's recommendation and hiring an un- qualified man as his daughter's musical tutor, as well as granting Mozart the smallest possible salary. He does, however, recognize when Salieri is being *cattivo*. The death of the emperor is the final blow to Mozart's support at court.

Constanze is the one character who grows and changes in the course of the play. She does not remain the high-spirited young woman in her early twenties whom Mozart playfully chases around the library of the Baroness Waldstädten; she quickly learns to deal with the realities of a philandering husband and dire financial straits. She supports her hus- band throughout, even to the point of being willing to give herself sexually to Salieri, if doing so will help Mozart's career. She also equals her husband in her frankness and honesty, even if it means telling Mozart how much she has always hated his father for constantly berating her. She is a good wife to the end. The last things she tells her dying husband is that "it was the best day of my life when you married me. And as long as I'm alive I'll be the most honored woman in the world" (*A*, 115). In what amounts to an epilogue, for reasons of self-interest more than for her husband's reputation, Constanze, now remarried and "retired to Salzburg to become a pious and final authority on all matters Mozartian" (*A*, 117), proclaims that "a sweeter-tongued man never lived," that their ten-year marriage was blissful, and that Mozart's music reflects his refined spirit. *Amadeus* is Shaffer's last play to have a woman in a minor role. In *Yonadab*, Tamar figures prominently in the intrigue, and *Lettice and Lovage* has two women as its principal characters.

Techniques

It is appropriate at this point to discuss the theatrical techniques, since the major technique is a pair of characters. Salieri serves as the narrator who introduces Mozart, Constanze, and the members of the court; and Greybig's comments prepare the audience to meet Salieri. But there is yet another level of introduction, this one provided by the two characters who introduce Greybig. They are the Venticelli ("Little Winds," in Italian). Shaffer calls them "purveyors of information, gossip and rumor" (*A*, 11). They are the first characters to speak on stage and create the play's mystery with their repetition of "I don't believe it" (*A*, 13–14). Just what is it that they don't believe? And why are their comments punctuated by off-stage whispers of *"Salieri!"*? The Venticelli provide the audience with what the Viennese public is saying. They speak very rapidly and produce the effect of a duet. Their first appearance serves as the overture for this "black opera." It is they who inform the audience that Salieri cries out during the night, and that he has driven Greybig to drink with his constant retelling of the tale, and with his recent confession of having murdered Mozart thirty-two years ago. They question him over and over to name the horrible and filthy truth that he knows, much as Dysart presses Alan about the details of what happened on the fateful night at the stables. Since they are Salieri's personal Venticelli, he pays them to keep him informed of the gossip in the city: "no one could survive in Vienna without paid informers" (*A*, 29). The first news they bring him is of Mozart's arrival. They also provide information about Mozart for the audience: he composed his first concert at the age of four, his first symphony at five, and a full opera at fourteen; and he is coming to Vienna to stay. (Could anyone in the eighteenth century have realized how permanent a part of the musical scene he was to become?) At other points in the play, they comment on the women in Mozart's life, his residences (the last of which is in a slum), his marriage, his extravagances, and how the members of the court react to him. In fact, they serve the function of the chorus in Greek tragedy. They are not the only choral effect in the play. There are also the "stage whispers" that fill the theater with Salieri's name. They have a similar choric effect to the one that accompanies the presence of Equus in that play. It is appropriate that Salieri's name is first spoken with a snake-like hissing.

Music of one kind or another, and to one extent or another, finds its way into *Five Finger Exercise*, *The Private Ear*, *The Royal Hunt of the Sun*, and *Yonadab*. In *Amadeus*, music is more than a theme or a way of providing melody on stage: it propels the action of the play. Mozart's exhibitionistic reworking of Salieri's march of welcome first makes Salieri an enemy of the young composer. Mozart's Serenade for 13 Wind Instruments provides proof to the audience of the Absolute Beauty of his music, and moves Salieri to declare war on God through Mozart. Mozart's operas tie into the plot and themes of the play. *Seraglio* provides the excessively ornamented aria for Katherina Cavalieri, and makes Salieri wonder at what price she got such special treatment from Mozart. *Così Fan Tutte* grows out of Mozart's involvement with Aloysia Weber, and then her sister, Constanze. *Don Giovanni* provides the figure of the judgmental father, and *The Magic Flute* (in the American version) of the forgiving father.

The techniques of flashbacks, masks, dreams, nicknames, and games tie *Amadeus* to Shaffer's other plays. Both *Equus* and *The Royal Hunt of the Sun* share the common trait with *Amadeus* of a narration in present time (be it the 1970s, the sixteenth, or the nineteenth centuries) of the events that transpired before the plays begin. There is also the evolution of Shaffer's use of masks from *The Royal Hunt of the Sun* to *Equus* to *Amadeus*. In the first, the masks are part of the spectacle of Peru. In the second, the actors who play the horses wear stylized masks. In *Amadeus*, the mask is an integral part of Salieri's plan to terrorize Mozart and drive him toward madness and death. Dreams have been a part of Shaffer's plays since *Five Finger Exercise*, in which Clive dreams that he is being smothered, that is, stifled. Pizarro dreams of the Incan emperor every night until they finally meet. Alan is haunted in his dreams by the horrible crime he committed against horses, and Dysart by the crime he believes he is committing against his patients. In the American version of *Amadeus* (to be discussed in a subsequent section), Salieri makes a reality of the dream that terrifies Mozart. Dreams will figure prominently again in *Yonadab*.[5]

Game-playing and false identities have been a mainstay of Shaffer's theater since his earliest plays. Clive Harrington plays a poseur game to stay in his mother's good graces, while Walter wears an orphan's mask to hide his true identity. Bob plays a friendship game with Ted in *The Private Ear*, and then plays host and chef for Doreen's benefit. Belinda and Julian play a game of silence with each other in *The Public Eye*. While

Clea plays at being Brindsley's charwoman and Harold plays the hand game in *Black Comedy*, the playwright is engaged in a game of reversal of light and darkness with the audience. Tom and Frank's entire relationship in *White Lies*, *The White Liars*, and *White Liars* is based on false identities. Dr. Dysart uses tricks as a part of Alan's psychotherapy, and Mark Askelon challenges the inhabitants of *Shrivings* to play the apple game with him.[6] Mozart's games with Constanze give Salieri his first impression of the musician, and make him decide that God is unfair in bestowing the qualities of genius on a man who likes doing everything backwards, from reversing the letters of his name to "Trazom," to claiming that "I'd want to kick my wife's arse instead of her face." (*A*, 35). Also, the minor technique of nicknames, which appears throughout Shaffer's dramatic production, is evident again in *Amadeus*. Louise Harrington calls Clive jou-jou and Walter Hibou. Ted calls Bob Tchaik; and Carol Melkett has a nickname for everything in *Black Comedy*, even Winnie Whiskey and Vera Vodka. The nickname "Secret Salieri" that Greybig bestows upon his employer is the most telling of all, since it is a clue to its recipient's character. Nicknames will appear again in *Yonadab*, and games will reach their pinnacle in *Lettice and Lovage*.

In the final moments of *The Royal Hunt of the Sun*, Old Martin relates what happened after the action of the play. Similarly, Salieri informs the audience of Constanze's second marriage. This union, in strong contrast to her first, is to a "Danish diplomat as dull as a clock" (*A*, 117). The final words on Salieri's last days come from the mouths of the Venticelli who quote from the conversation book that Beethoven maintained after he went deaf. In this way the reader learns that Salieri's attempt at suicide failed, and that he was taken to be "quite deranged. He keeps claiming that he is guilty of Mozart's death, and made away with him by poison" (*A*, 121). Finally there is the item in the *German Musical Times* of 25 May 1825: "In the frenzy of his imagination he [Salieri] is even said to accuse himself of complicity in Mozart's early death. A rambling of the mind believed in truth by no one but the poor deluded old man himself" (*A*, 121). Werner Huber and Hubert Zapf observe that some of the elements in the play come from Mozart's operas, such as the blackmail by the father figure in *Seraglio*, and the masks, eavesdropping, and intrigues in *Seraglio*, *Figaro*, and *Don Giovanni* [intrigues also abound in *Così Fan Tutte*]: Cherubino from *The Marriage of Figaro*, like Salieri, hides from view in an armchair; and the Papageno character (*Magic Flute*) engages in word games like Mozart and Constanze.[7]

Revised Version

Shaffer routinely makes changes in his plays between their British and American openings. Sometimes those changes are as minor as in spelling (*honour* to *honor*), sometimes they involve replacing a reference that is comprehensible to a British audience with another that is understandable by an American audience. For example, he changed the jingle that Alan sings about Typhoo tea in the British production of *Equus* to one for Doublemint gum in the American production. He cut an incident from the second act of *The Royal Hunt of the Sun* and put it into the first in order to please American theatergoers who like the second act of a play to be shorter than the first. (He regrets having made that change.) What took real courage was tampering with *Amadeus* after the success the original version enjoyed in London, both at the box office and from the critics: it broke all previous records at the National Theatre and won the Evening Standard Award and the London Drama Critics Award for the best play of 1979. But Shaffer was not satisfied with the work and he explains his reason in the preface of the revised version. He says he became obsessed with "purity of clarity, structural order and drama."[8]

Shaffer's chief complaint with the original version is that Salieri personally does not have enough to do with Mozart's ruin; he wanted Salieri to be at the very center of the action. Some of Salieri's actions in the revised version also appear in the original, but now from the start and throughout, Salieri makes a concerted effort to bring about personally Mozart's ruin. Salieri sets out to learn Mozart's weaknesses so that he can use them against him. One by one, the members of the court turn against Mozart. In one instance, Rosenberg is so furious at Mozart for producing *Figaro* with the dance sequence and thereby making Rosenberg look like a fool before the emperor, he vows that he'll "do anything to get back at him!" (*AA*, 67). Salieri uncomfortably agrees with the emperor that there are just so many notes that the ear can hear in one evening, and that Mozart uses too many of them. And Salieri knows how to plant seeds and manipulate others. *He* suggested to Mozart to include the secret rituals of the Masons in *The Magic Flute*. *He* then gets Van Swieten to attend a performance, to which the Mason can respond to Mozart in only one way: "You have betrayed the Order" (*AA*, 84). Salieri needs to drive a wedge between Mozart and the Masons, so that the Masonic brothers will no longer provide a source of income for the young composer. Salieri gets a bonus that he never expected: Mozart receives only enough money from

The Magic Flute to keep him in drink, and the more he drinks the more he hastens his own demise.

Shaffer wanted Salieri to be the active figure in the final atrocity, and therefore has Salieri use Mozart's own words against him. Mozart tells Salieri that he has a recurring dream in which a figure wrapped in gray comes to him; he has no face, just a mask. Mozart has so lost touch with reality that he can no longer tell if the figure really did appear before him to commission him to compose a Requiem Mass. What Salieri does is turn Mozart's dream into reality. Rather than having a melodramatic and frightening Messenger of Death, Shaffer decided on a poetic but dangerous Messenger of God to request the Mass. With each appearance Salieri sees that Mozart looks more and more crazed. The unmasking is as much a shock to Mozart as is the haunting. From behind, he unmasks Salieri and in horror hears, "Ecco mi. Antonio Salieri. Ten years of hate have poisoned you to death" (*AA*, 88). Years later, Salieri writes a false confession of having killed Mozart with arsenic, so that he could be remembered for something.

Salieri is also adept at manipulating the audience. He calls the members of the audience friends and shows how they would act no differently from him in circumstances similar to his. This time, the house lights come on to foster the direct communication Salieri has with the audience. When he sings to the audience in *recitativo secco*, he has the intention of turning the play into an opera and of using the invocation to serve the purpose that opera has always had—that of conjuring up ghosts. In both versions, Salieri refers to the audience as "the yet to kill." Announcing the central mystery of the play, the Venticelli ask, "Why on earth would he do it?" (*AA*, 4). Both *Equus* and *Yonadab* have at the core that same question. Salieri has a way of justifying his actions, shifting blame, and coming off looking like the good guy. He claims that he has an affair with Katherina not out of lust, but rather to erase "in sweat the sense of his little body, the Creature's preceding me" (*AA*, 51). In the final scene of act 1, Salieri blames Mozart for his own toying with blackmail and adultery. Yet when Mozart's father dies, Salieri offers, "Lean on me!" (*AA*, 69). After that offer, how could Mozart or anyone else suspect him of evil intentions?

Certainly not Constanze, who confides in Salieri. She relates that Leopold Mozart unfairly calls her a spendthrift, when the truth is she just does not have enough money to manage. She does not want her husband to know that she has spoken so frankly to Salieri. While Mozart has nightmares in his sleep, Constanze lives a continual nightmare while she is awake. She is able to exorcise some of the hurt that Leopold has caused her by using his letters as kindling. Once again, she remains the good wife to the end, encouraging Mozart, and begging him not to die. In this version Shaffer exaggerates Constanze's cockney speech and common mannerisms—"Ta very much" and "They're delish"—thus feeding the American audience a British stereotype it enjoys watching on stage. Like Doreen in *The Private Ear*, Constanze lets on that she is no fan of classical music. In fact, she goes to Salieri's apartment not when Mozart is working, but while he is at a concert of music by Sebastian Bach, which Mozart did not think she would enjoy.

For a couple of reasons, Shaffer decided to eliminate the role of Greybig. In the first place, he wanted to keep Salieri at the center of the evil deeds, thereby leaving Greybig without any real function in the play. Furthermore, if Greybig taunts Mozart, Salieri cannot know first-hand the young man's reactions. Shaffer also wanted to eliminate all of the unkind remarks that Greybig makes about Mozart's "sexual rot"; in this version, Mozart is said to die of kidney failure. The one loss to the play is the inspired line in which he tries to get to Salieri's conscience by announcing that *Frau* Mozart is here to see him.

Shaffer makes up for the loss of Greybig by enhancing the role of the Venticelli, who deal with Salieri much more personally than they did in the original play. It is they who tell him of Mozart's childhood musical accomplishments, and who first bring Mozart's music to him. They also let him know that Mozart is dosing himself with medicine to quell the anxiety that has arisen out of his envy of the court composer. An addition that greatly pleases the playwright is the inclusion of the performance of *The Magic Flute*. He finds it "rowdy and vigorous" and like *The Private Ear*, *The Royal Hunt of the Sun*, and *Equus*, it contains elements of mime. It also allows him to trace Mozart's mental journey from *Don Giovanni* to *The Magic Flute*, during which time the father figure evolves from the harsh Commandatore to that of Sarastro, who extends his hands in a gesture of forgiveness and love. Shaffer did have to trade off references to *Così Fan Tutte* in order to include this new scene, so as not to devote too much stage time to opera. The revised version replaced the original in London, and, with the exception of Roman Polanski's production in Warsaw and then in Paris, it became the basis of the presentations around the world.[9] In the New York production Sir Ian McKellen played the part of Salieri, Tim Curry that of Mozart, and Jane Seymour was Constanze. As in London, Peter Hall directed and John Bury designed the sets. Shaffer, Hall, McKellen, and Bury all won "Tony" Awards.

Sources

Just as Shaffer conceived his idea for *The Royal Hunt of the Sun* when he happened to be reading William Prescott's *History of the Conquest of Peru*, he also began working on *Amadeus* in a similarly accidental manner. Colin Chambers[10] reveals that Shaffer conceived the idea for *Amadeus* when he was "idly reading an account of a storm at the burial of Mozart which drove away mourners but which is not mentioned in the Vienna meteorological records . . ." C.J. Gianakaris[11] reports that Salieri is the only member of the entire Viennese Court who attends Mozart's funeral. That fact intrigued Shaffer. Shaffer has also stated that the story was inspired by a legend that an unnamed figure came to Mozart and requested that he compose a Requiem Mass. Mozart, in his failing state, came to believe the Mass was for him. The play started to take form from the playwright's mental picture of Mozart surrounded by a spectral haunter, the haunter's assistant, and the musician's wife.[12]

Mozart needs little introduction to the reading public, but some background information on Antonio Salieri may be in order. He was born in Legnago, Italy, on 18 August 1750, and died in Vienna on 7 May 1825. In 1774, he became court composer, and after 1775 his influence was felt in every aspect of Viennese musical life. He served as Court Kapellmeister for over fifty years, from 1778 to 1824. His work dominated the Parisian opera from 1784 to 1788. He was, in fact, concerned with the social welfare of musicians. There is apparently little evidence that he was engaged in an intrigue against Mozart, or in his making any derogatory comments about his junior musician at court. In fact, Mozart reported that Salieri gave *The Magic Flute* a warm reception. As in the revised play, Salieri did attend a performance of the opera with his mistress. There is no evidence to support rumors that he poisoned Mozart.[13]

One literary source did develop that last theme. *Mozart and Salieri*, a play written by Alexander Pushkin in 1830, has just those two characters and takes place in two scenes. In that plot, Salieri's jealousy of Mozart leads him to poison the man. (Shaffer has said that he did not read that play before writing his own.) In 1897, Nicolai Rimsky-Korsakov turned Pushkin's play into an opera.

Mozart's letters are most revealing about his spirit and his relationship with his family. They also bear out references in the play.[14] He wrote of what "a great chatterbox" (*Letters*, 168) he was and as being "always merry as usual" (*Letters*, 145). His enthusiasm of wanting to kiss the emperor's hand a hundred thousand times is borne out in a letter to his sister requesting that she "kiss Mamma's hands for [him] 1,000,000,000,000 times" (*Letters*, 117). There is also evidence of his facility with languages in another letter to his sister: "Hodie nous avons begegnet per strada Dominum Edelbach, welcher uns di voi compliments ausgerichtet hat, et qui sich tibi et ta mère empfehlen lässt. Addio" (*Letters*, 237). He also deliberately reverses the digits in a number, so that when Constanze was nineteen, he wrote to his father that "my wife is almost ninety-one" (*Letters*, 820). The incident of measuring Constanze's calves also seems to have basis in fact. His letter to Constanze states that "you had let a chapeau [young gallant] measure the calves of your legs" (*Letters*, 802). He alluded to the scene at the masked ball [in the movie] in another letter about dress-up valets.

There is other information from Mozart's letters that appears in the play. For example, on one occasion he wrote his father that the emperor was proposing to establish German opera in Vienna; and on another occasion that Count Rosenberg had issued a commission to hunt for a libretto, and that Stephanie (to whom Shaffer refers in the play), the manager of the opera, had found one. Mozart reported that Stephanie, who was rude and had the worst reputation in Vienna, was friendly to him. A reference to a cabal against the young composer, which Mozart mentions to Salieri in the play, appears in a letter that Leopold wrote to his daughter: "'Le Nozze di Figaro' is being performed on the 28th for the first time. It will be surprising if it is a success, for I know that very powerful cabals have ranged themselves against your brother. Salieri and all his supporters will again try to move heaven and earth to down the opera" (*Letters*, 897). Sophie Haibel (Constanze's younger sister) wrote to Georg Nicholas von Nissen (Constanze's second husband) that Constanze "simply could not tear herself away from Mozart" (*Letters*, 977) as he approached death. Finally, Mozart wrote many letters from 1788 through 1791 to Masonic brother Michael Puchberg, in which he asked for money and referred to his financial straits.

The letters are also revealing regarding Mozart's relationship with his father, apparently quite a dominant man. Mozart attempts to convince his father that "Constanze is a respectable honest girl of good parentage, and I am able *to support her*" (*Letters*, 811). The letter goes on to show that Leopold has expressed reservations about the marriage and has offered what the younger Mozart refers to as "well-meaning advice." It is also apparent from the letter that Mozart was not going to wait for his father's consent to the marriage. Unfortunately, none of the letters that Leopold wrote to his son after 1781 is included in the volumes from which these quotations were taken. However, the father's feelings are easy to imagine by the following letter from his son: "Well, it is over! [He has married Constance without his father's consent.] I only ask for your forgiveness for my too hasty trust in your fatherly love" (*Letters*, 813).

The letters also reveal that Leopold did not hesitate to criticize his son, as Mozart states in the play. On one occasion Leopold expresses how disappointed he is in his son, who is "ready to accept, without due consideration and reflexion, the first wild idea that comes into [his] head or that anyone puts there" (*Letters*, 492); and on another occasion, he admonishes his son *"to endeavor to get to know others through and through"* (*Letters*, 483), especially in Vienna where "the court is packed with people who look on strangers with suspicion and who put spokes in the wheels of the very ablest" (*Letters*, 346). Much of his advice focuses on finances: "Economy is most necessary" (*Letters*, 346); and "Where there is no money, friends are no longer to be found. . . ." (*Letters*, 389). Nor does he hesitate to remind his son of his religious and filial obligations: he must neither become lax about going to confession nor about the welfare of his parents, "or else your soul will go to the devil" (*Letters*, 479–80). He also insisted on being right: *"With regard to October 11th. I must finish my case for the prosecution.* I know that I am right and that you made a mistake . . ." (*Letters*, 330). In some letters to his father, Mozart closed "your most obedient son" (*Letters*, 363).

Admirers of Mozart on both sides of the Atlantic were up in arms about Shaffer's depiction of a man of rough language and coarse actions. Shaffer's source for those characteristics are Mozart's own letters.[15] He did make many undignified and particularly scatological references, of which the following written to his cousin Maria Anna Thekla Mozart, are a few examples: "I shit on your nose and it will run down your chin" (*Letters*, 358); and "Shit-Dibitari, the person at Rodampl, licked his cook's arse, to others as an example" (*Letters*, 644). He addressed her "Dearest Coz Fuzz!" and didn't mind closing: "W.A. Mozart Who shits without a fart" (*Letters*, 104). The names he invented for Rosenberg are not so surprising in the light of the following letter to his father: "A great crowd of nobility was there: the Duchess Smackbottom [incidentally a game he plays with Constanze], the Countess Makewater, to say nothing of the Princess Dunghill. . . . " (*Letters*, 327). There is also a factual basis for the Requiem Mass that the Messenger commissions from Mozart. In reality a Count Welsegg sent a messenger in disguise to Mozart to commission a Mass, and then passed it off as his own work.

Over six years passed between the premieres of *Equus* and *Amadeus*. In light of Shaffer's detailed research and meticulous writing, the lapse in time is not surprising.

The Film

The most familiar version of *Amadeus* is the 1984 motion picture directed by Miloš Forman. After what Shaffer had seen of his earlier plays (especially *Equus*) translated to the screen, he was not anxious to sacrifice *Amadeus* to a similar fate, even for the million dollars he was to receive for writing the script. He reluctantly accepted the offer on the condition that not a line went into the movie unless he and Forman agreed on it.[16] To produce the script, Shaffer and Forman locked themselves away in a farmhouse in Connecticut for four months. Shaffer spent twelve hours a day writing and reviewing his work with the director, and then rewriting. The two artists traveled to Europe to scout out locations for shooting the film. Vienna no longer has an eighteenth-century look, so they decided on Prague, in Forman's native Czechoslovakia, as the site. The Tye Theatre, where *Don Giovanni* was first performed in 1787, is the setting in the film for the performance of *The Marriage of Figaro*. The sixteenth-century Gryspek Palace so impressed both writer and director, that they decided to construct the scene of Mozart's meeting with the emperor around it.

Since Forman believes that a film drinks up music and that there cannot be too much of it, the result is a movie that Shaffer calls a "fantasia on events in Mozart's life."[17] Neville Marriner conducted the Academy of St. Martin-in-the-Fields, with Ivan Moravec at the piano. Music takes precedence over the action in this picture; the scenes were written to complement the music, and not the other way around. Miloš Forman was able to do with *Amadeus* what Sidney Lumet failed to do with *Equus*: he kept it from looking like a filmed play. While Lumet had Richard Burton recite his monologues directly into the camera, Forman had Salieri, played by F. Murray Abraham, make his confession to a priest in the mental hospital to which he is taken after he attempts suicide, the point at which the film begins rather than ends. To prove how Salieri's music has been forgotten in Vienna in his own lifetime, Salieri plays some of his most popular pieces for the priest. The priest fails to recognize any of them, but has no trouble recognizing Mozart's work. Forman was able to have incidents or lines from the play become part of the opera sequences, staged by Twyla Tharp. And so Mozart's life becomes the basis of his art. For example, Katherina Cavalieri's singing lesson with Salieri turns into her showy performance in *Seraglio*—with Mozart conducting. Constanze does not have to confront Mozart about having sex with the women with whom he works; he betrays himself. After the performance, Mozart introduces his fiancée to the emperor. Cavalieri did not know of Mozart's engagement and reacts to the sexual betrayal. In a later scene, after living it up at a brothel, Mozart returns home only to find that his wife has taken off for Baden. Constanze's yapping mother later turns into the Queen of the Night in *The Magic Flute*, and Mozart's and Constanze's PAPAPA game from the play becomes the Papageno-Pagagena duet from the end of the second act in that same opera.

The movie shows what the play only mentions, and soliloquies are replaced by visual images. In the film, the audience sees the two musicians as children: Mozart perform blindfolded for royalty; Salieri shares a picnic with his parents, who aspire only to mediocrity. In the play, Mozart brags about his great ability at billiards while Salieri bemoans the fact that his own most inspired notes cannot approach the quality of his rival's casual compositions. In fact, Mozart composes opera as he rolls a billiard ball around the table. The film also shows him dictating absolutely perfect music from memory, a boast that he made in the play. Constanze's reference in the play to how much Mozart likes to dance becomes a spectacular film scene of a masked ball. The day in which Salieri declares war on God and brings the first act of the play to its dramatic conclusion is summed up in a single image in the film: Salieri removes a crucifix from the wall and throws it into the fire.

The characters and their relative importance in the story undergo a transformation from the play to the motion picture. Martha A. Townsend[18] suggests that the inclusion of the character of the priest as Salieri's confessor is a way of allowing the composer to talk to himself, that is, to reflect on his life. He does not have Greybig or his Venticelli in the film to do his bidding and gather information about the young composer, so he engages a young maid whom he pays to serve the Mozarts. Just as in the play Mozart is anonymously presented a daily supply of wine, so in the film a servant is also provided him, and paid for anonymously. The film leaves out all references to poisoned wine as well as to the Masons.

Shaffer admits that he was less faithful to the historical facts in the film than in the play, and that change is nowhere more evident than in the final sequence, in which Salieri offers to help Mozart complete the

Requiem Mass by working with him all night long. What Salieri is really offering to do is kill the younger composer by working him to death; in Mozart's state of failing health anything but rest can end his life, and Salieri knows that. It may also be the only time in the film that Salieri demonstrates real passion derived, no doubt, as much from observing the process of Mozart's musical genius as from taking an active part in ending Mozart's life. From his bed Mozart dictates notes and Salieri transcribes them. Salieri also intends to pass off the Mass as his own work on the death of his friend. Mozart uses this occasion to instruct Salieri on the proper use of tonic and dominant notes. Again there is a visual—and practical—application of a reference in the play, one in which Mozart criticizes the music of Italian composers for their boring use of tonic and dominant notes, and their apparent fear of complexity in music. Throughout the scene, the theater is filled with the sound of notes that Mozart is dictating. The writing of the Mass turns out to be a self-fulfilling prophecy that Mozart does, in fact, compose for his own death. It also shows that Mozart never distrusts the man who is set on destroying him. He even asks Salieri to forgive *him*.

The movie shifts the focus of attention from Salieri to Mozart and plays up such subplots as Mozart's relationship with vaudevillians, his inability to play court politics, and his relationship with his father. The episode with the vaudevillians shows the playful side of the composer's personality, which reveals itself only with Constanze in the play: the boy now also has drinking buddies. He also goes further than in the play in stepping out of bounds in his comments to members of the court. This time Shaffer has him criticize and argue with the emperor himself. When His Majesty comments that *Seraglio* has "too many notes," Mozart asks arrogantly just which notes he should eliminate. The emperor seems not to take offense: he is a jovial man, who previously asked if he might play Salieri's march of welcome for Mozart's entrance just for fun.

Mozart's relationship with his father is presented through more than just the voice-over letters. Leopold is a character in the movie. The audience now sees him kissing the ring of the archbishop and begging him to forgive his son after their falling-out. As in the letters, Leopold is concerned about his son's finances—and his choice of a wife. At the party during which Constanze allows the men to measure her calves, it is Leopold who is offended by her immodesty, not his son, who tries to explain to his father that it is only a game. Mozart insists on a penalty when it is his turn, and his penalty is appropriately enough a musical one. In part, he plays Salieri's music while he is facing backwards and maintains an expression on his face that makes the court composer look like the "musical idiot" to whom Mozart refers in the play. This scene gives further proof of the musical gymnastics for which Mozart's father trained his son, and to which Salieri also refers on stage. To add insult to the injury he causes Salieri, who has been observing secretly from behind a mask (he is still "Secret Salieri"), Mozart ends his impersonation by making the sound of a fart and driving his audience wild—all at Salieri's expense. The senior Mozart remains unamused by his son's antics, the kind for which the factual father chastised his son in one of his letters. The first appearance of the father on film shows him in the cloak and hat that became the film's logo, as well as the symbol of the Commendatore in *Don Giovanni*. The mask that his father wears to the dance completes the costume that Salieri uses when he commissions Mozart to write the Requiem Mass. In composing *Don Giovanni*, Mozart allows the figure of his father as Commendatore to accuse his son before all the world. In that way, Mozart is able to experience catharsis and free himself from the unresolved guilt that he experiences after his father's death. It is during the performance of *Don Giovanni* that Salieri devises his scheme to have Mozart write the Mass. It sounds, in fact, as if Mozart were composing the Mass for his father: the figure who comes to him says that the Mass is for "a man who deserved a Requiem Mass and never got one."

The character of Constanze evolves from stage to screen just as it grew in the course of the play. She has turned into a young woman who shows much gumption. On her own initiative, without any prodding from Salieri, she takes her husband's music to the court composer in order to further her husband's career—and to see some money come in for the family. There is no attempted seduction, and Constanze trusts Salieri enough to confide in him about her financial problems: money just seems to slip through her husband's fingers, she tells him. She argues with Leopold when she can no longer stand his constant criticism of her; she thinks that her husband has gone mad when he insists on writing music for the vaudeville theater rather than working on the Mass, which is bringing money into the house (she also sees the Masked Figure in the film); and orders Salieri out of the house when she returns from Baden and finds her husband on his deathbed. While on stage, Salieri has only the members of the audience to absolve as representatives of the "mediocrities everywhere"; on film, he has an asylum full of patients to whom he is able to offer absolution from his wheelchair as he giggles on the way to the toilet and makes a sign of self-sanctification. The film won eight

Academy Awards including honors to Shaffer, Forman, and Abraham. It took the "Oscar" for best picture of the year in 1984.

Themes and Motifs

Amadeus is a veritable catalogue of the themes and motifs in Shaffer's dramatic writing throughout his career. References to many of those themes and motifs have already appeared in this chapter's studies of the plot and characters. This section will include others and will fill in additional details. There is a complexity of themes that involves worship and envy, genius and mediocrity, passion and divinity, trust and betrayal, and finally, divine justice. All are intermingled and interdependent. This section attempts to separate as well as integrate them.

Salieri, in his opening monologue, speaks of the function of operas as the "raising of gods," so that is an appropriate place to begin this discussion. There are the eternal gods and legends, the kind that so fascinate Dr. Dysart and control Alan in *Equus*. Here the "god" is music, which is inextricably bound to God, for whom sacred music is written and who disposes who will and who will not compose works to his glory. In the opening moments of the motion picture, the priest tells Salieri: "All men are equal in God's eyes." Salieri finds that statement hard to believe and cynically replies, *"Are* they?" Salieri's driving desire since childhood has been to serve God through music, to have the talent to fulfill that ambition, and to have his work rewarded with fame. It is Salieri's burden in life to have the ambition and to have received rewards for work that does not derive from talent which is divinely inspired nor touched with genius. His work is mediocre.

For Salieri, there is a connection between music and divinity. What he worships is the sound that Mozart can create in his Masonic funeral music; he knows that it is in those notes that God lives. There are three references in the revised version of the play that demonstrate the extreme to which there is identification in Salieri's mind between music and religion. He tells the audience that: "It is only through music that I know God exists. Only through writing music that I could worship" (*AA*, 95). Shaffer's characters know the need for worship and sometimes engage in unconventional practices in its name, from adoration of the sun to sexual acts with a horse. Salieri says too that music is God's art. Every composer who has felt the inspiration to write a Mass or other sacred music has believed that same notion. Salieri also performs an act which shows that not only is music divine, but that Mozart is Salieri's personal god of music: *"He tears off a corner of* [Mozart's] *music paper, elevates it in the manner of the Communion Service, places in his tongue and eats it"* (*A*, 88). Here too, is proof of one critic's assertion that Salieri's machinations are elevated to "metaphysical skirmishes" rather than being "petty jealousy" (Gianakaris 1981, 47). Salieri is prepared to end the war, if only God will enter *him* once. In the final sequence of the film, when Salieri is in Mozart's apartment, the court composer sees the quill pen with which Mozart composes his music and touches it with the reverence usually reserved for sacred objects. And in the music of *Figaro*, Salieri can hear divine absolution. Nowhere else in his work is the playwright so eloquent as in his description of Salieri's reaction (quoted earlier) to the adagio in Mozart's Seranade for 13 Wind Instruments. Salieri, by hearing Mozart's music, receives the vicarious experience of being touched by the divine, much as Dysart is moved by Alan's midnight rides, and Pizarro by Atahuallpa's belief that he is the Son of the Sun. As with Alan's rides on Nugget, the religious and sexual impulses border on each other. What is so painful to Salieri is not just that he does not have the touch of the divine and yet can recognize it when he does hear it, but that it emanates from a filthy-mouthed, irreverent, infantile boor, and not from him, who leads a virtuous life in exchange for the talent to honor God with his music. It just isn't fair. How can a just God choose Mozart and not him? It is what he sees as God's betrayal of him that causes Salieri to declare war on God. While he never received divine reward—only earthly riches—Salieri has received divine punishment for his sins: thirty-two years of obsolescence have been his constant reminder of and torture for his scheme against Mozart. In the movie, Salieri no longer believes that he killed Mozart; he now blames God for the act. Salieri did nothing more than fulfill the Divine Will.

How can Salieri create great music blessed with genius and inspiration when his talents are modest and his life devoid of passion? If Salieri employs nothing in his music but a boring repetition of tonic and dominant notes, it is because his music is a reflexion of his spirit. He is yet another of Shaffer's characters who, like Pizarro, Dysart, Mark Askelon, and later Yonadab, cannot experience passion. At the core of Salieri's struggle with Mozart, or rather with God, is the kind of envy that his lack of passion has inspired in him. There is a twist in this play from the basic situation in *The Private Ear*, *The Royal Hunt of the Sun*, *Equus*, and *Shrivings*, in that only one of the men embroiled in the competition recognizes it. Mozart is largely unaware of what Salieri is trying to do to him.

Perhaps there is some complexity, and a touch of humanity, in Salieri. He claims in the revised version of the play to feel pity for Mozart—the kind of pity that he believes God cannot feel. In saying so, Salieri both sets himself above God and proves once again to be a hypocrite. It is in Salieri's power to stop using Mozart as the battleground in his own war against God. But even if he feels a modicum of pity, the emotion that dominates Salieri is envy—envy of the ability to create music that demonstrates perfection. If Salieri envies Mozart's talent, Mozart envies Salieri's success. The Venticelli report that Mozart doses himself with medicine out of envy of the court composer's success, and for the economic rewards Salieri receives for his compositions. Salieri, in fact, identifies with Mozart, and tells him just before the unmasking: "I eat what God gives me. Dose after Dose. For all my life. His poison. We are both poisoned, Amadeus. I with you: you with me" (*AA*, 88).

Here it is appropriate to discuss the play's title and its relation to the theme. The eighteenth century's great composer was called Wolfgang Amadeus Mozart. (His baptismal name was Johannes Chrysostomus Wolfgangus Theophilus Mozart.) The musician preferred the Latin form Amadeus to its Greek equivalent Theophilus. He also used Amadé and Gottlieb when signing letters. All of these forms translate into Beloved of God. If that translation is the one that Shaffer had in mind, Mozart, and not Salieri, is the center of the play. But Amadeus may also be rendered as Lover of God, which accurately describes the protagonist, at least in the first act of the play. While one critic finds it an "unexpected twist" that Salieri and not Mozart is the narrative focus (Gianakaris 1981, 39) of the play, so it is in *Equus*, in which Alan is a more interesting character to watch than Dysart.

The title *Amadeus* might lead the reader to believe that the play is about a blessing. In fact, it is about Salieri's curse—or better yet, his quadruple curse. Salieri is cursed by a mediocre talent while he aspires to genius; he is cursed with just enough musical ability to recognize Mozart's greatness; he is cursed by the oblivion into which his name falls in his own lifetime. The last is the harshest curse with which Salieri has to live. He admits in the original version of the play: ". . . I cannot accept this sentence. A statue in my hometown. Two lines of reference in books of scholarship" (*A*, 118–19). So Salieri decides to "Starve out the God!" (*AA*, 70). In addition, *Mozart* is cursed by falling under the thumb of the man who is determined to ruin him. While Mozart is dictating the Requiem Mass to Salieri in the movie, the actors from *The Magic Flute* appear at the door to give Wolfgang his share for the performance. Salieri gives the money to his victim and leads him to believe that it came from the mysterious figure, and that Mozart will receive another hundred ducats if he completes the Mass in twenty-four hours. After the interruption at the door, the word with which Mozart continues his dictation is *maledictus*, the curse.

Salieri's final curse is that of not knowing how to forgive. He cannot forgive himself for being mediocre, Mozart for being musically superior to him, or God for being unfair to him. In addition, he also sees Mozart as a man who *does* know how to forgive himself. Mozart is able to create the figure of the Commendatore, who is the great accuser, and then progress to Sarastro, the forgiving father figure in *The Magic Flute*. Thus, Salieri has yet another reason to envy Mozart. And so he attacks Mozart, not just professionally, but also religiously, and with the kind of blasphemy that does not characterize a Lover of God: "God does not love you, Amadeus! God does not love! He can only *use!*" (*AA*, 88). Of course, Salieri is forced to recognize that nothing he did against Mozart was the cause of the younger man's death. He also believes that Mozart did not die from whatever physical ailments he might have had: "The cause of his death is simple. God blew—as He must—without cease. The pipe split in the mouth of his eternal need" (*A*, 116). God needed Mozart as his vessel on earth; when the need for him no longer existed, God ended his life. In addition to just that of teaching God a lesson, Salieri has another reason for wanting Mozart dead: he wants to have some peace in life, and he cannot have it while Mozart lives. If Salieri cannot kill Mozart, he at least wants to reduce him in stature: "Reduce the man, reduce the God" (*AA*, 89). Salieri is able to accomplish that end during the unmasking. He reduces Mozart to a child screaming for and singing to his Papa.

Sooner or later the motif of the father-son relationship emerges in most of Shaffer's plays. This theme has been an unhappy one since the radio play "The Prodigal Father," as well as in many of the plays from *Five Finger Exercise* through *Yonadab. Amadeus* is no exception, and here the situation in the play also existed in real life. But this play unites the theme of jealousy and the motif of the father. Mozart believes of his father that "he's jealous. Under everything, he's jealous of *me!* He'll never forgive me for being cleverer that he is. . . . Leopold Mozart is really just a jealous, dried up old turd . . . and I actually detest him" (*A*, 92). Mozart speaks these words to Salieri, and yet he seems to seek out father figures. Perhaps the reason is that his own father was always so critical of him, wanted him to know his place, and "lectured" him by mail. It therefore is not easy for men in the play to deal with Mozart, because he sees in them substitute fathers. He tells Van Swieten that he reminds him of his father because the Mason brother doesn't understand why Mozart would want to set the "rubbish" in *Figaro* to music. In a positive light, he calls the emperor "Père de tous les musiciens!" (*AA*, 24). Shaffer's Mozart had a relationship with his father that encompassed both love and hate. In the film, Mozart ridicules the picture of his father, but in the play latches onto Salieri as a replacement for his father when Leopold dies. Mozart always believed that he had betrayed his father by talking against him, and feels similar emotions towards Salieri. Shaffer states that he has Salieri offer himself as a father to Mozart as a way of increasing the human contact between them.

Salieri was never completely satisfied with his parents for the same reason that Clive Harrington in *Five Finger Exercise* could not accept his: they embodied mediocrity. While Louise Harrington aspires to social status, Salieri's parents had status quo as their goal. The nature of mediocrity vis-à-vis genius is one of the themes of the play; it is at the core of Salieri's envy of Mozart. Mediocrity, however, is built into Salieri's job as court composer. He has to sacramentalize ordinary persons and compose musical monuments to mundane events. His job is to celebrate average lives. There are touches here of *The Royal Hunt of the Sun*—the desire for immortality, be it in a history book or a musical score. As a child, Salieri saw as miracles the death of his father, and the friend of the family who took him away forever from Legnago to the road that led him to Vienna. To paraphrase Pizarro, his whole life was a road to that day. Salieri had no reason not to leave Italy, because like Mark Askeon, he has no territorial allegiance. He also knows no feeling of patriotism. His sole contact with Lombardy is through sweets.

One final theme worthy of mention is that of trust and betrayal, represented perhaps best in the relationship of Young Martin and Pizarro in *The Royal Hunt of the Sun*. In the progression of the three versions of *Amadeus* from London to New York to Hollywood, Mozart is ever less suspicious of Salieri, and by the film version trusts him completely. Pizarro feels betrayed when Atahuallpa fails to resurrect himself. Mozart feels betrayed by far less than that—because Leopold will not care for his grandson for a few months while Mozart seeks employment, perhaps in London. Ironically enough, it is to Salieri that he complains of betrayal: "In the end, you see, everyone betrays you—even the man you think loves you best" (*A*, 91). That is quite a statement from the man who innocently asks all of the members of the conspiracy against him at court: "We're all friends here, aren't we?" (*AA*, 33). The themes of worship, sex, divinity, envy and rivalry, and the motif of father-son relationships, again dominate the play in *Yonadab*.

Reviews and Critical Analyses

This section will include reviews of the original production in London, on the revised version in New York, commentary in scholarly articles, reviews of the film and video, and an example of the reviews in continental Europe. As is usually the case with Shaffer's plays, the reviewers either loved or hated *Amadeus*. James S. Bost[19] found the original version to be a brilliant version of drama and music in a play that has the symmetry, precision, and elegance of a Mozart symphony. The production, he thought, touches greatness. For R.W. Apple, Jr.,[20] *Amadeus* was nothing less than the "theatrical event of the season"; and for L. Poyser,[21] it was "one of the best theatre productions for many a year," the foul language notwithstanding. Not every reviewer was in agreement with those who were lavish in their praise of the play. James Fenton[22] liked neither the text nor the production: "Appalling new play by author of *Equus*, plasticated production by Peter Hall. Paul Scofield mediocre as Salieri, Simon Callow and Felicity Kendal do their best as the Mozarts." A month later the same reviewer[23] wrote what was little more than an attack on the playwright as well as on the play: he called the play "perfectly nauseating" and now found "appalling" too generous a word for it. He found Mozart depicted with "dreadful and offensive banality" because he is seen through the eyes of a very, very bad dramatist—perhaps the worst serious English playwright since John Drinkwater. The critic for the London *Financial Times*[24] could not find any life in the story and called the project as unimaginative and as "hollow as a strip-cartoon." For the reviewer of *Variety*,[25] the play represented "history as outlandish speculation"; a clever, provocative, and playful "stunt." Benedict Nightingale[26] was moved to ask if the play deserved Paul Scofield's and Peter Hall's considerable talents.

There is substantial attention paid to the level of language in the play. Although Steve Grant[27] accused the play of being "grossly unhistorical" (even if it is "slavishly authentic" in its details), creaking with the mechanics of drama, of being silly and self-indulgent, and occasionally overblown with empty rhetoric ("pure Shaffer"), he does not deny that it is a feast for the ears. In a scholarly article, Michael Hinden[28] calls the language of Shaffer's plays (particularly *The Royal Hunt of the Sun*, *Equus*, and *Amadeus*) "flowing oratory" in speeches that, despite their overabundance of dramatic language and lack of spontaneity, approach music. In a similar vein, Sarah Booth Conroy[29] quotes Jane Seymour (who played Constanze in New York) on the musical qualities of the writing: "It is a fugue. The timing has to be just right. Another character gives you a line. And you come back with your retort. It's like Mozart's music; his music goes up and it comes down and just when you think it's going to end, it crashes and crashes into something else."

American reviewers were generally more impressed by the work than were their British counterparts. Robert Jacobson[30] (who mispells Shaffer's name in *Opera News*) thought that even if the play was not a masterpiece, it makes for an extraordinary evening in the theatre—a fascinating situation, elegant direction, and riveting performances. The difference in reception may have been influenced by the changes Shaffer made to the text. Clive Barnes[31] found it Shaffer's best play to that date, with a text far superior to the one used in London. In a subsequent review,[32] he removed any reservations that he might have had after seeing the London production. Ronald Gelatt[33] was heartened to see that there was still room for a play of ideas; "a brilliantly diverting inquiry into the nature of genius" is what Nicholas Kenyon[34] called it. Even if the play raises more questions than it answers, it remained for Edwin Wilson[35] scene after scene of highly charged drama, "the most ingenious and engrossing theater piece we have seen in some time." The best that Jack Kroll[36] could say was that *Amadeus* is "a brilliant surrogate for 'great' theater." Then there were the reviews in the *Village Voice*. Michael Feingold[37] called Shaffer the real mediocrity, and Julius Novick[38] thought that Shaffer keeps writing the same play—and that it never fails to fascinate. Needless to say, it didn't please John Simon,[39] who was cruel enough to call his review of the "middlebrow masterpiece" "'Amadequus,' or Shaffer Rides Again." There is also no way for Shaffer to please Robert Brustein,[40] who attempted to identify Salieri with the playwright; the review is unfavorable throughout—especially toward Shaffer.

Reviews appeared again after there were changes in the cast: Frank Langella assumed the role of Salieri; Dennis Boutsikaris, Mozart; and Suzanne Lederer, Constanze. Clive Barnes[41] praised Shaffer's consummate skill in creating characters, and his knowledge of music, but also called the playwright Broadway's "top supplier of what might laughingly be called serious plays." Barnes admitted that *Amadeus*, like *Equus*, demands thought on the part of the audience. *Variety*[42] liked *Amadeus* better after the second viewing than after the first and called it "one of the outstanding plays of the recent past, likely to become a permanent addition to the international repertoire." But Stanley Kauffmann[43] called his review in the *Saturday Review* "Shaffer's Flat Notes," because the playwright once again reduced the possibility of large-scale epic with gimmicks. He too called the mediocrity that Salieri addressed at the end of the play its author. In Paris, Roman Polanski played Mozart, as well as directed the play. He is in complete agreement with the playwright that *Amadeus* is an opera in which the monologues are arias and the dialogues duets.[44] One reviewer[45] saw Mozart in French poetic terms as a sort of young Rimbaud, both showy and ill-behaved.

In "A Playwright Looks at Mozart: Peter Shaffer's *Amadeus*," Gianakaris shows himself to be in agreement with reviewers who commented on how Shaffer engages the audience in his plays through a "fascinating conundrum regarding human behavior drawing on the special metaphoric and physical attributes available to the theater" (Gianakaris 1981, 38). He shows, too, why Mozart was such a threat not just to Salieri but also to the whole Viennese musical establishment of the eighteenth century, the Age of Reason, in which Mozart was "an aberration whose potential artistic success became an offense to the grand order of the universe" (Gianakaris 1981, 40). From another perspective, William J. Sullivan[46] blends literature with serious psychology in his approach to the polarity of the two antagonists. Werner Huber and Hubert Zaft (see note 7) analyze the psychological, sociological, theological, and musical dimensions of the relationship between Salieri and Mozart. They also describe Salieri's dual role as the central speaker and detached observer, who serves as mediator between the stage and the audience in the present; and the prominent figure in the events in the past. They believe that Salieri's self-pity is what finally causes his destruction, and that his rebellion against God is no more than a cover-up for his self-hatred. Rodney Simard's[47] approach is at once literary, historical, sociological, and philosophical. He comments: "in his postmodern version of the Faust legend, Shaffer once again returns to materials, examining systems of belief in a situation wherein cause and effect seem to have broken down in a society that assumes just such a system: Salieri's rage emanates from his sense of virtue wronged."

There remains to consider the review of the motion picture. Vincent Canby[48] regarded the film as a major achievement, and thought it more humane than the play. David Ansen[49] saw it as an expansion of the play, from an operatic dance of death to a biography, love story, drama of revenge, and story of a young musical rebel, with Mozart at center stage—a feast for the eyes and ears that makes the point that genius is not always visible to the naked eye. Richard A. Blake[50] saw in the film Shaffer's statement on the human condition: helpless madness. Perhaps the most original approach of all was David Thompson's.[51] He called Salieri the most striking and ambivalent character on film since *Psycho*'s Norman Bates, and then proceeded to compare the two characters. *Opera News*[52] reviewed the videocassette, but took the opportunity to observe that the original production of the play was written with a "theatrically florid style that was also literate, sensitive and intelligent." The reviewer noted that the play was then shortened and modified in a desperate attempt to satisfy "hit-hungry New York," and that the film is no more than a costume parade at the "level of quick-sell pop entertainment." Richard Corliss[53] agreed, and called *Amadeus* an unfilmable play turned into great movie entertainment.

Summation

Mozart's music in general and his operas in particular are an important element in the play. If *Peter Grimes* provides a key for understanding *The Private Ear*, *The Magic Flute* may well serve a similar purpose in *Amadeus*. There are, at the very least, references in that opera that suggest the characters and motivations in the drama. For example, there is the character of Sarastro, who rules the Temple of Wisdom and sings about hypocrites' power. He performs an aria on the manly love and brotherhood that Mozart wanted to depict in his *Seraglio*; the words describe the fraternal love in an order such as the Masons:

> In diesen heil'gen Hallen
> kennt man die Rache nicht,
> und ist ein Mensch gefaleen,
> führt Liebe ihn zur Pflicht.
> Dann wandelt er an Freundes Hand,
> vergnügt und froh ins besser Land.
> In diesen heil'gen Mauern,
> wo Minsch den Menschen liebt,
> kann kein Verräter lauern,
> weil man dem Feind vergibt.

(In these sacred walls we do not know revenge; and when a man has fallen, love comes to his aid. Then a friend's hand guides him, satisfied and happy, to a better land. Within these sacred walls where men love each other, no betrayer lurks; we forgive our enemies.)

In the same opera, the character Tamino reminds Papageno of his duty to obey the Order. Some of Papageno's lines also apply to Shaffer's Mozart: "Ich bin zum Ungluck schon geboren. / Ich plauderte, und das war schlecht, / und drum geschiert es mir schol recht!" (I was really born to bad luck. I chattered away, and that was bad, so I got what I deserved). There is also the aria about vengeance, that the Queen of the Night sings and Monostatos's warning to Pamina: "Mein hass soll dich verderben!" (My hate will ruin you.) Disguises and deception—in a comic manner— dominate *Così Fan Tutte*. The retribution with which Salieri struggles in the final years of his life is also the theme of *Don Giovanni*, in which evil deeds are punished with the fires of hell. The first line of the final chorus of that opera applies to Salieri's situation: "Questo è el fin di chi fa mal!" (This is the end of the evildoer!) What Salieri has done is trade religious belief for an existential hell on earth. In the final scene of the movie *Amadeus*, when Mozart is dictating his Requiem Mass to Salieri, Mozart begins with the words *Confutatis maledictus*. At that point he asks if Salieri believes that a bad man is consigned to eternal flames after his death. Salieri says that he does, and thereby acknowledges that he has condemned himself, through his hate and revenge, to such an eternity. There may also be a passage in *Così Fan Tutte* that foretells Mozart's death: "Questo è il fin di chi fa mal! / E de' perfidi la morte / alla vita è sempre ugual." (This is the end of doers of evil! It is the death of sinners and always will be.)

Did Salieri leave poisoned wine for Mozart, or was he content in tormenting him emotionally? Was the wine that somebody was leaving really poisoned? Was Mozart bedeviled by his financial problems to the point where he could no longer face living? Were the Masons implicated in his death? What exactly did kill Mozart? Shaffer deliberately leaves those questions unanswered, as does history.

Like Dysart before him and Yonadab after him, Salieri is a prisoner. Dysart ends the play by referring to the bit he has in his mouth that will not come out. Yonadab is condemned to a lifetime of hanging from the Tree of Unattachment. Salieri is a prisoner of the self-recognition of his mediocrity and of the reality of his obscurity. While a previous section cited only historical sources for the play, there are also literary and biblical ones. Shaffer's Salieri bears a resemblance to John Milton's Lucifer in *Paradise Lost*, another character who is unable to accept God's supremacy and revolts against it; for this lack of faith he is cast into hell. Lucifer is unable to understand God, and, as a fallen angel, becomes his adversary. Ultimately, he enters into the body of a serpent. Salieri is also a literary echo of Satan in the biblical Book of Isaiah 14: 12– 15: "How art thou fallen from heaven O day-star, son of the morning! How art thou cut down to the nations! And thou saidst in thy heart, I will ascend into heaven, I will exalt my throne above the stars of God; and I will sit upon the mount of congregation, in the uttermost parts of the north; I will ascend above the heights of the clouds; I will make myself like the Most High. Yet thou shall *be* brought down to Sheol, to the uttermost parts of the pit." The chorus of boys (Die Knaben) in *The Magic Flute* sing of mortals who will become like the gods. That is the theme of Shaffer's next play, *Yonadab*, in which Isis and Osiris (of whom Sarastro in *The Magic Flute* is the High Priest) are the prototypes of mortals' ambitions to achieve divinity.

Chapter Eight
Yonadab

Yonadab, like *Shrivings*, exists in two different forms. The text of the play that was produced in London has not been published; the published text has not yet been staged. The play opened in Olivier Hall of the National Theatre on 4 December 1985 and later went into repertory there. As with *Amadeus*, Sir Peter Hall directed the work and John Bury designed the sets and lighting. Dominic Muldowney composed the musical score. Alan Bates originated the role of Yonadab, subsequently assumed by Patrick Stewart, who created the part of King David. Wendy Morgan played Tamar. Leigh Lawson and Anthony Head played the roles of Amnon and Absalom, respectively. For reasons mentioned later in this chapter, the play never reached New York. The point of departure for the story is chapter 13 of the Second Book of Samuel. The immediate source is Dan Jacobson's 1970 novel, *The Rape of Tamar*, to which the production was almost slavishly faithful. As in the chapter on *Amadeus*, this chapter will examine the original text and then the changes in the revised version. This study will examine the play's structure, plot, and characters, and relate them to themes, motifs, and techniques in the plays already discussed, and will show that despite the aforementioned source, *Yonadab* too bears Peter Shaffer's inimitable mark.

Set, Structure, and Plot

As in *Equus*, the set of *Yonadab* is sparse, and as in *The Royal Hunt of the Sun*, it represents an exotic culture. Here, through minimal use of props, the set evokes "the remote and primitive culture of David's Kingdom,"[1] three thousand years ago. The playwright suggests that the various locations of the throne room and Amnon's and Absalom's residences be indicated by means of different-colored awnings. The main props are rugs, cushions, lamps burning naked flames, and braziers; also, curtains, and Amnon's bed. The playwright indicates that there should be a sky to show blazing noons, sunsets, and starry nights. Except for two scenes in the countryside and one in a great tent, the action takes place in

Jerusalem. The structure of *Yonadab* is very much like that of *Equus* and *Amadeus* in that the protagonist is also the narrator of the work. It is closer to *Equus* than *Amadeus* in form, because the narration occupies the same time frame as the action, and is not presented in flashback. Like these other two plays, it is written in two acts, which are subdivided into scenes to indicate a change of time, place, or action. As in *Amadeus*, each act in *Yonadab* begins with a monologue of introspection, presents others throughout the play, and ends with yet another such monologue. Analyses of the monologues will appear in this book's sections on characters and themes.

After Yonadab's monologue of introduction, in which he calls himself a "special correspondent," he states that he is the nephew of King David, and that the play is about unnatural acts—incest, rape, and murder; struggles between fathers and sons; and fraternal rivalries. That said, Yonadab introduces the players, who are already assembled on stage and ready to have lunch as a family. First, he presents his father, Shimeah, brother of the king; then the king himself; finally the king's children: Amnon is the debauched first-born son, heir apparent to the throne. Absalom, for his physical beauty, is the king's favorite son, the man Shimeah believes will inherit the throne. The others—Adonijah, Cheleab, Ithream, Shepatiah, and the youngest boy, Solomon—appear on stage but take no part in the plot. This is also true of Bathsheba, the queen, but not of Tamar, the king's only daughter, one of the major players in the drama. Priests, servants, bodyguards, and musicians come and go. The early scenes show Shimeah's lowly position at court, and how totally ignored Yonadab is by all but Amnon, who calls him a friend. The relationships between the two fathers and their children, the princes and the princess, and Amnon and Yonadab are also subjects for subsequent sections. On the day in question, Amnon tells Yonadab to visit him that evening, and he will not be put off by Yonadab's lame excuse that he must tend to family business.

Befitting the ritual significance of meals in the Jewish tradition, Yonadab says that everything important in the play takes place during meals. After the king has made his entrance and the family has sat down to eat, David blesses the bread and adds his own blessing toward brothers who eat together in peace and who have no secrets from each other in their hearts. There is polite table conversation about each other's health, about the length of Absalom's handsome hair, and about how long it has been since the king has been in the countryside, where his subjects ache to see him. Absalom hopes that this is the year his father will accept his invitation to come to Baal Hazor for the sheepshearing. David, Yonadab observes, is far too canny to leave the capital. The king begs his daughter to honor the table with a song, but she is stubborn and refuses to grant her father's request until she hears that her brother Absalom would also like to hear her sing. It does not take much cajoling to get the king to accompany his daughter on the lyre. When Amnon almost faints and knocks over a dish because Tamar's veil brushes against him, the princess sulks and refuses to continue.

The scene shifts to Amnon's house, where he is clearly upset. He grabs a knife and begs Yonadab to cut off his genitals. Only that act will keep Amnon from having the sinful thoughts that have been tormenting him for a month. He wants to have sex with his half-sister Tamar. (The conversation in which Amnon makes this revelation to Yonadab is reminiscent of the interplay through which Dysart tries to learn Alan's secret.) A magician that Amnon consulted in secret told him that it is possible that the lustful demon entered his body when he saw Tamar smile innocently at him, and then snap her fingers. Amnon wishes he were dead, and if he acts on his illicit desires he may be: the penalty for incest is stoning. Amnon's predicament sets Yonadab's imagination in motion. He tempts Amnon, just as the serpent tempted Eve in the Garden of Eden. He says that not only is Amnon allowed to have intimate knowledge of his sister, but that it is ordained that he do so; it is his obligation as a prince to know sexual secrets forbidden to lesser men, and to join the ranks of Isis and Osiris, Akhenaton and Nefertiti, Tammuz and Ishtar: all brothers and sisters, and also kings and queens, who become gods and goddesses after their sexual unions. Yonadab tells Amnon that he must agree not to repeat anything that he has told the prince. Furthermore, he has a plan to turn Amnon's fantasy into a reality, but first Yonadab must leave for a week in the country. Like Pizarro, who holds Atahuallpa prisoner, Yonadab has a prince's destiny in his hands.

Yonadab lets one week turn into two before he returns to Amnon. As Yonadab had planned, the interim gave Amnon plenty of time to stew in his anxiety, a method that Dysart used to get Alan to talk. By now, Amnon is highly disturbed, unkempt, and barely in control of himself. But Yonadab makes Amnon believe that he has changed for the better, and that there is now a sense of wonder in his princely cousin. This sense of wonder is Yonadab's fabrication, and Amnon's babbling about achieving divinity through sexual union with his sister is the result of a week-long fast in which nothing but water passed through his lips—and of having had the time to assimilate into his own thinking the words with which Yonadab left him. And now Yonadab has a plan, elegant in its simplicity, to get Tamar into Amnon's bed. Amnon must feign being sick, and since he has been away from court for two weeks, he will be able to get his worried father to do anything to help him. That anything is to send Tamar to nurse him back to health, as she does for her father, whom she is able to restore to health by preparing her special pancakes. Through the kind of miracle that got Salieri out of Legnago, and the emperor to attend the rehearsal of *The Marriage of Figaro*, Amnon really does fall ill—probably self-induced through the power of suggestion— and he knows that the pay-off for his suffering will be a powerful one.

The king is filled with grief over his son's condition, and also with guilt for having thought that Amnon has not been at court because he was out drinking and whoring. The overwrought father is prepared to do whatever it takes to restore Amnon's health—even send Tamar to care for him. The royal physician gives Amnon a potion to make him sleep, so now both father and son can rest easy until the morning. Amnon sleeps for seventeen hours with Yonadab at his bedside, as the prince ordered. Amnon feels unworthy of having a father who thinks of everything. He awakens totally renewed and unwilling to mention the events that Yonadab has planned for that evening. If the act itself is no longer taboo for Amnon, discussing it is. He plans to fast all day in thanksgiving for his recovery and to sit in the sun: "It will restore me completely. Get me up" (1.7). Amnon cannot resist asking if Yonadab is jealous, and thereby gives his cousin the opportunity to broach the subject that may very well be Yonadab's motive in setting up the seduction: "You are about to commit one of the great forbidden acts—and all I can do is look on . . . That's all lesser men can do. Of course I'm jealous" (1.7).

And now he must ask the question: Will Amnon let him watch? It would not be the first time that Amnon has indulged him in this way. Despite Yonadab's assurances that he will remain out of sight, Amnon will not hear of it: "That was a screw. . . . This is a sacred act" (1.7). Just as Bob threw out Ted for betraying their friendship, so Amnon orders Yonadab out of his house. Yonadab tries to convince the prince that he owes him that much for having set up the whole affair, but succeeds in doing nothing but angering Amnon so much that the prince threatens to beat Yonadab with his belt. At that very moment Tamar arrives, beautifully clothed in rich silks and with eyelids powdered with malachite. She assures her brother that in her hands he will be completely cured tonight. Unfortunately for Amnon, she has her servant with her, which works to Yonadab's advantage. Amnon has no choice but to allow his cousin to watch the night's events if Yonadab can get rid of Micah, the servant. But Tamar needs her maid's help with the preparation of the food: "I cannot make batter myself, Amnon: that's servant's work" (1.7). Yonadab intervenes and through lies and flattery makes Tamar believe that it is her father's will that she serve her brother alone: "It was the particular wish of your father that you serve the Prince without assistants. We believe that he has a royal affliction which only someone of royal blood can tend. . . . It was my understanding that none of your assistants must remain" (1.7). At that point Micah insists that it would be unheard of to leave her mistress, that she would be whipped for doing such a thing. Amnon takes his clue from her last statement and tells her that she will be whipped if she stays. And now Micah makes a drastic error by saying that she would not leave even if the Princess ordered it. Tamar slaps her face and orders her out. Now Amnon betrays his promise to Yonadab, who is to escort Micah back to the palace personally. And Yonadab betrays the prince; he uses his usual lie of pressing family business, flattery, and a bribe to get Micah to see herself back to the palace. Then Yonadab slips back into Amnon's house and hides himself behind a huge stone vase from which he can look into Amnon's bedroom. He can also hear every word that brother and sister are saying. He hears Tamar say that she hates Amnon and would like to hang him up by his ears because he's always sneering, and that he is a worse bitch than any girl.

Amnon dismisses his own servants, and Tamar begins to sing and to cook her special pancakes for her brother. The manner in which the hidden Yonadab reports the preparation of the food is one link between this play and others by Shaffer: "What first happened was a smell. Vapour of olive oil from a pan: grated fruit from another—then mixed with honey and coriander. (AMNON GIVES A LOW MOAN). And now a sound: sizzle as each pancake was dropped into the skillet and favoured with a spoonful of the sweet mixture at the sweet hands of the girl. (AMNON GROANS LOUDER). . . . Sizzle and smell and song . . . (HE WRITHES AND GROANS LOUDER, FINALLY SHOUTING) *Tamar!*" (1.7). The most immediate antecedents for those lines are in *Amadeus*: they show a reaction (and a structure) similar to Salieri's when he hears Mozart's serenade; they also reflect his reactions, which border on sexual stimulation, when he is in the immediate presence of sweets. The writhing and groaning bear a resemblance to Alan's reaction as he rides Nugget at the end of the first act of *Equus*. There is yet another connection—this one with the film made from *The*

Private Ear, called *The Pad (And How to Use It)*. In it, there is a scene on food's erotic value. Part of Ted's technique in seducing Doreen is to prepare and eat dinner with her. They are having chicken, and Ted has to choose between the leg and the breast—a difficult choice for him. The manner in which both eat the food is no less than sexual foreplay.

In *Yonadab* the food has an aphrodisiac effect on Amnon, both because Tamar is preparing it and because he knows that it is only a suggestion of what else the night holds in store for him. Unfortunately for Tamar, she inadvertently reinforces his expectations: " 'Here—foretaste of things to come!' (SHE LIGHTLY RUBS HER HONEYED FINGER ON HIS LIPS)" (1.9). Without knowing what she is letting herself in for, Tamar innocently makes some other mistakes. She giggles when Amnon says that he will protect her in the absence of any servants; she brings up the subject of all of his women; she consents to sit next to him on his bed; she smiles when he compliments her eyes—"two priceless jewels"—and she puts her hand over his mouth to stop him from talking blasphemy. Her biggest mistake is not getting out of the house when he tells her that she is his sickness and that he wants her to be his wife. She is horrified by his talk of incest and tries humoring him, but by that time it is too late. There is no mistaking that what finally occurs is a rape: "He grabs her—pulls her back. She breaks towards the bed. He turns, furious, and slowly advances" (1.9). Her pleas that he not rob her of a chance to marry and not ruin her life are to no avail, nor are her attempts to leave the scene: "Amnon hurls himself forward and seizes her. He thrusts a hand over her mouth—pinions her—and together they sink down to the floor." And yes, Yonadab observes every move.

Amnon betrays Yonadab again and slowly draws the curtain across the bed, thus frustrating Yonadab by allowing him to see no more than the silhouettes of their bodies. He can hear Amnon's "groans of physical victory," but he cannot observe the act, which is supposed to make Amnon divine. Yonadab is as disappointed as was Pizarro when Atahuallpa failed to resurrect himself. He is not the only one who is disappointed. Amnon is shattered when the act that was supposed to make him a god turned out to be "just another fuck"—which is all he wanted until Yonadab filled his head with thoughts of divinity. To add psychological abuse to the physical injury that Amnon has already caused his half-sister, he blames her: it is somehow *her* fault that she did not turn him into a god. All he can figure out is that the "wicked bitch" must have used witchcraft on him—why else would he have been willing to touch her? Unlike *Equus*, in which the first act ends with Alan's masturbatory ride on Nugget, the curtain does not fall with the rape, nor with the violent accusations against Tamar. He spits at her feet and orders her out of the house as he would any other whore. But still the act does not end. It continues until the audience sees Tamar's reaction to all that has just happened to her, and so it is in the reaction rather than the action that the key to the next act resides.

Alone at dawn, Tamar walks through the labyrinth of streets. She is not the Princess of Israel at this moment—she is a violated, defiled, and frightened young woman, whose chances for happiness have been destroyed. She can't even scream when she opens her mouth. She knows what little sympathy a woman in her situation can expect to receive, if she can even get anyone to believe that she was really raped, so she begins an act of self-abasement. She mimes scooping up dust from the ground and pours it over her head; she dirties herself with chicken droppings and gashes her cheeks with a stone. Now that she looks like she has been through a gruesome, physical ordeal, she can bring herself to tell passersby: "I am Tamar, daughter of the King. My brother Amnon has raped me and thrown me in the street" (1.11). Over and over she repeats the words until they take on a musical rhythm, picked up by the onlookers, the voices of the city, in a manner reminiscent of both the Venticelli in *Amadeus* and Alan's chant as he rides Nugget. As if led by destiny, Tamar finds herself at the home of her brother Absalom. He puts his cloak around her, draws her gently to him, and kisses her on the brow as the lights go down on the first act.

The second act begins, as did the first, with a lengthy monologue spoken by Yonadab. The subject matter of that speech is better analysed in the sections of this book on characters, themes, and techniques. As he finishes speaking, the lights come up on the throne room; it is noon of the day on which the first act ended. Absalom is crying out for justice for his sister: he demands that Amnon be put to death like the beast he is. The king is trying to be calm and speak moderately to his son, who has now been ranting for an hour. The king wants to know, first of all, where Tamar is, and when he learns that she is at Absalom's house he is offended that she did not come to her father for comfort and support. King David feels shamed by her actions, and Absalom is exasperated by his father's inability to understand that it is *she* who is shamed and ashamed. David is astute and suspicious of Absalom's motives: Could he be trying to eliminate his rival for the throne? Absalom insists that his interest is in seeing that his father uphold the law; if his father will not uphold the law, no one else will either. But the king will not allow his son to dictate to him. He is being more of a father than a king when he says: "Amnon is my son, and I will decide his fate" (2.2). He makes Absalom swear that he will not harm Amnon in any way. Absalom does so, but vows that Amnon will never sit on the throne.

Absalom summons Yonadab to his house and demands to know what part he played in the rape. Yonadab denies any involvement, and Absalom's bodyguards are unsuccessful in beating the truth out of him. Yonadab goes to Amnon's house in the hope that his friend will show enough loyalty to protect him. Yonadab tries to convince Amnon to go to Absalom and throw himself at his brother's mercy; Absalom will have no choice but to grant forgiveness as proof of his royal character. But Amnon wants Yonadab to go as his ambassador. Yonadab tantalizes Amnon by telling him that no one sees Absalom, who is shut up in the house with Tamar. Amnon wonders if perhaps it is they—Absalom and Tamar— who are ordained to become divine through forbidden sexual union. Amnon's plan is for Yonadab to forgive Absalom for his beating, and then beg forgiveness for Amnon. And Yonadab feels something compelling driving him to Absalom.

Yonadab delivers Amnon's message—or a version thereof—begging Absalom to whip him (Amnon) and stand on his face, but to spare his life. That is the lesser of the two ways in which Yonadab betrays his cousin; Yonadab also declares to Absalom that he is now ready to serve him instead of his brother. Absalom is no dummy and observes: "Men get the friends they deserve. Betrayers get betrayed" (2.9). And once again Yonadab tries to play the game that failed so miserably last time; he plants the word *ordained* in Absalom's mind. Something drives Yonadab to Absalom. "I had to see him. I had to see them both! . . . An excitement was taking me over such as I'd never known with Amnon" (2.15). It is probably something more compelling than Absalom's physical beauty that attracts Yonadab to him; it is the appeal of being responsible for the mating of a full brother and sister rather than just the half-siblings that Tamar and Amnon are. He tells Absalom that Amnon believes that he was ordained to be with Tamar as husband and wife. He tempts Absalom with the pitch about being chosen to share in divinity. And he succeeds. Absalom wants to know the signs of proof of the terms of such ordination, and Yonadab tailors the answer to fit Absalom. The prince must be a virgin, as Absalom is.

During this conversation, a new Tamar enters the scene. She is more beautiful than ever before and speaks with great gentleness. She still totally ignores Yonadab. She does confirm, however, and Absalom later acknowledges, that Yonadab told lies in the matter of the rape. With that issue settled, Yonadab feels free to tell Absalom that he is choosing his princely cousin for higher things—things he read in wicked books, forbidden by the priests. Given that Tamar's steps were "guided" to Absalom's house after the rape, they are ordained to rule as equals. The discussion leaves Absalom trembling with excitement. The following scene shows how Tamar has Absalom eating not just figuratively, but also literally, out of her hand. The two agree that they cannot trust Yonadab. The plot thickens when Tamar relates a dream in which she and her brother ride into the city demanding justice. Her words echo others that Yonadab once spoke, and Tamar is moved to ask Absalom: "What if he's been sent to us—like a Messenger" (2.11). And Absalom relates the dream that he has had every night since Tamar came to him. Absalom wants to be Tamar's husband now, but she will not consent until he kills Amnon. He, of course, took an oath before his father not to do so.

In a turn of events that Absalom could not have expected, Yonadab volunteers to kill Amnon for him. Absalom has to refuse the offer since to accept it would be an act of cowardice on his part, and the guilt would still be with him. Yonadab advises Absalom to get Amnon out of Jerusalem for the murder, and Absalom vows to his sister that the moment Amnon dies, his bodyguards will become hers and only she will be allowed to command them—and that soon she will be a new kind of queen.

Back at the royal palace, Absalom begs forgiveness from his father for his stubbornness, and once again asks him to come to Baal Hazor as proof that he has forgiven his son. Once again the king declines. At that point, Absalom announces that Amnon will be the guest of honor as proof that Absalom has forgiven his brother. Amnon is, of course, suspicious of the invitation that Yonadab conveys to him; Yonadab lies that he begged to be invited also, but this is, after all, an event between princes. There is no doubt in Yonadab's mind that the event will end in Amnon's death. And he is content. At Baal Hazor Absalom has Amnon send away his servants, and invites him to dance. On Absalom's nod, his bodyguards lunge their spears at him. No sooner is Amnon dead than Tamar turns away from Absalom and disappears. She too lied to Absalom. The servants bring the news that all of his sons have been put to death by Absalom. But Yonadab saves the day. He tells the king that the news is not true, and that Amnon alone is dead.

Yonadab finds Tamar alone in the countryside and he is alarmed that Absalom is not with her. From her the audience learns the aftermath of the murder of her half-brother. She never intended to have Absalom as her husband, and after the evil deed told him to run into the desert and die. And now Yonadab, who has betrayed everyone else in the play, betrays himself. He shouts at her the words "one more fuck," and Tamar knows where he must have heard them. She lets him know that she never had the dreams she claimed, and that from the start she sought out Absalom to destroy him. She didn't get to Absalom's home by magic, exactly; her maid pointed it out on the way to Amnon's. She also lets Yonadab know that he may as well run off somewhere too, because he has no life left in Jerusalem.

The closing moments of the play show Tamar's new-found feminism; commentary on that aspect of the play will appear later in this study. She does have the satisfaction of knowing that she gets to treat her (male) bodyguards as dogs, and that some women will respect her in a very special way. It was because of her—a woman—that Amnon's body returned to Jerusalem slung over a mule, and with dung falling into its mouth. The last scene functions as an epilogue, much as in *The Royal Hunt of the Sun*, to let the audience know what happened after the principal action of the play. Tamar, in a stylized gray wig, beats the ground with her hand as she intones: "And Tamar the Princess took a timbrel in her hand, and sang unto the women of Israel! . . . Behold the Prince was cast down! . . . His head was shattered as a winepot. Yea—as a winepot is broken on stones! The feet of the mule did trample: the feet of his sister made dance!" (2.20). Absalom died as he was fleeing from his father—his hair got caught in a tree, and he was hanged. And King David mourned, far more for Absalom than for Amnon. As for Yonadab, he hangs forever from the metaphorical "Tree of Unattachment," and no one cuts him down.

Characters and Themes

In many of Shaffer's plays (notably *The Royal Hunt of the Sun, Shrivings, Equus* and *Amadeus*), the characters, especially the protagonists, are closely bound to the play's themes. In *Yonadab* the individual characters so completely embody the themes of the play, it would be forcing the issue to attempt to discuss characters and themes in separate sections. For that reason the characters, as individuals and in their relations with each other and their motivations, as portrayed in the production at the National Theatre, are analyzed together within this section. It is also in this section that those characters and themes are placed in the context of and related to the works that preceded *Yonadab*. The next section will deal with the revised version.

Yonadab is the most complex character in Peter Shaffer's dramatic repertoire. He is, perhaps, too complex, and therefore his motives are not always clear, and seem to contradict each other. He is driven by a need for acceptance (and for being taken seriously), as well as by envy and a desire to revenge his rejection; he has a need for belief—worship—and for a glimpse at divinity so that he can believe in something. At the core of his problem, as he reveals late in the play, is his need to please and win acceptance from his father. All of these motives have appeared previously in Shaffer's plays. It is as important to consider Yonadab's relationship with himself as well as with the other characters.

The English transliteration of the Hebrew word used to describe Yonadab in the Bible is *khokhom*. There is considerable latitude in translating the term. It can mean intelligent or scholarly. Shaffer used a translation from the other end of the spectrum—subtle or cunning, the same words used in English to describe the serpent in the Garden of Eden. There is as much ambiguity in the character as in the word, which has a variety of translations. Just as Salieri soon expects to be, like the members of *Amadeus*'s audience, Ghosts of the Future, Yonadab thinks of himself as already dead—and spiritually he is: "That's my life now I'm dead. Tied to telling the same tale over and over" (1.1). He thus links himself immediately with other Shaffer characters who came before him. Salieri tells his tale over and over, as does his valet Greybig. Old Martin's life consists of telling the story of Pizarro, and he is as dead to any feeling and meaning in his life as Martin Dysart and Mark Askelon are.

The first motive that Yonadab admits to is that of his desire to have revenge against the king, who never took seriously Shimeah's suggestion that his son Yonadab might be a prospect for marriage to Tamar. When the king dismissed the idea out of hand, Yonadab became bitter and jealous of the members of the court who dismissed him so easily. The king's response did nothing for the self-esteem of one who acknowledges himself as a low man with low insights. He knows, too, that he lacks credulity, and he blames that trait on the lack of women in his life. This last trait is one that he shares with Clive Harrington and Bob. Alan's is the most extreme case; there is a woman present, but Alan is not psychologically equipped to establish a relationship with her. Yonadab's source of sustenance, like Dysart's and Julian's, is other individuals' mysteries.

Yonadab is critical of both Jews and Jewish Law. He refers to Jews sarcastically as the "Top People in the world" (1.3) and the "absolute darlings of a single absolute Deity" (1.4), and says that they stole everything beautiful in their culture from the more creative neighboring nations. He criticizes everything from the dietary to their sexual laws. He complains that the priests who determine what may or may not be eaten do not have the slightest knowledge of gastronomy. He also wonders out loud if the God of the "Stone commandments enforced by stoning" (2.21) has any qualities other than wrath and revenge—as with Alan's judgmental and vengeful Equus. He condemns Israel for giving an infants' nostrils first smell the smoke of sacrificed animals, and their ears' first sound the war-call of the rams' horns. It was Judaism's turn to bear the brunt of Shaffer's antireligious sentiment, just as the Catholic Church was criticized in *The Royal Hunt of the Sun*, as was Christian fundamentalism in *Equus*. He mentions that "the yapping prohibitions of the Priests might just have led me to lie with some fellow a little prettier, just for the defiance of it" (1.3). There seems to be some ambiguity about Yonadab's sexuality in the other references that he makes too. For example, he talks of being attracted by both "the dark animal [Amnon] and the light [Absalom]," focusing entirely on their physical characteristics; furthermore, he describes the latter as "that older boy you worshipped at school—the one you longed to notice you: frank eyed, good at games, streaming all day with idealism" (1.2). But Yonadab's sexuality really is not a major issue in the play, unless it is the real motive behind his wanting to watch the sexual act Amnon forces on Tamar. He is accustomed to hearing about Amnon's latest women, and just as uninterested as Harold is in hearing Brindsley's tales in *Black Comedy*.

Amnon's sexual drives *are* important in the play, and Yonadab uses them to have revenge. He is able to use Amnon (as much as Amnon uses him) because he has managed to win the prince's trust. Trust and betrayal by so-called friends were themes in all of the one-act plays except *Public Eye*. The themes also figured in *The Royal Hunt of the Sun* and *Amadeus*. In *Yonadab*, misplaced trust brings about the destruction of the royal family. In part it is Yonadab's cunning, but equally at fault is Amnon's naïveté in trusting a man to the point of calling him the best friend any man has had since the Day of Creation. Amnon needs to believe that such is the case, so that he can unburden himself about the dark secret and forbidden passion that burns within him, and he abuses that trust in order to satisfy his own needs.

Another such need is belief. Yonadab says, "I believe in nothing" (1.1). He has in him the same kind of void that plagued Pizarro, Mark Askelon, and Martin Dysart: "I can endorse no single creed I have ever observed anybody else professing. I had never been able to commit this self to one idea or cause outside it—and even less to one person" (1.1). No, he is not a man who can extend friendship or accept religion. And that is his next problem: Yonadab desperately needs and wants to believe. He envies the men around him who can prostrate themselves in prayer and believe that someone is listening to their pleas. All Yonadab can do is simulate prayer and belief. But if he truly believes in nothing, how can Yonadab say that the play's events are ordained, and that his plots and plans are to no avail?

Yonadab is successful in creating belief in Amnon. He convinces his cousin that his sexual union with his sister will turn both partners into gods. Despite the fact that Yonadab knows that he has fabricated this entire nonsense, he starts to believe it himself. His need is to have a glimpse at divinity compels him to watch the rape. For once he is not interested in looking at bodies, but in seeing inside skulls, in experiencing vicariously what feeling individuals know directly. He is a biblical-era Dysart: "What could I see remotely commensurate with what was happening inside his skull? Inside hers I could just imagine: dimness—shock waves—finally perhaps a kind of numbed accomodation" (1.9).

What Yonadab can understand is the spiritual pain that Amnon suffers over what turned out to be "just another fuck": "This is the worst pain he can know. To recognize his own mundane, immutable human-ity" (1.9). He understands that pain so well because it is at the core of his existence. What Yonadab wishes for is some way to escape from the "basic entanglement with being human" (1.1). Life for him is empty and meaningless. The letters of the Hebrew alphabet serve as a metaphor for that essential lack of meaning: "Study these letters slowly forming words: dissolving to make others, others and others. They [the lovers] are like the consonants on some Hebrew parchment—hoops and humps—squirms and squiggles—indecipherable without the dots and dashes which are the vowels. And what vowels of imagination can I insert to make these consonants of flesh yield even remotely the meaning they have for him who forms them so compulsively? . . . You have entered in fact into Yonadab's world, my friends—watching experience as a dog watches a newspaper: seeing the signs for things: perpetually illiterate" (1.11). Yonadab is, so to speak, a spiritual and emotional "illiterate." He can watch, but not comprehend. He can make no meaning out of or give any meaning to life. He aspires to do so by being the cause of something monumental.

Yonadab's dealings with Amnon and Tamar lead to the prince's death. But Yonadab believes that he has done Amnon a good turn because he had a death that the world will remember: "You didn't just slide into oblivion. . . ." (2.7). Yonadab managed to keep Amnon from suffering the fate that plagued Salieri. If, in Amnon's eyes, Tamar is responsible for not transforming him into a god, Yonadab levels a similar accusation against Amnon: "That's why I ran from you, Amnon. That's why I had you killed in the end. Just for that! For one more fuck. . . . You deserved to die, Amnon! Because you were human forever!" (2.7).

Amnon's relationship with Tamar in the play is mostly limited to the rape. The Bull (as his father calls him) is in his late twenties, and behaves something like Mozart: he is maladroit and ill at ease. He is the king's spoiled son. His emotional disturbance is as difficult for him to conceal as Dysart's. He is, in a way, Yonadab's spiritual double, since both men think that they are dead. Amnon became a slave to Tamar in much the same way that Salieri became a slave of Mozart's music—it happened instantly. For Salieri, it took only a few notes of Mozart's adagio, and for Amnon, the snapping of Tamar's fingers. Amnon could never reveal that what he felt for her was sexual desire, so Yonadab cloaked those base feelings in lofty mysticism for him. Amnon uses an anti-Jewish attitude that he probably learned from Yonadab to tempt Tamar to be his wife. He tells her that in Israel she is considered beneath him, and that Judaism admits no female spirit. It is impossible to know if Amnon was a blasphemous person before he fell under Yonadab's spell, but he certainly is by the night of the rape. He tries to point out to Tamar the shortcomings of Judaism as compared to heathenism: "You prayed to a tree and it rustled for you—its blossoms scented you more if you stroked it! . . . there was no voice saying 'Forbidden!—I am a jealous God!' That's what we brought to the world. Javeh the Jealous. And all our natural loves are tied up tight" (1.9). Amnon's imagery is sexual, and his view of God negative. He is an ancient Alan who has confused the two concepts in his mind. Amnon's vision of the Hebrew God is the model for Alan's concept of Equus. As Amnon sees no gentleness in the Jewish God, so Alan saw no forgiveness in his horse/god. Having abandoned the ethical beliefs of Judaism, Amnon can proceed with ruthless abandon in his savage violation of his sister.

King David, whose sole function in the play is that of a father, may be partly responsible for Amnon's actions. Amnon is not a sensitive musical lad (like Clive and Bob), yet King David encourages his son in his sexual exploits and seems proud of them: "Your eyes are not clear. Have you perhaps been drinking? (AMUSED). Or something else, eh—eh, eh? . . . Amnon the Bull, ha? . . . Amnon the bad bull! (HE CHUCK-LES DELIGHTEDLY) (1.2). During Amnon's illness, David is absolutely overcome with guilt: "My fault. My fault and my sin. Behold it. Over and over these seven days, when this boy still did not appear at Court, I said to everyone: 'He is drinking. He is whoring. My son is vicious.' And all the time I cursed him, he was growing sick: Observe all of you the injustices of a father. So I am punished. Rightly—punished. . . . You have a wicked father, Amnon! A selfish, wicked father! . . . I'm unworthy to have good children" (1.6).

Their father may also be responsible for the friction between Amnon and Absalom. As King David praises Amnon's sexual prowess, so is he lavish in his praise of tall, handsome, and virile Absalom: "I declare before all—this is the most beautiful man of the whole tribe" (1.2). David adores Absalom, even if he fears his ambitions for the throne. He cannot restrain himself in his demonstration of affection for the young man who is twenty-five in this version, twenty-two in the revision: "Come here—to my heart! Hear how it beats for you. . . . Who would believe such a beauty could come from the loins of an ugly thing like me?" (1.2). When Absalom returns to the court from Baal Hazor despite the rumor that he is dead, David is so relieved that he asks that his eyes be closed forever if he is ever angry with his son again. He enfolds him in his arms and kisses him on the mouth. After Absalom's death the king is in such grief that he wishes he had died in his son's place. The father's special source of pride is Absalom's long and handsome hair, about which he goes on and on. It is the final irony that David should cause Absalom's death by pursuing his son, whose hair catches on the branch of a tree. Yet, when Absalom demands Amnon's death, King David cannot help but suspect his motive: "So that there may be one less rival for the throne?" (2.2). And when David sees that his eldest son is becoming jealous, he reassures him: "I love you as deeply as only a father can love his first-seen son!" (1.2). Nor does he omit his other sons. He praises Adonijah's judgment, Ithream's manly grace, and Shepatiah's strength. The only son nobody but his mother pays much attention to is the baby of the family, Solomon. Like all children (and Salieri), he is happy to be left alone with all the desserts he can handle. Through Solomon, Shaffer plays with the audience's knowledge of history. What part could this child possibly play in the struggle among the other sons for the throne of Israel?

There is always a hidden message in what David says to his sons: "How may I serve *you* [Amnon] today? If I can grant you some desire it would please me deeply. Perhaps then we would see you more often. We've missed you" (1.2). But only he has the right to chastise his son for avoiding the court. If Absalom tries to do so, the king jumps to Amnon's defense of his right to keep hidden. David's great concern is for peace among his children, and he finds a way of hiding that message in the blessing over bread: "Blessed be He who has given us bread. And blessed is he who eats it in peace with his brothers: in whose heart is no secret thing. Selah." (1.2).

If King David is lavish in his praise of Absalom the "Shiner," he is absolutely doting in his attention to the young and beautiful Tamar, his only daughter. "Perfection," he says of her. "I shall make it official. I'll have it inscribed on tablets of porphyry: The Lord has blessed my issue with perfection!" (1.2). With her, the king can be playful; with him she can be cool, insolent, and smug, the "immemorial daddy's girl" (1.2), whose only goal is to marry well. The ordeal of the rape changes all that, and now, like Yonadab, she too resorts to manipulation in order to get revenge against Amnon in particular, and men in general. The Tamar of the final scenes of the play is irreverent and bitter: "Cursed be Amnon. Cursed be the King. Cursed be Absalom his brother, beloved of the King! And cursed above all cursed be the One God of the King—God of Men." Then, in a disgraceful parody of the ritual that Jewish men perform each morning, Tamar dons a prayer shawl on stage (although not so specified in the script), and recites: "I thank thee O God for not making me a woman!" (2.19). Her bitterness derives from the pathetic vision she has of her future: "'Is that Tamar? You just be joking! . . . Whatever did anyone see in her to cause all that trouble?' Or they'll be kind—'Cut the best slice of meat for Auntie Tamar, will you. She hasn't got much in her life, poor cow!'" (2.19). If she has come to treat men like dogs, it is because of what she has heard men say about her day after day, as they hold the victim responsible for the crime: "'There she goes—the slit: she's the cause of it all. Poor old Amnon, what chance did he have? She played the flute: he wanted to *be* that flute: slitty girl to play flutes! She shook a rattle: he wanted to be shaken: slitty girl to shake rattles! She smiled: we know about smiling. She danced: we know about dancing. She cooked: we know about cooking. She's a *slit*, what more do you need to know?'" (2.19).

David's reactions to the rape and to Absalom's plans for justice for his sister seem out of character for him. He refuses to take action against his first-born son, and accuses his "beauty" of trying to eliminate his rival for the throne. But worst of all, he shows no sympathy for what his daughter has suffered. He turns the situation around so that *he* is the offended party—offended because Tamar sought refuge with Absalom and not with him: "She imagines I'm too feeble. Too weak to be her champion. Or simply to old, perhaps?" (2.2). David's problem is that he has never overcome his past, despite the fact that he was chosen by God to be the second King of Israel. In his mind, he, like Pizarro, is still the boy who tended sheep and goats. He imagines Tamar thinks "'Let him go back to sheep and goats! That's all he's good for now'" (2.2). In what has become a cliché of fathers telling their children about their own childhoods, David recalls that when he was young he had no great father to grant his every wish: "Big men did not serve little goat-boys!" (1.2). And he prophetically advises his other sons as he strokes little Solomon's ears: "Be careful even of the smallest—for he may be magnified above you all!" (2.2).

Father-son relationships appear throughout Shaffer's plays, and are never smooth. This play is complicated by the presence of two sets of fathers and children. Yonadab's relationship with his father, Shimeah, is more important to his motivations and to the plot than are David's relations with his children. Shaffer provides the introduction to Shimeah through Yonadab's lofty recitation of a genealogy, which sounds like something out of the Bible (or *Equus*): "Yonadab, son of Shimeah . . . third son of Jesse the Bethlemite. . . . Son of Obed!—Son of Boaz!—Son of Salma!—Son of Nachshon!—Prince of the Tribe of Judah!" (1.1). Shimeah remembers his brother as being a "relentless little bully who worked his way up from being armor-bearer for Saul and by doing particularly nasty acts of valour: in particular *smiting*, which means hacking with bronze swords" (1.1). Shimeah's position in the court is "wretched," and he can only hope that Yonadab's future at court will be brighter than his own. He criticizes his son for picking Amnon for a friend: "With all the Princes around, you have to arselick that one! The obvious loser! The absolute loser! . . . If you are going to cultivate a Prince in this Court, pick the right one! Is that so hard?" (1.2). (This diatribe sounds a lot like Stanley Harrington criticizing Clive for his choice of friends in *Five Finger Exercise*.) Yonadab reminds his father that Amnon happens to be the heir to the throne, but is open to his father's suggestion as to which prince he *should* "arselick." Shimeah does not hesitate to call his son a half-wit, to remind him that no one likes him, and to report that the king sees how much time Yonadab spends with Amnon. When

Yonadab tells Absalom that he cannot appear at his house because he has family business, Shimeah exposes his son as a liar. In effect, he betrays Yonadab for his own good: it is a chance for Yonadab to get on the good side of the king's favorite.

After the rape, tensions between father and son intensify. Shimea's rebuke of Yonadab belies the date of the action, and has the ring of a conversation that could take place today: "So—are you satisfied? . . . Didn't I say to you one thousand times—drop him, that beast? . . . You realize of course I'll never be able to show my face at court again. Because you've shamed me—that's why! You have shamed me as no son has ever shamed his father!" (2.2). Shimeah's expertise in instilling guilt feelings in his son are as highly developed as any parent's, pre- or post-Freud. Shimeah is also capable of bestowing praise and showing affection when Yonadab wins approval from members of the royal family. He pulls his son's cheek when Absalom invites Yonadab to Baal Hazor. And when Yonadab gives the King the news that, despite rumors that all of his sons have been killed, Amnon alone is dead, David crawls to the throne on which Yonadab has positioned himself, clutches the man's knees, and climbs up his body. Yonadab reacts: "Behold the climax of my life. I stand before my father, wearing a king for a pendant!" And perhaps for the first time in his life, Yonadab has won his father's approval. Shimeah proudly embraces his son, tells him of his job well done, and calls him "My good son!" (2.17). Yonadab admits to what has been the motivating force in his life: "For the first time in my life I find myself approved. I am buoyed up by a great wave of joy. My life is changing so fast!" (2.18).

By the end of the play, David's two sons are dead, and his daughter is a crone, left beating the floor with her hand. Nor is Yonadab's position in life an enviable one in the play's final moments. Like Dysart who ends *Equus* by referring to the bit in his mouth that never comes out, Yonadab describes himself as "attached to the tree of Unattachment . . . Who can cut me down?" (2.20). The playwright's words call to mind those that describe Absalom's death in II Samuel 18: 9: ". . . and he was taken up between heaven and earth." Yonadab must live the rest of his life in emotional limbo.

Revised Version

For reasons that were completely out of the control of the playwright, in particular assembling an acceptable cast and finding a director, the revised version, which Shaffer wrote for Broadway, has not yet been produced.[2] That turn of events may have been a blessing in disguise for the author, since the largely Jewish audience in New York may have stayed away from a play that makes derogatory remarks about Old Testament Law as well as of the Jewish nation at that time, not to mention comments which border on blasphemy.

In the preface of the revised and published version, Shaffer wrote that he reworked about eighty percent of the text. The purpose in the revised version is to present the fruit of Yonadab's plotting, that is, "the shaming of the House of David."[3] Shaffer also used the play to explore his own feelings about the Old Testament, that "blood-splattered chronicle of death and deception, racial arrogance and magnificence . . ." (LLY, vii). He also became obsessed "by the figure of a cynic lured for a moment into the possibility of Belief: an anguished figure forever caught between the impossibility of religious credo and the equal impossibility of perpetual incredulity" (LLY, 7). To the playwright's credit, he was willing to move away from Jacobson's novel and have the plot take on new patterns of development. As he had done previously with Amadeus, Shaffer reworked the script to give the story greater clarity, the action more tension and texture, and the characters better delineation than in the first version. For the author, "Yonadab exists in a world of superstition, of prophecies, interlocking dreams and the deep-running insistence of Semitic fear and willfulness. It is a world of desert and judgement: the limitless void of sand and the exact limitation of the Law. This new stylization should make it come alive with an exact and extraordinary vividness" (LLY, 7). This section examines the substantive changes that Shaffer made in the language, plot, characters, themes, and stagecraft of the original version.

The stylization to which Shaffer referred becomes immediately evident in the new cast of characters and a description of their functions in the play. There are no longer any brothers but Amnon and Absalom in the cast. Also gone are Shimeah, Adoram the physician, Bathsheba, bodyguards, and servants. Those from among that category are now replaced by six Helpers, who are dressed in white robes and seated around the outer stage as the curtain rises. Their facial characteristics are obliterated by white stocking masks. They never speak, but do make sounds. Their effect is very similar to that of the actors who compose the chorus of horses in Equus. Yonadab's age is no longer given as late twenties or early thirties—he is now middle-aged.

Once again the play begins with a monologue by Yonadab. To set the mood, he begins with the Hebrew words from the biblical book of Samuel, which state that Yonadab was a friend of Amnon and a subtle man. He defines the meaning of "subtle" as "devious." He gives the citation for his quotation, and continues by saying that two references describe him alternately as cunning and kind, "creating between them a kind of invisibility" (*LLY*, 87). He finds that an appropriate way of defining himself, since Yonadab, like Clive in *Five Finger Exercise*, has a problem with self-definition. Yonadab goes on to say that he has been living in limbo for eternity. Whereas the original version called this a play about unnatural desires, the revision calls it a tale of deceit, in which each character deceives and is in turn deceived. For Yonadab, this is the story of Yonadab the Despised, son of Shimeah the Ignored, who brought about the ruin of the House of David. If Salieri could not be remembered for his music, he was content to be remembered for having destroyed Mozart; similarly, if Yonadab couldn't do anything good in his life, at least he did something infamous.

Anachronisms are once again written into the text. In this monologue, Yonadab is speaking as a twentieth-century Jew to an audience that has certain images of modern Jews, and he asks his listeners to "banish from your minds all images of cowed men cringing in Ghettos, or kind men creating cultural centres" (*LLY*, 88). The Jews in this tale he deems as neither cringing nor kind, but smiters of all of the ancient "Ites" they could get their hands on—Ammonites, Caananites, Jebusites, Amelekites, Hivites, Hittites, Perizites, Moabites—and all in the name of the God of the Commandments. He also makes sure that the audience abandons the image of a peaceful David lying down in the green pastures of the Twenty-third Psalm for one in which he is living in a city of stones and stonings. The first action in this version is, in fact, a maimed stoning accompanied by the approval of the crowd and the shrill of rams' horns.

Yonadab paints an ugly picture of biblical Jerusalem: "The air stank of blood. Human blood in the gutters: animal blood from the altars. And beyond in the desert, for miles, the blood of our chopped enemies soaking the sand" (*LLY*, 89). Yonadab depicts himself as the only "delicate" man in the tribe—another similarity between him and Clive Harrington, Bob in *The Private Ear*, and Mark's son David in *Shrivings*. This quality clearly distinguishes him from a God who is not nearly so delicate, and sets up the dichotomy of Yonadab the Sensitive vis-à-vis Yaveh the Savage, an image all too close to that of Equus the god. In reality, however, the appropriate nickname for him is Yonadab the Destroyer. He finally broaches his real problem—Yonadab doubts God's existence. He then identifies himself with the dramatic Pizarro and Dysart by confessing that his religion—his by birth—is simply not enough for him. Yonadab is just as unrelenting in his depiction of the king's sons, a "ghastly brood: ambitious, dark-souled bullies, scared of Daddy, licensed to sneer at me: and every one of them watching the old man for signs of falling" (*LLY*, 90). And no kinder is the detail with which he introduces King David: "Some years before, David had a Hittite man killed in order to possess his wife, Bathsheba. It was said that as a punishment God killed the first son they had together—and then placed a sword for ever in the midst of his other children" (*LLY*, 90). That punishment is the genesis of the story of the play. The next bit of stagecraft is a foreshadowing of Yonadab's speeches to both Amnon and Absalom. Two of the Helpers assume poses that suggest Egyptian god-figures, one male and one female.

Yonadab is a victim of his own desires and fantasies. He has always wanted to escape from Jerusalem, "the world of perpetual anger," to the land he dreamed about as a boy, the Kingdom of Perpetual Peace, "ruled over jointly by a King and Queen, young and deep in love. Both beautiful—and both eternal" (*LLY*, 90). He wanted to live in a world where flutes, not rams' horns, filled the air, a land that did not have rams "dragged shitting to slaughter for a ravenous God" (*LLY*, 90). Despite his claims, Yonadab is not a pacifist in the tradition of *Shrivings*'s Gideon Petrie. Perhaps the closest Yonadab comes to being Gideon is through his unconventional sexual needs and his images of his imaginary king's "exquisite brown shoulders." He does admit that his fantasies had more to do with sexual than celestial matters.

Now the princes appear on stage. Amnon is stocky and powerful, "'thick' in several senses of the word . . . innocent and engagingly stupid. . . ." Absalom is a "glorious beauty—handsome and well tended . . . ardently emotional and dangerous and immature. . . ." (*LLY*, 91). It is impossible to see into Absalom, and Amnon's thickness makes him regard Yonadab as a brilliant scholar. The king tries to cheer his brooding son, the Bull, by imitating horns and charging motions, but he will not be amused. Yonadab introduces Tamar as the "Sex Interest in this story. . . . Single most spoilt creature in the Kingdom" (*LLY*, 95). She tries to be such a good girl to Daddy that *she* reminds *him* to say the appropriate blessing before eating. This time when Tamar sings her song at Absalom's request, she pays particular attention to him. Yonadab knows intuitively why Amnon has summoned his cousin to his house and he can hardly contain himself from bringing up the subject of uncovering the nakedness of Amnon's sister. It is now that Yonadab, like Salieri, conceives of his plot "to bring things down. . . . Ruin to the great who despise me" (*LLY*, 98). He takes on not only the royal family, but also "Yaveh the Prohibitor." Yonadab, like Salieri, challenges God to stop him in his plans.

Those plans begin with flattery. Yonadab tells his cousin that he is an exceptional man, and not just mere muscle (as his father thinks). He convinces Amnon not to condemn congress with Tamar as an abomination because "what would be blasphemy in ordinary people is—is learning in you" (*LLY*, 100). Amnon is suspicious but deeply impressed as he listens to Yonadab's words on blessed sibling unions: "They couple together with a pleasure unimaginable to the rest of mankind—and achieve Immortality! When they die, they both pass into another world, where they love each other for eternity" (*LLY*, 100). The combination of a fairy-tale ending and fantastic sex—with immortality thrown in—is too much for Amnon to resist. Yonadab also convinces Amnon that even the plans of gods need the help of man. Yonadab is drunk on the idea of ruin and of seeing if the "Great Punishers" will to do anything to stop him from seeing Tamar "wriggling on her back. . . . That lofty little Princess reduced forever to the level I lived on every day" (*LLY*, 102). He wants Tamar the Insolent to join Yonadab the Insulted, and have her brothers sneer at *her* for a change. Amnon sees in the plan his chance, not Absalom's, to reign. Yonadab can hardly claim in this version that he wanted to do any more than watch Amnon and Tamar have sex. He can no longer make claims of wanting to watch the bestowal of immortality when he regards Amnon's drivel as "half-digested mysticism" from a "randy, pseudo-intellectual, nearly mindless dummy dressed up as a prince!" (*LLY*, 104). Amnon returns Yonadab's favor with the promise that the companions of the immortal can become immortal, too. The first truth Yonadab speaks is that he is not worthy.

What Yonadab considers to be Amnon's self-inducted ailments in the earlier version of the play, he now sees as being brought on by the sheer terror of abusing his two fathers—the earthly and the heavenly. Yonadab, too, is concerned with those two fathers: "I tried with all my being to imagine myself David—a Priest King influencing the universe" (*LLY*, 109). He shares Salieri's ambition and envy in wanting to be God's instrument on earth: "Unknowable God confirmed as surely as the existence of myself! *Oh, the wonder of that! To be its entire resounding instrument!*" (*LLY*, 109).

There are significant changes in both the scene preceding and the scene of the rape itself. Amnon requests of his father that Tamar cook for him because he needs her goodness to offset his evil. Absalom strenuously objects to the request, even to the point of challenging the decision of his father and king. David contemplates Yonadab and calls him perceptively the "Man of Eyes." He jovially prods Amnon's genitals and leaves. Absalom makes it Yonadab's personal responsibility to take care of his sister. Yonadab speculates that the younger brother is jealous of his elder sibling. Left alone with his friend, Amnon confides how reassuring it is to have Yonadab watching over him: "There are very few one would trust to watch at a time like this. It's a mark of how I trust you" (*LLY*, 111). Yonadab is watching someone else, who must surely intervene and stop him in his evil tracks: "Surely Yaveh must show His hand now and stop it! How far would He let it go?—and what would his punishment be?" (*LLY*, 111). The music, which plays at all significant moments in this version, grows sinister. Yonadab's attitude is far more willful than before, and he is even arrogant around royalty. He insists that Tamar's servant leave or he will have to inform the king that his daughter has disobeyed his wishes. He comments that "members of your family tend to be willful, Princess" (*LLY*, 116). He assures the members of the audience that what he witnessed was seen by no one else but him, their Special Correspondent, and that they are "some of the most privileged viewers in the history of royal scandal" (*LLY*, 119).

Amnon is less menacing in this rape scene than in the original. He also expects the act to change his sister from a spoiled child into a loving woman. Like Salieri, who is convinced that God needed Mozart to be his vessel on earth, Amnon believes that the gods need Tamar and him to fulfill a special mission on earth. Tamar thinks that her half-brother must be possessed by a demon, which is speaking through him. She resists his advances and is clearly frightened. They circle each other and engage in a rhythmic repetition of the word "please." Tamar prays to the Eternal for mercy and tries to humor Amnon, and even to run. And then occurs the most unrealistic change in her behavior: "(*He folds her tightly in his arms. Hypnotized, she does not resist.*)" (*LLY*, 125). Amnon raises his arms to release Tamar, but she does not move. Amnon's actions, similar to those of Alan in *Equus*, are described: "Like a priest with a sacred scroll he laid her for unwrapping on his altar" (*LLY*, 126). Amnon bows to Tamar and calls out "Holy! Holy! Holy!" before he tears off his robe and stands naked before her. Tamar stares at him. The music becomes savage and menacing as Tamar cries out. What Yonadab saw in the silhouettes reflected on the curtain was despair, as Amnon seeks "to hurt himself through her to *freedom*. Seeking a bliss to end his need for bliss" (*LLY*, 127). The description of the rape calls to mind Alan's wild ride on Nugget: "There on the fall of a Jerusalem drape I saw, writ enormous—

like a parody of our Hebrew Consonants—the archaic alphabet of the Book of Lust. I watched in horror as their bodies slipped and shaped—seemed to form words. . . . Hoops of the hunted woman writhing! Humps of the hunting man riding!—round and round in the forest of his fury where all paths lead back to the same blank clearing! Shapes of hurting and being hurt" (*LLY*, 127). What does Yonadab see in this scene? Perhaps a man, like Alan, yearning to touch a nonexistent god; perhaps "the oldest puppet show in the world": "Man bobbing on a non-apparent string—held by the jerking hand of that very God . . ." The equation between sex and religion is again apparent, as it was in *Equus*.

After the rape, Yonadab, "creeping like a spy," follows behind Tamar at a safe distance through the streets of Jerusalem. He is confused when her steps lead her to Absalom. He knows that if she tells her brother what Amnon has done to her she will be signaling her own ruin, but he knows too that she will do it: *"Oh these children of David!—these idealists!* Like her deluded brother she is going to make her own stab at the sublime—*at making things mean more than they do or even can!"* (*LLY*, 130). The reaction is typical of a cynic—Mark Askelon comes to mind. The townspeople mime shock and outrage, Absalom promises justice, and Yonadab ends the first act with another monologue, expressing his motive: "Ruin! Ruin to the House of David! And I the ruiner! Yonadab the family joke—Lord over them all! Lord over Him too above—*Yaveh the Non-God!"* (*LLY*, 131). In his head he hears the yell of emptiness of Amnon, the Bull in chains. Yonadab's belief in the meaninglessness of life is confirmed by "a pumping man, a wriggling woman and an empty world—that's all there is" (*LLY*, 132). And yet there remains in him a slight hope that he can change his life because Yonadab the Cynic *needs* to believe in "The Birth of Godhead."

Act 2 opens again at court, where Absalom is demanding justice for his sister. David sits on his throne with his prayer shawl drawn over his face, while Yonadab is concerned only with saving his own skin. Yonadab again engages in an introductory monologue, this time telling the audience that this is a story about demons—specifically, the Demon of Mischief, who lives in the despised man; and the Demon of Credulity, who lives in the cynic. Both exist in Yonadab: the first destroyed Amnon, and the second destroyed Yonadab himself. In *Amadeus*, Salieri engages the audience and asks who among them would not take the kind of revenge that he does. Yonadab makes a similar plea for understanding as he again speaks anachronistically: "If you could have your choice today, my dears—smart and modern dears as you are, festooned with your computers and your calculators—which would you finally rather witness? Men and women walking out into the sky on to further and further stars, filling the universe with more of *You*—or you walking here, but in another state of Being, freed from the conditions which enslave you now? A state in which you grew more wise, each day, not less. More filled with adoration, not less" (*LLY*, 134). His plea, his hopes, and his suppositions echo Dr. Dysart's, and appeal to an audience who seeks deeper meaning and greater satisfaction in their lives. And divine choosing, as in *Amadeus*, falls not on individuals of great refinement and virtue, but on an "over-sexed dummy and a petulant little prick-teaser. . . . " (*LLY*, 134).

Back at Absalom's house, all Tamar is interested in learning is if her father will act on her behalf. Again Yonadab lies—swears to God—that he knew nothing of Amnon's purpose in wanting Tamar to care for him. After his beating, he thanks heaven that he has no broken bones. Does he believe or doesn't he? He does seem to believe that his dream about his being beaten had prophetic powers. Yonadab remains indoors while Jerusalem is "moaning for a stoning" (*LLY*, 139).

A drunken, quaking Amnon comes to believe that both he and Yonadab are merely instruments to bring about the real Choosing, that of Tamar and Absalom. Yonadab is disgusted by the whole story and wants to hear no more of it. He is also afraid of further involvement, but finally decides that his best move is to ingratiate himself to Absalom: Amnon "the lump" is no longer of any use to him: "Shit-scared, I went back to that dangerous beauty" (*LLY*, 144). Absalom can only accuse him of being the companion of a beast, and therefore a beast himself. Yonadab insists "I am myself," as did Clive Harrington. When Absalom slaps Yonadab for kissing his sister's hand and forbids him even to speak to her ever again, Yonadab's new, defiant side comes to the surface: "You're all the same—David's savages!" (*LLY*, 146). Despite Absalom's claims not to be interested in the "blasphemous filth" about becoming a god by bedding his sister, he cannot conceal his interest in learning the signs that prove that he is the Chosen One. He declares that he is still a virgin at twenty-two. (Yonadab knows that only a twenty-two-year-old virgin could get so upset as he did over a loss of virginity.) Absalom unties his hair, and Yonadab must confess that Absalom and Tamar, two beings he has long disliked, are "holding me there by the rope of pure beauty" (*LLY*, 149).

As Alan and his father caught each at a pornographic cinema and Alan realized his identification with his father, so Yonadab catches the king wandering the rooms of his palace beseeching heaven, just as Yonadab does—or wishes he could do. The king's language is simple as he begs that mercy for his son win out over justice for his daughter. Yonadab locks himself in his house out of fear that a voice may advise the king: *"Yonadab did it. Kill Yonadab for Justice!"* (*LLY*, 151). After three nights of dreaming of Absalom's gaining the throne, Yonadab is summoned to him in the middle of the night, just as Dysart summoned Alan. Absalom insists that the king cannot refuse to judge Amnon for blasphemy, if for nothing else. In an uncharacteristic statement, Yonadab feels compelled to say that Amnon was once his friend, and that he will not deliver him to death. Absalom's motive is to become king and excel at being a man of peace, something his father has never been. The Secret Salieri theme reappears when Absalom confesses that he has no idea of who Yonadab really is. Neither does Yonadab. As an "Advanced Voyeur," he feels compelled to hide yet again and observe Tamar and Absalom together. This technique not only allows Yonadab to spy, but it also allows the audience to indulge *its* voyeuristic desires. Yonadab wishes he had never stayed around for this scene, which explains the reason for the events in the Bible.

Tamar tempts her brother by reading the gossip around Jerusalem about how she is a witch, and that she put a spell on Amnon by making him pancakes. She also claims that she no longer hates Yonadab, and even sees him repeatedly in one particular dream, where he is not "creepy" the way he is in life. And so, she puts her own scheme into motion. Absalom confesses that when Tamar was raped it was as if something had been torn in his virgin body as well. He tells her of his dream, of how he believes that they are chosen—and that he loves her, to which she responds in kind in both words and actions. She surrenders herself to him. As Yonadab watches them mingling their beauty, he finally thinks he understands the force of prayer, and again dares to hope that he too can know belief: *"Let it be!* I know Gods cannot walk on earth: *let it be!* I know lovers cannot infect Kingdoms: *let it be!* Let there be an end to this world of blood-soaked worship—and to my own world too, which owns no worship. *Make me see it!* Change my unchanging world! Set this manipulating man at last in ways of *Meaning! Why else was I born with such urgency of spirit, and nothing for urgency to move?"* (*LLY*, 160). And so again he joins Pizarro, Mark Askelon, and Dr. Dysart in his need for belief.

Yonadab sighs aloud, the lovers hear him, and Yonadab begs them to forgive him—he confesses to having heard everything. Absalom leads him to believe that this is Yonadab's destiny—to tell them to fulfill their own. But how can this be? As he himself proclaims: "I'm Yonadab! *I'm Nobody!*" (*LLY*, 161), his true self-image. Absalom and Tamar have not yet consummated their love. Absalom believes that David must topple as a part of the prophecy, but that he and his sister must complete their love now. Absalom, like Salieri, turns against God (or his law) in the name of justice. Tamar again insists on justice first. She is able to involve Yonadab in the plan to kill Amnon by promising him that he will be their Chief Counsellor when they reign. (She knows how to appeal to Yonadab's self-interest.) Absalom finds it hard to believe that Yonadab would conspire to kill his former friend; but now that he calls himself Yonadab the Soothsayer, his ego takes over: "It's actually a fairly easy role to play if you have been starved for attention all your life" (*LLY*, 163–64). In his usual oxymoronic way, Yonadab counsels violence for peace: raise the sword once, and like magic the result will be the Kingdom of Peace. One more bullet, one more bomb (two more anachronisms), and the exorcism of war is completed.

Curiously enough, it is David who suggests that Amnon will join Absalom in Baal Hazor, and one has to wonder at the father's motive. Can he really believe that the Shiner has truly forgiven the Bull and that peace has returned to his family? Perhaps he believes that his prayer has been answered. In the attitude that has come to characterize Yonadab in this version of the play, he is firm with Amnon about the prince going to Baal Hazor with his brother, and if he doesn't want to go, he can "stay in this room for the rest of [his] life" (*LLY*, 168). Yonadab piles one lie on top of the other for his bringing this news rather than Absalom: Yonadab asks Absalom to let him come; he is vain and wanted to deliver the good news by himself. He'll say anything to get the brother to go to the meeting about which he feels uneasy. And Yonadab makes a confession—he watched the rape. Of course, that minor betrayal no longer matters to Amnon. What Yonadab wants to know is why Amnon pulled the curtain for the first time in his life. Amnon explains that he wanted to turn his bed into a temple for the holy act.

The rug under which Amnon is ambushed and killed is no longer a plain piece of wool; it is now emblazoned with the Star of David, so that the blood on it might symbolize King David's reign. At the appropriate moment, the Helpers stamp their feet, the way the horses do just before Alan puts out their eyes. The sound of mourning fills the theater. After bearing the news of his son's death to the king, David asks Yonadab if it was he who planned Amnon's murder: "The Watching Man. I have waited many years for this. Always your eyes on me. In the end I knew it would come through you" (*LLY*, 171). He also suspects that Yonadab was responsible for what happened to Tamar: "I know you. Don't strike yourself: make others strike" (*LLY*, 171). David cannot imagine what death is harsh enough for Yonadab in punishment for all that he has taken away from the king. Yonadab is just as arrogant with the king as with the princes: "It was you—not I—*You* did it! . . . All-seeing David: what did you see?" (*LLY*, 172). But Yonadab confesses to ruining the royal family because David's anointed eyes saw nothing: "I worked it all. Your daughter ruined—your son speared like a boar! And nothing stopped me! *God did nothing*! Just kept you blind and left me to do it!" (*LLY*, 172). In the reversal of the blessings that the biblical Isaac and Jacob bestow upon their sons, David puts a curse on his nephew: "Be a Watcher and no more, for life. See it as through a veil drawn before your eyes. Be as a dead man in the midst of the living—warmed by nothing. . . . a bitterness even beyond death" (*LLY*, 172). And the curse sticks: Yonadab's life is a living death, devoid of all feeling and meaning. Yonadab in return jeers the king that there is no death harsh enough for him, for being a blind ruler. Finally, he turns to the audience swearing that he dismissed King David; and Ghosts—just like Sophie in *White Lies*—never lie. He joins Salieri in the world of Ghosts. Yonadab does see a ray of hope for himself: "I *am* an Instrument! I have condemned Kings and brought them low. I have beheld Amnon rebuked! Absalom reformed! Tamar reborn! May not Yonadab be reborn also?" (*LLY*, 173). He can only hope that the design that began in lust can flower in love. He is ready to receive any sign of rebirth, which he himself cannot effect.

Yonadab is alarmed when he sees Tamar returning from Baal Hazor without Absalom. In a scene in which the action takes place in three separate corners, the audience views what transpired between brother and sister after Amnon's murder. Tamar tells Absalom that he is cursed for having broken his oath not to kill his brother. Then Micah appears in the flashback, so that the audience can learn how Tamar knew which was Absalom's house: "When men are determined to believe nonsense there's no preventing them" (*LLY*, 175). Tamar also reveals to Yonadab how she beat him at his own game of hide and overhear by finding the home. She believes that God will forgive her because she was doing his work. She claims, in fact, that God spoke to her: "*"Thou*, Tamar, must do it! What no man will do for me. *Avenge!* . . . I will not suffer Unrighteousness to go unpunished in Israel!'" (*LLY*, 176). Tamar believes that it is she who is his Instrument. Tamar confesses to Yonadab that she worshipped Absalom and wept every night over what she had to do. But God was unyielding; he hardened her heart and made her kill. She believes that at a certain point Absalom wanted her because "he smelt the blood on me. . . ." (*LLY*, 177). In the end, Absalom became just another Bull.

Yonadab now loses all hope in the Kingdom of Peace, because Absalom was the last chance for establishing it. Tamar never really had that expectation, and, in an attitude that may be realistic or cynical, she believes that it would not have taken Absalom long to tire of her, and maybe even throw her into the street as a whore, just as Amnon did. She also contradicts herself and claims that she *was* guided to Absalom's house by the Lord's hand for the sake of the people. She believes that she has restored justice to Israel through Amnon's murder, that she has made Israel whole again, that she has "sweetened Israel in the nostrils of the Lord!" (*LLY*, 179). Like the psalm says, *she* will make a new song unto the Lord, so that Israel is again worthy to be his chosen people. Her song takes on the aspect of prayer, ending in "Amen! Selah!" Raising a spear, Tamar becomes a warrior-priestess holding the words of her song to her breast, where no other lover will ever be. For Yonadab, it is a song that shrinks its singer with each repetition, and her only crown now is her gray wig: "And she sat for life in her palace and sang to her savage God, the stink of vengeance the incense of her Faith. She knew more joy in the memory of killing than ever she would have known in the making of children" (*LLY*, 180). While Tamar is able to turn her pain into meaning, Yonadab "sat banished on my dreary estate, and new *none*. No meaning. Ever. One moment of hope—then dark forever" (*LLY*, 180). He gets little consolation from the fact that no one could ever abuse, delude, or disappoint him ever again. Yonadab envies Tamar as much as he despises her. To him none is more hateful than those "who stink of Faith, and murder in its name" (*LLY*, 181). But worst of all are those who bear King David's curse and who have no sustenance beyond themselves. What is more lethal, Yonadab must finally question, belief or nothing?

Literary Techniques and Theatrical Effect

Many of the techniques of language and stagecraft are familiar from Shaffer's earlier plays. They include dreams, nicknames, and spectacle—both visual and aural. Dreams have been a clue to character since Clive's in *Five Finger Exercise*. In *Yonadab* there are two dreams, and both are significant. The first is Yonadab's early in the second act. This is a dream he has over and over again: "In it two figures were riding on gigantic horses—straight towards me. The road was the high road to Jerusalem. The horses huger than any I'd ever seen—and light streamed out of their hair, and out of their riders. Through the light I saw their faces:—*Tamar and Absalom*, wearing crowns of light! 'Married' they cried out. 'Married! We come to make proper justice!' Then they laughed—and the horses laughed—and rode over me" (2.7). This dream effectively sets the second act in motion. Yonadab is positively feverish over the idea of "two brothers hooked on the same sister! Two Princes on the same myth!" (2.8). In an effort to deceive Absalom and stir up Yonadab's imagination, Tamar claims that she has the same dream in every detail. (The image of gigantic horses sounds like the picture that Alan Strang had hanging in his room.)

The second dream is Absalom's, and it also occurs in the second act. He relates it to Tamar: "I see you with my brother Amnon. It's as if I am hidden in the very room, watching. I am stuck to the floor, powerless to help! . . . And I hear him shout at you 'Out! Get out!' And I shout 'Come to me! . . . I'll take you in, and keep You forever'" (2.11). He claims to have had that dream every night since Tamar came to him. Has he had the dream, or is his saying so a part of the deceptions that dominate the play? And if he had it, might it not have been self-induced and brought on by amorous, if not sexual, desires toward Tamar, thereby making his self-delusion as bad as his brother's? The "fever" that the first dream produces in Yonadab parallels the fever that Amnon suffers. The fever, or heat, that Amnon experiences could well be a manifestation of sexual heat. This metaphoric expression for sexual desire has many precedents. The best example may be Federico García Lorca's play *La Casa de Bernarda Alba* (The House of Bernarda Alba), in which the heat of the Spanish summer intensifies the sexual body heat of the characters.[4] Amnon also makes a connection between heat and evil desires, and he begs to be consumed in fire, perhaps suggesting the flames of hell—the ultimate connection between Yonadab and Salieri.

Shaffer involves the audience in wordplay with a humorous tone. For example, in Yonadab's opening monologue, he refers to the letters B.C. and indicates that the C stands for descendant of his people. He also uses language that comes from the Bible, such as in the line "Thou shalt not uncover the nakedness of thy sister Tamar" (1.3), and "May your days fatten, Absalom, until the fat runneth over" (1.2). Yonadab uses a variation of that last line when he wishes that the guards' days fatten "until they burst you" (2.9). Humor is mixed with sarcasm when

Yonadab tells Amnon that the crowd is no longer waiting for him in front of his house because "there are other people in this city to be stoned besides you" (2.8). Sometimes the playwright uses Yiddishisms, which he expects many members of the audience to understand. Shimeah, for example, calls his son "clever-dick": "I thank God for sending me such a clever-dick son!" (1.2). Tamar translates the Yiddish phrase *es gezinte heit* when Shimeah tells his father to eat and be well. Finally, Shimeah refers to Solomon as "Solly the silly." These are further examples of anachronisms: Yiddish did not exist in the time of King David. And nicknames appear again, Yonadab is alternately called Yonadab the Untouchable, the Friend, the Incredulous, the Subtle, the Voyeur, and Yonny.

There are similarities in the stagecraft between this biblical epic and the historical epic, *The Royal Hunt of the Sun*. There is the music—here sistras, rattles, timbres, a lyre, and of course, rams' horns. David's throne room has the spectacle about it of Atahuallpa's. The bloody scene of Amnon's death is much like the Spaniards' massacre of the Incas. Here the bodyguards use staves. The use of sharp objects for killing goes back to Arieh's use of a knife rather than a gun in the war for the free State of Israel in "The Salt Land." Bob uses a needle to destroy his recording of *Madame Butterfly*. In a comedic mode, Colonel Melkett and Harold Gorringe take pointed objects from a piece of Brindsley's sculpture in *Black Comedy* and chase Brindsley around the room with them. And Alan uses a pick to put out the eyes of the horses. For aural effect, the porters stomp their feet to show disapproval, as do the horses in *Equus*. The actors' make-up is garish, and suggests vaudeville more than serious drama.

In the program notes, Shaffer wrote that the dominant image in his head as he was creating the play was that of curtains: "a girl carried through the streets behind the curtains of her litter; the endless curtains of the Middle East, hiding what must not be seen; secret beds and secret cupboards; and above all the curtain suspended before the eyes of Yonadab." Curtains are a metaphor in the play. On stage, two different sets appear that bear the story in Hebrew from the Book of Samuel. The first does not have vowels, and depicts Yonadab's total lack of comprehension of the world around him, and perhaps the meaninglessness of life. The second curtain provides the vowels, and some understanding of what is happening in the play. Michael Hinden[5] calls this work Shaffer's "ultimate play of veils." It is always with a veil between him and the rest of humanity that Yonadab sees life.

Criticism and Summation

Once again the reviews ran the gamut. Benedict Nightingale[6] praised Shaffer's courage and derring-do this time in making the court of King David the site of the debating chambers of the playwright's mind. He pointed out how Yonadab is obsessively embattled with the God he intellectually rejects. He lamented that Shaffer was not able to bring the play to life, and that the manipulation of the plot is all too visible. Yonadab lacks the substance and consistency of character, he wrote, that Salieri possessed; he seems to shift and change according to Shaffer's whim and needs for the story. The reviewer for *Variety*[7] found *Yonadab* disappointing after *The Royal Hunt of the Sun* and *Amadeus*. The play, he felt, is overwritten, has little to say, and is not redeemed by its visual and melodramatic impact. Irving Wardle[8] saw the play as Yonadab's vision of what life ought to be. His objection with the play was that it lays claim to ultimate questions about humanity's place in the universe, and reduces those questions to theatrical structure. Michael Coveney[9] complained that the story is crudely and inefficiently laid out, and that Yonadab is a crude emcee, a sore thumb, a creep, and a bore. The reviewer would have settled for another battle between two protagonists. Not so for Michael Billington,[10] who was tired of the old formula. He wrote that *Yonadab*, like all of Shaffer's major plays, is a conflict between cold calculation and dangerous ecstasy, with God as the invisible protagonist, and that "this time you can hear Shaffer audibly cranking up the material to fit his governing obsession." While he believed that Shaffer's Yonadab has the credulity that Jacobson's lacks, he found the drama unsatisfying because of the contradictions in Yonadab's personality, which ranged from an "ironic smartyboots" to someone "racked by spiritual possibilities." In addition, Bilington thought the play lacked narrative suspense, and he believed that the author tried to inflate the theme through heightened language.

Esther Fuchs[11] turned the play into an opportunity for a feminist discourse on the political aspect of rape and of male domination versus female subjugation. Her complaint is less with the play than with the Bible, which is more interested in the effect of the rape on Amnon and Absalom than on the victim. Fuchs believes that Tamar *had* to be raped, so that she could not become the queen. Jack Kroll[12] calls Yonadab a biblical Salieri, who needs to believe that great individuals can turn the basest acts into some kind of divinity. He called the protagonist Shaffer's "most human, most scathingly funny spokesman" and the work

"Shaffer's most daring, personal and honest play." Billington complained that this is Shaffer's fifth play on the same basic theme, and that
it is time for him to start translating the direct experience of life into
drama rather than seeking out stories about his own fixations. Billington
got his wish: *Lettice and Lovage* came next.

Chapter Nine
Lettice and Lovage
and
Whom Do I Have the Honour of
Addressing?

Lettice and Lovage

After writing four plays rooted in philosophical and metaphysical themes, with male protagonists and women only in secondary or minor roles, Shaffer departed sharply from that format with *Lettice and Lovage*. For the first time since 1965, Shaffer wrote a comedy—but this one was intended specifically for the talents of Dame Maggie Smith, who created the roles of Doreen in *The Private Ear* and of Belinda in *The Public Eye*. Smith, who requested the play, was reunited with Richard Pearson, who portrayed Charles Sidley in the second of those one-act plays. Like *The Private Ear* and *The Public Eye*, *Lettice and Lovage* also opened at the Globe Theatre in London; it had its premiere on 27 October 1987, under the direction of Michael Blakemore. That year the play won the Evening Standard Drama Award for the best play of the year.

    A. Structure and plot. *Shrivings*, *Lettice and Lovage*, and *The Gift of the Gorgon* are Shaffer's only plays in three acts. The structure of the first scene of *Lettice and Lovage* is particularly important. It is divided into four sections, which are essentially the same situation repeated with variations. In those variations reside proof of Shaffer's talent for writing comedy, a test for Maggie Smith's skills . . . and the beginning of Lettice's problems. The curtain raises, accompanied by lugubrious Elizabethan music, on the grand hall of Fustian House in Wiltshire, England. The set is dominated by an oak Tudor staircase. All four variations of the first scene take place in the same physical setting and with essentially the same anonymous characters, a group of tourists. What keeps changing is the weather, the details of the dialogue, and the reaction of the tourists. The weather mirrors the spirits of the characters on stage.

In the first segment, the tourists are downcast and bored on this gray and rainy day as Lettice Douffet, the guide appointed by the Preservation Trust, recites the prepared text on the house: date of construction, number of steps, type of design, and the family's motto *lapsu surgo* (Latin for "by a fall I rise"). The tour of this exceedingly dull house comes to its end with Lettice's one highlight story of the staircase incident (from which the family's motto derives), which took place on the Feast of Candlemas, 1585. On that night, Queen Elizabeth I honored John Fustian with her presence. As he was accompanying the queen to the banquet that awaited at the bottom of the staircase, Her Majesty tripped on the hem of her dress and would have fallen down all fifteen steps, but for Fustian's grabbing her arm and saving her. In appreciation, the queen dubbed him knight on the spot. The tourists can all but keep awake as they dispiritedly file pass the dejected tour guide to the strains of more lugubrious music.

Scene 1B takes place several days after 1A. The weather has improved somewhat, but the crowd is equally bored as Lettice mechanically recites in a much faster monotone than before the approved text of her speech. When she notices that the members of the group are paying more attention to a crying baby than to her talk, she has a sudden inspiration to liven her talk up a bit and points out the "Staircase of Advancement." Having invented a name, she also invents a legend to go along with it. Improvising as wildly as Clea in *Black Comedy,* she devises the following story: "Her Majesty . . . was wearing a dazzling dress with a hem onto which had been sewn one hundred pearls, dredged from the Indian Ocean, and sent as a present by an Ottomite Sultan!"[1] The host was able to leap down half the staircase and save the queen. Now the interested crowd wants to see the steps, and Lettice is in the position to go on with her yarn. Not only did the queen dub Fustian a knight, but "she then tore off the six largest pearls from her treacherous hem and bade him set them in the handle of the sword which had just ennobled him" (*LL,* 6–7). Unfortunately, they cannot see the sword because it has been stolen. Lettice even has details about the menu of the banquet in 1585 because Elizabethan food is an enthusiasm of hers. The meal no doubt included hedgehogs glazed with egg yolks—a particular delicacy of the time. There was probably also infant rabbit, torn from its mother's breast or cut from the womb. The crowd found this talk quite charming, and

Lettice smiles happily as her listeners depart to sprightly Elizabethan music.

This reception only encourages her to enhance her exaggerations the third time. It is an even brighter day than in segment 1B, and Lettice is "happily dramatic" about her narration: "You are looking now at what is indisputedly the most famous staircase in England!" (*LL*, 7). She has elevated its name to "The Staircase of Aggrandisement." After some remarks about the foods served at the banquet—which included peacocks and swans—she tells of the evening when the queen, "in a blaze of diamonds presented to her by the Czar Ivan the Terrible" (*LL*, 8), slipped and would have fallen if her host had not leapt to her rescue. She describes the reaction of the beribboned guests, frozen in suspended time like Renaissance statues, and wide-eyed with terror until Fustian "springs forward—upward—rises like a bird—like feathered Mercury—*soars* in one astounding leap the whole height of these stairs, and at the last possible moment catches her in his loyal arms . . . 'Adored and *Endored* Majesty! Fear not! You are safe!—And your hedgehogs await!'" (*LL*, 8). But this time she can't get away with her improvements on history and embellishment of the truth. One member of the tour identified as Surly Man (and who on stage looked rather like Frank Strang did) is an Elizabethan scholar and wishes to know the source of her information. She responds to him as Sophie might have spoken: "Excuse me, but there is a hostility in your voice which implies that I am saying an untruth. That it is lacking in veracity" (*LL*, 9). She is willing to compromise on the details of the Herculean feat, but insists that the account of the rescue is written in the family chronicle, which is hidden away "from the eyes of those who would use it for aggressive and uncharitable purposes" (*LL*, 10). The other members of the group speak out with approval of her reply, and look disparagingly at the man who would discredit her. She declared the tour concluded and invites the members to leave such "tokens of appreciation" as they see fit in the saucer that she has provided for that purpose. Most thank Lettice effusively, and she even smiles at the Surly Man, who marches off crossly. He is going to be trouble for Lettice, as the final segments of the scene reveals.

Scene 1D takes place on a brilliant day. The tourists are dressed in summer attire and enter the stage to lively music. Among this group is Lotte Schoen, a severe-looking lady in her late forties, with "aggressively plain" dress and hair, and guidebook in hand. Lettice is mid speech as the lights come up on the set. She has now exaggerated the story to the point that the daring feat, which would be unachievable by the greatest Olympic athlete today, saved the Virgin Queen Elizabeth from almost certain death. Lettice is no longer content to stop at just one legend of the "Staircase of Wound and Woe." She now tells of the wedding celebration for Miss Arabella Fustian, who was about the enter into matrimony with "the handsomest young lordling in the region" (*LL*, 11). Her father's eyes welled up with tears at the vision of his exquisite daughter, whom he was about to escort to church. At that moment, the family mascot charged toward the kitchen below at the smell of the roasting meats. He charged into the young woman and sent her rolling down the fifteen stairs. The fall left her legs forever deformed.

Lotte calls out that what Lettice is saying is absolutely intolerable, and that the two of them must speak at once in private. Lotte dismisses the rest of the group, but Lettice does not let them get away until she has mentioned the "tokens of appreciation." Miss Schoen identifies herself as representing the personnel department of the Preservation Trust, and reminds Miss Douffet that she is not permitted to accept tips, nor to fabricate what is supposed to be history. She summons Lettice to appear in her office in London the following morning. All that Lettice can see is how deceitful and rude Miss Schoen had been: she spied on her and then humiliated her in front of all the tourists. Lettice's response to what Miss Schoen calls her duty is a gem of a speech: "To embarrass your employees—that is your duty? To creep about the Kingdom with a look of false interest, guidebook in hand—and then pounce on them before the people in their charge?" (*LL*, 16). Lettice is dismayed as she realizes that she is to be judged in the morning. The scene ends with music as grim as her spirits.

The second scene of act 1 takes place in Miss Schoen's office, where the contrast between the assertive administrator and her meek receptionist is worthy of the author of *Black Comedy*. Miss Framer, the assistant, has done some investigations into Lettice's background and has discovered that she briefly held a job at the Tower of London, in the Department of Edged Weapons. She guarded the swords and axes, and left with a rather cautious recommendation. She will soon be dismissed again, and the audience is about to see a foreshadowing of the third act. Lettice dutifully appears at the "Bar of Judgement" and likens Miss Schoen to an executioner about to perform the fatal act: "The headsman always asked forgiveness of those he was about to decapitate" (*LL*, 22). Miss Shoen says she would appreciate it if Lettice eliminated historical analogies from the conversation. Lettice's defense for her fabrications is that she worked in the dullest house in England where nothing happened for four hundred years, and that in the words of her late mother, her job is to "Enlarge! Enliven! Enlighten!" the house that is haunted by the Spirit of Nullity. She was thus carried "further and further from the shore of fact down the slip-stream of fiction" (*LL*, 26). As proof that what she was doing was proper, she refers to her public: "Where people once left yawning they now leave *admiring*. I use that word in its strict old sense—meaning a State of Wonder" (*LL*, 26). And then there are all of the letters of appreciation that she has received. She dumps the proof of the vox populi on Miss Schoen's desk. But the office has received twenty-two letters of complaint about the liberties that Lettice takes with historical fact, and of course fact must prevail over fantasy. Miss Schoen will try to think of something to write as a reference for Lettice. This scene between the two women contains further elements that serve as a foreshadowing of the big events to come—Lotte Shoen's headache, a "blood red" garment, and most of all, Lettice's contagious spirit, which affects even Lotte's "grey integrity." Before Lettice's grand exit, which ends the first act, she sheds her black cloak in the manner of Mary Queen of Scots at the moment of her execution, and reveals a nightdress of brightest red—the color of martyrdom.

The plot of the rest of the play is rather easy to narrate. The second and third acts, each of a single scene, take place in Lettice's flat in the Earl's Court section of London, several weeks after the first act. The living room is dominated by two thrones from her mother's theatrical company, and have the grandeur of the chair that David Askelon made for Gideon Petrie. As act 2 opens, Lettice is talking to Felina, Queen of Sorrows, her cat, in the first person, as if it were the cat speaking, in a manner that is reminiscent of Sophie of *Lies* and *Liars*. Lettice has Felina talk of the tragedy of her life, of how she has been reduced to eating canned cat food—the "Munchies of Affliction"—instead of feasting on crayfish and scallops. There is in this speech a reflection of Lettice's own life—not the exciting life that her mother had in a traveling theatrical company, but merely a dull day-by-day existence in a particularly drab area.

All of a sudden, Lettice has a most unlikely visitor. It is Lotte Shoen—"The Executioner." Lettice is reluctant to admit her, but finally consents to invite her "Down to the Dungeon." Lotte is hesitant about entering because she has an aversion to cats. As in the first act, the terminology and references in this act foreshadow the events that take place later in the play. Lotte comes not to gloat over Lettice's present condition, as Lettice accuses, but to offer her former employee a position as a guide on a tourboat that Lotte's neighbors own on the Thames. They require someone who has enthusiasm for history, and Lotte thought of Lettice, not because she regrets having dismissed her (Lotte believes that she had to do it), but because Lettice has been on her conscience. Lettice has been less than successful about keeping herself employed since she was fired from the Preservation Trust. She had a job, for less than a week, promoting cheese in a store on Oxford Street. She was fired for "improving upon" the set sales pitch; history seems to repeat itself in her life. But how could she mouth empty words about cheese when she has a passion for Elizabethan foods? Miss Schoen requires one promise from Lettice before securing the job on the tourist boat for her: "no departures of any kind from the strictest historical truth" (*LL*, 41). While the pay is not enormous, there are tips—this time legitimate. The letter of recommendation that Lotte wrote on Lettice's behalf mentions her extensive knowledge of history and the letters that the guide received from appreciative tourists. She has been selectively honest for Lettice's benefit, and Lettice is touched to the point of tears by her former employer's confidence in her.

Rather than leaving at this point, now that her mission is complete, Lotte asks for a cup of tea, coffee, or even Coca-Cola, for which she admits a fondness. She obviously does not want to leave. Lettice offers Quaff, her own adaptation of a sixteenth-century potent cordial composed of mead, sugar, vodka, and lovage—an herb, whose name derives from "love" and "ache"; it is the medieval word for parsley. Lettice assures her guest that the pleasures of Quaff are both herbal and verbal. And so they are for Lotte who, like Miss Furnival in *Black Comedy*, is unaccustomed to strong drink. It has the effect on her that Alan wants a truth drug to have on him: verbosity. The two ladies talk of their past and current lives, of their likes and dislikes. The details and techniques in their conversation is subject matter for subsequent sections. All that need be mentioned here is their common dislike of the modern architecture that afflicts London. After Lotte has had several refills of Lettice's alcoholic concoction and is about to leave, she confesses that her motive in coming this evening was Lettice's uniqueness as a human being, and her theatrics at the office. Miss Shoen drops to her knees, and Lettice is afraid that she has made her ill. She allows Lettice to remove her wig and reveal beneath it Lotte's gray hair. They decide to go out for dinner, and Lettice lays her cloak ceremoniously on the floor in the manner of Sir Walter Raleigh assisting Queen Elizabeth. Lettice employs a line she used in the tour at the

Fustian House when she tells her new friend: "Come, madam. Your hedgehogs await!" (*LL*, 59).

The opening lines of act 3, which takes place in Lettice's flat on an afternoon six months after act 2, are a mystery to the audience. No one has any idea of why the front door is broken, or why Mr. Bardolph, a solicitor, is asking Lettice questions. These moments are as incomprehensible as the beginning of the conversation between Julian Christoforou and Charles Sidley at the opening of *The Public Eye*. (Richard Pearson played the role of Sidley in that play and of Bardolph in this one—both dry, middle-aged professionals.) He is trying to gather information to use in Lettice's defense at her trial for attempted murder. Appropriately enough, he is seated in the chair that Lettice's mother used in her theatrical company—it is called the Falstaff chair. (Bardolph was one of Falstaff's highwaymen in *Henry IV*.) Lettice awaits Lotte, who will set the record straight. Mr. Bardolph doubts that she will be able to do so, since Lotte is the principal witness for the prosecution. Lettice can hardly believe that "my shield and my buckler" would betray her in this way, but must accept the fact that history repeats itself. Two can play at betrayal. At that point, Lettice consents to tell the story of what happened on the night in question. Mr. Bardolph tapes the conversation in the interest of accuracy.

The charge against Lettice is the attempted murder of Lotte, whom the police found lying on the floor with blood pouring out of her head, and Lettice standing over her head with ax in hand. Lettice does not deny the accuracy of the report, even though she calls the police a bunch of liars; what she objects to is the charge. Mr. Bardolph says that according to Mr. Pachmani, a neighbor, this was not the first time he heard violent noises emanating from her flat: "Cries. Bumps. Voices raised in fury, and sometimes apparently in screaming and pleading. He is emphatic about this. He says that such quarrels were a constant companion to his evenings. . . . he has said that he would rather forfeit his chance of Paradise than spend another winter living—as he put it—above those two demented infidels." (*LL*, 70). In a manner similar to Dr. Dysart's insisting that Alan must know about the events of the evening that led up to his crime, Bardolph insists on knowing what took place at Lettice's home. She answers in one word: executions. The solicitor cannot believe his ears, and so Lettice elaborates on the events that took place between acts 2 and 3. For six months, the two women acted out the trials and executions of heroic historical figures. While Lotte usually played the part of the executioner, on the evening of the alleged crime Lotte wanted to play the part of the victim, Charles I, who was executed on 31 January 1649. Naturally, they enacted this execution on the anniversary of the event. At this moment, Lotte lets herself in and startles Lettice. She insists that Mr. Bardolph turn off the tape recorder, and tells him that Lettice is a compulsive storyteller. She does, however, fill in the details of that evening. While she was in the hospital, she responded "yes" to the police officers who asked if she had been hit with an ax. The police logically concluded that Lotte must have been attacked, although it was not necessarily her intention to convey that message. Be that as it may, Lettice reminds her that as a result of that statement, she is going on trial. Lotte is certain that they will think of a way out of the problem.

Now Lettice does betray Lotte's wishes. Despite her friend's solid reputation, Lettice insists that they must reveal in court what happened that night. Mr. Bardolph resumes taping, and with prodding from Lettice, both women reenact that night's events. When the solicitor is satisfied that Lettice committed no crime, he tells Lotte that she must declare in court exactly what the two women told him. Lettice will be acquitted, and the judge will berate them for acting like foolish school-girls. When Mr. Bardolph leaves, the women have a hard time facing each other. Lotte accuses Lettice of wanting to take revenge for her dismissal; when word of the trial gets out, Lotte will not be able to show her face at the office—job for job, tit for tat. Lotte accepts part of the responsibility for having allowed herself to get lured into the world where Lettice hides in the past. She returns Lettice's keys and leaves the flat, despite Lettice's protests that she would never do anything to hurt her friend. With Lotte's exit, the sky darkens to reflect Lettice's spirits.

The play could well end here, but it does not. Shaffer states that he wanted the work to have a happy ending befitting the genre of comedy. Lettice goes free, Lotte leaves her job, and together the two women cook up a new adventure. They will compile a list of the ten ugliest buildings in London and do enough damage to them that the structures will have to be torn down. With Lotte's knowledge of architecture and Lettice's of weaponry, they are a natural team. Best of all, the police will never suspect ugliness as the motive, nor two completely unknown women as the perpetrators. Lettice has the last line of the play, which she models on the ending of the second act: "Come madam. Our targets await" (*LL*, 95). They point a formidable weapon at the audience as the curtain falls.

B. Revised version.   In 1988, Maggie Smith suffered an accident, and Geraldine McEwan assumed her role. Sara Kestleman took the role of Lotte, which Margaret Tyzack had originated. (McEwen played the roles of Belinda and Doreen in *The Public Eye* and *The Private Ear* in New York.) Shaffer rewrote the ending of the work and it played in its new version for another year in London. *Lettice and Lovage* opened at the Ethel Barrymore Theatre in New York on 25 March 1990 with Smith and Tyzack in their original roles, directed again by Michael Blakemore. Shaffer and Blakemore earned "Tony" nominations, and both Smith and Tyzack won "Tony" Awards for their performances. Shaffer made the changes because he wanted to add elements to the play that would produce laughter—he succeeded. The playwright also came to believe that the original ending was forced, and he wanted one that would be organic and natural, that grew out of the situation. Instead of going out to destroy buildings, in the revised version the two women organize E.N.D. Tours, which provides guided tours of the fifty worst buildings in London.

In the rewritten form, Lotte returns in the final moments of the play because she can't stand to see Lettice reduced to "sniveling, feeble, whining rubbish! That's not You! *I won't have it*."[2] Lotte confesses that she hated her job and that she is glad to be rid of it. And she won't let Lettice live in the past, in history, which she has glamorized. She can't hide in her basement playing games: "We are two able, intelligent women. *I* am an experienced organizer of tours. *You* are without a doubt the most . . . original tour guide. That gives us something" (*L&L*, 95). In E.N.D. Tours, Lotte will provide the information about the architecture, and Lettice will provide the commentary to the tourists. The advertising that Lotte will prepare will include elements that come right out of the plot of the play: "'E.N.D. Tours presents Lettice Douffet's *Dramatic* Guide to Disgusting Buildings! Hear her Devastating Denunciation of Modern Design! Before your very eyes she will show you how *Beauty* has been *murdered*—and by whom'" (*L&L*, 96; emphasis added). Lettice is alive again, and contrives the talk she will give at the (imaginary) Computex House—she models it on her talk about the grand staircase at Fustian House:

Ladies and gentlemen—these grim stairs were recently the scene of the most dramatic protest yet to he made in Britain by ordinary people against a modern brutalist architecture. Last Christmas Eve, a brilliant snowy night—though nobody could see it because of the tinted solar glass—six typists, unable to bear the prospect of working in this place another day, walked up all seven hundred gray and granolithic steps—joined hands on the topmost landing up there . . . and together hurled themselves into the stairwell below, singing

the Hallelujah Chorus. They landed *precisely where I stand now!* . . . For this
reason it is now known as the Staircase of Secretarial Solace. (*L&L*, 97–98)

As a final touch, Lotte proposes that they present each guest with a gift
at the end of the tour—a glass of Quaff. And with that, the two characters
toast the audience.

Which ending is better is a matter of taste. The second is certainly
upbeat and gives the play a perfectly circular action. The first is plausible
if the audience believes that the two women, who have a taste for
performing mock executions on each other, could not be satisfied with
less than acts of violence. But maybe Lettice's arrest taught them a lesson.

C. **Characters and motifs.**   On the surface, *Lettice and Lovage* is a
complete departure for Shaffer from plays in which two male protagonists engage in a battle of wills. An examination of the characters and
later of the themes will reveal that while the sex of the protagonists is
now female, the battle between reason and passion and the theme of the
need for fantasy in life are still present in this play.

1. **Lettice.**   Lettice Douffet, a woman in middle life, rivals any of
Shaffer's other creations for the position of most optimistic, spirited, and
imaginative character, which is as it should be; her name derives from
laetitia, the Latin word for gladness. Her last name is of French origin and
explains her preference—like Louise Harrington's—for sprinkling her
speech with French words. Her lively traits are apparent from the way she
conducts the tours around Fustian House, to the way she handles herself
in Lotte Shoen's office. She is a woman who lives on her interests, which
she indulges passionately. Those interests include history in general, the
Elizabethan age in particular (especially food and weaponry of that era),
language, and theater. There is, in fact, a touch of theater in everything
she does. She inherited her passion for history from her mother, whose
theatrical troupe performed only Shakespeare's historical plays.

The subject of history appears in many of Shaffer's works. There are
references to the classical world in the early detective novels, as well as in
Equus; to Renaissance history in *The Royal Hunt of the Sun*; and to modern
history in "The Salt Land," *Five Finger Exercise*, and *White Liars*. As such,
the precedents are abundant for the references that occur in *Lettice and
Lovage*. Those references begin during the tours, and are usually more
fanciful than they are historic. Sometimes the information amounts to
trivia. Lettice states, for example, that the word "marmalade" is a
corruption of the French *Marie est malade* because Mary Queen of Scots
used to take a conserve of oranges and sugar when she had headaches, and

at those times her maids would whisper among themselves, "Mary is sick." (References to headaches—Queen Mary's and Lottes—are a foreshadowing of events to come in the carefully plotted and structured play.) There is also titillating historical gossip, such as the Lettice's revelation that Marie Antoinette had sexual relations with her own son. Lettice also relates to Lotte solid references to the history of England. She begins the afternoon of her dismissal, when she appears with a black cloak that conceals a red dress, as did Queen Mary at her execution—the queen who wished to be executed in a color that reflected the crime ("whoring"), of which she had been accused. Lettice's mother also taught her that history gives one a sense of place. The themes of lack of place and homelessness find their way into plays from "The Salt Land," in which the Jews are wandering from Europe to Israel to find a place to be at home, to *Shrivings*, in which Mark bemoans the fact that his son will always be a "mongrel" and never know a place that he can call home. The theme also appears in *Five Finger Exercise*, in which Walter left his homeland behind, and in *Equus*, in which Dysart's final monologue expresses his fear that industrial modern life, symbolized by multilane highways, may one day extinguish altogether the very idea of place.

Lettice inherited her affinity for theatrical behavior from her mother, who directed an all-woman dramatic troupe, which presented Shakespeare's plays in French. It was her mother who taught Lettice that the watchwords of life must be enlarge, enliven, enlighten. Her mother played such great roles as those of Richard III, Marc Antony, and Falstaff—Lettice's favorite character in all of drama. The reversal of sexual roles never seemed to present a problem. From her mother, Lettice also learned a respect for language, and for the appropriate usage of each word. Her mother believed that "language alone frees one" (*LL*, 25). Lettice is careful, for example, of who may use the word "dear" in addressing her. She doesn't allow Lotte to say it to her at the beginning of the second act because "I am not 'dear' to you. I am not dear at all" (*LL*, 39). Nor does she permit Mr. Bardolph to call her "my dear Miss Douffet" (*LL*, 63).

Dysart's disgust with and distrust of modern civilization reappears in the form of Lettice's fear of living in the present and finding solace in the past. Hers is the world of the homemade and of the tansy (a medieval omelet). In fact, she tells Lotte that she feels like a stranger in the world that surrounds her: "It's like a mesh keeping me out—all the new things, every day more. *Your* things. Computers. Screens. Bleeps and Buttons. Processors. Every day more . . . Bank cards—phone cards. Software.

Discs, JVC, VCR, ABC, DEF . . . The whole place—the whole world
I understood isn't there!" (*LL*, 90–91). But it is not in Lettice's character
to abandon her optimism. In her speech to the cat, she tells her pet that
sooner of later "the whole world will see my triumphant restoration to
the throne!" (*LL*, 36). As the rest of this subchapter will reveal, Lettice's
natural exuberance is contagious.

    2. **Lotte.** The relationship between Lettice and Lotte is much like
that of Don Quixote and Sancho Panza. As in Cervantes's masterpiece,
Lotte is so won over by Lettice's approach to life that by the third act she
will not allow Lettice to give up her dreams and sit at home feeling sorry
for herself. Her attitude reflects Sancho's, who won't hear of his master
giving up his impossible dreams and succumbing to death. Closer to
home, it is a variation of Sidley's respect for facts versus Belinda's for her
spirit, as well as of the contrast between Dr. Dysart and Alan Strang, in
which Dysart begins to appreciate Alan's world of fantasy. The play is, in
part, about Lettice's transformation. Lotte Schoen has a name that is at
odds with her being. The playwright describes her as being anything but
schön, the German word for pretty. She inherited that name from her
father, of course, who, like Walter's in *Five Finger Exercise*, was German.
Like Walter himself, her father came to England from Germany as a
refugee. Other Germans in Shaffer's works are the professor who is one of
the suspects in *Withered Murder*; Schuppanzigh, the electrician in *Black
Comedy*; and the Nazis, who lurk in the background of "The Salt Land,"
and in Sophie's past.

    Lotte's father published books for Perseus Press on other civilizations
(about which Dysart liked to read)—and some of these books are known
to Lettice. After Lotte's mother ran off with someone from her office and
her father sold his business for too little money, her fate was similar to
that of the young Louise: she and her father had to move from the family
home into a small flat. Lotte's father had as much of an influence on her
as Lettice's mother had on her daughter. He taught her about the
"Communal Eye." Here is the first hint of an affinity between the two
ladies, just as Lettice hates the mechanical aspect of modern civilization,
Lotte is offended by its lack of beauty: "The disgusting world we live in
now could simply not have been built when that eye was open" (*LL*, 50).
This talk foreshadows both the confession that Lotte is soon to make
about her past, and the plan that the two companions devise for the
future. Lotte resents the fact that she had to inherit her father's eyes: "I
wish I was blind, like everyone else" (*LL*, 50). She wishes she did not have
the ability to see more than the common eye of the rest of society sees. She

wishes that her eyes were not so talented as Salieri's ears in knowing the difference between beauty and mediocrity. She goes so far as to call herself an idolater—she marvels in architecture what Salieri worships in music, what Young Martin admires in Pizarro, and what Dysart envies in Alan Strang. The blindness of Oedipus (mentioned in *Five Finger Exercise*) and the horses in *Equus*; Julian Christoforou's detailed description of his public eyes, Sophie's attraction for Vassilli and her point of association with Tom in *White Lies*; Pizarro's attention to Atahuallpa's coal black eyes; eyes as the beauty of Lois and Giulia in *Shrivings* and the sexiest part of a man's body for Jill in *Equus*, are all linked with Lotte's fascination with sight. Lotte, the name by which this character is known, is a shortened form of Charlotte. Despite the French origin of her name, she has nothing kind to say about the French. During the meeting in which she fires Lettice, Lotte accuses the French of thinking that they invented civilization, and later on in the play, that their spirit thrives on stinginess. (Nor did Lettice's mother have much good to say about the French after the Frenchman to whom she was married abandoned her within three months of their wedding.) Lotte's first and Lettice's last name is, therefore, an onomastic bond between them.

The role of Lettice is a masterful creation, but that of Lotte is the one that shows the most growth and development in the course of the play. In fact, Lotte's life begins to change the moment they meet. Lotte expresses to Lettice that the process began when she first came to visit her former employee: "My life began again when I first walked down those stairs [to Lettice's basement flat]. I actually believed it might. . . . I knew them well from the Perseus Book of Staircases" (*LL*, 94). Stairs, then, are another motif in the play, and one that links the beginning of the play with the ending. Lettice loses her job over the wild tales she tells about the staircase in Fustian House. Lotte changes both of their lives when she descends the steps familiar to her, and which take her to Lettice. Under the influence of the Quaff, which forges the bond between the two women, Lotte begins to speak in earnest. During the first visit that Lotte pays to Lettice, she makes all kinds of confessions. The first is that Lettice has been on her conscience since the dismissal. The letter of recommendation that Lotte writes shows that the spirit of Lettice's imagination has already started to work its magic on Lotte: the woman who lives by facts and accuracy is willing to exceed somewhat "the limits of veracity" in assisting Lettice with finding employment. She makes a very telling comment about how she feels about the work that she does at the Trust. Lotte says that her present position keeps her at the "Non-Doer's Desk."

Just as Julian Christoforou has always had a hard time finding a job worthy of him, and as Dysart has lost faith in what he is doing professionally, so Lotte wants to do more than push paper. The wig she wears is really a metaphor for false appearances she presents to the world. It hides her true identity, the rebellious spirit, which exists just beneath the surface. It takes another person to bring out that identity in her. This time it is Lettice.

Two other concepts are closely related to that of "Non-Doers," and they are the The Mere People (versus persons of spunk), and ghosts—in the sense in which Salieri used the word. Lotte and Lettice are kindred spirits because they respect the heroic figures who had spunk, the opposite of the Non-Doers or the Mere People, those who seem to be the only persons left in contemporary society. Becoming such a person is a real fear that Lotte has: "Ghosts! They're the worst! That's what we must never become ourselves—you and I. Not that there's not danger of it in your case. . . . Gentlewomen who live in the past and wring their hands . . . They should all be selling fragrant cushions in our gift shops. Or Tudor House tea towels" (LL, 47). At this point it is fair to indicate a major difference between Lotte and Lettice. While Lotte is taking a course to learn the use of computers and processors, Lettice is intimidated by the gadgets of the modern age, as a quotation in the previous section reveals.

Previously it was Jim who brought out Lotte's spunk. He was a fellow student of architecture with "Scottish passion buried inside him" (LL, 52). They were a matched set and brought to the fore the passion and idealism in each other. She relates to Lettice the kind of spirit that her relationship with Jim was able to awaken in her, and at the same time provides a foreshadowing of the ending of the original version of the play: "Why should all the bombs just fall on beauty? Why shouldn't one at least be used on ugliness—purely as protest? Witness that someone at least still has eyes!" (LL, 51). And so she entered into a pact with Jim to blow up the Shell Building in London. In order to go undetected in her examination of the intended building, she had to dress up as a man—in overalls, cap, and a false mustache. That is another example of sexual reversal in the play, as with the theater company of Lettice's mother, and the mock trials and executions that Lettice and Lotte reenact. A source of remorse in Lotte's life is that she could not go ahead with her part in the bombing. She regrets not only that Jim left her and that she did not complete her studies to become an architect, but more so that she betrayed him. With her plans now to blow up buildings with Lettice, to renew E.N.D.—Eyesore Negation Detachment—which she and Jim created, she has a chance to make up for the past, with Lettice replacing her former conspirator.

The theme of betrayal runs throughout Shaffer's plays. Walter felt betrayed by the Harrington family in his hopes of becoming a British subject; Bob is betrayed by his supposed friend Ted in their competition over Doreen; Frank and Tom betray each other in the *Lies/Liars* plays. Pizarro betrays not only Atahuallpa's, but also Young Martin's trust in him. Mark Askelon betrays everyone at Shrivings. Further, Salieri ruins the young musician who trusted him; and Yonadab, the king, Amnon, and Absalom betray each other, and maybe even themselves in the process. As a result of Lotte's betrayal, she believes that both she and Jim reduced their lives, as Dysart also believes he has done. Like Alan, who blames a placebo for making him confess his crime to Dr. Dysart, Lotte blames Lettice's alcoholic concoction. The truth is that both were ready to unburden themselves and start anew.

It is, therefore, not a new Lotte who emerges, but an honest one who can now be true to herself, and to the real feelings at work within her. Lettice describes to Mr. Bardolph just what their friendship has been like since they identified in each other their common enthusiasm for the heroic figures in history: "In this room I watched her perform one small but thrilling act [her portrayal of Charles I] which could *only* have been ventured by someone longing in her heart to do what her tongue denounced. . . . In an equally small way I was able to gratify that longing. She finally consented to take part in historical charades of my devising" (*LL*, 71).

And so the games began. Since all the charades take place between the end of act 2 and the opening of act 3, the audience or reader learns about them through Lettice's and Lotte's retelling to Mr. Bardolph. The two ladies venture to reenact "how a few monumental spirits turned history into legend" (*LL*, 71), words that recall what Salieri said about Mozart's special talent in opera. Each week the pair would choose a different figure, then relive the trials and executions. Lettice's dual passions of history and theater merged with games into a single act. Games (and tricks) have been important throughout Shaffer's literary and dramatic production. Mr. Verity used them to expose murderers in the detective novels. Clive engaged in different types of games with his sister (amusing) and with his mother (pathetic). Ted dressed up as a chef to amuse—and win—Doreen. Julian played the silence game with Belinda; Clea pretended to be a charwoman in *Black Comedy*; Tom's and Frank's entire relationship was based on practical (and serious) jokes with each other. Mark Askelon played the Apple Game, and Dr. Dysart the truth game. Wolfgang and Constanze played childish games with each other. But Lettice's and Lotte's games end in the charge of attempted murder. Whatever embarrassment Lotte felt when she started playing the games soon turned to excitement. The games are metatheater, and Lettice reminds the solicitor that "without danger, Mr. Bardolph, there is no theatre!" (*LL*, 73).

Seeing the secret side of Lotte gives Lettice a new respect for her, and that respect turns into affection. After the final "execution" in which Lotte is injured, Lettice demonstrates deep concern for her: "[Lotte] was in such a state! I tried to quiet her. . . ." (*LL*, 86). She has assumed the role that Dr. Dysart had after Alan's abreaction. By the end of the play, her feelings are so strong that she would rather cut off her own hand than harm a hair on Lotte's head. Likewise, Lotte springs to Lettice's defense and assures the solicitor that Lettice would not hurt a fly. She will turn hostile witness for the prosecution and maintain her companion's innocence. Shaffer has made the following statement on his play: ". . . I truly meant my comedy *Lettice & Lovage* to be about love, because in fact—though obviously not in a sexual way—Lettice seduces everyone she meets: she seduces Lotte Schoen to her appreciation of life, and she seduces Bardolph from his wintery profession into something wholly different. That's not love in the romantic sense, but it is love of the spirit" ("Conversation," 34). And yes, Lettice is successful in getting the staid solicitor to mock playing the drum as Lettice and Lotte replay the events of the fateful night, in which Lotte, as King Charles, marched through London to his execution.

Lotte was equally inventive in her plans for the executions. The women needed an execution block and could never find one at auction, so Lotte devised the idea of making their own, a process which involved taking a bus (they couldn't afford a cab) to a forest in Epping and talking the bus driver—a pedantic man, in Lotte's words—into letting her take the lumber onto the bus by convincing him that she and Lettice were research scientists: "'We are fungus experts from the Ministry of Health. We have found a very rare variety of fungus growing on this log. It could prove of the utmost benefit to medical research—provided it is not scraped off in the meantime'" (*LL*, 82). The search for a block and the "executions" are not Lotte's first experience at games with Lettice. They play their first game on Lotte's initial visit in the second act. Lettice wants to find out information about Lotte, but not in any conventional way. Instead they reverse their usual roles in life; Lettice becomes the interviewer, and Lotte must answer her questions as if she were looking for employment. It is in this way that Lettice—and the audience—learn everything from Lotte's name to her family's history. This initial game apparently whets Lotte's appetite for the others that followed.

   D. Themes.   As is usual in Shaffer's plays, there are several themes interwoven in the plot. One of the main subjects is modern-day London, and it includes such subtopics as architecture and xenophobia. There are also the big subjects of spirit versus reason and reality versus fantasy. Modern architecture may well serve as a metaphor for both the absence of beauty and for what is wrong with contemporary society. The need for imagination and for an element of fantasy in life is a trait that Lettice inherited from her actress mother. It has put her in the same group as so many other of Shaffer's characters, who face the battle of reason versus spirit and reality versus fantasy.

   In her tours of Fustian House, Lettice started out by spouting facts from history, but they were not interesting enough for either her or her clients. The facts needed the element of fantasy to be satisfying. Lettice explains what occurs during her tours as something that is out of her control: "Fantasy floods in where fact leaves a vacuum" (*LL*, 25). Again there is a tie-in with the theater, which as much made up the reality of her mother's earning a living as it satisfied her need for fantasy in portraying the great Shakespearean roles; when Lettice's mother played Richard III, she was royalty. The line between fact and fiction thus became blurred for Lettice's mother, just as it did for Sophie, who knew the difference between fact and fantasy, but who needed some creativity to keep her from the harsh truth of reality. After all, it took Julian Christoforou's imagination to soften Charles Sidley's reality and make life livable for him. A stage direction in act 3 reads, "Lettice hides her eyes from its glaring flood" (*LL*, 91). Her reaction is the same as Brindsley's, who needs to be in the dark and protected from the truth that light reveals.

   Until Lettice wins Lotte over to her way of dealing with life, the two women are engaged in the same kind of Apollonian-Dionysian battle that characterizes *Equus*. Nothing that Lettice does at Fustian House is quite so drastic as Alan's blinding of the horses, and this play's ending is quite the opposite of that in *Equus*. *Lettice and Lovage* is a comedy, so spirit wins out over reason; *Equus* is a modern tragedy, so Dr. Dysart's rationality prevails. Just as Lotte learns about fantasy, Lettice learns about reality. The fact is not lost on her that she is going to be tried in a real court and may end up in a real prison. Again fact and fantasy border each other. Her real trial will take place because of an act that only looks like a crime, but that was in fact a game.

Having experienced games with her newly-found partner, Lotte does not want to give them up and go back to grim reality. Thus, it is she who decides they must destroy the ten ugliest buildings in London: "We have to make some statement in the world—about the world we both hate so much" (*LL*, 92). It is now Lotte's plan that wins over Lettice and captures *her* imagination. Lettice affirms: "We're a team. A natural team. An expert in architecture and an expert in weaponry. It's a formidable combination" (*LL*, 93). She finds irresistible the fact that Elizabethan weapons will be attacking modern buildings.

In this way, the theme of the need for beauty versus the ugliness of modern society meshes with the theme of reality and reason versus fantasy and spirit. Salieri found beauty in the world through music; Lotte finds it in architecture. (The subject of London's unsightly modern architecture touched a responsive chord in that city's audiences, and is one of Prince Charles's causes.) Now Lotte disagrees with the facts in history books that the destruction of London took place during World War II; no, it took place *after* the war: "We [Lotte and Jim] use to walk through the city endlessly together, watching it be destroyed. That was the true Age of Destruction—the late fifties and sixties" (*LL*, 51). They witnessed the process of destruction in which mediocrity rushed in where once there was beauty, and saw British heritage being erased from the London cityscape: "There would be gangs of workmen all over the place, bashing down our heritage. Whole terraces of Georgian buildings crashing to the ground. I can still see those great balls of iron swinging against elegant façades—street after street! All those fanlights shattered— enchanting little doorways—perfectly portioned windows, bash bash bash!—and no one stopping it" (*LL*, 51). First she proposed stopping it to Jim, and now she makes the same proposal to Lettice.

And so the city of London becomes a subject in the play. Lotte finds justification for the terrorism that she proposes in the crime that takes place all over London: "This city is actually crammed with fanatics from all over the globe fighting medieval crusades on our ground. Isn't it time we became a little fanatic ourselves—on its behalf?" (*LL*, 47). It is with those lines in the second act that the plot thickens and the playwright foreshadows the play's ending. The reference to fanatics leads to the element of xenophobia in the play. There are comments in the section on Lotte about her attitudes toward the French. Those comments are mild compared to what Lettice has to say about her neighbor, Mr. Pachmani. He is of unspecified nationality, and she holds him responsible for the Arabic graffiti that she reads on the walls. What Lettice says about him is what the vox populi of London says of the nonwhite immigrants to their city. In the following speech, she is referring to her broken door: "Since I lack the money to repair it, I am now at the total mercy of every marauder in London. Including Mr. Pachmani—probably a rapist—and almost certainly making plans upstairs at this very minute to overthrow several governments" (*LL*, 68). Her accusation is, of course, fantastic, and probably goes beyond what even she herself believes about him, but it reflects the fear of Londoners. What seems to escape her notice is that the only violence and projected violence in the play takes place between Lotte and her in one of their flats, and later against public buildings. Once again there is the question of fact versus fantasy. Shaffer never has Mr. Pachmani appear on stage, and the only information the audience receives about him is the thirdhand account that Mr. Bardolph relates to Lettice of what the police told him, and Lettice's wild fears about the man's potential for danger. Xenophobia is an uncharacteristic trait in a play by Shaffer. In *Five Finger Exercise*, there is sympathy and understanding for the German character, and there is certainly respect and regard for the Greek Julian Christoforou. *The Royal Hunt of the Sun* presents the Incan value system as superior to that of its European invaders. That Lettice and Mr. Pachmani occupy the same apartment building unites the past of the city with its present and future.

In the final moments of the play, Lotte paraphrases Lettice's opening of the play in her comments on the stairs that lead to Lettice's flat. She claims that her words come from the Perseus Book of Staircases: "Humble as it appears, this is actually the most extraordinary set of stairs in England. . . . many witnesses agree that it is unquestionably endowed with miraculous properties. . . . Enlargement for their shrunken souls; Enlivenment of their dying spirits; Enlightenment for their dim prosaic eyes" (*LL*, 94–95). With those words, Lotte shows that Lettice's conversion of her spirit is complete. The motto of Fustian House now takes on an additional meaning. "By a fall I rise" refers to Lotte's physical and Lettice's professional fall, both of which led to their enhanced lives.

E. Reviews and summation. Some reviewers were so taken by Maggie Smith's tour de force performance that they had little to say about the script—without which there is no play.[3] Others did consider the themes and language. Irving Wardle[4] saw that the play would touch the rage of Londoners, who bemoan what their city became at the hands of the postwar planners. He appreciated the original and often hilarious treatment that the important and much-neglected subject received from Shaffer. Wardle summed up the play as an uproarious farce of savage indignation. In his follow-up review of the revised version, Wardle[5] found an improved balance between the two parts, and a text that enlivened the comic detail of the play. While Clare Armistead[6] saw the play as essentially a "present" for Dame Maggie Smith, and one that doesn't really tell a story, she did say it is "a celebration of history and individuality of character and art and civilization and a joy in the humour of nonsense and sense." Benedict Nightingale[7] identified the theme of poetic impulse in conflict with the prosaic, of fact versus fantasy. He called Lotte jealous of the very impulse she attempted to defeat in Lettice. He thought the play more "laughing gas" than "intellectual wind" and that it sentimentalizes England's past, the relationship between the characters, and Lettice herself. With musical vocabulary previously used to describe *Amadeus*, Peter Lewis[8] called the play ". . . a concerto for a virtuoso with solo cadenzas. . . ."

In anticipation of the opening on Broadway, Gordon Rogoff[9] alerted the public to the coming of a "sweet, rambling comedy . . . alive with verbal bounce and grumbling melancholy." *Variety*[10] acknowledged that "Shaffer is in a class by himself in the manufacture of sophisticated, erudite, skillfully constructed plays that satisfy the middlebrow legit public on both sides of the Atlantic." For Edith Oliver[11] the play was a source of continuous delight, but for Frank Rich[12] it was no more than a slight if harmless confection of lackadaisical dramatic structure and shallow characterizations.

Other critics did not consider the characterizations to be shallow, and saw amorous implications in the relationship. Thomas M. Disch[13] saw a genteel, wholesome, and consistently funny play about "two women in late middle age [who] meet, quarrel, fall in love, and in lieu of having sex, design for themselves a *folie à deux* that resembles in its bizarre intimacy the divine madness of the hippocidal hero of *Equus*." In a similar vein, Frank Rich's[14] review of the London production called Lettice Shaffer's "sexually ambiguous answer to Auntie Mame." For Sheridan Morley,[15] the play is "a very odd love story." That, in fact, is what Shaffer intended to write, as the quotation in a previous section reveals. John Simon[16] (who never has a good word to say about Shaffer) accused Shaffer of once again lacking the courage to write what should have been a lesbian love story. Shaffer has in fact done anything but shy away from depicting characters who demonstrate a wide diversity of sexual preferences. There *is* a lesbian attraction in *Withered Murder*, not to mention homosexual males in *White Liars* and *Black Comedy*. Homosexuality lurks just below the surface in *Five Finger Exercise*. Gideon Petrie found equally strong sexual impulses in everything from men and women to flowers and mathematics. Alan Strang could find sexual satisfaction only during masturbatory rides at midnight on a horse. Yonadab is a voyeur. Michael Hinden observes that the dialectic of *Lettice and Lovage* is framed in terms of "aesthetic pleasure versus Puritanism, which is defined as hatred of all that is beautiful or voluptuous" (Hinden, 164). Like Salieri, the only good Lotte perceives is in beauty.

Whom Do I Have the Honour of Addressing?

Shaffer wrote this radio script for Smith after her accident, and hoped that she might be able to perform it while she was recuperating. However, other problems with her health prevented her from accepting the role. As a result, Dame Judi Dench performed it on BBC Radio on 20 November 1989. Shaffer was very pleased with the work, and hopes that he will be able to adapt it for either television or the stage. Since it is a comparatively short, one-woman monologue, it makes sense to consider plot, characterization, themes, and motifs in one section, as an integrated reading.

The drama takes place in the Clapham, London, flat of Mrs. Angela Parsons, a woman in her fifties. It opens and closes to the sound of "When You Wish upon a Star," a song composed for the motion picture *Pinocchio*. (The word "star" in the context of this work takes on an additional meaning). There are three props in the play. The first and most important is a tape recorder, which serves a different function here from its uses in *Equus* and *Lettice and Lovage*. As in *Amadeus*, this play takes place on what the speaker believes will be her last day on earth, since Angela, like Salieri, is planning to commit suicide. She is using the tape recorder (although she knows as little about technology as does Lettice) to leave her final message to the world. All but the first words and final moments of the play constitute that message. Everything in between is the explanation of why she has decided to end her life. She, like Salieri, addresses her remarks to posterity. This recording is the only statement she has ever made concerning her life . . . and death. She suspects that by tomorrow it will explode like a bomb on the millions of individuals who could potentially hear it.

The second prop is a bottle of whiskey, which Angela, like Miss

Furnival, is tasting for the first time. As in *Lettice and Lovage*, where there is constant foreshadowing, Angela compares the tape to a spool of film; film plays a major part in this monologue. "Whom do I have the honour of addressing?" are words she heard from Tom Prance, a twenty-four-year-old American film idol at the London premiere of one of his movies. That question changed her life and may now end it. Despite criticism from her partner Connie at Swift Scripts, a firm which types plays and filmscripts, Angela is not only a devotee of the movies in general, but she also attends every star-studded premiere that takes place in her city. There is a certain parallelism between Angela and Connie in this play, and Lettice and Lotte in act 1 of theirs. Angela describes Connie as "a rather embittered woman, who thinks her life's mission is to take people down a peg."[17] Connie's view of film stars it that they, like Brindsley and Frank (*Liars*), need constant adulation. The Tom in this work, like his namesake in *The White Liars*, is a handsome entertainer, a turn-on whose skin is like the white satin of the other Tom's singing outfit. Tom Prance uttered the title question to Angela at the premiere when she criticized the long fake fur coat he wore, which she thought made him look like Mae West. She objected not only to the hideous garment, but to the fact that it hid his gorgeous "God's-gift" body, which she had seen in one of his films. The crowd envied the attention she received from the star; that envy is also a foreshadowing of things yet to come.

Angela wrote to him in care of his studio in Hollywood, and as fate would have it, Tom himself, and not his personal assistant Bud, opened the letter. He answered it, and thus began what turned into a correspondence between the middle-aged Englishwoman and the young American. If *Lettice and Lovage* contains derogatory remarks about the French and Arabs, in *Whom . . .* the target is Americans, who are referred to as nitwits who know nothing about proper grammar or vocabulary; they are also hypocrites, who care only about appearances, and who are "goody-good on top and filth underneath" (*W*, 38).

Angela is suffering from a kind of personal and professional malaise. Her life, like Doreen's, is one of typing an original and two carbons. At just the time that her life and job seemed empty—like Bob's in *The Private Ear* and Dr. Dysart's—when she could no more take the dreariness that surrounded her than could Sophie, she had an offer that promised to take her away from all that. Angela, like a host of other characters in Shaffer's plays, is another casualty of the institution of marriage. She follows in the tradition of such other unsatisfactorily married couples as the Harringtons, Sidleys, Dysarts, and Petries. It was, in fact, her being totally ignored by her husband of only two years that turned her to the movies, which became something of a drug—some more foreshadowing—for her. She was beside herself with joy when Tom Prance, rated as one of the handsomest men in the world, wanted her to move to Los Angeles to work at the drug rehabilitation center he owned. Tom Prance, "Hero to the Young" and "Clean Right Fellow," wanted her over every woman in his own city because he liked the way British English sounds, and he wanted a "Margaret Rutherford type" to greet him each morning. It may have been no more flattering to hear herself referred to by that image than it was for Louise Harrington to learn that Walter thought of her as a mother, but how could she not accept such a tempting offer? Connie's face was "absolutely puckered with jealousy" (*W*, 18) when Mr. Tom Prance called the office and asked for Angela by name, so that he could invite her to his hotel.

Not only Americans are concerned with appearances and images. In Shaffer's works there are also the socially-pretentious Louise Harrington, Carol Melkett, and Tom's mother in *The White Liars*, not to mention Ted, and Frank and Sophie of *The Private Ear* and *The White Liars*, respectively. And Angela. Before she went to Tom's hotel, she had her hair done at an expensive parlor in Mayfair, and bought a new outfit on Regent Street. When Tom finally did ask her to move to Los Angeles, time froze for Angela: "The film, which I sometimes imagine as my life, became a freeze" (*W*, 20). This is only the first of many references in which life becomes film and vice versa. Both Tom and Angela were going to fulfill their fantasies: he would have a "real English Lady Assistant," and she would live in Los Angeles among "sun and palm trees and ice tinkling in tall glasses" (*W*, 21). Connie does not approve of Angela's acting on a "childish whim." Connie was not only envious, she was furious. Angela was about to act like a fool, and at the same time betray her partner. The theme of betrayal looks back to the earlier plays, and it also looks ahead in this one. Like so many other characters, from Bob and Young Martin to David Askelon, Alan Strang, and Amnon, Angela was about to put her trust in another person: Tom would look after her— until he betrayed her.

Tom did not meet Angela personally at the airport, but rather sent his assistant Bud, who acted hostilely toward the woman. Her concern, after so many hours of crossing the globe, was about her appearance. Bud drove Angela to what would be her residence, the penthouse of the drug rehabilitation center. She found the pale pink walls and strawberry-patterned sofa quite feminine and assumed that Tom had the place redone for her. While whiskey-guzzling Bud was a worry for Angela right from the start, Tom made a delightful companion for her. However tired he might have been, every evening after leaving the studio he stopped by the penthouse to see her. His visits were ritualistic. After his characteristic knock at the door (to the beat of Beethoven's ba ba ba *ba*), he asked if she was receiving "picture performers" that evening. Then he would enjoy a Diet Coke, and while Angela spoke he lay on the sofa. Angela, of course, looked forward to each evening with her "visiting young god," with whom she was falling in love. They talked of Tom's life—his childhood had been anything but pleasant. His mother had abandoned him at birth, and he grew up in orphanages. His knowledge of grammar and literature was self-taught. Tom was not only an actor by profession, but by avocation. He enjoyed imitating Charlie Chaplin and Buster Keaton, whose films were included in Tom's large private collection. He would send videocassettes to Angela via Bud, who always treated her with a total lack of respect.

Angela started assuming more and more responsibility with the clients until she was playing the role of a bona fide psychiatrist; her lack of qualifications was unimportant since what the clients really wanted was an old-fashioned mother to look after them. After three months, Angela felt as qualified as anyone else at giving therapy. At the same time, Tom's intimacy (never sexual) with her intensified. He even confessed that he too had taken drugs until an older person helped him get off them. She, like Julian Christoforou, had found her professional and personal niche. Only Bud did not warm up to her, and in fact seemed sinister. Tom explained his attitude was that of a "loner." She did not like Bud's hands or eyes, the two parts of the body to which Shaffer makes frequent references in his plays. His hands, unlike Tom's, were not those of a hugger; they were for repairing automobile engines and pouring whiskey. On the one occasion that his eyes were not hidden behind mirrored glasses, Angela saw that they were a very pale gray, as if he had spent his life in the dark.

His life, in fact, was uglier than Angela could ever have imagined, as she found out on the day that was to change her relationship with Tom and lead her to thoughts of suicide. She came home to find Bud, who had a key, "shooting up" cocaine on her sofa. It was the act of revenge to which his jealousy of her had led him: Angela had taken over his "little pink pad" (*W*, 31). In a frenzy, Angela rushed to Tom's studio, and despite the red light indicating shooting in progress and the presence of the crew, Angela burst in and told the actor what she had just witnessed.

Life is again compared to a film: Angela felt as if she and Tom were in the movie about tropical passion, in which Tom was cast.

From that moment on, Angela's situation went from bad to worse. For the first time since she arrived in Los Angeles, Tom did not show up that night. The next day Bud appeared with another film for her to watch, and Angela had a premonition that something horrible was about to happen. She imagined herself in a woman-in-danger movie. Nothing could have prepared her for what she saw in that film: a naked Tom wearing a studded leather harness and with a look of joy on his face in a submissive position to a menacing Bud. Tom's secret life is now revealed. It seemed to Angela that Tom was deliberately mocking her from the screen, as Bud laughed at her from behind the penthouse door. Before Bud exited, he left Angela a pile of such films "for [her] viewing pleasure" (*W*, 35).

The next time Angela saw Tom, he was an icy-cold, cruel judge—the way Clive Harrington felt his father behaved, and the way Alan perceived Equus to act. And to continue the associations with *Equus*, Tom "sat there looking all pained and Jesussy, talking about failure of imagination!" (*W*, 37). "Jesussy" recalls Equus the horse-god. Tom confessed that it was Bud who had gotten him off drugs. Angela's arrival on the scene had driven Bud to use them again out of jealousy. And if Tom must chose between Bud and Angela, his priority was Bud. In a rage, Angela slashed Tom's forehead with the video and left him scarred, perhaps for life: "He gave a scream—exactly like a girl—and shot off the sofa and ran to the mirror!" (*W*, 38). Tom's life and livelihood are in his looks, his image. The arguing and fighting that ensued made Angela feel as if she were in a film. When she awoke from the horror, Bud was standing over her with her packed bags, and telling her that she was leaving immediately.

Angela has spent the last two days back in Clapham feeling something like the violated Tamar, who was more of a temptress than a victim in the eyes of society: "What will they say when they hear this tape? . . . 'Silly F. Bitch! What a stupid thing to do—for a boy nearly young enough to be her grandson! Why didn't she stay in London where she belonged?'" (*W*, 41). And so the third prop is the pills with which she will commit suicide—ultimately the most destructive use of drugs— after she leaves the note "Please Play This." Like Salieri, she will not be mocked; and like Tamar, she will have her revenge. There is a bit of ambiguity over her motive. Is it solely that Tom tried to make her feel guilty for Bud's use of drugs? His choosing Bud over her? Or for a motive that approximates Louise's action against Walter: "That'll show you,

won't it? What we can do if we choose—we Margaret Rutherford types!"
(*W*, 41). All she wants now is to ruin Tom's life the way she destroyed his
looks by involving him in scandals of suicide and kink: "It'll be the end
of you, my dear!" (*W*, 42). Angela had no idea that she could be so cruel.

And then she vacillates. Perhaps she has done him enough harm by
blemishing his absolute beauty and thereby ending his career in the
movies. But she'll save his reputation by erasing the tape before she
commits suicide, if she commits suicide, instead of turning Tom's and
Bud's lives into a living hell of doubt over when she might decide to
reveal their secret. She ends the radio play with the line "Whom do I have
the honour of erasing?" (*W*, 45), and with the mystery of whether or not
she kills, or "erases," herself or takes further revenge on her American
victims.

The two plays in this chapter are a pair in their portrayals of what
damage middle-aged Englishwomen can cause when provoked, and thus
join the plays *Five Finger Exercise* and *Yonadab* on the theme of a woman's
revenge. These plays also lay to rest reservations that critics had about
Shaffer's lack of significant female characters.[18] This chapter analyzes
much of the more recent work that Shaffer has done in depicting
individuals who are dissatisfied with their lives—their marital relations
and sexual lives, their professional and personal battles—those individuals who in fact, or in their own minds, compose a part of society's
misfits.

Chapter Ten
The Gift of the Gorgon and Conclusion

The Gift of the Gorgon

The Gift of the Gorgon had its official opening on 16 December 1992 at The Pit, the experimental theater of the Royal Shakespeare Company at the Barbican Centre in London. The play was presented in repertory until 11 March 1993. The Pit was modified from a theater-in-the-round format to seat 190 persons on three sides of the theater. The stage was almost bare, the lighting was exposed (as in *Equus*), and the fourth wall, where the proscenium arch would be in a conventional theater, was made of gray glass through which the audience could see a stylized cliff of the Greek island of Thira, where the present-day action takes place. On entering, the audience was confronted with a stage dominated by a wooden coffin that faced the main section of seating, across a large desk; a few wooden chairs; a coat rack; a suitcase and attaché case; and a basket of books. The cast, under the direction of Sir Peter Hall, included Dame Judi Dench as Helen Damson, Michael Pennington as Edward Damson, and Jeremy Northam as Philip. Mr. Shaffer rewrote feverishly during previews and then had to have heart surgery, which prevented his attending the opening. A note that he posted backstage read, "To the company of *The Gift of the Gorgon*. I am sorry not to be able to thank you and greet you individually tonight. Unfortunately it is the night before surgery, and the doctors refused permission. (As skilled knife-men, they have a keen fellow-feeling with the Critics.) I want to tell you that I have enjoyed working with you all tremendously. You're terrific people and a terrific company. Good luck tonight and always. I'll hope to see you all soon. Love, Peter Shaffer." The text of the play has not been published at the time of this writing, and all quotations are as they were spoken at the performance on the evening of 9 January 1993. Since the play is not yet in final form, no study of it at this time can be definitive. What follows is an integrated reading of plot, characters, techniques, and themes of the original production.

The play is written in three acts, with no subdivisions into scenes. The segments in the present (1993) take place at the widow Damson's villa, which she occupied with her husband until his death; and in flashbacks in England, beginning in 1975. As in *Shrivings*, the present action takes place over a weekend. The first act begins with the overvoices that re-create the correspondence between Helen and Philip, "an assistant professor at an undistinguished college in America's Middle-West." He keeps asking permission to come to Greece to interview Helen, and she keeps denying it. Damson was Philip's father, a father whom the professor never met (making this situation more extreme than those in *Shrivings* and "The Prodigal Father"), and Philip is anxious to write the biography of Damson, a prominent playwright. Without waiting for her consent, Philip travels to Greece and after considerable objection the recently widowed Helen reluctantly receives him. It does not take her long to warm up to the likable and dedicated twenty-eight-year-old professor, and she consents to tell him about her late husband, but on one condition: he must take a pledge on his father's desk and altar that he hear the whole story about Damson, and write a book that tells the truth about his life and death. Philip agrees, and Helen assures him, "You will never forgive me." During the rest of the play Philip sits at his father's desk and writes down every word that comes out of Helen's mouth. He, therefore, like Yonadab before him, is depicted as an onlooker rather than as an active participant of life.

The theme of the contrast between individuals of passion versus those of reason has been a trademark of Shaffer's work, and most provocatively presented in *Equus* and *Amadeus*. In order to begin his exposition on this contrast of passion and reason, Shaffer introduces the two men in Helen's life, her father and her future husband. In 1975, Helen was working on her doctorate in classics at Cambridge University, where her father was a professor. Her father, like Gideon in *Shrivings*, is a man of moderate temperament and president of the Peace League. In sharp contrast to her father is the man Helen meets at the library and who later becomes her husband, the aspiring playwright who calls himself Edward Damson. Like Mark Askelon, he advocates violence; unlike Askelon, he demonstrates the passion of Alan Strang and Wolfgang Amadeus Mozart. To justify his support of violence, he uses Mark Askelon's example: What is the appropriate response to a violent act, if not violent retribution? For Damson, "pure revenge is pure justice." He endorses Clytemnestra's murder of her husband in Aeschylus's *Agamemnon* as justified because the adulterous wife was feeling rage, and Damson insists, "Don't piss on the rage": it is that rage that embodies passion. He detests pacifists and their philosophy.

Like Mark Askelon and Francisco Pizarro, Damson has no faith in conventional religion and institutions; his faith is in the theater, "the only religion that can never die." It is the theater alone that illuminates life. But it needs new "priests" who can make it blaze again. He is dedicated to becoming one of those priests.

To that end he needs Helen. He pleads with her, "Be my savior," and thereby defines what is to become her role in life. She is to be Athena to his Perseus: she will be the voice of wisdom, reason, and moderation in his life. Her role, then, is like that of Hesther Salomon in *Equus*. In contrast, Damson will be Perseus, who, in Greek mythology, married Andromeda after rescuing her from a sea monster. As Damson sees it, he can "deliver" Helen, but only after she delivers him. In part, Damson is escaping from his drab past, just as Sophie in the three *Lies/Liars* plays is escaping from hers. There is nothing heroic in his background; he is the son of a Russian father who finds life in a bottle of vodka. Helen's father wants his daughter to have nothing to do with Damson, who wastes his time and who has no future; but acting on her passion, Helen marries him.

While most of the play takes place in flashbacks, at significant moments the play returns to the present and becomes a dialogue between the widow and the young professor. At these times, after a drink, she warns the son about details yet to come and prepares the audience for the strong curtains that end each act, and for the final climax. One bit of information that Philip learns is his origin. He was conceived before Helen's marriage to Damson, while his father was off for "two weeks on a packaged tour," the kind of sterile vacations that Dr. Dysart laments. These interludes also give Philip the opportunity to explain himself. He says that his father's "worship of theatre" is also his own "disease." It was the deciding factor in his becoming a professor of drama.

Shaffer intends here to contrast father and son. To his mind, the playwright is the passionate person who creates and the professor the passive person who analyzes. In fact, throughout the play, Philip sits on the sidelines and takes down his father's every word. Shaffer generally has a target for his biting criticism: in *Equus* it was fundamental Christianity and possibly the psychiatric profession; in *The Royal Hunt of the Sun*, *Amadeus*, and *Shrivings* he attacks Catholicism, the musical establishment of eighteenth-century Vienna, and a host of social institutions; in *Yonadab*, orthodox Judaism gets the brunt of his wrath. In *The Gift of the*

Gorgon he attacks the academic profession. If *Five Finger Exercise* contains an autobiographical element of the young Peter Shaffer, *The Gift of the Gorgon* is the play that comes closest to reflecting the attitude of the mature Shaffer: the protagonist is, after all, a playwright who believes that in drama extremity is the point, an idea that echoes words Martin Dysart spoke ten years earlier. Shaffer attacks what he calls "dry sticks" who conduct boring seminars on drama, and the endless line of academics who sit and analyze his thoughts because they have no thoughts of their own. Finally he insists, "Playwrights do not exist to provide professors with a livelihood." It is for this reason that a large basket of books remains on stage throughout the play—the books are the studies that professors have sent to the dramatist in an effort to prove that they are worthy of studying him.

Helen contrasts her father and husband in the way she describes her trips to Greece. As a child she visited the country six times with her father. They were passionless experiences because her father was a passionless man. But her one trip with Damson before they were married was different from her childhood trips. She describes an event that is to gain significance in the third act. Damson, then only her boyfriend, asks her to soap him down in the shower. After the shower, he appears clad in a towel (although he is presumably naked) and passionately performs a Greek folk dance. Upset by this memory, Helen runs off the stage crying; Philip can no longer control himself and screams, "I want my father," the father who abandoned him before his birth; and the maid informs Philip that he should return at six o'clock that evening. On that note, act 1 comes to an end.

As act 2 opens, Helen restates the agreement to Philip that she will relate the whole story about his late father and that he will listen to it. And so she continues. After Helen and Damson returned from Greece they were married, despite her father's objections. She spent the rest of her married life as her husband's muse and supporter, at the cost of pursuing her own career. The message that Damson learned from his mother is reminiscent of ideas in *Five Finger Exercise* and in Shaffer's own life: theater is frivolous; it is not real work. Perhaps it was that notion, or perhaps the idea of failure, that kept Damson from completing a play during the early period of his marriage.

Viewers of *The Royal Hunt of the Sun, Equus,* and *Yonadab* have become accustomed to the element of spectacle in Shaffer's plays. The present work is no exception. A plank drops from the back of the set onto the desk to reveal the heavily stylized figures of Athena and Perseus in the

Temple of Athena. Damson sees himself as Perseus and Helen as the nurturing Athena. Also in the play-within-the-play is a mirror in which Damson and presumably the members of the audience are supposed to take a look at themselves. Damson is suffering the punishment of the Gorgon, who in Greek mythology were monsters named Stheno, Ewryale, and Medusa; they had snakes for hair and turned men into stone. The Gorgon (here, Medusa) prevents Damson from writing by turning his mind into stone, by inflicting him with "creative paralysis." Damson must kill the Gorgon to be free of its curse. But killing the Gorgon is dangerous because while the blood from its right side saves, the blood from its left side kills. Damson must understand and assume his position of playwright-as-god. He must write in blood-red ink on special paper that must be cut with a special blade. Writing must be a ritual in his religion of the theater. And he must immortalize the two values of Beauty and Violence. Damson vows to Helen that he will now see a play through to completion. While she is not the classical Helen whose face launched a thousand ships in the Trojan war, she does launch her husband's career. And so he writes his first play, "Icons," about the Byzantinian empress Irene. It has spectacle, masks, and violence. The character Constantine, whose worst crime was that he destroyed beauty, must have his eyes put out so that he will be prevented from seeing his god. (The parallels to *Equus* are so obvious that they need not be enumerated here.) His play is a huge hit, and Damson becomes an overnight success.

Helen now lives on Damson's need of her, and his plays became their children. One of the terms of their marriage was that Helen abort the real child of his that she was carrying. Under her care he writes his second play, this time about Cromwell's England. Helen objects to the violence and fears the audience's reaction to it, but Damson insists "it's the playwright's duty to appall" and also to reestablish the theater's moral authority, just as it is the playwright's prerogative to create truths. He further believes that rage should not be allowed to fester; it must be the impetus for acts of terror. Helen insists that humanity can and must stop acts of bloodshed. When Damson believes that he has lost his wife's support, he accuses her of wanting to castrate him. Helen is beside herself and is unable to continue narrating these events to Philip. In the act's final image, Damson tellingly pours a bottle of red wine over himself.

Damson's view of Helen changes in the third act. While he still sees her as Athena at the beginning of the act, he sees Athena as having a dual spirit, part of which is jealousy. To his mind, Helen has become his

Medusa, and Damson believes that it is humanity's obligation to question gods and not obey them. The gruesome head of Medusa circulates on a pole before the audience. The reference here to Medusa brings Shaffer's work full circle—Clive in *Five Finger Exercise* makes a reference to her when he walks in on his mother and a disheveled Walter. Despite his wife's advice and pleas, Damson writes a play about the I.R.A's acts of terrorism and a pacifist reaction to them. Through the technique of broadcasting reviews over a loudspeaker, the audience learns that the play fails miserably (even Damson's unsophisticated father is disappointed by it), and Damson flees England for his villa in Greece. For five years he becomes compulsively secretive, seeks refuge in alcohol and avoids his wife. He indulges himself instead by picking up American backpackers at the local taverna, bringing them home, and having sex with these women, who are young enough to be his daughters, with his wife in the house. His rank insensitivity parallels a similar act that Mark Askelon commits in front of his wife.

Philip finally has to ask the question that is personally important to him: Did his father ever mention him? Helen knows that the answer will be hard for Philip to hear, but according to their pledge she must say all and he must hear it. Until a year ago, Helen never knew that her husband had a son. She learned of his existence when Philip sent a copy of the published version of his doctoral dissertation about his father's work to Damson. Damson never bothered to read the book; he threw it into the basket with the rest of the uninspired academic trash that professors kept sending to him. Damson believed that he had a reason to disregard his son's professional efforts. Once, when he was on a lecture tour in America (from which he returned early), he secretly observed his son participating in a seminar on Damson. When he saw what a bore his son was—much like Helen's now-dead father—he left, unable to tolerate the "dry sticks" who were draining the life out of his plays. Damson did learn a lesson from his son: drama had been dismissed for the less-challenging media of movies and television, the new "icons of irrelevance." He left the United States convinced that American English had been reduced to the words "wow" and "shit" and further convinced that he had wasted his life.

Upon Damson's return to Greece, Helen tells him that she is leaving him in the morning. Since Damson has always been so self-absorbed, he had never taken notice of what he had done to his wife, and that it was her life and not his that has been squandered. He begs her to indulge him in one last ritual this night, lathering him with his special soap, and she consents. He wants "justice, clear and clean for us both." Unbeknownst to her, Damson conceals in his ritualistic bar of soap the blade that he uses for his ritualistic slicing of paper. After his shower, he enters the stage in a towel, blood streaming from his body. Once again, it is a sharp object that is the means of destruction in a Shaffer play. His death is his gift to his wife. The previous symbols—the soap; the knife, whose cutting sound was magnified over a loudspeaker; the blood-red wine, with which the second act comes to an end—all participate in the climax. He goes to the cliff and throws himself off. When his body is discovered, everyone believes he had suffered an accident.

Helen, who has always been the voice of moderation, now wants revenge. She wants to hurt her late husband by destroying his posthumous reputation, and she will do it through the book that his own son had pledged at the beginning of the play to write. But Philip has another idea: he wants to write a book that will make his late father "live and glint," and give no hint of his suicide. In what amounts to an epilogue, which gives circular action to the play, there is another exchange of letters between widow and professor in which she finally consents not to expose her husband's secret, much to his son's relief. On the desk that served as the altar for his writing, Damson appears. He is stomping rhythmically (as he did in the dance at the end of act 1) through Helen's conscience, just as Equus stomped through Alan's. *Amadeus* ends with Salieri absolving the mediocrities of the world; this play ends with Helen's repeated cries to her dead husband, "I forgive you. I forgive." Maybe it is even a collective pardon of professors, this play's mediocrities of the world.

Expectations ran high for a new play by Peter Shaffer, and tickets for the entire run of *Gift of the Gorgon* were sold out before the play opened. Critical reception of the play was mixed, but generally unfavorable. The *Daily Telegraph* titled Charles Spencer's[1] review "A Masterpiece of Higher Tosh." In excessively strong language, he called the play "as ripe a slice of phoney baloney as you are ever likely to come across." He finds it both pretentious bilge and terrific entertainment. Alastair Macauly[2] sees Damson as entertaining but not persuasive, and questions why Shaffer needs to write such characters into his work. He enjoyed watching the play, despite the formulaic structure, which prepares the audience for a melodramatic climax. Benedict Nightingale[3] believes that Dench, rather than Shaffer, brings the evening to life. Paul Taylor[4] finds no surprise or redeeming value in "all the ponderous paraphernalia you expect from this author's work." However, Michael Billington[5] finds it a powerful work and concedes that "whatever its excesses, it is bracingly theatrical, endlessly alive and fiercely ambitious." He finds the ending unresolved on the issue of vengeance versus clemency, but respects Shaffer for the "sheer recklessness [which] allows him to go for the big issues." Peter Hepple[6] suspects that Shaffer is "producing memories that will linger and will resound . . . in years to come." Frank Rich[7] found this "compelling but unsettling piece . . . compelling when it champions the power of epic theater against the onslaught of cineplex literalism or when it deals with its moral themes in the domestic arena." The highest praise came from London's *Time Out* magazine, which rated the play the number-one critics' choice for the week of 30 December 1992–6 January 1993, and calls it "a complex well-produced piece of theatre with a Rolls-Royce company that includes an extraordinary performance from Michael Pennington" (94). Shaffer is a master at reworking his plays and with some trimming and refining, he should be able to do for this play what he did for *Amadeus* and *Yonadab*.

Conclusion

Peter Shaffer's success as a dramatist has been phenomenal. He has enjoyed such great success because his work is as much a pleasure to the mind as literature, as it is a feast for the eyes and ears as theater. His success is the result of the combination of research, talent, insight, and involvement in every aspect of production. He has gone beyond winning awards from critics and inspiring scholarship from academics, who are fiercely devoted to the man and his work—and the present writer is no exception—to having had an influence on society. The conclusion to this book summarizes some of those reactions from scholars, dramatists, the world of music, and society at large.

As is the case with any body of work that becomes the subject of scholarship, writing on Shaffer's plays runs the gamut from acutely perceptive to embarrassingly sophomoric, from treating big themes to splitting hairs; some of this criticism has become tiresomely repetitive. The readers of that research can decide for themselves which works fall into which categories. The studies listed in this book's bibliography appear because they are either an excellent example of the genre, or in some way present a unique point of view worthy of consideration.

Shaffer seems also to have had an effect on other playwrights. James M. Welsh finds John Pielmeier's 1982 drama *Agnes of God* a gimmicky imitation of *Equus* (Welsh, 123). Perhaps Pielmeier awarded the author of *Equus* the sincerest form of flattery. More recently, Miguel Delibes's

La guerra de nuestros antepasados (Our ancestors' war), which had a success-ful run in Madrid during the 1989–90 theatrical season, also owes a debt of thanks to Shaffer. *Guerra* is a two-character play whose plot is limited to the therapy sessions between a psychiatrist and his patient, who was sentenced to death for murder. Once again, the doctor attempts to uncover what details in the patient's past led up to the crime.

Shaffer seems to bring even words and names into fashion with his works. For example, Robert Vavra titled his 1977 book of photographs of horses *Equus*.[8] C. J. Gianakaris mentions the cartoon in *The New Yorker* that depicts two men talking at a bar; one is telling the other, "Everywhere you go it's Wolfgang Amadeus Mozart, Wolfgang Amadeus Mozart. I've had it up to *here* with Wolfgang Amadeus Mozart" (Gianakaris 1983, 88). The wide appeal of *Amadeus* is difficult to explain. Who would have thought that anyone but serious theatergoers, music lovers, and the odd intellectual would would care to sit through what amounts to a series of monologues on the nature of genius and mediocrity, as well as speculations on who or what killed Mozart? Richard Corliss's review of the film in *Time* magazine raises similar questions: Who will be interested in the movie? Can it make money? He answers those questions by calling Shaffer's Mozart the punk rebel of whom there is a little in all of us (Corliss, 74–75). The play—and perhaps even more so the movie—made Amadeus a household name and brought Mozart's music to the largest audience it has ever had. The soundtrack was a best-seller among members of the general public who would generally not *think* of buying a recording of Mozart's music. Even the "Wireless," the gift catalogue of Minnesota Public Radio, advertises the recording *The Sublime Mozart* as containing "twenty favorites from the movie *Amadeus*." Is it a mere coincidence that in 1989 Decca produced the Amadeus Winds's recording of the piece of music that makes the theatrical Salieri declare war on God through Mozart?

Shaffer is probably responsible for granting Salieri the fame for which he hungered. Since *Amadeus*, there has been a resurgence of Salieri's music. For example, while it is not surprising that *Time and Life*'s series of Great Ages of Music contains a 1985 volume called *The Age of Mozart*, it is surprising to find that it includes Salieri's Sinfonia in D Major (Veneziana). In the same year, Hungaton brought out Salieri's 1799 opera *Falstaff*. (How typical of Salieri to chose as subject matter at-tempted seduction, deceit, and jealousy, as well as a glutton for the title character.) While *Falstaff*, with its simplistic music and heavy use of recitativo, is a far cry from both *Così Fan Tutte* and *Figaro*, it might have borrowed from the former the devices of tricks and disguises, and from the latter laundresses as characters. In addition, its libretto by Carlo Prospero Defranceschi includes the line "Così tutte le donne facesser come noi" (if only women could do as we do), which cannot help but bring to the listener's mind Mozart's *Così Fan Tutte*, written nine years before *Falstaff*. In effect, Shaffer has made Salieri's scheme work: his name has not fallen into oblivion. Lettice thinks that Lotte is too hard on herself. The same may be said of Salieri. While his music is no match for Mozart's, it is not so bad as Shaffer's character might lead the audience to believe. In "Finishing Salieri: Another Act to *Amadeus*," Frank X. Mikels and James Rurak[9] suggest that Salieri's real problems are self-hatred and self-pity; the former kept him from ever being free, and the latter finally destroyed him. Just as Mozart had turned the drama of his own life into grand opera, so Shaffer turned his love of opera into great drama.

A part of the explanation of the success of Shaffer's plays may lie in his ability to titillate the audience with subject matter that is timely and controversial. In the 1950s, he hinted at the then-taboo subject of homosexuality in *Five Finger Exercise*. In 1970, the subject was the peace movement in *The Battle of Shrivings*; and in the same decade, in *Equus*, Shaffer provided analysis-crazed theatergoers a glimpse into what the lives of their own therapists might be, turning the tables, so to speak. When the Palestinians were in the news, he produced *Yonadab*, which depicts Jews as oppressors of primitive peoples. Shaffer tackled historical figures with the demythification of King David, Pizarro, and Mozart, and thereby dramatized the other side of history, if not exactly as it was, at least as it might have been. *The Royal Hunt of the Sun* is really as much about Martin as about Pizarro; he is a character parallel to Pizarro in his loss of faith. Shaffer shows Mozart through the eyes of a jealous second-rate composer, and King David's family through the eyes of a vengeful character who is hardly a footnote to biblical history. In fact, King David, who is regarded as a great hero in Jewish history, becomes a secondary character in the play, and the future King Solomon, who built the Temple, is written out altogether in the final version of the play. It is, then, history's mediocrities and forgotten souls, the onlookers of greatness, who become the central focus in Shaffer's works.

The original preface of this book stated that Shaffer had no social ax to grind, but it appears that he has a philosophical statement to make in his attempts at describing the mental anguish of alienated souls and the level to which their sense of failure can reduce them. In his attempts to describe the human condition, Shaffer tackles themes that are traditionally the subject matter of philosophers, psychologists, and theologians. Rodney Simard sees Shaffer's characters as "individuals divided within themselves, lacking a firm sense of self, and representing modern questers in search of integration. The dramatization of the *angst* and despairs of the contemporary, alienated individual, locked in subjective perceptions, is both Shaffer's subject and technique" (Simard, 100) The body of this book has studiously avoided identifying the playwright with any of his characters, except where he himself did so regarding *Five Finger Exercise*. He has also made other autobiographical references. For example, at the 1983 Modern Language Association Convention, the playwright acknowledged that his plays illuminate his own experience; and in an interview with the London *Times*, he described his own internal battle: "There is in me a continuous tension between what I suppose I could loosely call the Apollonian and the Dionysiac sides of interpreting life, between, say, Dysart and Alan Strang. . . . I just feel in myself that there is a constant debate going on between the violence of instinct on the one hand and the desire in my mind for order and restraint. Between the secular side of me the fact that I have never actually been able to buy anything of official religion—and the inescapable fact that to me life without a sense of the divine is perfectly meaningless."[10] He acknowledged in the same interview that agonized insights into the working of the human soul are what keep him writing. If the same subjects keep surfacing, he acknowledges, it is because all the plays are products of the same brain.

Perhaps the duality of his spirit accounts for the epic proportions of *The Royal Hunt of the Sun, Equus, Amadeus,* and *Yonadab,* versus the classical structure of *Five Finger Exercise, The Private Ear, The Public Eye, Black Comedy, The White Lies /(The) White Liars,* and *Shrivings*—the one-set play that Shaffer says in the above-mentioned interview he does not like. He touches the ground trod upon previously by Jung, who noted what human beings hope but often fail to receive from religion. *Yonadab* states that the religion of his birth is just not enough for him. Shaffer appears to be extending that statement to society-at-large. Even back in 1963, Shaffer confronted the subject of religion and concluded that religious ritual trivializes the concept of God.[11] And Pizarro in *The Royal Hunt of the Sun* goes so far as to say, "Dungballs to all churches that are or ever could be" (*RH*, 71). And so Shaffer's characters seek replacements for God and mainstream religion. Pizarro finds it in the sun, Alan in horses, Dysart in Greek civilization, Gideon in pacifism, David

Askelon in Gideon, and Salieri in music. They are the lucky ones: Mark Askelon and Yonadab find nothing to give meaning to their lives.

In agreement with the playwright, who wants to exercise the public's "imagination muscle," Bernard Beckman[12] insists that Shaffer creates theatrical, not literary, images. Yet the doctoral dissertations[13] that appear on his plays treat them as serious literature—as does this critic.[14] And literary critics are more consistently appreciative of Mr. Shaffer's efforts than are theater reviewers. The truth of the matter, of course, is that Shaffer's work is both theatrical *and* literary, which accounts for both his awards for drama and the scholarship that he has inspired. Despite his statement that he does not like to see an actor "delivering a sequence of lectures to the audience" (Connell, 7), that is exactly what he has Dysart, Salieri, and Yonadab do; the last two characters speak to the audience without even the pretext of merely delivering a monologue. It appears that Shaffer wants to do more than just illuminate his own experiences—he seems to want to turn the stage into a mirror in which the spectators can see themselves. His mission is very much like Lettice Douffet's: he wishes to Enlarge, Enliven, and Enlighten—but also to Exorcise, and certainly to Entertain.

Notes and References

Preface–1979

1. The exception is the chapter on *Shrivings*, where this organization is less appropriate than in the other chapters.

2. See, for example, Robert Brustein, *The Theatre of Revolt: An Approach to Modern Drama* (Boston, 1974); Ruby Cohn, *Currents in Contemporary Drama* (Bloomington, IN, 1969); John Elsom, *Post-War British Theatre* (London, 1976); Martin Esslin, *The Theater of the Absurd* (Garden City, NY, 1969); Arnold P. Hinchliffe, *British Theatre 1950–70* (Totowa, NJ: Rowman and Littlefield, 1974), hereafter referred to in the text as Hinchliffe; Frederick Lumley, *New Trends in Twentieth-Century Drama: A Survey since Ibsen and Shaw* (New York: Oxford University Press, 1967); J.L. Styan, *The Dark Comedy: The Development of Modern Comic Tragedy* (Cambridge: Cambridge University Press, 1962); John Russell Taylor, *The Angry Theatre: New British Drama* (New York: Hill and Wang, 1969); George Wellwarth, *The Theater of Protest and Paradox: Developments in the Avant-Garde Drama* (New York: New York University Press, 1964).

3. Such as Hinchliffe's study, *Harold Pinter* (New York: Twayne, 1967).

Chapter One

1. Two of the sketches that Shaffer wrote for the British television series "That Was the Week That Was" appear in a collection by the same name. The intention of the program was to be as topical and satirical as it was comical and entertaining. The first of Shaffer's two contributions is "But My Dear," a one-scene dialogue between Senior Officer and Junior Officer (whose name is Fairy) on "good taste" in letters. The conversation evolves into a comic and ironic tirade by Senior Officer against homosexuals. The second piece is called "The President of France" and is a satirical speech delivered by the chauvinistic French president to the Council of Europe in 1990. Both pieces are as pointed and biting as they are creative and entertaining.

2. Peter Shaffer in "Labels Aren't for Playwrights," *Theatre Arts* (February 1960), 21; hereafter cited in text as "Labels."

3. Don Ross, "Peter Shaffer Is an Enemy of 'Togetherness,'" *New York Herald Tribune* (2 January 1960), sect. 4, 3; hereafter cited in text as Ross.

4. The British "Pantomime" for children is a traditional Christmastime entertainment; it is not mime theater.

5. "Joan Littlewood Panto," 20 December 1963, 7.

6. 20 December 1963, 18.

    7. 20 December 1963, 4.
    8. 20 December 1963, 13.
    9. 20 December 1963, 4.
   10. 22 December 1963, 14.

Chapter Two

    1. Peter Shaffer, *Five Finger Exercise*, (London: Samuel French, 1958), 1;
hereafter cited in text as *FFE*.
    2. Charles R. Lyons observes that Louise's interest in culture "constitutes
a pose more than an animating energy." See "Peter Shaffer's *Five Finger Exercise*
and the Conventions of Realism" (hereafter cited in text as Lyons), in *Peter
Shaffer: A Casebook*, C. J. Gianakaris, ed. (New York: Garland Publishing, 1991),
48. Louise, therefore, is playing a "culture game" with the family as Clive plays
a "poseur game" with her.
    3. Many years after writing the play, Peter Shaffer acknowledged the
autobiographical element in the work: "Unquestionably it expressed a great deal
of my own family tensions and also a desperate need to stop feeling invisible. . . .
In its defense I can say that the repression I speak of [that of a career in writing,
which is frivolous, as opposed to one in business, which is serious]—a reticence in
the play which somewhat reflected my own at the time—injects a kind of fear into
its rage which I do not find appropriate even now." See the preface of *The Collected
Plays of Peter Shaffer* (New York: Harmony Books, 1982), vii, viii, hereafter cited in
the text as *CP*.
    4. ". . . One day he [Shaffer] picked up a book labeled 'Five Finger
Exercise' . . . for the exercise of five interrelated elements and how they react
to one another and how they strengthen each other, or weaken each other if you
use them wrong." From Joseph A. Loftus, "Playwright's Moral Exercise," *New
York Times*, 29 November 1959, sect. 2, 3; hereafter cited in text as Loftus.
    5. "Strangers at Breakfast," *Reporter* 22 (7 January 1960), 36–37.
    6. *The Angry Theatre: New British Drama* (New York: Hill and Wang,
1969), 275.
    7. *McGraw Hill Encyclopedia of World Drama* (New York: McGraw Hill,
1972), vol. 4, 83–85.
    8. Review in *Observer* (20 July 1958), 13.
    9. 12 December, 1959, 100–102.
   10. Review in the *New York Journal American*, 3 December 1959.
   11. Review in the *New York Daily Mirror*, 3 December 1959.
   12. *The Theater of Protest and Paradox: Developments in the Avant-Garde
Drama* (New York: New York University Press, 1964), 254.
   13. See Peter Shaffer, "Scripts in Trans-Atlantic Crossings May Suffer
Two Kinds of Changes," *Dramatic Guild Quarterly* (Spring 1980), 29.
   14. Review by Michael Walsh, 17 July 1958, 5.
   15. Unsigned review in the *Times* (London), 17 July 1958, 4.

16. Review by J. C. Trewin, 2 August 1958, 200.
17. Review by Eric Keown, 23 July 1958, 118–19.
18. Review by Alan Brien, 25 July 1958, 133–34.
19. Signed "Reuter," 4 December 1959, 15.
20. Review by Brooks Atkinson, 3 December 1959.
21. John McClain; see note 10, above.
22. See, for example, both John Russell Taylor works, 9; Hinchliffe, chapter 4, entitled "1956 Annus Mirabilis."
23. Taylor believes that Shaffer used the same method in *Five Finger Exercise* that Ionesco used in *La Cantatrice chauve* (The Bald Prima Donna), that of stripping bare the characters and their way of life. See both Taylor works, 274.

Chapter Three

1. Peter Shaffer, *The Private Ear {and} The Public Eye* (New York: Stein and Day, 1964), 22; hereafter cited in the text as *PE*.
2. Review in the *Daily Telegraph*, 11 May 1962, 16.
3. Review in *Cue*, 19 October 1963, 28.
4. "Broadway in Review," *Educational Theatre Journal* 15 (1963), 358–65.
5. Review in the *Illustrated London News*, 26 May 1962, 860.
6. Review in the *Evening Standard*, 11 May 1962, 21.
7. Review in the *New York Daily News*, 10 October 1963.
8. Review in the *Christian Science Monitor*, 12 May 1962, 4.
9. Review in the *Daily Express*, 12 May 1962, 7.
10. Review in *Films in Review*, October 1972, 504.
11. Review in *Time*, 11 September 1972, 78.
12. Peter Shaffer, *Black Comedy {including} White Lies* (New York: Stein and Day, 1967), 52; hereafter cited in the text as *BL*.
13. At this point, Brindsley places the raincoat over the Wedgwood bowl; later, however, it is the porcelain Buddha that breaks. This is a mistake on Shaffer's part.
14. For a discussion of the identification between Sophie and Tom, see Jules Glenn, "Anthony and Peter Shaffer's Plays: The Influence of Twinship on Creativity," *American Imago* 31 (1974), 270–92.
15. Peter Shaffer, *The White Liars {and} Black Comedy* (New York; Samuel French, 1968), 3; hereafter cited in the text as *WL*.
16. Mel Gussow in *Newsweek*, 20 February 1967, 102–13; and Walter Kerr in the *New York Times*, 13 February 1967, 42.
17. Unsigned review in *Time*, 17 February 1967, 70; and Walter Kerr in the *New York Times*, 13 February 1967, 42.
18. "What Comes after a Smash?" *Times* (London), 29 June 1976, 8.
19. Review in *New Statesman*, 9 July 1976, 59.

Chapter Four

1. Peter Shaffer, *The Royal Hunt of the Sun* (New York: Stein and Day, 1964), v; hereafter referred to in the text as *RH*.

2. I am using the spelling of the names as they appear in the play.

3. Gene A. Plunka, *Peter Shaffer: Roles, Rites, and Rituals in the Theater* (Rutherford, NJ: Fairleigh Dickinson University Press, 1988), 101.

4. See William H. Prescott, *History of the Conquest of Peru* (New York: Fred De Fau and Co., 1847), vol. 1, 343. Another historian, Philip Ainsworth Means, relates that Atahuallpa's real friend among the Spaniards was Hernando De Soto; see *Fall of the Inca Empire and the Spanish Rule in Peru: 1530–1780* (New York: Charles Scribner's Sons, 1932), 35.

5. Marshall Cohen, "Theater 66," *Partisan Review* (Spring 1966), 269– 76. Bettina L. Knapp, *Antonin Artaud: Man of Vision* (New York: David Lewis, 1969), 202, reads: "Peter Schaffer's [sic] *The Royal Hunt of the Sun* is, in my opinion, a virtual transposition of Artaud's metaphysical drama *The Conquest of Mexico.*" The two seminal works on epic theater are Antonin Artaud, *The Theater and It's Double*, Mary Caroline Richards, ed. (New York: Grove Press, 1958); and Bertolt Brecht, *Brecht on Theatre: The Development of an Aesthetic*, John Willett, trans. and ed. (New York: Hill and Wang, 1964). *Royal Hunt* demonstrates aspects specified by both of these theorists, whose philosophies on epic theater are quite different from each other. For Artaud, epic theater should have poetry in its language and spectacle—such as music, dance, and pantomime—on stage. For Brecht, epic theater has to appeal to the spectators' reason and present a remote past, which leaves the spectators with a feeling of alienation. Shaffer commented on how Cajamarca, Peru, seemed far more remote to British audiences that to American theatergoers, to whom it appeared to be not too far from Cheyenne; see "Scripts," cited in Chapter 2, note 13, 30.

6. In *La Nef*, 63/64 (March–April 1950), 159–65.

7. 27 October, 1965.

8. Review by Henry Hewes, 13 November 1965, 71.

9. Review by Theophilus Lewis, *America* 113 (20 November 1965), 648–49.

10. Review by John Chapman, 27 October 1965.

11. Review in *Plays and Players*, June 1969, 70.

12. Review in *Plays and Players*, February 1965, 34.

13. For example, Milton Shulman, *Evening Standard*, 8 July 1964, 4; and Charles Marowitz, *Encore* (March–April 1965), 44–45.

14. For example, John Simon, *Hudson Review*, 18 (Winter 1965–66), 571–74; and Howard Taubman, *New York Times*, 14 November 1965, sect. 2, 1.

15. See both John Russell Taylor works, 277.

16. Robert Brustein, *The Third Theatre* (New York: Alfred A. Knopf, 1969), 109.

17. Malcolm Rutherford, *Spectator* (17 July 1964), 82, 84.

18. Article in *New York Times*, 14 November 1965, sect. 2, 1.
19. (Garden City, NY, 1970).
20. "To See the Soul of a Man . . . ," *New York Times*, 24 October 1965, sect. 2, 3.
21. "In Search of a God," *Plays and Players*, October 1964, 22.
22. Comparative studies between *The Royal Hunt of the Sun* and other plays of the Spanish conquest of the New World include Dennis A. Klein, "Epic Theatre of the Conquest: Jaime Salom's *Las Casas, una hoguera en el amanecer* and Peter Shaffer's *The Royal Hunt of the Sun*," *Estreno* 18 (Fall 1992), 34–36; Betty Osorio de Negret, "La sintaxis básica del teatro: Ensayo comparativo de dos tradiciones sobre la prisión y muerte de Athuallpa" (The basic syntax of the theater: Comparative essay of two traditions about the imprisonment and death of Athuallpa), *Lexis: Revista de lingüística y literatura*, 8 (1984), 113–29; and two essays by Peter L. Podol: "Dramatizations of the Conquest of Peru: Peter Shaffer's *The Royal Hunt of the Sun* and Claude Demarigny's *Cajamarca*," *Hispanic Journal* (Indiana, PA), 6 (1964), 121–29; and "Contradictions and Dualities in Artaud and Artaudian Theatre: *The Conquest of Mexico* and the Conquest of Peru," *Modern Drama*, 26 (1983), 518–27.

Chapter Five

1. For B. A. Young (*Financial Times*, 6 February 1970, 3) the play is just not believable. Milton Shulman (*Evening Standard*, 6 February 1970, 24) saw in the play the archetypal Thinker and Artist, rather than real people. He found the play to be an interesting literary exercise, with flashes of profundity, poetry, and wit. There is no lack of intelligence in the work for Eric Shorter (*Daily Telegraph*, 6 February 1970); Philip Hope-Wallace (*Guardian*, 6 February 1970, 8); or Jeremy Kingston (*Punch*, 11 February 1970, 236).
2. Note in Peter Shaffer, *Equus {and} Shrivings* (New York, 1976), 111; hereafter cited in the text as *ES*. Copyright ©, 1974 by Peter Shaffer. Reprinted by permission of Atheneum Publishers.

Chapter Six

1. For a psychiatrist's comments on this detail as well as on the twinship between Alan and Dysart, see Jules Glenn, cited in Chapter 3, note 14.
2. I am referring here to De Nizza's speech in which he criticizes Incan society for depriving its citizens of unhappiness, want, and inequality. Similarly, Dysart is reluctant to alleviate Alan's pain because it is "his pain. His own. He made it. . . . to go through life and call it yours—*your life*—you first have to get your own pain. Pain that's unique to you. You can't just dip into the common bin and say 'That's enough!' . . . He's done that" (*ES*, 80).
3. James M. Welsh suggests that Dysart serves the triple function of priest-sacrificer, priest-confessor, and priest-exorcist. See "Dream Doctors as

Healers in Drama and Film: A Paradigm, an Antecedent, and an Imitation,"
Literature and Medicine 6 (1987), 123; hereafter cited in text as Welsh.

    4. I am indebted to Dr. Susan Wolfe of The University of South Dakota
for bringing her linguistic talents to this passage.

    5. Gene A. Plunka observes that Alan's existential search is for the kind
of freedom that a horse has. He seeks to free himself from his father's repressive-
ness, his mother's religion, and society's mechanization. From Alan, Dysart
learns the meaning of freedom. See "The Existential Ritual: Peter Shaffer's
Equus," *Kansas Quarterly* 12 (1980), 87–97.

    6. Sexual and religious fervor have always been two sides of the same
coin. Witness, for example, Bernini's statue of St. Teresa, for which, according
to artistic lore, the artist is said to have used the expression of a woman during
orgasm to capture the rapture of direct communication with God. John Weight-
man views Alan's rides as *"ejaculatio sacra,* or ecstatic communion with God-
beast." See his article, "Christ as Man and Horse," *Encounter* 44, no. 3 (March
1975), 46.

    7. In *"Equus:* A Psychiatrist Questions His Priestly Powers," *Hastings
Center Report* 5, no. 1 (February 1975), 9–10, Morris Bernard Kaplan states that
Dysart's therapeutic methods work on Alan because Alan trusts the doctor and
wants to be freed from his psychological entrapment.

    8. For a Jungian analysis of the play, see Ronald J. Lee, "Jungian
Approach to Theatre: Shaffer's *Equus,*" *Psychological Perspectives* 8 (Spring 1977),
10–21.

    9. I appreciate the help of Dr. Brent Froberg, a professor of Greek, for
translating *dys* for me.

    10. See R. D. Laing, *The Politics of Experience* (New York: Pantheon Books,
1967), for a full treatment of this subject.

    11. The Holy Bible (New York: Nelson and Sons, 1901). All biblical
quotations are from this edition, and are accompanied by citations of chapter and
verse.

    12. See Richard Lewinsohn, *Animals, Men and Myths* (New York: Harper
and Brothers, 1954), 85.

    13. George Gaylord Simpson, *Horses: The Story of the Horse Family in the
Modern World and through Sixty Million Years of History* (New York: Oxford
University Press, 1951), 30.

    14. In *The Classical Journal* 65 (1970), 245.

    15. "High Horse," in *Guardian,* 8 August 1973, 8; "Christ as Man and
Horse," *Encounter* 44, no. 3 (March 1975), 46.

    16. D. H. Lawrence, *Mornings in Mexico {and} Etruscan Places,* 2nd ed.
(London: Heinemann, 1965), 68; hereafter cited in text as Lawrence.

    17. D. H. Lawrence, "The Rocking-Horse Winner," in *The Complete Short
Stories,* vol. 3 (New York: The Viking Press, 1962), 794.

    18. See Rafael Martínez Nadal, *"El Público." Amor, teatro y caballos en la*

obra de Federico García Lorca ("The Audience." Love, theater, and horses in the work of Federico García Lorca; Oxford: Dolphin, 1970); also the English version, *Lorca's "The Public": A Study of His Unfinished Play "El Público" and of Love and Death in the Work of Federico García Lorca* (London: Calder and Boyars, 1974); Julian Palley, "Archetypal Symbols in *Bodas de sangre*," *Hispania* 50 (1967), 74–79; and Juan Villegas, "El leitmotif del caballo en *Bodas de sangre*," *Hispanófila* 29 (1967), 21–36.

19. Federico García Lorca, *Obras completas*, 15th ed. (Madrid: Aguilar, 1969), 905; hereafter cited in text as García Lorca.

20. All translations are my own.

21. For a Jungian analysis of horses, see Una Chaudhuri, "The Spectator in Drama/Drama in the Spectator," *Modern Drama* 27 (1984), 281–98. This "response-oriented" analysis of *Equus* that contrasts written drama from performed theater also contrasts the Brechtian and Artaudian aspects of the play. Hélène L. Baldwin argues that *Equus* does not exemplify Artaud's definition of "Theater of Cruelty." See "Equus: Theater of Cruelty or Theater of Sensationalism?" *Philological Papers* (West Virginia University), 25 (1978), 118–27. I. Dean Ebner characterizes the horse-as-god element of the play as a metaphor for a yearning for transcendence. See "The Double Crisis of Sexuality and Worship in Peter Shaffer's *Equus*," *Christianity and Literature* 31, no. 2 (Winter 1982), 29–47.

22. I thank Dr. Larry Vonalt of the University of Missouri–Rolla for this insight.

23. See W. L. Warren, *King John* (Berkeley: University of California Press, 1981), 81.

24. In *El mono piadoso y seis piezas de café-teatro* (The pious monkey and six coffee-house plays) (Madrid, 1969), 63.

25. See note 15.

26. James M. Welsh (cited in note 3) observes that the square represents the world of reality and the circle around it the world of imagination (123). Una Chaudhuri (cited in note 21) believes that the section of on-stage seating gives the Brechtian effect of a lecture/demonstration that the spectators are observing.

27. Aristotle, *Rhetoric {and} Poetics*, trans. by Rhys Roberts and Ingram Bywater, respectively (New York: Modern Library, 1954), 230; hereafter cited in text as Aristotle.

28. In "Scripts," (Chapter 2, note 13), Shaffer points out how different from each other were the reactions of British and American audiences. The British found the play cruel to animals, while the Americans found it cruel to psychiatrists. Shaffer insisted that he did not intend to be unkind toward psychiatry.

29. During an interview at the playwright's New York penthouse on 6 January 1978, Shaffer emphasized that first and foremost a dramatist must tell a story that will keep the attention of the audience.

30. In "*Equus*: Modern Myth in the Making," *Drama and Theatre* 12, no. 2 (Spring 1975), 132.

31. Samual Terrier, "*Equus*: Human Conflicts and the Trinity," *Christian Century* (18 May 1977), 472–76.

32. Martin Gottfried in *New York Post*, 25 October 1975; and Walter Kerr in *New York Times*, 5 October 1975, sect. 2.

33. John Simon, "Hippodrama at the Psychodrome," *Hudson Review* 28 (Spring 1975), 97–106.

34. Martin Gottfried in *New York Post*, 24 February 1977, 18.

35. Howard Kissel in *Women's Wear Daily*, 18 October 1974.

36. Edwin Wilson in *Wall Street Journal*, 28 October 1974.

37. Review by Walter Kerr, 3 November 1974, sect. 2, 1.

38. Review by Douglas Watt, 25 October 1974.

39. John Leonard in *New York Times*, 26 May 1976, 24; John Simon in *New York* magazine, 11 November 1974, 118.

40. Blurb that appeared frequently, as on 31 May 1976, 4.

41. See "The Anger in *Equus*," *Modern Drama* 22 (1979), 61–66.

42. In "Existential Ritual" (cited in note 5), 96.

43. See my bibliography for references to four of Glenn's articles.

44. "Psychoanalyst Says Nay to *Equus*," *New York Times*, 15 December 1974, section 2, 1.

Chapter Seven

1. Peter Shaffer, *Amadeus*, (London: André Deutsch, 1980), 8; all further references to the British version are from this edition; and are hereafter cited in text as *A*.

2. Michael Hinden comments that there is a hollowness about Salieri and that he is a static character who cannot grow because he knows everything from the start. See "When Playwrights Talk to God: Peter Shaffer and the Legacy of O'Neill," in *Critical Approaches to O'Neill*, John H. Stroupe, ed. (New York: AMS Press, 1988), 199–213.

3. Gene A. Plunka observes that Louise and Stanley Harrington fight with each other through Clive. That situation is therefore parallel to the one that exists in *Amadeus*. See "'Know Thyself': Integrity and Self-Awareness in the Early Plays of Peter Shaffer," in *Peter Shaffer: A Casebook*, ed. C. J. Gianakaris (New York: Garland Publishing, 1991), 61.

4. Salieri speaks to Mozart in Italian when he asks for his forgiveness, both at the beginning of the play, when he talks to the long-dead composer "*Perdonami, Mozart! Il tuo assasino ti chiede perdono!* . . . *Pietà: Mozart, Mozart: Pietà*" (*A*, 17)], and face-to-face in their final confrontation ["*Eccomi!*—il tuo assesino! . . . Eccomi: il tuo Vittima" (*A*, 113)]. Similarly, Mark Askelon uses Italian to ask forgiveness of his dead wife in *Shrivings*.

5. For a full study of this subject, see Dennis A. Klein, "A Note on the Use of Dreams in Peter Shaffer's Major Plays," *Journal of Evolutionary Psychology* 9 (1989), 25–31.

6. For a thorough study of games in some of the plays, see Dennis A. Klein, "Game-Playing in Four Plays by Peter Shaffer: *Shrivings, Equus, Lettice and Lovage,* and *Yonadab,*" in *Peter Shaffer: A Casebook,* ed. C. J. Gianakaris (New York: Garland Publishing, 1991), 133–50.

7. In "On the Structure of Peter Shaffer's *Amadeus,*" *Modern Drama* 27, no 3 (September 1984), 299–313.

8. Peter Shaffer, *Amadeus* (New York: Harper & Row, 1981), ix. All subsequent references to the American version are from this edition, and are hereafter cited in text as *AA*.

9. For a detailed treatment of the differences between the two versions, see C. J. Gianakaris, "Shaffer's Revisions in *Amadeus,*" *Theatre Journal* 35, no. 1 (March 1983), 88–101; hereafter cited in text as Gianakaris 1983.

10. In "Psychic Energy," *Plays and Players* 27, no. 5 (February 1980), 13.

11. In "A Playwright Looks at Mozart: Peter Shaffer's *Amadeus,*" *Comparative Drama* 15, i (Spring 1981), 38; hereafter cited in text as Gianakaris 1981.

12. Peter Shaffer, "Figure of Death," *Observer* (London), 4 November 1979, 37.

13. According to *The New Grove Dictionary of Music and Musicians,* vol. 16, ed. Stanley Sadic (London: Macmillan, 1980), 415–20.

14. All quotations from Mozart's correspondence come from *The Letters of Mozart and His Family,* 2d ed., 2 vols., trans. and ed. Emily Anderson, prepared by A. Hyatt King and Monica Carolan (New York: St. Martin's Press, 1966); hereafter cited in text as *Letters*.

15. C.J. Gianakaris states that Shaffer took almost no liberties with historical fact in his portrayal of Mozart in *Amadeus*. See "Fair Play?" *Opera News* 27 (February 1982), 18, 36.

16. For a detailed treatment of the production of the script, see C.J. Gianakaris, "Drama into Film: The Shaffer Situation," *Modern Drama* 28, no. 1 (March 1985), 83–98; and Michiko Kakutani, "How 'Amadeus' Was Translated From Play to Film," *New York Times,* 16 September 1984, sect. 2.

17. In "Paying Homage to Mozart," *New York Times Magazine,* 2 September 1984, 38.

18. See "*Amadeus* as Dramatic Monologue," Literature/Film Quarterly 14, no. 4 (1986), 214–19.

19. Review, *Theatre Journal* 32, no. 4 (December 1980), 521–23.

20. "Portrait of Mozart As a Loudmouth," *New York Times,* 11 November 1979, sect. 2, 8.

21. In a letter to the *Sunday Times* (London), 30 December 1979, 10.

22. Blurb on *Amadeus, Sunday Times* (London), 18 November 1975, 38.

23. "Can We Worship This Mozart?" *Sunday Times* (London), 23 December 1979, 43.

24. B.A. Young, Review of *Amadeus,* 5 November 1979, 15.

25. Signed Pit, Review of *Amadeus,* 14 November 1979, 90–92.

26. "In London, the Talk is of *Amadeus*," *New York Times*, 23 December 1979, sect. 2.

27. "Much Ado about Mozart," *Observer* (London), 11 November 1979, 16.

28. "Trying to Like Shaffer," *Comparative Drama* 19, no. 1 (1985), 15–16.

29. "The Infinite Variety of Jane Seymour," *Horizon* (February 1981), 59.

30. "Viewpoint," 31 January 1981, 4.

31. "*Amadeus*: A Total Triumph," *New York Post*, 18 December 1980, 39.

32. "Change Aids *Amadeus*," *New York Post*, 31 December 1980, 17.

33. "Peter Shaffer's *Amadeus*: A Controversial Hit," *Saturday Review*, November 1980, 11–14.

34. "More on the Don," *New Yorker*, 24 March 1980, 122.

35. "Peter Shaffer's Astigmatic View of God," *Wall Street Journal*, 19 December 1980, 25.

36. "Mozart and His Nemesis," *Newsweek*, 29 December 1980, 58.

37. "Eine Kleine Nicht Musik," 24–30 December 1980, 82–83.

38. "Mozart and Shaffer's Craft," 24–30 December 1980, 82.

39. *New York* Magazine, 29 December 1980/5 January 1981, 62–63.

40. "The Triumph of Mediocrity," *New Republic*, 17 January 1981, 23–24.

41. "Looking at Langella in 'Amadeus,'" *New York Post*, 26 July 1982, 20.

42. Signed Humm, "Broadway Followup: Amadeus," 23 December 1981, 70.

43. February 1981, 78–79.

44. See Daniele Heymann, "Une féroce petite musique de nuit," *L'Express* (international edition) 22 January 1982, 12–13.

45. Robert Kanters, "'Amadeus': les silence de Mozart," *L'Express* (international edition) 12 February 1982, 7.

46. See "Peter Shaffer's *Amadeus*: The Making and Un-Making of the Fathers," *American Imago* 45, no. 1 (Spring 1988), 45–60.

47. *Postmodern Drama: Contemporary Playwrights in America and Britain* (Lanham, MD: University Press of America, 1984), 163; hereafter cited in text as Simard.

48. Review of *Amadeus*, *New York Times*, 19 September 1984, C23.

49. "A Genius Despite Himself," *Newsweek*, 24 September 1984, 85.

50. "God's Grandeur," *America*, 13 October 1984, 210.

51. "Salieri, Psycho," *Film Comment*, February 1985, 70–75.

52. Richard Hornak, "Taster's Choice," 15 February 1990, 35.

53. Mozart's Greatest Hit," *Time*, 10 September 1984, 74–75; hereafter cited in text as Corliss.

Chapter Eight

1. All citations from the staged version are from the unpublished manuscript. Quotations will hereafter be identified by act and scene.

2. For details about the failure to have the play produced on Broadway,

see C. J. Gianakaris, "A Conversation with Peter Shaffer (1990)," in *Peter Shaffer: A Casebook*, ed. C. J. Gianakaris (New York: Garland, 1991), 27; hereafter cited in text as "Conversation."

3. Peter Shaffer, *Lettice and Lovage {and} Yonadab* (London: Penguin Books, 1989), vii. All references to the revised version are from this edition, hereafter cited in text as *LLY*.

4. I make a similar point in my book *Blood Wedding, Yerma, and The House of Bernarda Alba: García Lorca's Tragic Trilogy* (Boston: Twayne, 1991), 138.

5. In "Where All the Ladders Start': The Autobiographical Impulse in Shaffer's Recent Work," in *Peter Shaffer: A Casebook*, ed. C. J. Gianakaris (New York: Garland Publishing, 1991), 160. Hereafter cited in text as Hinden.

6. In "Peter Shaffer Creates Another Envious Outsider," *New York Times*, 22 December 1985, sect. 2.

7. In "Shows Abroad," 11 December 1985, 138.

8. "Spy of History," *Times* (London), 6 December 1985, 13.

9. "Yonadab/Olivier," *Financial Times* (London), 5 December 1985, 25.

10. Review of *Yonadab*, *Manchester Guardian*, 6 December 1985, 10.

11. "The Rape Type-Scene in the Biblical Narrative: The Desire of Violence," paper presented at the convention of the Modern Language Association, 30 December 1985.

12. "Four from the London Stage," *Newsweek*, 13 January 1986, 64–65.

Chapter Nine

1. Peter Shaffer, *Lettice and Lovage* (London: André Deutsch, 1988), 6. Further references to the original version are from this edition; hereafter cited in text as *LL*.

2. Peter Shaffer, *Lettice & Lovage* (New York: Harper & Row, 1989), 94. Further references to the revised version are from this edition; hereafter cited in text as *L&L*.

3. For example, Walter Kerr, "Stage View: About a Pointsettia and a Women with Five Hands," *New York Times*, 22 April 1990, sect. 2, 5–6; William A. Henry III, "Just What the Doctor Ordered," *Time*, 2 April 1990, 71–72; and Edwin Wilson, "Theater: Maggie Smith's Tour de Force," *Wall Street Journal*, 2 April 1990, A11.

4. Review of *Lettice and Lovage*, *Times* (London), 28 October 1987, 21.

5. Review of *Lettice and Lovage*, *Times* (London), 17 November 1988, 20.

6. "Shaffer's Pen," *Plays and Players*, November 1987, 6–8.

7. "Peter Shaffer Turns On the Laughing Gas," *New York Times*, 22 November 1987, sect. 2.

8. "And Finally Another Rewrite," *Times* (London), 22 October 1988, 32.

9. "Broadway Redux," *Connoisseur*, January 1989, 32.

10. Review signed Humm, 28 March 1990, 103, 106.

11. "To the Ladies," *New Yorker*, 9 April 1990, 80.

12. "One and Many Maggie Smiths," *New York Times*, 26 March 1990.

13. Review of *Lettive & Lovage*, *Nation*, 7 May 1990, 644.

14. "Critic's Notebook," *New York Times*, 25 February 1988, C28.

15. Review in *Plays and Players*, December 1987, 16–17.

16. "Maggie and Margaret," *New York Magazine*, 9 April 1990, 102–3.

17. Peter Shaffer, *Whom Do I Have the Honour of Addressing?* (London: André Deutsch, 1990), 6; hereafter cited in text *W*.

18. For example, Robert Asahina, "Theatre Chronicle," *Hudson Review*, 34, ii (Summer 1981), 263–68, comments that Shaffer's plays became devoid of significant female characters to dramatize "to him a grander passion: the mutually destructive need of two men for each other" as well as to heighten the homoerotic tension between them. In *Whom Do I Have the Honour of Addressing?* it is the female protagonist who brings about that result in the two secondary male characters.

Chapter Ten

1. *Daily Telegraph* (London), 18 December 1992, 15.

2. *Financial Times* (London), 18 December 1992, 11.

3. "Dench Boils Over Amid the Lava," *Times* (London), 17 December 1992, 28.

4. "A Revenger's Tragedy," *Independent* (London), 18 December 1992, 15.

5. *Guardian* (London), 18 December 1992, sect. 2, 9.

6. *Stage and Television Today* (London), 31 December 1992, 11.

7. "Three New British Plays with Serious Messages," *New York Times*, 23 December 1992, C9, C12.

8. New York: William Morrow and Co.; forward by James A. Michener.

9. In *Soundings*, 67, no. 1 (Spring 1984), 42–54.

10. Brian Connell, "Peter Shaffer: The Two Sides of Theatre's Agonised Perfectionist," 28 April 1980, 7; hereafter cited in text as Connell.

11. "Peter Shaffer's Personal Dialogue," *New York Times*, 6 October 1963, sect. 2, 3.

12. "The Dynamics of Peter Shaffer's Drama" in *The Play and Its Critic: Essays for Eric Bentley*, ed., Michael Bertin (Lanham, MD: University Press of America, 1986), 199–209.

13. The most recent is John Clair Watson, "The Ritual Plays of Peter Shaffer" (unpublished), (University of Oregon, 1987), which treats, in part, characters' attempts to transcend the human condition.

14. Mr. Shaffer has expressed to me his concern that I am reducing his gestural theater to the printed page. I assured him that I am elevating his plays to the level of literature.

Selected Bibliography

PRIMARY SOURCES

Most of Shaffer's works are available in various editions. Only the editions used in this study are listed here.

Plays

Amadeus. London: André Deutsch, 1980. Original version of the play.
Amadeus. New York: Harper & Row, 1981. Revised version.
Black Comedy {including} White Lies. New York: Stein and Day, 1967.
Collected Plays. New York: Harmony Books, 1982. Contains the plays from *Five Finger Exercise* through *Amadeus*, and the final version of *White Liars*.
Equus {and} Shrivings. New York: Atheneum, 1976.
Five Finger Exercise. London: Samuel French, 1958.
Lettice and Lovage. London: André Deutsch, 1988. Original version.
Lettice & Lovage. New York: Harper & Row, 1990. Revised version.
Lettice and Lovage {and} Yonadab. London: Penguin Books, 1989. Revised version of *Yonadab*.
The Prviate Ear {and} The Public Eye. New York: Stein and Day, 1964.
The Royal Hunt of the Sun. New York: Stein and Day, 1964.
The White Liars {and} Black Comedy: Two One-Act Plays. New York: Samuel French, 1968.
Whom Do I Have the Honour of Addressing? London: André Deutsch, 1990.

Unpublished Plays

Yonadab, as produced in London.

Novels

How Doth the Little Crocodile?, with Anthony Shaffer. New York: Macmillan, 1957.
Withered Murder, with Anthony Shaffer. New York: Macmillan, 1956.
The Woman in the Wardrobe. Drawings by Nicolas Bentley. London: Evans Brothers, 1951.

Unpublished Radio and Television Scripts

"The Prodigal Father," aired on BBC radio, 14 September 1957.
"The Salt Land," produced by ITV, 8 November 1955.

Miscellaneous

Frost, David, and Ned Sherrin. *That Was the Week That Was*. London: W. H. Allen, 1963. Contains two sketches by Shaffer.

SECONDARY SOURCES

Books

Anderson, Emily, trans. and ed.; prepared by A. Hyatt King and Monica Carolan. *The Letters of Mozart and His Family*. New York: St. Martin's Press, 1966. Factual basis of *Amadeus* through Mozart's correspondence.

Aristotle. *Rhetoric {and} Poetics*. Trans. by Rhys Roberts and Ingram Bywater, respectively. New York: The Modern Library, 1954.

Artaud, Antonin. *The Theater and Its Double*, edited by Mary Caroline Richards. New York: Grove Press, 1958. Artaud's theory of epic theater. Applies to studying *The Royal Hunt of the Sun*, *Equus*, and *Yonadab*.

Brecht, Bertolt. *Brecht on Theatre: the Development of an Aesthetic*, trans. and edited by John Willett. New York: Hill and Wang, 1964. Brecht's theory of epic drama applies to studying *The Royal Hunt of the Sun, Equus, Amadeus,* and *Yonadab*.

Brustein, Robert. *The Third Theatre*. New York: Alfred A. Knopf, 1969. Contains an essay entitled "Peru in New York: *The Royal Hunt of the Sun* by Peter Shaffer."

Burgess, Anthony. *A Clockwork Orange*. Afterword and glossary by Stanley Edgar Hyman. New York: W.W. Norton and Co., 1963. A novelistic treatment of the question of society's right to cure antisocial behavior. Worthwhile background reading for *Equus*.

Cavendish, Richard, ed. *Man, Myth and Magic: An Illustrated Encyclopedia of the Supernatural*. New York: Marshall Cavendish Corp., 1970. Volume ten has a section on horses and their symbolic value.

Chiari, J. *Landmarks of Contemporary Drama*. London: Herbert Jenkins, 1965. Praise for *Five Finger Exercise* and disdain for *The Royal Hunt of the Sun*, in the chapter of "Concluding Remarks."

Cirlot, J. E. *A Dictionary of Symbols*, 2nd ed. Trans. by Jack Sage. New York: Philosophical Library, Inc., 1971. A standard reference work on literary symbols, including horses.

Cohn, Ruby. *Currents in Contemporary Drama*. Bloomington: Indiana University Press, 1969. Commentary on Shaffer in the context of modern British drama and a comment on *The Royal Hunt of the Sun*.

Elsom, John. *Post-War British Theatre*. London and Boston: Routledge and Kegan Paul, 1976. Comments on Shaffer's early major plays, as well as comparisons between Shaffer's work and that of his contemporaries.

Esslin, Martin. *Reflections: Essays on Modern Theatre.* Garden City, NY: Double-day and Co., 1969. The chapter "Brecht and the English Theatre" mentions *The Royal Hunt of the Sun.*

García Lorca, Federico. *Obras completas,* 15th ed. Madrid: Aguilar, 1969.

Gassner, John, and Edward Quinn, eds. *The Reader's Encyclopedia of World Drama.* New York: Thomas Y. Crowell Co., 1969. Notes on Shaffer's life and plays, through *Black Comedy.*

Gianakaris, C.J. *Peter Shaffer.* New York: St. Martin's Press, 1992. A concise and intelligent presentation from the detective novels through *Whom Do I Have the Honour of Addressing?*

————. ed. *Peter Shaffer: A Casebook.* New York: Garland Publishing, 1991. Collection of essays by diverse hands; some of whose chapters are listed in the section on articles.

Gilliatt, Penelope. *Unholy Fools. Wits, Comics, Disturbers of Peace: Film and Theater.* New York: The Viking Press, 1973. One of the many articles is on the production of *Black Comedy* in Chichester.

Grau, Jacinto. *Teatro,* 2nd ed. Buenos Aires: Losada, 1960. The theme and protaganist of *Las gafas de don Telesforo o un loco de buen capricho* parellel those of *The Public Eye.*

Greene, Naomi. *Antonin Artaud: Poet Without Words.* New York: Simon and Schuster, 1970. A discussion of *La Conquête du Mexique,* which some critics think influenced *The Royal Hunt of the Sun.*

Hemming, John. *The Conquest of the Incas.* New York: Harcourt Brace Jovanovich, 1970. Contains background information, which is useful for an appreciation of *The Royal Hunt of the Sun* as historical drama.

Hinchliffe, Arnold P. *British Theatre, 1950–70.* Totowa, NJ: Rowman and Littlefield, 1974. Space does not permit the critic to "explain why the Shaffer brothers were so successful in the West End . . ." (149), in this book, which contains valuable background information on the British theater.

Holy Bible, The; Containing the Old and New Testaments. New York: Nelson and Sons, 1901.

Homer. *Complete Works. The Iliad.* Trans. by Andrew Lang, Walter Leaf, and Ernest Myers.

The Odyssey. Trans. by S. H. Butcher and Andrew Lang. New York: The Modern Library, 1950.

Jung, Carl G. *The Archtypes and the Collective Unconscious,* 2nd ed. Trans. by R.F.C. Hull. Princeton, NJ: Princeton University Press, 1975. A reference work on archetypal symbols.

————. *The Portable Jung.* Ed. and intro. by Joseph Campbell. Trans. by R.F.C. Hull. New York: The Viking Press, 1972. Contains ideas applicable to characters in *Royal Hunt, Shrivings, Equus, Amadeus,* and *Yonadab.*

Kernodle, George R. *Invitation to the Theatre.* New York: Harcourt, Brace and World, 1967. Commentaries on *The Royal Hunt of the Sun* as epic theater and on the film version (which Shaffer did not write) of *Five Finger Exercise*.

Klein, Dennis A. *Peter and Anthony Shaffer: A Reference Guide*. Boston: G. K. Hall, 1982. A critical bibliography through 1980.

———. *Peter Shaffer*. Boston: Twayne, 1979. Original version of the present book.

Knapp, Bettina L. *Antonin Artaud: Man of Vision*. New York: David Lewis, 1969. The critic views *The Royal Hunt of the Sun* as a "virtual transposition" of *La Conquête du Mexique*.

Kupferberg, Herbert. *Amadeus: A Mozart Mosaic*. New York: McGraw-Hill, 1986. Anecdotal biography of character in *Amadeus*.

Laing, R. D. *The Politics of Experience*. New York: Pantheon Books, 1967. A psychiatrist's beliefs on who should and should not be cured of individualizing personality traits.

Lambert, J. W. *Drama in Britain 1964–1973*. Harlow, Essex: Longman Group, 1974. Background reading on such institutions as the National Theatre.

Lawrence, D. H. *The Complete Short Stories*. Vol. 3, 2nd ed. New York: The Viking Press, 1962. Contains "The Rocking-Horse Winner."

———. *Mornings in Mexico {and} Etruscan Places*. London: Heinemann, 1965. 2nd ed. Intro. by Richard Aldington.

Lewinsohn, Richard. *Animals, Men and Myths*. New York: Harper and Brothers, 1954. Trans. from the German. The role of horses in the classical Greek world.

Maschler, Tom, ed. *New English Dramatists*. Vol. 4. Harmondsworth, England: Penguin Books, [1962]. Includes the text of *Five Finger Exercise* and introductory comments on the play.

Macgraw Hill Encyclopedia of World Drama. New York, 1972. Mention of Shaffer's plays through 1970, a paragraph each on *Five Finger Exercise* and *The Royal Hunt of the Sun*, as well as a biographical sketch of the playwright.

Means, Philip Ainsworth. *Fall of the Inca Empire and the Spanish Rule in Peru: 1530–1780*. New York and London: Charles Scribner's Sons, 1932. Background reading for the historical events on which *The Royal Hunt of the Sun* is based.

Nasso, Christine, ed. *Contemporary Authors: A Bio-Bibliographical Guide to Current Authors and Their Work*. Detroit: Gale Research Co., 1977. A chronology with criticism on some of Shaffer's plays appears in volume 25–28.

Parker, John, original compiler. *Who's Who in the Theatre: A Biographical Record of the Contemporary Stage*, 15th ed. London: Pitman and Sons, 1972. A one-paragraph biographical and professional résumé through 1970.

Plunka, Gene A. *Peter Shaffer: Roles, Rites, and Rituals in the Theater*. Rutherford, NJ: Fairleigh Dickinson University Press, 1988. Chapters on the early and minor works and the plays from *Five Finger Exercise* through *Amadeus*. The chapter on *The Royal Hunt of the Sun* is particularly good.

Prescott, William H. *History of the Conquest of Peru*. 2 vols. New York: Fred De Fau and Co., [1874]. Shaffer's source for *The Royal Hunt of the Sun*.

Richards, Stanley, ed. *Best Plays of the Sixties*. Garden City, NY: Doubleday and Co., 1970. Includes *The Royal Hunt of the Sun*, as well as a biographical sketch.

Ruibal, José. "Los ojos" in *El mono piadoso y seis piezas de café-teatro*. Madrid. Escelicer, 1969. A Spanish play about watchful eyes.

Sadie, Stanley, ed. *The New Grove Dictionary of Music and Musicians*. London: Macmillan, 1980. Vol. 16 contains a biographical sketch of Antonio Salieri.

Salem, Daniel. *La Révolution théâtrale actuelle en Angleterre*. Paris: Denoël, 1969. Remarks on *Five Finger Exercise, The Royal Hunt of the Sun, Black Comedy*, and on Shaffer himself.

Simard, Rodney. *Postmodern Drama: Contemporary Playwrights in America and Britain*. Lanham, MD: University Press of America, 1984. Contains a chapter on Shaffer called "Peter Shaffer: Epic Psychoquester."

Smith, Warren Sylvester. Essay on Peter Shaffer in *Dictionary of Literary Biography, Vol. 13: British Dramatists Since World War II*, edited by Stanley Weintraub. Detroit: Gale Research Co., 1982, 451–69. Basic biographical information; lists of plays through *Amadeus* on stage, radio, television, and in print; synopses of plays, with some insights and comparative observations; photographs of some productions.

Styan, J. L. *The Dark Comedy: The Development of Modern Comic Tragedy*. Cambridge, England: Cambridge University Press, 1962. Styan enumerates and comments on the essential elements of dark comedy.

Taylor, John Russell. *Anger and After: A Guide to the New British Drama*. London: Methuen and Co., 1962 and 1969.

————. *The Angry Theatre: New British Drama*. New York: Hill and Wang, 1969. This is essentially the same book as the entry above, and the two 1969 editions mention *The Public Eye, The Private Ear, Black Comedy*, and *The White Liars*, while the 1962 edition does not.

————. *Peter Shaffer*. Ed. by Ian Scott-Kilvert. No. 244 of the Writers and Their Work series. Harlow, Essex: Longman House, 1974. An essay on the plays from *Five Finger Exercise* through *Equus*.

————. *The Rise and Fall of the Well-Made Play*. New York: Hill and Wang, 1967. Contains only a brief comment on *Five Finger Exercise*.

Thomas, Eberle. *Peter Shaffer: An Annotated Bibliography*. New York: Garland Publishing, 1991. Bibliography through *Lettice & Lovage*. Compiler used, in part, secondary sources, and readers should beware of errors.

Vinson, James, ed. *Contemporary Dramatists*. Preface by Ruby Cohn. New York: St. Martin's Press; and London: St. James Press, 1973. John Elsom prepared the biographical sketch, bibliography, and notes on Shaffer's works.

Wakeman, John, ed. *World Authors 1950–1970*. New York: H. W. Wilson Co.,
    1975. Biographical sketch and commentary on the plays.
Wellwarth, George. *The Theater of Protest and Paradox: Developments in the
    Avant-Garde Drama*. New York: New York University Press, 1964. Well-
    warth's inclusion of Shaffer is limited to the comment that *Five Finger
    Exercise* is an example of a play in which a dramatist tries to exorcise his
    middle-class background by denigrating it.
Yarmolinsky, Avraham, ed. *The Poems, Prose and Plays of Alexander Pushkin*. New
    York: The Modern Library, 1936. Contains the play *Mozart and Salieri*, an
    early dramatic treatment of the material in *Amadeus*.

Articles

Artaud, Antonin. "La Conquête du Mexique." *La Nef* 63/64 (March–April
    1950): 159–65. An outline of the play which some critics believe that
    Shaffer used as a model for *The Royal Hunt of the Sun*.
Baldwin, Hélène L. "Equus: Theater of Cruelty or Theater of Sensationalism?"
    Philological Papers (West Virginia University) 25 (1978): 118–27. Bald-
    win argues that *Equus* does not fulfill Artaud's definition of Theater of
    Cruelty.
Bidney, Martin. "Thinking about God and Mozart: The Salieri's of Puškin and
    Peter Shaffer." *Slavic and East European Journal* 30 (1986): 183–85. Com-
    pares the protagonists in the two plays.
Buckley, Tom. "'Write Me' Said the Play to Peter Shaffer." *New York Times
    Magazine*, 13 April 1975. Shaffer reveals details of the actual case that
    inspired *Equus* and talks about his play.
Chambers, Colin. "Psychic Energy." *Plays and Players* 27, no. 5 (February 1980):
    11–13. Interview with Shaffer; information on the background of the
    writing of *Amadeus*.
Chandhuri, Una. "The Spectator in Drama/Drama in the Spectator." *Modern
    Drama* 27 (1984): 281–98. On Brechtian and Artaudian elements in
    Equus.
Clum, John M. "Religion and Five Contemporary Plays: The Quest for God in
    a Godless World." *South Atlantic Quarterly* 77, no. 4 (Autumn 1978):
    418–32. Quest for transcendence in *The Royal Hunt of the Sun* and *Equus*, as
    well as in Ionesco's *Hunger and Thirst*, Albee's *Tiny Alice*, and Stoppard's
    Jumpers.
Gianakaris, C. J. "The Artistic Trajectory of Peter Shaffer." In *Peter Shaffer: A
    Casebook* ed. C. J. Gianakaris, 3–23. New York: Garland, 1991. Overview
    of Shaffer's career.
———. "A Conversation with Peter Shaffer (1990)." In *Peter Shaffer: A Case-
    book*, ed. C. J. Gianakaris, 25–38. New York: Garland, 1991. Interview
    with Shaffer. Information on productions of *Yonadab* and *Lettice & Lovage* as
    well as on a future project.
———. "Drama into Film: The Shaffer Situation." *Modern Drama* 28 (1985):

83–98. Why Shaffer's plays before *Amadeus* failed as films, particularly *Equus*. Process of converting *Amadeus* successfully to the screen.

———. "Placing Shaffer's *Lettice and Lovage* in Perspective." *Comparative Drama* 22 (1988): 145–61. Analysis of characters and relationship with earlier plays.

———. "A Playwright Looks at Mozart: Peter Shaffer's *Amadeus*." *Comparative Drama* 15 (1981): 37–53. Study of historical and dramatic protagonists.

———. "Shaffer's Revisions in *Amadeus*." *Theatre Journal* 35 (1983): 88–101. Changes from original to revised version.

———. "The Theatre of the Mind in Miller, Osborne, and Shaffer." *Renascence* 30, no. 1 (Autumn 1977): 33–42. Insights on *Equus*.

Glenn, Jules. "Anthony and Peter Shaffer's Plays: The Influence of Twinship on Creativity." *American Imago* 31 (1974): 270–92. Dr. Glenn, a psychiatrist, demonstrates how the two main characters in many of Shaffer's plays are "doubles" and exhibit the characteristics typical to twins.

———. "Twins in Disguise: A Psychoanalytic Essay on *Sleuth* and *The Royal Hunt of the Sun*." *Psychoanalytic Quarterly* 43, no. 2 (1974): 288–302. A study of the close kinship between the protagonists in the two plays and of their twin traits.

———. "Twins in Disguise. II. Content, Form and Style in Plays by Anthony and Peter Shaffer." *The International Review of Psycho-Analysis* 1, no. 3 (1974): 373–81. Explores further the twin elements in *Sleuth*, as well as in Anthony's *Frenzy* and Peter's *Black Comedy, The White Liars, While Lies,* and *The Public Eye*.

———. "Twins in the Theater: A Study of Plays by Peter and Anthony Shaffer." In *Blood Brothers*. Ed. By Norman Kiell. New York: International Universities Press, 1983, 277–99. Considers *Equus* and *Amadeus*.

Hays, Peter L. "Shaffer's Horses in *Equus*, the Inverse of Swift's." *Notes of Contemporary Literature*, 17, iv. (September 1987): 10–12. Studies the difference between Shaffer's and Swift's use of equine imagery.

Hinden, Michael. "'Where All the Ladders Start': The Autobiographical Impulse in Shaffer's Recent Work." In *Peter Shaffer: A Casebook*, ed. C. J. Gianakaris, 151–69. New York: Garland, 1991. Insights into *Yonadab* and *Lettice and Lovage*, with references to the earlier works.

———. "Trying to Like Shaffer." *Comparative Drama* 19 (1985): 325–35. Responds to those critics who find that *The Royal Hunt of the Sun, Equus*, and *Amadeus* use spectacular theatricality to disguise a lack of substance. Analogy with O'Neill.

———. "When Playwrights Talk to God: Peter Shaffer and the Legacy of O'Neill." *Comparative Drama* 16 (1982): 49–63; reprinted in *Critical Approaches to O'Neill*. Ed. by John H. Stroupe. New York: AMS Press, 1988, 199–213. Shaffer as the best English-language playwright of O'Neill's legacy; use of masks, mime, spectacle, and monologues; theme of spiritually- and metaphysically-isolated protagonists. *Equus* compared to *The Great God Brown*, and *Amadeus* to *The Iceman Cometh*.

Huber, Werner and Hubert Zapf. "On the Structure of Peter Shaffer's *Amadeus*." *Modern Drama* 27 (1984): 299–313. Play as dramatic composition and theatrical artifact; thematic and structural complexity; functions of protagonists.

Jones, Julian Ward, Jr. "The Trojan Horse, *Timeo Danaos et dona ferentis*." *Classical Journal* 65, no. 6 (1970): 241–47. Sheds light on the religious consideration of equine imagery.

Kakutani, Michiko. "How 'Amadeus' Was Translated from Play to Film." *New York Times* 16 (September 1984): section 2. Background information on producing the script.

Klein, Dennis A. "*Amadeus*: The Third Part of Peter Shaffer's Dramatic Trilogy." *Modern Language Studies* 13 (1983): 31–38. First of many studies to compare *Amadeus* to earlier plays.

————. "Breaking Masculine Stereotypes: The Theatre of Peter Shaffer." *University of Dayton Review* 18, no. 2 (1986–87): 49–55. Images of men in the plays.

————. "Family Relations in Peter Shaffer's *Yonadab*." *Modern Jewish Studies* 7 (1990): 78–84. Study based on original version of the play.

————. "Game-playing in Four Plays by Peter Shaffer: *Shrivings, Equus, Lettice and Lovage*, and *Yonadab*. In *Peter Shaffer: A Casebook*, ed. C. J. Gianakaris. 133–50. New York: Garland, 1991. The theme as it evolved from *Five Finger Exercise* and the one-act plays to the plays (except *Amadeus*) of the 1970s and 1980s.

————. "A Note on the Use of Dreams in Peter Shaffer's Major Plays." *Journal of Evolutionary Psychology* 9 (1989): 25–31. Dreams on *Five Finger Exercise, The Royal Hunt of the Sun, Equus, Amadeus*, and *Yonadab*.

————. "Peter Shaffer's *Equus* as a Modern Aristotelian Tragedy." *Studies in Iconography* 9 (1983): 175–81; reprinted in *Contemporary Literature Criticism*, vol. 60, Roger Matuz, ed., 367–69. Detroit: Gale Research, 1990. Classical features of the play.

————. "*Yonadab*: Peter Shaffer's Earlier Dramas Revisited in the Court of King David." *Comparative Drama* 22 (1988): 68–78. Comparisons with *The Royal Hunt of the Sun, Equus*, and *Amadeus*.

Lee, Ronald J. "Jungian Approach to Theatre: Shaffer's *Equus*." *Psychological Perspectives* 8, no. 1 (Spring 1977): 10–21. Jungian psychology used in the study of the play.

Londré, Felicia Hardison. "Straddling a Dual Poetics in *Amadeus*: Salieri as Tragic Hero and Joker." In *Peter Shaffer: A Casebook*, ed. C. J. Gianakaris, 115–25. New York: Garland, 1991. Character study that calls upon roots that go back to Aristotle and proceed through European drama.

Lyons, Charles R. "Peter Shaffer's *Five Finger Exercise* and the Conventions of

Realism." In *Peter Shaffer: A Casebook*, ed. C. J. Gianakaris, 39–56. New York: Garland, 1991. Traces elements in the play to realistic drama of the nineteenth century and compares it to other works of this century.

Osorio de Negret, Betty. "La sintaxis básica del teatro: Ensayo comparativo de dos tradiciones sobre la prisión y muerte de Atahuallpa" (The basic syntax of the theater: Comparative essay of two traditions about the imprisonment and death of Atahuallpa.) *Lexis: Revista de lingüística y literatura* 8 (1984): 113–29. Compares *The Royal Hunt of the Sun* to indigenous plays.

Pennel, Charles A. "The Plays of Peter Shaffer: Experiment in Convention." *Kansas Quarterly* 3, no. 2 (1971): 100–109. An early article on Shaffer's theater, from *Five Finger Exercise* through *The Battle of Shrivings*.

"Philip Oaks Talks to Peter Shaffer." *Sunday Times* (London), 29 July 1973, 33. An interview with Shaffer about his work and the theater in general.

Plunka, Gene A. "The Existential Ritual: Peter Shaffer's *Equus*." *Kansas Quarterly* 12 (1980): 87–97. Concerns Alan Strang's existential search for freedom.

Podol, Peter L. "Contradictions and Dualities in Artaud and Artaudian Theatre: *The Conquest of Mexico* and the Conquest of Peru." *Modern Drama* 26 (1983): 518–27. Compares *The Royal Hunt of the Sun* with Artaud's *Conquest of Mexico* and Claude Demarigny's *Cajamarca*.

———. "Dramatizations of the Conquest of Peru: Peter Shaffer's *The Royal Hunt of the Sun* and Claude Demarigny's *Cajamarca*." *Hispanic Journal* (Indiana, PA), 6 (1984): 121–29. A comparative study.

Rogoff, Gordon. "Richard's Himself Again: Journey to an Actor's Theatre." *Tulane Drama Review* (Winter 1966): 29–40. Rogoff on the work of the National Theatre.

Shaffer, Peter. "Figure of Death." *Observer* (London), 4 November 1979, 37. Background information on the creation of *Amadeus*.

———. "In Search of a God." *Plays and Players* (October 1964): 22. Shaffer on *The Royal Hunt of the Sun*.

———. "Labels Aren't for Playwrights." *Theatre Arts* (February 1960): 20–21. An early interview, in which Shaffer reveals that he wants to write in a variety of styles.

———. "Scripts in Trans-Atlantic Crossings May Suffer Two Kinds of Changes." *Dramatists Guild Quarterly* (Spring 1980): 29–33. On changes that the dramatist makes in his plays between their premieres in London and New York.

Simon, John. "Hippodrama at the Psychodrome." *Hudson Review* 28 (Spring 1975): 97–106. An unwarrantedly severe critique of *Equus*, as well as an attempt to prove that the play is somehow a defense of homosexuality, and a dishonest one at that.

Stacy, James R. "The Sun and the Horse: Peter Shaffer's Search for Worship." *Educational Theatre Journal* 28, no. 3 (1979): 325–35; reprinted in *Peter*

Shaffer: A Casebook, ed. C. J. Gianakaris, 95–113. New York: Garland, 1991. Not Shaffer's, as the title suggests, but rather the fictional Pizarro's and Alan Strang's search for worship.

Sullivan, William J. "Peter Shaffer's *Amadeus*: The Making and Unmaking of the Fathers." *American Imago* 45, no. 1 (Spring 1988): 45–60. An excellent study that combines literature and psychology.

Terrier, Samuel. "*Equus*: Human Conflicts and the Trinity." *Christian Century* (18 May 1977): 472–76. A Christian approach to *Equus*.

Tobias, Tobi. "Playing without Words." *Dance Magazine* (May 1975): 48–50. Tobias is primarily concerned with the role of the horse-actors in *Equus*.

Walls, Doyle W. "*Equus*: Shaffer, Nietzsche, and the Neurosis of Health." *Modern Drama* 27 (1984): 314–23. *Equus* compared to Nietzsche's ideas in *The Birth of Tragedy*.

Witham, Barry B. "The Anger in *Equus*." *Modern Drama* 22 (1979): 61–66. *Equus* as an extension of the "angry young man" plays of the 1950s.

Doctoral Dissertations

Lawson, Wayne Paul. "The Dramatic Hunt: A Critical Evaluation of Peter Shaffer's Plays." Ph.D. dissertation, written at The Ohio State University, 1973. Lawson places Shaffer within the context of British drama and analyzes the plays from *Five Finger Exercise* through *The Battle of Shrivings*.

Watson, John Clair. "The Ritual Plays of Peter Shaffer." Ph.D. dissertation, written at the University of Oregon, 1987. On *The Royal Hunt of the Sun*, *Equus*, and *Amadeus*.

Troxel, Patricia Margaret. "Theater of Adultery: Studies in Modern Drama from Ibsen to Stoppard." Ph.D. dissertation, written at Princeton University, 1987. Adultery "as a means to explode form and setting" in Shaffer's and others' contemporary plays.

Plunka, Gene Alan. "The Existential Ritual in the Plays of Jean Genet, Peter Shaffer, and Edward Albee." Ph.D. dissertation, written at the University of Maryland, 1978. Studies the influence of Artaud's idea of getting the audience to release "basic animal urges, desires or instincts" through ceremonial rites and rituals. Applied to *The Royal Hunt of the Sun* and *Equus*.

Simard, Rodney Joe. "Postmodern Anglo-American Dramatic Theory." Ph.D. dissertation, written at the University of Alabama, 1982. Attempt of Shaffer and other playwrights "to reconcile form to meaning and philosophy to technique"; the existential realism of their generation's concerns.

Index

Index 261

227, 228, 229, 234, (ballet), 122;
(film), 121–22, 151
Establishment, The, 2, 237
Five Finger Exercise, 13–38, 44, 47, 66,
67, 88, 89, 94, 95, 96, 109, 141,
143, 144, 158, 159, 176, 182, 185,
190, 194, 208, 209, 210, 213, 217,
219, 220, 221, 223–24, 228, 230,
244n3; (film), 38
Follow Me! (film version of *The Public
Eye*), 52
Gift of the Gorgon, The, 225–32
How Doth the Little Crocodile?, 2, 5, 213
Lettice and Lovage, 61, 67, 68, 144, 199–
219, 220
Merry Roosters' Panto, The, 11–12
Private Ear, The, 39–44, 51–52, 66,
68, 94, 129, 130, 131, 133, 143,
144, 147, 156, 163, 176, 185, 213,
220, 221
"Prodigal Father, The," 9–11, 19, 86,
88, 95, 158, 226
Public Eye, The, 39, 44–52, 66, 96, 102,
133, 143, 176, 205, 210, 211, 212,
215, 217, 220, 222
Royal Hunt of the Sun, The, 48, 68, 69–
81, 87, 93, 95, 96, 101, 107, 120,
124, 125, 127, 128, 131, 133, 138,
141, 143, 144, 145, 147, 156, 159,
160, 168, 175, 177, 178, 182, 185,
191, 196, 208, 211, 213, 217, 221,
227, 234, 235; (film), 81; (opera), 81
"Salt Land, The," 6–9, 81, 94, 95, 96,
196, 208, 209, 210
Shrivings, 47, 68, 75, 81, 82–96, 107,
128, 129, 131, 133, 134, 144, 156,
159, 175, 176, 178, 185, 191, 203,
209, 211, 213, 214, 220, 226, 227,
230, 244n4
"Warning Game, A," 52

White Liars, 66–68, 144, 203, 208,
213–14, 215, 219, 227
White Liars, The, 44, 63–66, 68, 87,
95, 96, 144, 203, 210, 213–14, 215,
220, 221, 227
White Lies, 52, 58–63, 65, 66, 68, 87,
95, 96, 144, 193, 203, 211, 213–14,
215, 227
*Whom Do I Have the Honour of Address-
ing?*, 68, 95, 219–24
Withered Murder, 2, 5, 210, 213, 219
Woman in the Wardrobe, The, 1–2, 4–5,
213
Yonadab, 43, 66, 68, 75, 87, 92, 93, 95,
127, 133, 134, 143, 144, 146, 156,
158, 160, 164, 165, 166–98, 213,
221, 223, 224, 226, 234

Shaw, Martin, 82
Shaw, Robert, 81
Smith, Maggie, 39, 52, 199, 206, 207,
217, 218, 219
Sommars, Julie, 52
Starr, Ben, 52
Stephens, Robert, 69
Stewart, Patrick, 166

Tandy, Jessica, 13
Tennant, H. M., 13, 82
Tharp, Twyla, 151
Topol, Chaim, 52
Tyzack, Margaret, 206, 207

Vavra, Robert, 233

Watson, Moray, 39
Wesker, Arnold, 38
Wilkinson, Marc, 69
William, Kenneth, 39
Wood, Peter, 39

The Author

Dennis A. Klein is professor of Spanish in the Department of Modern Languages at the University of South Dakota in Vermillion. Dr. Klein holds bachelor's and master's degrees from the University of Kansas, and received his Ph.D., with a specialization in modern Spanish drama, from the University of Massachusetts. He has been widely published on the subjects of Hispanic and British drama, and also serves as head bibliographer in Spanish for the Modern Language Association's *International Bibliography*. Dr. Klein served as a contributing editor for *García Lorca: An Annotated Primary Bibliography* and *García Lorca: A Selectively Annotated Bibliography of Criticism*, both edited by Francesca Colecchia. He recently published *"Blood Wedding", "Yerma," and "The House of Bernarda Alba: García Lorca's Tragic Trilogy* in Twayne's Masterwork Studies series. He was also a contributor to *Peter Shaffer: A Casebook*, edited by C. J. Gianakaris. This book is his third single-authored volume on Peter Shaffer.